SYNTAX and SEMANTICS

VOLUME 15

SYNTAX and SEMANTICS

VOLUME 15

Studies in Transitivity

Edited by

Paul J. Hopper

Linguistics Program
State University of New York at Binghamton
Binghamton, New York

Sandra A. Thompson

Department of Linguistics
University of California, Los Angeles
Los Angeles, California

ACADEMIC PRESS
A Subsidiary of Harcourt Brace Jovanovich, Publishers
New York   London
Paris   San Diego   San Francisco   São Paulo   Sydney   Tokyo   Toronto

ACADEMIC PRESS, INC.
111 Fifth Avenue, New York, New York 10003

United Kingdom Edition published by
ACADEMIC PRESS, INC. (LONDON) LTD.
24/28 Oval Road, London NW1 7DX

LIBRARY OF CONGRESS CATALOG CARD NUMBER: 72-9423

ISBN 0-12-613515-0

PRINTED IN THE UNITED STATES OF AMERICA

82 83 84 85   9 8 7 6 5 4 3 2 1

pd
1-25-84

CONTENTS

The Origins of Grammatical Encoding of Events   409

DAN I. SLOBIN

Transitivity and Objecthood in Japanese   423

NOBUKO SUGAMOTO

CONTRIBUTORS

Numbers in parentheses indicate the pages on which the authors' contributions begin.

JUDITH AISSEN (7), *Department of Linguistics, Yale University, New Haven, Connecticut 06520*

PETER AUSTIN (37), *Department of Philosophy, La Trobe University, Bundoora, Victoria 3083, Australia*

JOËLLE BAILARD (49), *Department of Linguistics, University of California, Los Angeles, Los Angeles, California 90024*

BARRY J. BLAKE (71), *Department of Linguistics, Monash University, Clayton, Victoria 3168, Australia*

BERNARD COMRIE (95), *Department of Linguistics, University of Southern California, Los Angeles, California 90007*

ALESSANDRO DURANTI (217), *Department of Linguistics, University of Rome, Rome, Italy*

DAVID GIL (117), *Department of Linguistics, University of California, Los Angeles, Los Angeles, California 90024, and Department of Linguistics, Tel Aviv University, Tel Aviv, Israel*

T. GIVÓN (143), *Ute Language Program, Southern Ute Tribe, Ignacio, Colorado 81137*

HELEN A. HAIG (161), *Los Angeles, California 90067*

JOHN HAIMAN (177), *Department of Anthropology, University of Manitoba, Winnipeg, Manitoba R3T 2N2, Canada*

YVONNE M. HÉBERT (195), *Department of Linguistics, University of British Columbia, Vancouver, British Columbia V6T 1W5, Canada*

PAUL J. HOPPER (1), *Linguistics Program, State University of New York at Binghamton, Binghamton, New York 13901*

LARRY M. HYMAN (217), *Department of Linguistics, University of Southern California, Los Angeles, California 90007*

IVAN KALMÁR (241), *Department of Anthropology, University of Toronto, Toronto M5S 1A1, Canada*

FRANTISEK LICHTENBERG (261), *Department of Anthropology, University of Auckland, Auckland, New Zealand*

CAROL LORD (277), *Department of Linguistics, University of California, Los Angeles, Los Angeles, California 90024*

PAMELA MUNRO (301), *Department of Linguistics, University of California, Los Angeles, Los Angeles, California 90024*

JOHANNA NICHOLS (319), *Department of Slavic Languages, University of California, Berkeley, Berkeley, California 94720*

DORIS L. PAYNE (351), *Summer Institute of Linguistics, and Department of Linguistics, University of California, Los Angeles, Los Angeles, California 90024*

JOANNE SHAYNE (379), *Department of Linguistics, University of California, Los Angeles, Los Angeles, California 90024*

DAN I. SLOBIN (409), *Department of Psychology, University of California, Berkeley, Berkeley, California 94720*

NOBUKO SUGAMOTO (423), *Department of Linguistics, University of California, Los Angeles, Los Angeles, California 90024*

SANDRA A. THOMPSON (1), *Department of Linguistics, University of California, Los Angeles, Los Angeles, California 90024*

PREFACE

When people talk (or write), they make an enormous range of decisions about how to PRESENT the thoughts that are in their heads: They structure their ideas according to what they intend to be "figure" and what they intend to be "ground," they decide what should be presented as "subject" and what as "object," whether an event should be presented as having actually occurred or as only a possibility, and so on.

Decisions as to how to present events and situations with respect to the people and things involved in them are decisions affecting the TRANSITIVITY of a clause in actual language use. Once these decisions are made, a number of grammatical choices follow automatically. For example, if you are speaking English, and you want to talk about someone's mountain climbing, you must decide whether you want to present this event as an attainment of some goal, or as an activity with no particular achievement being referred to. The resulting difference in the grammar of the two clauses resulting from this choice is a difference of transitivity:

(1)   a. *Janine climbed **the mountain**.*
        b. *Janine climbed **up the mountain**.*

In (1a), which expresses the attainment of a goal, implying that Janine reached the top, the noun *mountain* is presented directly after the verb as its direct object, while in (1b), which does not imply that she necessarily reached the top, it is presented in a position more removed from the verb, not as its direct object, but in construction with a motional preposition.

Each of the papers in this collection addresses itself to some facet of this issue of the decisions speakers make about how to present events and situations with respect to their participants, and the grammatical consequences of such decisions.

Scholars pursuing questions of discourse, universal grammer, language typology, semantics, and grammatical description and theory will find much here to ponder and to respond to; we offer *Studies in Transitivity* in the spirit of furthering dialogue and discovery.

INTRODUCTION

PAUL J. HOPPER
SANDRA A. THOMPSON

To modern linguists, the concepts of traditional grammar often seem elusive and tantalizing. Although by encountering these concepts in a variety of languages we are repeatedly being made aware of their importance, we are nonetheless at a loss to provide an explicit characterization of their range and functions. This elusiveness pervades both elementary concepts like "noun" and "verb," and more complex relational terms like "reflexive" and "transitive." The transitivity relationship, the theme of this volume, is a particularly troublesome one. Clauses typically contain references to one or two *participants*. These participants are to an overwhelming degree asymmetrically arranged, and this asymmetry—or its absence—is found time and again to have consequences for grammar (morphology and syntax). Indeed, the number, kind, and interrelationships of the participants are frequently the basis for the organization of the entire verb system into conjugational and aspectual classes. In other words, in many languages (and perhaps covertly in all languages) the transitivity relationship lies at the explanatory core of *most* grammatical processes.

Nonetheless, transitivity has in general not been treated by linguists as a unitary phenomenon, but almost always as a by-product of something else. This was especially true of transformational grammar, which in its

1

most naive formulations casually dismissed this rich and central relationship as a nonproblem; thus Chomsky (1966) declared: "Consider now
the problem of a proper notation for the other contextual features, e.g.
transitivity. Clearly the best notation is simply an indication of the context in which the item can occur. Thus the feature [+Transitive] can be
represented simply [+___NP]" [p. 45]. A consequence of this view of
transitivity is, of course, that the verb *to be* must be treated as a transitive
verb, to mention only an example from English; the vast and largely
systematic array of grammatical and semantic circumstances under which
other verbs designated as "transitive" by these schema are treated as
intransitive in the world's languages must be either ignored or deferred
to a "superficial" level of case-marking, etc.

The more sophisticated treatment by Lyons (1968) pointed out that
no formal grammar handled the facts about transitivity correctly (p. 332),
and concluded that there is some notion of a "normal" transitive sentence, in which an agent does something to an object (p. 359). Lyons's
discussion recalls a long-standing assumption of classical grammar, that
the term "transitive" is properly applied to actions which "affect" an
object. Such actions are *hrémata metabatiká* "predicates which 'go beyond' (the subject)." Other predicates are *hrémata ametábata* "predicates which do not 'go beyond' (the subject)" (cf. Schmidt 1973 for these
points and further significant discussion of transitivity). Lyons views
untransferred predicates, in which there are two participants and yet the
action is not instigated by an animate agent, as intrusions on the ideal
notion of transitivity:

> The notional basis for the system of transitivity has superimposed upon it in various
> languages many transitive constructions which do not satisfy the conditions of the
> ideal system. For example, *Wealth attracts robbers* is a perfectly acceptable transitive
> sentence of English, in spite of the fact that *wealth* is an inanimate noun. It may very
> well be that sentences like this should be thought of as 'parasitic' upon the more
> 'normal' type of transitive sentence with an animate subject [p. 359].

Lyons's treatment falls short of proposing a continuum of transitivity;
indeed, his theoretical assumptions seem to preclude such a possibility.
He distinguishes "intransitive" sentences from "pseudo-intransitives"
of the *John smokes* variety, which have undergone "Object-deletion"
(pp. 360–361), yet he has no corresponding category of "pseudo-
transitives" into which the type *Wealth attracts robbers* might be fitted.

That many phenomena in different languages could be better captured
through a notion of more/less transitive has been noted in a number of
individual studies. Brewer (1970) makes use of such a concept in his
account of Old Spanish direct objects marked with *le* and *lo*. He concludes his study by observing:

... a relationship between afficience and imperfective aspect, effect and perfective aspect suggests itself and calls for investigation. Another implication is that the concept of verbal transitivity may need revision. Perhaps it would be more accurate to think in terms of *how* transitive verbs are than in terms of an absolute division into the transitive (which includes both afficient and effective verbs) and the intransitive (non-afficient and quasi-afficient verbs) [p. 146].

Ferguson (1958:319–320) suggests "less transitive" and "doubly transitive" as parameters for certain facts of Classical Arabic verb derivation. Some notion of transitivity as a continuum seems to be implicit in the work of Bolinger on the English passive; thus in his paper of 1978 he observes that the passive in English favors subjects which are "on the scene" and "affected by" the action of the verb. In *George was run into coming out of the subway,* the interpretation is of a collision rather than a chance encounter. G. Lakoff (1977:244–245) suggested that the "agent–patient sentence" was a prototypical concept in the sense of E. Rosch (cf., e.g., Rosch 1978), determined by the presence of a number of parameters; these included properties of the agent (e.g., acts deliberately, uses his hands or an instrument), of the patient (e.g., is definite, is changed by the action), and of the action (a single, "overlapping" event). The debate over *kill* and *cause to die* could thus be settled by viewing *kill* as more prototypical of agent–patient sentences, in that *kill* denotes a single event, with spatiotemporal overlap between the agent's action and the patient's change.

The exact parameters of a transitive (i.e., fully transitive) clause as they are relevant to grammatical universals and to discourse were the theme of an extensive study carried out in the late 1970s by the editors of this volume (Hopper and Thompson, 1980). This work established the following parameters whose aggregate resulted in the *cardinal transitivity* of a clause (p. 252):

	High transitivity	Low transitivity
A. PARTICIPANTS	two participants or more (A and O)	1 participant
B. KINESIS	action	nonaction
C. ASPECT	telic	atelic
D. PUNCTUALITY	punctual	nonpunctual
E. VOLITIONALITY	volitional	nonvolitional
F. AFFIRMATION	affirmative	negative
G. MODE	realis	irrealis
H. AGENCY	A high in potency	A low in potency
I. AFFECTEDNESS OF O	O totally affected	O not affected
J. INDIVIDUATION OF O	O highly individuated	O nonindividuated

On the basis of these parameters a *Transitivity Hypothesis* was proposed as a language universal:

If two clauses (a) and (b) differ in that (a) is higher in Transitivity according to any
of the features A–J, then, if a concomitant grammatical or semantic difference appears
elsewhere in the clause, that difference will also show (a) to be higher in Transitivity
[p. 255].

In other words, we predicted that the grammatical or semantic markings
of transitivity would covary in the clause in the same direction with
respect to cardinal transitivity. The list of features involved in the Transitivity Hypothesis contains some that are not usually associated with
the primary meaning of the term "transitive," taken in the sense of
'having a direct object'; yet our research showed that in language the
morphosyntactic structures used to signal a progression toward, or a
recession away from, cardinal transitivity were similar to those signaling
the presence or absence of a second participant, that is, an object. For
example, languages that indexed the object in the verb frequently failed
to do so when the object was nonreferential, or when it was not fully
affected. Or an action would be cast in a syntactic form appropriate for
one participant if the action was conceived as being incomplete or in-
effective, or if the agent was acting involuntarily. Typologically there
was something very central about the marking of participants which
spilled over into all the other parameters of cardinal transitivity, and
which showed that the classical notion of transitivity as being more than
the mere presence of a grammatical object was essentially correct.

But these 10 parameters, besides having a cumulative grammatical
value, also seemed to have a unified discourse function. To a greater or
lesser extent they contributed to the construction of "foreground"—the
chief, event-centered, sequential actions of a discourse. Other grammatical functions (e.g., number, gender) appeared to make no such contribution, and were also irrelevant to the grammatical transitivity of a
clause.

The need for further research along these lines is evident. Single-
language studies of the morphosyntax and semantics of the transitive
clause are required, as many important links between grammar and semantics are missing even from otherwise extensive and competent linguistic descriptions. Still more urgent is the need for continued discourse
analysis as a basis for studying the relationship between grammatical
form and pragmatic function. The notion of "foregrounding" in discourse
must be refined and either empirically validated or replaced by a more
sophisticated parameter.

At the time that earlier versions of our 1980 paper were being circu-
lated, there began to appear a number of other studies, some of them
written in direct response. The thematic coherence of these papers encouraged us to ask the authors for permission to publish them as a single

volume. The topic of the volume was to be simply "Transitivity"; no unified approach or other conformity was imposed on the authors. The book thus contains papers written in extension of our own work, papers that ignore it, and papers that criticize it. Together they constitute, we hope, a significant advance in our understanding of a core area of language—the grammar and pragmatics of actions and their participants.

ACKNOWLEDGMENTS

We wish to express our gratitude to Carol Lord for her concerned and careful editorial assistance.

REFERENCES

Bolinger, D. (1978) "Passive and Transitivity Again," *Forum Linguisticum* **3**, 25–28.
Brewer, W. B. (1970) "Extent of Verbal Influence and Choice between *le* and *lo* in Alphonsine Prose," *Hispanic Review* **38**, 133–146.
Chomsky, N. A. (1966) "Topics in the Theory of Generative Grammar," in *Current Trends in Linguistics* Vol. 3, Indiana University Press, Bloomington.
Ferguson, C. (1958) "Review of Fleisch, *L'arabe classique*," *Language* **34**, 314–321.
Hopper, P. J., and S. A. Thompson (1980) "Transitivity in Grammar and Discourse," *Language* **56**, 251–299.
Lakoff, G. (1977) "Linguistic Gestalts" in *Papers from the Thirteenth Regional Meeting, Chicago Linguistic Society,* University of Chicago.
Lyons, J. (1968) *Introduction to Theoretical Linguistics,* Cambridge University Press, London.
Rosch, E. (1978) "Principles of Categorization," in E. Rosch and B. Lloyd, eds., *Cognition and Categorization,* Lawrence Erlbaum, Hillsdale, N.J.
Schmidt, K.-H. (1973) "Transitiv und Intransitiv," in G. Redard, ed., *Indogermanische und allgemeine Sprachwissenschaft, Akten der IV. Fachtagung der Indogermanischen Gesellschaft, 1969,* Ludwig Reichert Vlg, Wiesbaden.

VALENCE AND COREFERENCE

JUDITH AISSEN

1. COREFERENCE AND REDUCTION IN CLAUSAL VALENCE

Despite the fact that we are far from having an adequate theory of meaning, the conviction that diverse syntactic constructions may reflect a semantic commonality has underlain cross-linguistic investigations into, for example, the syntax of relative clauses, the syntax of questions, and the syntax of causative constructions. The very labels "relative clause," "question," "causative construction" refer to this presumed semantic commonality rather than to any syntactic similarity or identity.

This paper is concerned with one aspect of the syntactic resolution of clause-internal coreference, a situation for which natural languages commonly have special syntactic and morphological devices, such as reflexive pronouns. Studies of the cross-linguistic possibilities for expressing clause-internal coreference include Faltz (1977), Keenan (1975), and Edmondson (1978).

Where there is coreference between subject and direct object of a clause, there are two common options: (*a*) a construction that is superficially transitive (more precisely, transitive in the final stratum, a notion to be defined in what follows) and where the direct object appears in the

7

form of a reflexive pronoun as in the following examples from English, Turkish, and Tzotzil:

(1)   *Peter saw **himself**.*

(2)   *Hasan **kendini** gördü.*
        'Hasan saw himself'.

(3)   *ʔiyil **sba** li Xune.*
        'Juan saw himself'.

and (b) a construction that is superficially intransitive (intransitive in the final stratum) and which hence by definition lacks a direct object at late levels of structure. The verb in such clauses is frequently specially marked. In Turkish and Dyirbal, for example, there are "reflexive" verbal suffixes which attach to transitive verb stems, yielding a verb that cannot cooccur with an overt direct object nominal:

(4)   a.   *Hasan yika-n-dɨ.*
                 wash-refl-past
             'Hasan washed himself'.
        b.   **Hasan kendini yɨkandɨ.*
                 self-acc

(5)   *Bayi   yaṛa   buyba-yir-iñu.*
        the-nom man-nom hide-refl-pres
        'The man hides himself'.

The arguments for final intransitivity of such examples will be reviewed in the third section of this paper. For the moment, it is assumed that these sentences are underlyingly transitive and are detransitivized by elimination of the direct object relation.

Given that coreference between subject and direct object may induce detransitivization, the question arises whether coreference between argument terms in other positions ever results in a reduction in syntactic valence.[1] Here it is argued that coreference between subject and indirect object can result in the reduction of a ditransitive clause to a mono-transitive one by elimination of the indirect object relation.[2] Affected

[1] The term VALENCE is used here in a somewhat extended sense. As I assume a theory that posits more than one level of syntactic structure, valence is used to refer to the number of nominal arguments in a clause at any level one chooses to specify. Thus, one can sensibly speak of the decrease or increase in a clause's valence from one level to another.

[2] The following definitions are assumed: A clause is INTRANSITIVE at some level if it contains a subject but no direct object at that level; a clause is MONOTRANSITIVE at some level if it contains a subject, direct object, and no indirect object at that level; a clause is DITRANSITIVE at some level if it contains a subject, direct object, and indirect object at that level.

structures thus lack an indirect object in the final stratum. Such an analysis is proposed for Tzotzil, a Mayan language of southern Mexico, and Georgian (following Harris 1976).

That coreference should induce reduction in syntactic valence is perhaps not surprising. A proposition whose predicate has n argument positions can potentially say something about n individuals, but if two positions are filled by the same variable, then the proposition says something about $n - 1$ individuals. Reduction by 1 in syntactic valence under the condition of coreference makes the syntactic valence equal to the number of distinctly filled argument positions of the corresponding predicate, as will be discussed further in the last section of this paper.

The paper deals with two related but distinct issues. The first is the argument that in some languages coreference between subject and indirect object of a clause results in structures that contain no final indirect object. The second is the question of how the nonexistence of a final indirect object is to be described within Relational Grammar. Contrary to certain claims of Postal, it is proposed here that grammatical relations may be canceled under certain conditions. It is further argued that if cancellation is not permitted, then the Motivated Chômage Law must be abandoned. The paper thus proceeds as follows: The second section briefly presents the theoretical assumptions underlying the analysis presented here, along with an explanation of the notation and some relevant definitions. The third section discusses the evidence for the final intransitivity of some reflexive constructions. The fourth section presents the argument for cancellation of indirect objects in Tzotzil and Georgian. The fifth argues for cancellation or, barring that, for abandonment of the Motivated Chômage Law, and the sixth concludes with some speculation on why coreferent clausemates induce reduction in syntactic valence.

2. ASSUMPTIONS AND NOTATION

The paper is couched in the general terms of Relational Grammar, as developed over a number of years by David Perlmutter and Paul Postal, because this framework makes available in a particularly direct way the notions necessary for dealing with grammatical relations.

In Relational Grammar, grammatical structure is represented as a network of relations holding among various elements. Relevant here are those relations which hold between the various nominals of a clause and the clause itself. The relevant nominal relations are subject ("1"), direct object ("2"), and indirect object ("3"), plus various oblique relations and the chômeur relation. Also relevant here are the relations head ("head") and possessor ("poss") which may be borne to a nominal. It is necessary to recognize a number of distinct syntactic levels, referred to as *strata*. Among these are the initial stratum, the level most closely linked to thematic (i.e., case) relations, and the final stratum, the one most closely linked to surface structure.

The relation that holds between two elements in a given stratum or in a sequence of adjacent strata is represented by an arc, and one element is said to govern the other. The governor (b) occurs at the tail of the arc, and the governee (a) at the head; the name of the relation (x) is written to the left of the arc and the names of the strata ($C_i, C_{i+1}, \ldots$) to the right:

(6)   a. b b. b
            $x \downarrow$ $x \downarrow C_i, C_{i+1}, C_{i+2}$
            a a

Graphically, the set of strata that constitute (part of) the syntactic representation of a sentence are displayed as a sequence of horizontal rows, the initial stratum being the highest and the final stratum the lowest. Such representations are called STRATAL DIAGRAMS. For example:

(7)

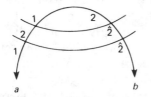

The arclike objects in (7) headed by a and b, which will be called PATHS, are not necessarily arcs. For an arc represents a single relation in all its strata whereas a path may represent more than one relation. Thus a path may represent a set of arcs. The members of a path have a special relation to one another, a relation which requires, inter alia, that each member arc have the same head. If a given arc belongs to a given path, I will say that the arc is along that path.

Diagram (8) is a partial representation of the relational structure of an English passive like *Mark was kissed by Betty*.

(8)

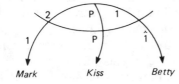

The diagram represents only the grammatical relations borne by the three elements that bear grammatical relations in the initial stratum. According to (8), *Mark* is the initial 2, but final 1. Relevant to later discussion is the fate of *Betty,* which is initial 1. Two proposed laws of Relational Grammar come into play here: the Stratal Uniqueness Law and the Chômeur Law (Perlmutter and Postal 1977, 1982a).[3] Informally, the Stratal Uniqueness Law specifies that no more than one nominal may bear a given *term* relation (i.e., 1, 2, 3) in a given clause in a given stratum. This law rules out a structure in which both *Mark* and *Betty* are final 1s. The Chômeur Law guarantees that *Betty* bears a special relation, called the CHÔMEUR RELATION ("$\hat{n}$" where $n = 1, 2, 3$) in the second stratum. Informally, the law says that if the term relation borne by some nominal a in one stratum is borne by a distinct nominal in the next stratum, then a bears the chômeur relation in that next stratum.

Following proposals in Relational Grammar, coreference will be represented by so-called multiattachment (Perlmutter and Postal, 1982b). In the earliest stratum of *John embarrassed himself,* the nominal *John* is both subject and object of the clause:

(9)

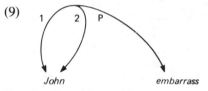

     John   embarrass

For details of how this structure is related to the surface structure within the theory of Arc Pair Grammar, see Johnson and Postal (1980).

It is assumed here that a well-formed stratal network must by some set of principles be associated with a surface structure—a structure that is suitable input to a set of phonological rules. This involves, among other things: (*a*) specification of which elements in the network appear in surface structure; (*b*) in the case of multiattachment, specification of how the various arcs which have the same head are realized in surface structure; and (*c*) specification of the linear order of elements. Surface structure will not be represented, but the following principle will be assumed: Only those elements which head arcs in the final stratum appear in surface structure.

It will be useful to have a way of talking about arcs that are adjacent along a path. We need to distinguish the following two cases:

(10)   a.   b.

         a   b   a

[3] See Gary and Keenan (1977) for a challenge to both of these laws and Perlmutter and Postal (1982a) for a response.

In both cases, a bears the 3 relation in one stratum and the 2 relation in the next, but only in (10a) are the two arcs along the same path. We will say that an arc B is the SUCCESSOR of an arc A if A and B are along the same path and A is an arc in the C_i stratum and B is an arc in the C_{i+1} stratum. The term CANCELLATION can be defined in terms of the notion of successor:[4]

(11)   **Definition.** Let A be an arc in a clause C with stratum C_i.
        Then, A is canceled if and only if:
        (i) C has stratum C_{i+1},
        (ii) A is not in stratum C_{i+1}, and
        (iii) A has no successor.

The following stratal diagrams show cancellation of a 2-arc in the second stratum:

(12)   a.   b.

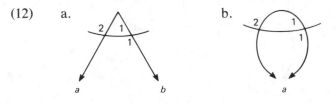

3. THE FINAL INTRANSITIVITY OF SOME REFLEXIVE CONSTRUCTIONS

A variety of facts may be cited in support of the final intransitivity of certain reflexive constructions.[5] Only two will be cited here.

Case-marking rules that distinguish final stratum intransitive and transitive clauses may be relevant to establishing the final (in)transitivity of reflexive clauses. In Dyirbal, for example, nonpronominal subjects of finally intransitive clauses are case marked differently,[6] the intransitive subject being marked in the absolutive case (Dixon's nominative, glossed in what follows as "nom") and the transitive subject in the ergative case (data from Dixon 1972:86–90):

(13)   a. *Bayi   yaṛa   bulgan.*
           the-nom man-nom big
           'The man is big'.

---

[4] I use the term SUCCESSOR here because I believe the relation it designates is the same one for which Johnson and Postal (1980) use that term. Their definition involves the primitive relation SPONSOR which I have not used here. I am indebted to David Johnson for discussion on this point and several others. He suggested the definition of cancellation.

[5] Edmondson (1978) includes a discussion of relevant evidence.

[6] For a contrary view, see Jake (1978), and also Dixon's reply (1979).

   b. *Bala   yugu   baŋgul yaɽangu buyban.*
       the-nom stick-nom the-erg man-erg hide
       'The man hides the stick'.

In clauses containing verbs with the so-called reflexive suffix, no direct object nominal may occur in the sentence; the subject is marked with absolutive case:

(14)(= 5)   *Bayi   yaɽa   buyba-yir- iñu.*
            the-nom man-nom hide- refl-pres
            'The man hides himself'.

If the subjects of final stratum intransitive clauses are marked absolutive, then the case marking in (14) follows if reflexive clauses are final stratum intransitives.

Somewhat more complex evidence for the final intransitivity of reflexive constructions is discussed in Postal (1977) with reference to facts discussed in Kayne (1975). Sentences like (15a)–(15b) are analyzed as initially transitive but finally intransitive:

(15)   a. *Paul se photographie.*
         'Paul photographs himself'.
     b. *Le juge s'est tué.*
         'The judge killed himself'.

The argument for final intransitivity is based on the treatment of reflexive clauses in causative constructions formed with the main verb *faire* 'to make/have someone do something'. Crucially, this construction distinguishes final stratum transitive and intransitive complement clauses. The final subject of a complement clause that is intransitive in the final stratum is (noninitial) direct object of *faire,* as in (16)–(17), whereas the final subject of a complement clause that is finally transitive is (noninitial) indirect object of *faire,* as in (18)–(19). (The pronominal forms of third person final direct objects are *le/la/les,* and those of third person final indirect objects *lui/leur;* final indirect objects are marked by *à.*)

(16)   *Il a fait partir **son amie**.*
      'He made **his friend** leave'.

(17)   *Il **l'**a fait partir.*
      'He made **her** leave'.

(18)   a. *Il fera [son enfant boire un peu de vin]*
      b. *Il fera boire un peu de vin **à son enfant**.*
         'He'll have **his child** drink a little wine'.

(19)   *Il **lui** fera boire un peu de vin.*
      'He'll have **him** drink a little wine'.

Assuming, then, that the final subject of a final stratum intransitive clause must be direct object of *faire,* but that of a final stratum transitive clause indirect object, the final transitivity of reflexive clauses can be determined. In (20)–(21), *le frère du juge,* final subject of a reflexive clause, is direct object of *faire;* hence the complement (reflexive) clause is finally intransitive:

(20)   a.   *La crainte du scandale a fait* [*le frère du juge s'être tué*]
         b.   *La crainte du scandale a fait se tuer **le frère du juge.***
         c.   **La crainte du scandale a fait se tuer **au frère du juge.***
              'Fear of scandal made **the judge's brother** kill himself'.

(21)   *La crainte du scandale l'/*lui a fait se tuer.*
         'Fear of scandal made **him** kill himself'.

From this discussion, it should be clear that the question of evidence for the intransitivity of reflexive clauses must be addressed within particular languages. Grammars of different languages vary in the ways that grammatical rules distinguish transitive and intransitive clauses. Thus far, we have seen evidence, from case marking and causative constructions, that in a number of languages reflexive clauses are intransitive in the final stratum. No evidence has been presented that the clause is detransitivized by cancellation of the direct object rather than in some other way (e.g., by demotion of the direct object to indirect object). Discussion of this issue is deferred to a later section; for the present, cancellation of the relevant grammatical relations is assumed.

4. CANCELLATION OF 1-COREFERENTIAL 3s

We turn now to the reduction of ditransitive clauses to monotransitive clauses by cancellation of the indirect object relation. Such indirect objects are always coreferential with the subject of their clauses (but see Note 15) and will be referred to here as *1-coreferential 3s.* Languages that appear to require cancellation of 1-coreferential 3s under at least some circumstances include Tzotzil (Mayan), Georgian, and Sierra Popoluca (brought to my attention by Will Norman).[7] English and Basque, in contrast, are examples of languages that do not.

4.1. Tzotzil

Although no indirect objects occur in surface structure in Tzotzil, it is necessary to assume their existence in nonfinal strata. A consequence

---

[7] Tzeltal and Chol, languages closely related to Tzotzil, also appear to have this rule.

of two independent facts is that every clause in which an indirect object occurs, save those where the indirect object is cancelled, is marked.

First, 3s advance to 2 in Tzotzil. As a morphological reflex of this advancement, *-be* is suffixed to the verb (see Aissen, 1982, for discussion). In the following, the (a) sentences have no specified 3 at any level; the (b) sentences have a 3 that has advanced to 2. Note that pronouns are generally omitted in surface structure. Basic word order is VOS.[8]

(22)   a.   *Ba y-ak' une.*   (L. 337)
                  go E3-give pts
                  'He went to give it'.

        b.   *ti mi ch-av-ak'-b-on   7ep tak'ine*   (L.75)
                  if icp-E2-give-*be*-A1 much money
                  'if you will give me a lot of money'

(23)   a.   *Ba x-chon li   nukul 7une.*   (L. 336)
                  go E3-sell the skin   pts
                  'He went to sell the skin'.

        b.   *Mi mu x-a-chon-b-on   l-a-   chitome.*   (L. 86)
                  ? neg icp-E2-sell-*be*-A1 the-E2-pig
                  'Won't you sell me your pigs?'

The verbs of the (a) sentences are not suffixed with *-be* and no specific indirect object is understood in these. In the (b) sentences, *-be* does occur (the *e* is elided before a following vowel-initial suffix), and these sentences have specific understood indirect objects.

There are two arguments that the initial 3s of the (b) sentences are final 2s. First, Tzotzil has a rule of verb agreement according to which the verb agrees with both final 1 and final 2 (if there is one) of the clause. Agreement works according to an ergative schema so that one affix marks intransitive subject and transitive object in a given person and a distinct affix marks the transitive subject in that person.[9]

---

[8] Tzotzil examples come either from Laughlin (1977) (cited by page) or from my own field notes. Language consultants were Maryan Lopis Chiku7 and Chep Jernantis Kontzares, both from the municipality of Zinacantan. The orthography used here represents [č] with *ch*, [š] with *x,* and [h] with *j,* and [ʔ] with *7.* The following abbreviations appear in the glosses: *icp*–incompletive aspect, *cp*–completive aspect, *neg*–negation, *?*–yes–no question particle, *pass*–passive, *pt*–particle, *enc*–enclitic, *be*–suffix *-be* as explicated in text, *E1, E2, E3*–ergative 1st, etc. person, *A1, A2*–absolutive 1st, etc. person, *refl*–reflexive, *emph*–emphatic.

[9] The ergative markers, which are used to cross-reference both transitive subjects on verbs and possessors on nouns, are always prefixes. There are two sets: one used with glottal stop-initial stems and one used with all other consonant-initial stems. (There are no vowel-initial stems, though initial glottal stop always deletes after the ergative prefix,

(24)   a. *L- i- s- maj.*
            cp-A1-E3-hit
            'He hit me'.
        b. *L-i-7ay.*
            cp-A1-go
            'I went'.
        c. *7i -j-*maj.
            cp -E1-hit
            'I hit him'.

In sentences like (22b) and (23b) where the verb is suffixed with *-be,* the absolutive affix obligatorily cross-references the notional indirect object. If the initial 3 is final 2 and agreement is with final 1 and 2, these facts follow directly.

---

making these appear to be vowel-initial.) The ergative prefixes mark person and may optionally cooccur with a set of suffixes which mark plurality:

	/____7	/____C	Plural suffix
1	*k-*	*j-*	*-tik* (inclusive)
			-tikótik (exclusive)
2	*7av-*	*7a-*	*-ik*
3	*y-*	*s*	*-ik*

The absolutive markers also come in two sets—a set of prefixes and a set of suffixes. Their distribution is determined as follows. The prefixes are used when the predicate has an overt aspect prefix, the suffixes otherwise (always with nonverbal predicates, and with some verb forms). In addition, the suffixes always mark the object when the subject is second person. A set of suffixes optionally occurs with the absolutive *prefixes* to mark plurality of either intransitive subject or direct object. The absolutive suffixes conflate person and number. There is no marker for third person singular.

	Absolutive prefix	Plural suffix
1	*-i-*	*-otik* (inclusive)
		-otikótik (exclusive)
2	*-a-*	*-ik*
3		*-ik*

	Absolutive suffix	
	sg.	pl.
1	*-on*	*-otik* (inclusive)
		-otikótik (exclusive)
2	*-ot*	*-oxuk*
3		*-ik*

Second, there is a rule of Passive in the language which promotes the 2 of a clause to 1:

(25)
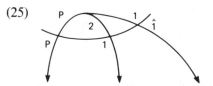

As predicted by the Chômeur Law, the initial 1 is a final chômeur. Passive clauses are finally intransitive and thus the verb agrees only with the final 1. The final 1-chômeur, if expressed, functions as possessor of a noun stem *-u7un* (e.g., *k-u7un* 'by me').[10] Advancement of 2 to 1 is marked on the verb by one of two suffixes: *-e* or *-at*. The only suffix possible with polysyllabic stems is *-at*. The following are some examples:

(26) *Ch-a-k'opon-at.*   (L. 38)
icp-A2-speak-pass
'You will be spoken to'.

(27) *Te   la ch - mak-e   ta be   y-u7un ti   vakax 7une.*   (L. 227)
there pt icp -stop-pass on road his-by the cow   pts
'He was stopped there on the road by this cow'.

The advancement analysis correctly predicts that in sentences where the verb is suffixed with *-be,* only the initial 3 will advance to 1 by Passive, for in such sentences, it is the initial 3 which is 2 (see also Note 11). The verbs of such clauses, which involve both Indirect Object Advancement and Passive, are suffixed both with *-be* (3 → 2) and *-at* (2 → 1) (*be + at → bat*):

(28)
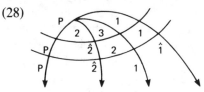

The verb agrees with the final 1, which is initial 3:

(29) *Ch-i-7ak'-b-at   jun tzeb.*   (L. 66)
icp-A1-give-*be*-pass one girl
'I am being given a girl'.

---

[10] The same noun stem is also used to express the cause of an event and the benefactive. Nonhuman passive 1-chômeurs can also be marked with the preposition *ta*.

(30)   *Mi l- a- 7ak'-b-at   7a- ve7el?*
        ?   cp-A2-give-*be*-pass your-meal
        'Were you given your meal?'

(31)   *Ch-7ak -b-at   s-lo7bol.*   (L. 351)
        icp-give-*be*-pass his-fruit
        'He is given fruit'.

In each sentence, the postverbal nominal is final 2-chômeur, put *en chômage* by the advancement of the 3. These chômeurs have no special marking.

Nothing has yet been said about structures in which 3s fail to advance to 2. No grammatical sentences correspond to such structures because of a constraint which rules out structures containing a 3 in the final stratum. This constraint is needed to rule out sentences that do not meet the conditions of Indirect Object Advancement, yet can be supposed to contain indirect objects.[11] The combined effect of the advancement rule and this constraint is that the presence of an indirect object in a clause of any grammatical sentence is marked by the verbal suffix, -*be*, marking its advancement to direct object.

To argue for the cancellation of 1-coreferential 3s, we turn to a Tzotzil construction called "possessor ascension" in Aissen (1979). If the 2 of a clause is possessed,[12] then under some circumstances the nominal that is possessor of the 2 may, and in other circumstances it must, bear the 3 relation to that clause as well. Like other 3s, these advance to 2, the verb is suffixed with -*be*, and the original 2 (the possessed nominal) goes *en chômage*. In Aissen (1979), this construction is characterized by the addition to the clause of a 3-arc headed by the nominal that is possessor of the 2. In this view, the nominal in question bears no relation to the clause in the first stratum, but is clausal 3 in a subsequent stratum, perhaps the second [see (33a)]. However, as noted in that paper, there is no evidence that this 3 is not an initial 3; what is clear is simply that under certain circumstances—namely, when the possessor of the 2 is a

---

[11] The details of this are laid out in Aissen (1982). Indirect objects cannot advance to direct object in intransitive strata (i.e., strata not containing a 2); yet no intransitive sentences containing indirect objects ever surface. Incidentally, the restriction of advancement to transitive strata together with the constraint on final 3s will rule out networks in which the initial 2 advances to 1, leaving a 3 which can neither advance to 2 nor remain a 3.

[12] In possessive phrases, the possessor follows the possessed nominal. Attached to the possessed noun is an ergative prefix marking the person of the possessor and optionally a suffix marking the number of the possessor; pronominal possessors are generally omitted:

(i)   *y-ok   li   Xune*   (ii)   *s-me7*
       E3-leg the Juan   E3-mother
       'Juan's leg'   'his/her/their mother'

third person pronoun—that nominal must also be clausal 3. The following condition guarantees this:

(32)   If a is the poss of b, and b is the 2 of a clause d, and a is a
         third person pronoun, then a must bear the 3 relation to d.

Both (33a), where a is not initial 3, and (33b), where a is, satisfy (32). Both diagrams show advancement to 2 in the final stratum.

(33)   a.   b.

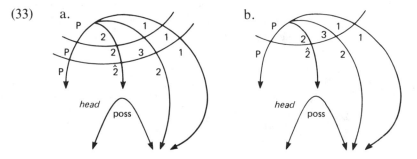

I assume that either structure is possible.

The contrast between (34b) and (35b) illustrates the requirement that third person pronominal possessors of 2s be clausal 3s.

(34)   a.   *7i -j-maj-be   y-ok.*
             cp -E1-hit-*be* his-leg
             'I hit his leg'.

        b.   **7ijmaj yok.*

(35)   a.   *Ch-i-s-tzak-be   li   j-k'ob-e.*   (L. 56)
             icp-A1-E3-grab-*be* the my-hand-enc

        b.   *Ta -s-tzak   li   j-k'ob-e.*
             icp -E3-grab the my-hand-enc
             'She grabbed my hand'.

One (possible) structure for (35a) is (36):

(36)

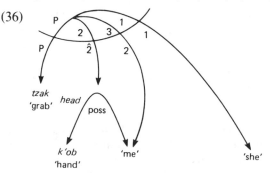

According to this structure, in the initial stratum 'me' is 3 and poss of the 2. It advances to 2 and the original 2 goes en chômage. The final 2 is first person and the verb agrees with it. Because 'me' is a pronoun, neither relation is realized in surface structure. In (35b), the poss of the 2 is not a clausal 3. One and the same nominal is initial and final 2; the verb agrees with it (third person) and -be is not suffixed to the verb.

Relevant for cancellation of 3s is the sentence synonymous with English 'He$_i$ hit his$_i$ leg' where the possessor of the 2 is 1-coreferential. The principles of Tzotzil syntax discussed earlier predict the following structure for the Tzotzil version:

(37)

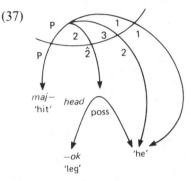

The possessor of the 2 is also the clausal 3 and as such advances to 2. In (37), the final 1 and 2 are coreferential. Generally, where final 1 and 2 are coreferential, the reflexive noun -ba (obligatorily possessed) occurs in place of the final 2:

(38)   7i -s-nak'   s-ba.
         cp -E3-hide his-self
         'He hid himself'.

The ergative affix on the verb shows that this clause is finally transitive, and hence that unlike French, for example, coreference between 1 and 2 in Tzotzil does not induce detransitivization.

However, a surface structure corresponding to (37) where -ba replaces the final 2, and the verb is suffixed with -be to mark advancement is ungrammatical:

(39)
         *7i -s-maj-be $\begin{Bmatrix} s\text{-}ba & y\text{-}ok. \\ \text{his-self his-leg} \\ y\text{-}ok & s\text{-}ba. \end{Bmatrix}$
         cp -E3-hit-be

Omission of sba yields a grammatical sentence, but the meaning is wrong. Sentence (40) is synonymous with English 'He$_i$ hit his$_j$ leg', with the possessor of the 2 and the 1 necessarily noncoreferential.

(40)   *7i -s-maj-be y-ok.*
        cp -E3-hit-*be* his-leg
        'He*i* hit his*j* leg'.

The translation of 'he*i* hit his*i* leg' is

(41)   *7i -s-maj y-ok.*
        cp -E3-hit his-leg

This sentence, in which the verb is not suffixed with -*be*, is also un-ambiguous, with necessary coreference between the 1 and possessor of the 2.

More generally, if the possessor is 1-coreferential, the verb may not be suffixed with -*be*, but if it is not, the verb must be. The obligatory presence of -*be* in (40) follows from principles already discussed: 3-hood is required for third person pronominal possessors of 2s, and advance-ment is required as well. However, the possibility of (41) under any reading has not been accounted for, nor the fact that (40) is unambiguous, lacking the coreferential reading.

The absence of -*be* in (41) and in all similar sentences suggests that these involve no advancement of the indirect object. There are at least three ways to prevent advancement: (*a*) 3-hood can be excluded when the poss of the 2 is 1-coreferential; as there is no 3, there will be no advancement; (*b*) we can allow 3-hood for the poss of the 2, but eliminate 3s which are 1-coreferential in such a way that they cannot advance; and (*c*) advancement of 3s to 2 can be restricted to those 3s which are not 1-coreferential. Possibility (c) can be dispensed with immediately. This solution requires not only that 1-coreferential 3s not advance, but also that the constraint that rules out final 3s be restricted to 3s that are not 1-coreferential. Further, these 1-coreferential final 3s would have to be obligatorily "silent." A grammar that imposes these restrictions is obviously missing something, and therefore this solution is considered untenable.[13]

Structures implied by (a) and (b) are given in (42) and (43), respectively.

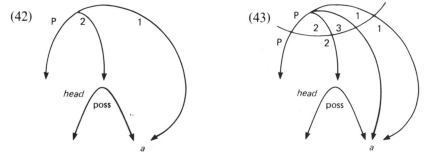

(42)   (43)

---

[13] Further, this solution does not extend to the Georgian data discussed in what follows.

Structures like (42) in which the poss of the 2 is not clausal 3 can be exempted from (32) by adding a further condition:

(44)   Iff a is the poss of b, and b is the 2 of a clause d, and a is a third person pronoun, then a must bear the 3 relation to d unless a is the 1 of d, in which case a may not bear the 3 relation to d.

In (43), the poss of the 2 is the 3, as required by (32), but the 3-arc is immediately cancelled because the 3 is 1-coreferential. The condition given in (45) would guarantee cancellation:

(45)   If a is the 3 of a clause d in a stratum C_i, and a is also the 1 of d in C_i, then the 3-arc is cancelled in C_{i+1}.

Cancellation of the 3 precludes the possibility of advancement to 2; hence there is no *-be*.

The argument for the structure in (43), and hence for Condition (45), over the structure in (42), and Condition (44), is that in other cases, having nothing to do with possessor ascension, there is evidence for 3-Cancellation. Thus (44), involving a condition on possessor ascension, is too limited, whereas (45) can account for these latter cases as well.

A type of indirect object not yet discussed is that representing a notional benefactive. Benefactives are expressed in one of several ways in Tzotzil. A benefactive may be expressed as possessor of the noun stem *-u7un* (see Note 10), which is a syntactic oblique.

(46)   *7i -s-komtzan jun kampana y-u7un jch'ul tottik . . .*   (L. 123)
         cp -E3-leave   one bell   his-for our holy father
         'They left a bell for our holy father . . .'

In this construction, coreference between subject and benefactive is indicated by the pronoun *-tuk* (itself necessarily possessed), which is similar in function to the English intensive reflexive. In this case, *-tuk* is possessor of *-u7un:*

(47)   *7i -s-meltzan jun falta y-u7un s-tuk.*
         cp -E3-make   one skirt E3-for her-self
         'She made a skirt for herself'.

More commonly in transitive clauses, the benefactive is expressed by a syntactic indirect object. Like other indirect objects, those corresponding to notional benefactives advance to direct object, with all the previously mentioned consequences for the morphology and syntax.

(48)   *Ch-a-j-mil-be-ik.*   (L. 131)
        icp-A2-E1-kill-*be*-2pl
        'I'll kill them for you(pl)'.

However, such benefactive indirect objects can only be interpreted as noncoreferential with the subject. Thus (49) can mean only that one person made a skirt for another:

(49)   *7i -s-meltzan-be jun falta.*
        cp -E3-make-*be* one skirt
        'She made her a skirt'.

The reading on which someone made a skirt for herself is expressed by (50) where the verb is not suffixed with -*be:*[14]

(50)   *7i -s-meltzan jun falta.*
        cp -E3-make one skirt

Sentence (50) was offered with no hesitation whatever on the part of the native speaker as a translation of the Spanish *Se cosió una falda para ella misma* ('She made a skirt for herself') which contains two overt reflexive morphemes (*se* and *misma*). The necessarily noncoreferential reading of (49) and the necessarily coreferential reading of (50) follow if (45) is part of the grammar of Tzotzil. The structure assigned to (50) is (51):

(51)

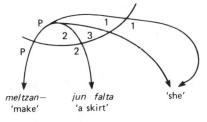

The interpretations of (49) and (50) do not follow from Condition (45).

Not surprisingly, (50) is ambiguous, having also a reading on which no benefactive at all is specified, 'She made a skirt'. On this reading, nothing suggests the existence of a 3 at any level. The ambiguity of (50)

---

[14] Again, if the benefactive indirect object advances to direct object instead of being cancelled, it would presumably be replaced by the reflexive pronoun *sba*. As with "possessor" indirect objects [see Example (39)], this is not possible:

(i)   **7i-s-meltzan-be* { *jun falta s-ba.*
        cp-E3-make-*be*   one skirt E3-self
                             sba jun falta }

       ('She made herself a skirt'.)

can be explained by positing a distinct syntactic structure for each reading. This ambiguity is not explained by assuming that (50) has the same syntactic structure under both readings with the two readings supplied by semantic interpretive rules. For it is still necessary to explain why (49), where the verb is suffixed with -*be*, cannot be interpreted with a 1-coreferential benefactive. This reading would have to be blocked independently.

To conclude this section, the absence of -*be* in clauses where 1-coreferential 3s are posited is accounted for by Condition (45), which requires immediate cancellation of all 1-coreferential 3s.[15]

4.2. Targets

There is one class of 1-coreferential 3s that are not cancelled: These bear a case relation I will term *target*. Verbs that take 3s corresponding to target ('y' in the following glosses) include *ten* 'throw x to/at y', *nap'an* 'stick x on y', *matz'an* 'stick x in/on y', *paj* 'prick y with x', *jis* 'shoot x at y', *bech'* 'poke x at y', *nib* 'rub x on y', *lam* 'spread x over y', *k'eb* 'pour x on y'.

In (52)–(54), the 3 is not 1-coreferential:

(52)   *Batan   naka me j-paj-b-ot*   *lok'el xupet k'ok'*.   (Laughlin
        get out lest   E1-insert-*be*-A2 out   firebrand   1975:262)
        'Get out or I'll stick a firebrand through you'.

(53)   *7i-j-paj-be*   *7akuxa li Xun-e*.
        cp-E1-insert-*be* needle the Juan-enc
        'I gave Juan an injection', or
        'I pricked Juan with a needle'.

(54)   *Ta s-k'eb-be   k'ak'al vo7*.   (L. 189)
        icp E3-pour-*be* hot   water
        'She poured boiling water on him'.

The syntax of target 3s is the same as that of other 3s. They necessarily advance to 2 with the same morphological and syntactic consequences.

Unlike other 3s, however, 1-coreferential 3s that are targets are not cancelled. Sentences (55)–(57) are exactly what we would expect in the

---

[15] The verb of a clause containing an unspecified but understood recipient also lacks -*be* [e.g., (22a) and (23a)]. One solution is to assume that such clauses lack a syntactic indirect object at all levels, the understood recipient being supplied by a semantic or pragmatic rule. The alternative is to assume that these verbs do take initial indirect objects, but that unspecified 3s are cancelled, like 1-coreferential 3s.

absence of cancellation. The verb is suffixed with *-be* and the final 2 is realized by the reflexive pronoun *-ba:*

(55)   *7i-j-paj-be   j-ba   7akuxa.*
        cp-E1-insert-*be* E1-self needle
        'I pricked myself with a needle', or
        'I gave myself an injection'.

(56)   *7i-j-mal-be   j-ba   k'ak'al vo7.*
        cp-E1-spill-*be* E1-self hot   water
        'I spilled the hot water on myself'.

(57)   *7i-y-ak'-be   s-ba   bala.*
        cp-E3-give-*be* E3-self bullet
        'He fired the bullet at himself'.

The structure associated with (55) is:

(58)

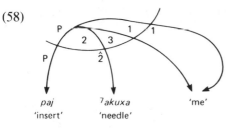

As (58) is ruled out by (45), (45) must be revised to require the advancement of 1-coreferential 3s exactly when these bear the case relation *target:*

(59)   (=45 revised) Iff *a* is the 3 of a clause *d* in a stratum C_i and
        a is also the 1 of *d* in C_i and *a* does not bear the case
        relation TARGET in *d,* then the 3-arc is cancelled in C_{i+1}.

Obviously, (59) is a possible rule only in a theory where information about both the syntactic relations and the case relation of a nominal are available simultaneously.

The existence of these facts thus interpreted constitutes an argument for the well-formedness of structures containing 1-coreferential 3s, and thus an argument for the well-formedness of the precancellation stratum in cancellation structures. Further, these facts rule out a number of otherwise possible analyses of the facts for which cancellation was proposed, for example, one in which *-ba* only realizes final 2s which are also initial 2s, or one in which a 1-coreferential 3 cannot advance to 2.

4.3. Reciprocals

An additional argument for the well-formedness of the precancellation stratum comes from reciprocal constructions. Expressions of reciprocal and reflexive coreference are syntactically and morphologically identical when the coreference holds between 1 and 2. Both are finally transitive and both use the noun -*ba*.

(60)   *7i-s-mak   la s-ba-ik   ta na.*   (L. 59)
       cp-E3-close pt E3-self-pl in house
       'They shut themselves up inside the house'.

(61)   *7i-s-nup   s-ba-ik.*   (L. 326)
       cp-E3-meet E3-self-pl
       'They met one another'.

Context determines whether it is reciprocal or reflexive coreference that is understood. Haviland (to appear) cites the following sentence as ambiguous:

(62)   *7av-ak' a-ba-ik   ta k'exlal.*
       E2-give E2-self-pl to shame
       'They exposed themselves/each other to shame'.

In this case nothing suggests any difference in syntactic structure at any stratum.

However, in the case of 1s and 3s, reciprocal and reflexive coreference are expressed differently (a fact also noted in Haviland, to appear). Whereas 3-Cancellation is required for the reflexive case (except as noted in the preceding section), it is disallowed for the reciprocal case. Instead, we get exactly the structure expected in a grammar where 3-Cancellation fails to apply [see (37)]. In (63)–(64), the verb is suffixed with -*be* and the noun -*ba* occurs:

(63)   *Ja7   7i-s-jak'-be   s-ba-ik*   (L. 61)
       emph cp-E3-ask-*be* E3-self-pl
       'So they asked each other . . .'

(64)   *Ch-[y]-av-be   s-ba-ik.*   (L. 262)
       icp-E3-plant-*be* E3-self-pl
       'They planted it for each other'.

The structures of (63)–(64) are the same as those seen in (37) and (58), with the final 2-relation realized by the noun -*ba*.

The difference between reflexive and reciprocals might be due to an unrestricted rule of 3-Cancellation, plus a semantic rule which associates the cancellation structure with (nontarget) reflexives and the others with reciprocals and target reflexives. Alternatively, 3-Cancellation could be restricted to, and required of, nontarget reflexive coreferents. It is not clear at present in what ways these proposals are significantly different.

4.4. Georgian[16]

Harris (1976, 1981) proposes an account of certain Georgian data which is very similar to the analysis proposed here for Tzotzil. There is evidence of an interesting kind for precancellation 1-coreferential 3s in the relevant structures.

In Georgian, at least two classes of 1-coreferential 3s are cancelled: 3s that correspond to notional benefactives and 3s understood as possessors of some other nominal in the clause. Harris proposes that these 3s are introduced by rules she calls Benefactive Version and Possessive Version. The first optionally promotes an oblique benefactive to 3; the second (optional in some circumstances, obligatory in others) raises certain nominal possessors to clausal 3. The following (a) and (b) sentences illustrate the nonapplication versus application of these rules. There are a number of obvious differences between sentences that involve the version rules and ones that do not. First, the verb agrees with a final 3, but not with a final oblique or final possessor. Thus, in the (b) sentences, but not the (a) sentences, the verb agrees with a 3. Second, final pronominal 3s may be omitted in surface structures, whereas final obliques and possessors may not be.

(65)   a.   *Gelam šeḳera   axali šarvali   šen-tvis.*
            G.-erg he-sewed-it new trousers-nom you-for
            'Gelam sewed new trousers for you'.

       b.   *Gelam še-g- i-ḳera (šen) axali šarvali.*
                  -2io-vv-   you
            'Gelam sewed new trousers for you'.

                                              (Harris 1976:153)

(66)   a.   *Mzia   çmends   dis   pexsacmlebs.*
            M.-nom she-cleans-it sister-gen shoes
            'Mzia cleans her sister's shoes'.

       b.   *Mzia u-çmends das   pexsacmlebs.*
                  3io-   sister-dat shoes
            'Mzia cleans her sister's shoes'.

                                              (Harris 1976:159)

[16] All of the Georgian data, as well as the analysis, are due to Harris (1976).

Crucial both to Harris's analysis and the current one is the morpheme glossed 'vv' for "version vowel." In (66b), it is conflated with the indirect object agreement marker, but in (65b), where it occurs independently, its form is /-i-/. Harris accounts for the conflated form by a morphological rule: $+h+i+ \rightarrow +u+$ (Harris 1976:157). The version vowel is always affixed to the verb of a clause containing an indirect object corresponding to notional benefactive or possessor. According to Harris's analysis, the version vowel is introduced by Benefactive and Possessive Version. I will assume this here, although it is not crucial to the argument.

We turn now to cases where indirect objects are coreferential with the subjects of their clauses. In such cases, the indirect object CANNOT occur in surface structure (either as a reflexive or as a nonreflexive pronoun) and, though the verb bears the version vowel, it does not agree with a final indirect object. The following is quoted directly from Harris (1976):

> In (14) below, the benefactive nominal is coreferential to the subject of the clause; in (15) the possessor is coreferential to the subject. In the (a) sentences, to which no version rule has applied, the benefactive nominal and the possessor are present in surface structure. But in the (b) sentences, to which the version rules have applied, the benefactive-nominal and the possessor are not present in surface structure. The ungrammaticality of the (*c) sentences show that it is not possible to apply version and leave the advancee in the clause as a reflexive; the grammaticality of (a) rules out the possibility that these sentences have ill-formed initial structures. In the (*d) sentences, the version marker, i-, has been added to the verb, but the benefactive and possessive have not been advanced.

(14)   a.   *gela   tavistvis aḳetebs   saçer   magidas.*
              Gela-nom self-for   he-makes-it writing table-dat
              'Gela is making a desk for himself'.

        b.   *gela iḳetebs   saçer magidas.*[5]
                   he-makes-self-it
              'Gela is making a desk for himself'.

        c.   **gela (tavis) tavs   iḳetebs saçer magidas.*
                   self's self-dat
              ('Gela is making a desk for himself'.)

        d.   **gela tavistvis iḳetebs saçer magidas.*
                   self-for
              ('Gela is making a desk for himself'.)

(15)   a.   *gela   çmends   tavis pexsacmlebs.*
              Gela-nom he-cleans-it self's shoes-dat
              'Gela$_i$ is cleaning his$_i$ shoes'.

        b.   *gela içmends   pexsacmlebs.*
                   he-cleans-self-it
              'Gela$_i$ is cleaning his$_i$ shoes'.

> c. *gela (tavis) tavs icmends pexsacmlebs.
>   self's self-dat
>   ('Gela is cleaning his shoes'.)
>
> d. *gela icmends tavis pexsacmlebs.
>   self's
>   ('Gela is cleaning his shoes'.)

It is the marker *i* on the verb, in addition to the meaning of the sentence, that tells us that Benefactive or Possessive Version has applied.

Notice that the (*c) sentences in (14–15) differ from the fully grammatical version sentences considered in sections 1. and 2. above only in that the derived indirect object is coreferent with the subject of the clause. . . .

It is worth pointing out that in (14–15) the version marker *i* standing alone without an object agreement marker indicates that a coreferential version object has deleted. If version had not applied, there would be no *i*. If the version object had not been coreferential, it could not have deleted without triggering Indirect Object Agreement (*m-i*, *g-i*, or *u-*). Although *i* is used elsewhere, it would never occur in exactly these forms for another morphological purpose. Thus, (14) and (15) are absolutely unambiguous. But in (16) and (17) there is nothing parallel to *i* to indicate the deletion of a coreferent nominal. [pp. 163–166; footnote 5 omitted]

Harris proposes a rule which deletes 1-coreferential indirect objects introduced by any of the version rules. As the version vowel is added by the version rules, its presence is accounted for. And as agreement is with FINAL indirect objects, absence of indirect object agreement in these cases is accounted for by the deletion rule. Whether or not one follows Harris in assuming syntactic rules of Benefactive and Possessive Version, as long as the presence of the version vowel is due to the presence of an indirect object corresponding to notional benefactive or nominal possessor in the clause, the presence of the version vowel in Harris's (14b) and (15b) is evidence for an indirect object in early strata of the network.

4.5. Cancellation Not Required

The claim being made here is the rather weak one that languages may require cancellation of a grammatical relation borne by a nominal under the condition of coreference, and not that all languages require this, or that languages with such-and-such properties require this. Two languages that appear not to require cancellation of 1-coreferential 3s are English and Basque.

English requires the presence of a reflexive 3 in surface structure if one is to be understood; in other words, the (a) and (b) sentences given here are not synonymous:

(67)   a. *He addressed the letter.*
        b. *He addressed the letter to himself.*

(68)   a. *He repeated the answer.*
        b. *He repeated the answer to himself.*

In Basque, the reflexive pronoun has the form 'my head', 'your head', 'his head'. When the 3 is 1-coreferential, it occurs in surface structure and the verb agrees with it, like any other 3:

(69)   *Ez diot nere buruari mikik eginen.*
                my   head-dat
        'I won't do any harm to myself'.   (LaFitte:94)

The verb *diot* agrees with a third person indirect object.

4.6. Range of Cancellation

Cancellation of the indirect object relation in Tzotzil and Georgian reduces the valence of the affected clauses from three nominal arguments to two. Thus, the effect is parallel to the detransitivization of reflexive clauses in French, Dyirbal, and Turkish. In both cases, cancellation of the lower of two grammatical relations borne by a single nominal reduces clausal valence by one.

The question remains whether there also exist oblique cancellations; in general, the range of cancellations remains to be discovered.

5. CANCELLATION AND MOTIVATED CHÔMAGE

The previous discussion presupposes the possibility of cancellation. However, within the framework of relational grammar, the question arises whether it is required, given that its effects can largely be achieved by combining demotion with the requirement of silence (invisibility) for certain nominals, both of which are needed independently.

The most relevant proposals are those of Postal (1977, 1982), who has proposed that detransitivization by demotion or apparent deletion of the direct object (as in the French reflexive case, and in various cases of antipassive) be accounted for by only two operations:

(70)   2-to-3 Retreat

(71)   1-to-2 Demotion

Postal (1977) proposes that the term "antipassive" be restricted to cases of 1-to-2 Demotion. In making an earlier direct object the indirect object, 2-to-3 Retreat detransitivizes the clause:

(72)
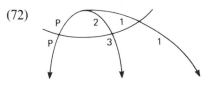

The effect of 1-to-2 Demotion is to place the original 2 en chômage. Relevant to us is a principle Postal (1977) refers to which will guarantee that the original subject will advance to subject: ". . . that the original subject does not stay direct object but reverts to subjecthood is attributed to a rule requiring the assignment of subjecthood to a direct object not coexisting at a stratum with a subject. This rule, not to be confused with Passive, can, I believe, be shown to be strongly motivated independently of all questions of Antipassive [p. 292]."

(73)
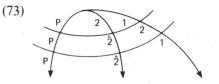

The absence of a final 2 makes the clause finally intransitive.

Cases in which the direct object chômeur or indirect object fails to surface in any form are attributed to the fact that certain nominals may be silent (i.e., assigned no representation by the phonology). In the case of detransitivization, the combination of demotion and silence has much the same effect as cancellation. In principle, the two proposals make different claims, but distinguishing cases will be hard to find.

However, if we are to do without cancellation in the case of detransitivization, we must be able to dispense with it in the cases of reduction of ditransitive clauses to monotransitive ones. If cancellation is needed for indirect objects, some good reason will be needed to exclude it in the case of direct objects. It is worth considering, then, whether operations analogous to (70)–(71) are available for eliminating indirect objects. If not, then some other solution is needed if cancellation is ruled out.

Consider first an operation analogous to 2-to-3 Retreat. The nominal relations lower than 3 to which an indirect object might revalue are the oblique relations, and the chômeur relation. But principles of relational grammar prohibit any revaluation to an oblique relation and any spontaneous demotion to chômeur. The Oblique Law rules out the network in (74) and the Motivated Chômage Law rules out (75):[17]

(74)   3   P   n
     Oblique   P   n

(75)   3   P   n
        3̂   P   n

The operation analogous to 1-to-2 Demotion [see (73)] would be demotion of the subject to indirect object, placing the latter en chômage. Crucially, however, the original subject must revalue to subject [as in (76a)], and in particular, the direct object in the second stratum must not; (76b) must be ruled out:

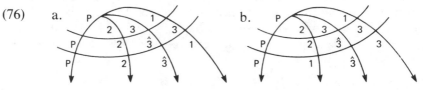

(76)   a.   P   1   b.   P   1
             2   3   3   2   3   3
          P   2   3̂   1   P   2   3̂   3
          P   2   3̂   P   1   3̂

If, per the passage quoted from Postal (1977), there is a principle which would force advancement of direct object to subject when the direct object does not cooccur with a subject at some stratum, then the wrong structure (76b) is forced and the right one (76a) ruled out in principle. Even if (76b) is not forced, its mere possibility must be ruled out. In short, operations analogous to (70) and (71) cannot eliminate indirect objects from clauses, given the assumptions of relational grammar.

If the Motivated Chômage Law is abandoned, however, analyses of the Tzotzil and Georgian facts which do not involve cancellation become available. One could hypothesize that in Tzotzil, 1-coreferential 3s spontaneously demote to 3-chômeur, with the provision that 3-chômeurs are necessarily silent. In Georgian, certain 1-coreferential 3s spontaneously demote to 3-chômeur, and are likewise silent. As final 3-chômeurs are not final terms, they will not trigger agreement in Georgian.

Thus, spontaneous demotion and silence do all the work of cancellation. Assuming that there is no way to distinguish a structure containing a final silent 3-chômeur (and no 3) from one containing neither a final 3-chômeur nor a final 3, the two analyses are not distinguishable on

---

[17] The Oblique Law rules out any network in which a nominal that does not bear a given oblique relation in the initial stratum bears that relation in a later stratum. The Motivated Chômage Law excludes networks in which a nominal bears the chômeur relation under conditions other than those allowed by the Chômeur Law. See Perlmutter and Postal (1982a).

empirical grounds. Further, once spontaneous demotion is allowed, an account of detransitivization by spontaneous demotion of the 2 plus silence is available, making it possible to relate the reduction in syntactic valence in transitive and ditransitive clauses.

6. MORPHOLOGY

Some linguists have attempted to relate the syntactic intransitivity of some reflexive constructions to their semantic properties (e.g., Lakoff 1977:257; Faltz 1977:Chap. 1, especially p. 14; Edmondson 1978). The relevant semantic property is that predicates of the form $F(x, x)$, where both argument positions of a 2-place predicate are filled by the same term, are different from those of the form $G(x, y)$ in that F denotes a property of individuals whereas G denotes a relation between pairs of individuals. In this respect, F is like any 1-place predicate.

Hence, if we take the DEGREE of a predicate to be the number of distinct variables in argument positions (cf. Mates 1972:72), then the degree of $F(x, x)$ is 1, while that of $G(x, y)$ is 2, and the cancellation of 1-coreferential direct objects makes the final syntactic valence of the reflexive clause equal to the degree of the corresponding predicate. In syntactically transitive reflexive constructions, the number of syntactic positions equals the number of argument positions itself. In general, any n-ary predicate which has identical variables in two argument positions will denote a set of $(n - 1)$-tuples of individuals, just like an $(n - 1)$-ary predicate with distinct variables in every argument position. Hence the reduction in syntactic valence observed in Tzotzil and Georgian can likewise be motivated by the apparent predisposition of languages to match syntactic valence to the degree of the corresponding predicate.

Such an account may shed some light on the fact, discussed by many linguists (among them Babby and Brecht, 1975; Baldi, 1974; Cranmer, 1976; Langacker and Munro, 1975; Napoli, 1974; and Perlmutter and Postal, 1982b), that constructions of the following sort have, in various languages, common morphology and/or syntax: reflexive constructions, reciprocals, passives, inchoatives, unspecified object constructions. Various common features have been proposed, but we may note that the logical representations of these constructions can all be analyzed as having predicates of degree $n - 1$, and as derived by elimination of one argument position from predicates with n argument positions. According to this view, the common feature of reflexives and passives is not, as Langacker and Munro argue, the nondistinctness of two argument positions but the relation of reflexives and passives, both with predicates of degree $n - 1$, to predicates of degree n.

In some languages, the morphology shared by these constructions can be linked to some common syntactic property (a common structure at some level—cf. Cranmer, 1976; Napoli, 1974) or a common syntactic operation. But in other cases, the morphology is so lexically restricted or the required syntactic derivations so implausible that the linking of morphology to shared syntax is undesirable. In such cases, the common semantic properties are an obvious key to the morphology.[18]

ACKNOWLEDGMENTS

I owe a special debt to Carol Rosen, for the idea of cancellation was hers. I believe she has developed it in her own way, and is not responsible for anything here. Many others have helped me to clarify my thoughts on the matters discussed here. I am grateful to all of them, especially Michael Aissen, Sandy Chung, Jorge Hankamer, David Johnson, David Perlmutter, Paul Postal, Jonathan Pressler, and Alan Timberlake.

REFERENCES

Aissen, J. (1979) "Possessor Ascension in Tzotzil," in L. Martin, ed., *Papers in Mayan Linguistics,* Lucas Brothers Publishers, Columbia, Mo.

Aissen, J. (1982) "Indirect Object Advancement in Tzotzil," in D. Perlmutter, ed., *Studies in Relational Grammar, I,* University of Chicago Press, Chicago.

Babby, L. H. and R. D. Brecht (1975) "The Syntax of Voice in Russian," *Language* 51, 342–367.

Baldi, P. (1974) "Reciprocal Verbs and Symmetric Predicates," in M. W. LaGaly, R. A. Fox, and A. Bruck, eds., *Papers from the Tenth Regional Meeting of the Chicago Linguistic Society,* University of Chicago.

Cranmer, D. J. (1976) *Derived Intransitivity: A Contrastive Analysis of Certain Reflexive Verbs in German, Russian, and English,* Max Niemeyer Verlag, Tubingen, Germany.

Dixon, R. M. W. (1972) *The Dyirbal Language of North Queensland,* Cambridge University Press, Cambridge.

Dixon, R. M. W. (1979) "A Note on Dyirbal Ergativity," in P. R. Clyne, W. F. Hanks, and C. L. Hofbauer, eds., *Papers from the Fifteenth Regional Meeting of the Chicago Linguistic Society,* University of Chicago.

Edmondson, J. (1978) "Ergative Languages, Accessibility Hierarchies Governing Reflexives and Questions of Formal Analysis," in W. Abraham, ed., *Valence, Semantic Case, and Grammatical Relations,* John Benjamins B.B., Amsterdam, The Netherlands.

Faltz, L. (1977) *Reflexivization: A Study in Universal Syntax,* unpublished doctoral dissertation, University of California, Berkeley.

---

[18] García (1975) discusses such an approach, albeit from a very different perspective, at great length.

García, E. (1975) *The Role of Theory in Linguistic Analysis,* North-Holland, Amsterdam, The Netherlands.

Gary, J. and E. L. Keenan (1977) "On Collapsing Grammatical Relations in Universal Grammar," in P. Cole and J. Sadock, eds., *Syntax and Semantics 8,* Academic Press, New York.

Harris, A. (1976) *Grammatical Relations in Modern Georgian,* unpublished doctoral dissertation, Harvard University, Cambridge, Massachusetts.

Harris, A. (1981) *Georgian Syntax: A Study in Relational Grammar,* Cambridge University Press, Cambridge.

Haviland, J. (to appear) *Sk'op sotz'leb: El Tzotzil de San Lorenzo Zinacantán,* Centro de Estudios Mayas, Mexico City.

Hopper, P. and S. Thompson (1980) "Transitivity in Grammar and Discourse," *Language* 56, 251–299.

Jake, J. (1978) "Why Dyirbal Isn't Ergative at All," in D. Farkas, W. M. Jacobsen, and K. W. Todrys, eds., *Papers from the Fourteenth Regional Meeting of the Chicago Linguistic Society,* University of Chicago.

Johnson, D. and P. Postal (1980) *Arc Pair Grammar,* Princeton University Press, Princeton, New Jersey.

Kayne, R. (1975) *French Syntax: The Transformational Cycle,* MIT Press, Cambridge, Massachusetts.

Keenan, E. L. (1975) "Logical Expressive Power, and Syntactic Variation in Natural Language," in E. L. Keenan, ed., *Formal Semantics of Natural Language,* Cambridge University Press, London.

LaFitte, A. P. (1944) *Grammaire Basque,* Bayonne, France.

Lakoff, G. (1977) "Linguistic Gestalts," in W. A. Beach, S. E. Fox, and S. Philosoph, eds., *Papers from the Thirteenth Regional Meeting of the Chicago Linguistic Society,* University of Chicago.

Langacker, R. and P. Munro (1975) "Passives and Their Meaning," *Language* 51, 789–830.

Laughlin, R. (1975) *The Great Tzotzil Dictionary of San Lorenzo Zinacantan,* Smithsonian Institution Press, Washington, D.C.

Laughlin, R. (1977) *Of Cabbages and Kings,* Smithsonian Institution Press, Washington, D.C.

Mates, B. (1972) *Elementary Logic,* Oxford University Press, New York.

Napoli, D. J. (1974) "In Chaos or Inchoative? An Analysis of Inchoatives in Modern Standard Italian," in R. J. Campbell, M. Goldin, and M. C. Wang, eds., *Linguistic Studies in Romance Languages,* Georgetown University Press, Washington, D.C.

Perlmutter, D. and P. Postal (1977) "Toward a Universal Characterization of Passive," in K. Whistler *et al.,* eds., *Proceedings of the Third Annual Meeting of the Berkeley Linguistic Society,* University of California, Berkeley.

Perlmutter, D. and P. Postal (1982a) "Some Laws of Basic Clause Structure," in D. Perlmutter, ed., *Studies in Relational Grammar, I,* University of Chicago Press, Chicago.

Perlmutter, D. and P. Postal (1982b) "Impersonal Passives and Some Relational Laws," in D. Perlmutter, ed., *Studies in Relational Grammar, I,* University of Chicago Press, Chicago.

Postal, P. (1977) "Antipassive in French," in J. Regal, D. Nash, and A. Zaenen, eds., *Proceedings of the Seventh Annual Meeting of the North Eastern Linguistic Society,* Department of Linguistics, MIT, Cambridge, Massachusetts.

Postal, P. (1982) "Some Arc Pair Grammar Descriptions," in P. Jacobson and G. Pullum, eds., *The Nature of Syntactic Representation,* D. Reidel, Dordrecht, The Netherlands.

TRANSITIVITY AND COGNATE OBJECTS IN AUSTRALIAN LANGUAGES

PETER AUSTIN

1. INTRODUCTION

Linguists describing the structure of Australian Aboriginal languages have generally taken as uncontroversial a dichotomy between transitive verbs (and clauses) and intransitive verbs (and clauses). The clearest statement of this position is in Dixon (1980) where we find that: "Every verb in an Australian language is strictly transitive—occurring with subject (A) and object (O) core NPs—or strictly intransitive—occurring just with a subject (S) core NP. It is usually a simple matter to determine transitivity [p. 378]." In most instances this statement appears to hold and verbs will divide neatly into the two classes. However, in a number of Australian languages, there are verbs that resist subcategorization in this way. In this paper I wish to focus on two types of deviation from the simple pattern, namely:

1. In some languages there are verbs that occur with an A NP (which is case marked as "ergative" if a common noun, "nominative" if a pronoun—see Silverstein, 1976; Dixon, 1979) and which can *never* take an O NP. An instance is Bandjalang.
2. In some languages there are verbs that occur with an S NP (case marked as "absolutive" if a common noun, "nominative" if a pronoun)

37

Syntax and Semantics, Volume 15

and a complement noun phrase which has some or all of the morpho-syntactic properties of a transitive object NP. Examples of this are found in Diyari, Bayungu, Djaru, Guugu Yimidhirr, and Yidiny.

In the following discussion it is shown that these two phenomena are related and that the verbs involved all take so-called cognate objects. An explanation of the morphosyntactic facts is proposed drawing on the framework of Hopper and Thompson (1980) who suggest that transitivity is a continuum and not a simple dichotomy. Cognate object constructions in Australian languages have a natural explanation in this framework.

2. COGNATE OBJECT CONSTRUCTIONS

2.1. Bandjalang

The Bandjalang language is spoken on the north coast of New South Wales. In the Waalubal dialect described by Crowley (1978) there are a number of verbs that occur with a transitive subject noun phrase but can *never* take a transitive object. They can all be characterized se-mantically as cognate object verbs where the understood object is highly specific. Crowley (1978:107) lists the members of this set as:[1]

ginyjaama	'defecate'	*banma*	'put on' (clothing)
jaluba	'urinate'	*yarrbi*	'sing'
birrma	'yawn'	*wulbi*	'make' (noise)
ngaarri	'dance'	*juuma*	'smoke' (cigarette)

Examples of their use in sentences are:

(1)   *Mali-yu jaajam-bu jaluba-ni.*
       that-erg child-erg   urinate-past definite
       'That child urinated (some urine)'.

(2)   *Mali-yu dandaygam-bu yarrbi-ni.*
       that-erg old man-erg   sing-past definite
       'That old man sang (a song)'.

Bandjalang has an antipassive construction (Silverstein, 1976; Dixon, 1979) which applies only to transitive verbs changing the A NP to an

---

[1] In these and following examples (except for Guugu Yimidhirr), original transcriptions have been changed to a practical orthography using digraphs, where *th, nh* and *lh* are laminodental stop, nasal and lateral; *rt, rn,* and *rl* are apicodomals (retroflexes); *j, ny,* and *ly* are palatals; and *ng* is a dorsovelar nasal. Long vowels are written double.

S NP and adding -*li*/-*le* to the verb root; an example is the pair (Crowley 1978:108):

(3)   *Ngaju juga-ala   nyabay.*
        I-erg   drink-pres water-abs
        'I am drinking water'.

(4)   *Ngay juga-le-ela   nyabay.*
        I-nom drink-antipass-pres water-abs
        'I am drinking water (repeatedly)'.

Now, the eight cognate object verbs can all appear in the antipassive and hence behave syntactically like normal transitive verbs:

(5)   *Ngay gala   juuma-le-ela.*
        I-nom this-nom smoke-antipass-pres
        'I here am smoking (a cigarette)'.

Thus, Bandjalang has a class of verbs that are transitive from a syntactic point of view yet can never appear in a clause with an overt transitive object noun phrase. Clearly, cooccurrence with A and O NPs cannot be a necessary and sufficient condition for defining transitive verbs, and some explanation of the apparently deviant behavior of these particular verbs is required.

2.2. Diyari

Diyari is spoken in the northeastern corner of the state of South Australia; data are from Austin (1981). In this language we find a construction type that poses problems for any simple definition of transitivity.

Diyari has a group of six verbs which occur with an S NP (in nominative or absolutive case depending on constituent type) and a further complement noun phrase whose head noun is marked as absolutive case. These verbs are:

yatha	'to speak' (a language)
kirli	'to dance' (a ceremony)
thurrara	'to lie, sleep'
pirrki	'to play' (a game)
wirri	'to wear' (clothing)
widi	'to be painted' (a pattern)

Examples of their use are:

(6)   *Nganhi diyari yawada   yatha-yi.*
        I-nom   Diyari language-abs speak-pres
        'I speak Diyari'.

(7)   *Thana   karna   pukartu wima   kirli-rna   wanthiyi.*
       they-nom person-abs ochre   ceremony-abs dance-ptcple aux
       'Those people danced the ochre ceremony'.

The nominal complements of these verbs occur in absolutive case as
(6) and (7) illustrate. In addition, they have two syntactic characteristics
in common with transitive object NPs (coded as absolutive or accusative
case depending on constituent type). First, when a demonstrative is
included in the complement NP it inflects for ACCUSATIVE case just like
an O NP. Thus, we have:

(8)   *Nganhi nhinha-ya   yawada   yatha-yi.*
       I-nom   this-acc-here language-abs speak-pres
       'I speak this language'.

Compare this with the transitive sentence:

(9)   *Ngathu nhinha-ya   nganthi   thayi-yi.*
       I-erg   this-acc-here meat-abs eat-pres
       'I eat this meat'.

Second, when nominalized a transitive verb can take an object nominal
immediately before it, forming a type of phrasal compound (no other
constituents can intervene between the object and nominalized verb but
phonologically they are not a single word). Examples of agentive nominalizations illustrating this are:

        nganthi thayi-rnayija   'meat eater'
        meat   eat-agent nominal

        ngapa thapa-rnayija   'water drinker'
        water drink-agent nominal

        kupa   nanda-rnayija   'child beater'
        child   hit-agent nominal

Nominalizations of intransitive verbs cannot take such a nominal element
preceding them; yet the six verbs that have been listed here can occur
in nominalizations with their complements which thus function syntactically like O NPs:

        yawada   yatha-rnayija   'language speaker'
        language speak-agent nominal

        wima   kirli-rnayija   'ceremony dancer'
        ceremony dance-agent nominal

As far as nominalization and case marking of demonstratives are concerned, complements of cognate object verbs in Diyari function exactly

like transitive objects. Their subjects, however, function like intransitive subjects.

2.3. Bayungu

Bayungu is spoken on the central coast of Western Australia; data are from Austin (1978). In Bayungu three basic clause types are found:

1. Intransitive clauses where the subject (S) NP is in absolutive (if a noun) or nominative case (if a pronoun or demonstrative). An example is:

(10)   *Ngunha kanyara nyina-yi.*
        that-nom man-abs sit-pres
        'That man is sitting down'.

2. Middle clauses where the subject is marked like an intransitive subject and there is a complement NP in dative case:[2]

(11)   *Yinha   kupuju   pirungkarri-yi ngurnu kaparla-ku.*
        this-nom child-abs fear-pres   that-dat dog-dat
        'This child fears that dog'.

3. Transitive clauses where the subject (A) is in ergative case (except for the first person pronoun which collapses S and A as nominative) and the subject (O) is in accusative (if a pronoun, demonstrative or noun with animate reference) or absolutive case (all other nouns). Examples are:

(12)   *Yulu   kupuju-lu ngunhanha kaparla-nha pujurrpa-nma*
        this-erg child-erg that-acc dog-acc   see-past
        'This child saw that dog'.

(13)   *Ngulu   kanyara-lu ngunhanha murla   warni-nmayi.*
        that-erg man-erg   that-acc meat-abs cut-past
        'That man cut that meat'.

There are two verbs in the Bayungu corpus which do not fit into this pattern; they take an intransitive subject and an absolutive case complement noun:

Verb		Complement	
ngurnta	'to lie'	*pungurn*	'sleep'
wangka	'to speak'	*kujurru*	'language'
		piyal	'story'

---

[2] A number of Australian languages have this type of construction—see Blake (1977) for discussion and examples.

An example is:

(14)   *Ngunha kanyara piyal   wangka-yi.*
        that-nom man-abs story-abs tell-pres
        'That man is telling a story'.

Unfortunately, I have no examples of these nouns cooccurring with a
demonstrative so I am not sure if they take accusative case-marked
demonstratives (like O NPs). However, there are some data that suggest
that these complements function like transitive objects.

In nonfinite clauses in Bayungu, transitive objects take case marking
that is different from the marking they receive in finite (main) clauses.
For present purposes all that is necessary is the information that in
certain nonfinite participial clauses O NPs take dative case marking, for
instance [cf. (13)]:

(15)   *Ngunha kanyara nyina-yi murla-ku warni-lkarra.*
        that-nom man-abs sit-pres meat-dat cut-ptcple
        'That man is sitting down cutting meat'.

Now, the complement of *wangka* 'say' is also marked with the dative
case in this type of clause:

(16)   *Ngunha kanyara nyina-yi piyal-ku wangka-rra.*
        that-nom man-abs sit-pres story-dat say-ptcple
        'That man is sitting down telling a story'.

It is clear that in (16) *piyal* is functioning like a transitive object as far
as the details of case marking are concerned, yet it occurs in clauses
with an S NP. Bayungu cognate object verbs thus resemble those of
Diyari.

2.4. Djaru

Djaru is spoken in the Kimberleys district of northern Western Australia; data are from Tsunoda (1978). Djaru has two verbs which Tsunoda
(1978:111) states are "intransitive" but take an "intransitive direct object," namely *marn-* 'to speak, talk' and *ruyu marn-* 'to play, perform
(a corroboree)'. Examples are:[3]

(17)   *Ngaju nga-rna jaru   marn-an.*
        I-nom aux-I   Djaru-abs speak-pres
        'I speak Djaru'.

[3] Tsunoda (1978:112) states that similar constructions occur in the neighboring languages
Malngin, Wandjira, and Ngardi.

(18)   *Mawun nga-lu   junpa   ruyu marn-an.*
       man-abs aux-they corroboree-abs perform-pres
       'The men are performing a corroboree'.

Tsunoda calls the complement nouns in (17) and (18) intransitive direct objects because they, like true direct object nouns, may be incorporated into nominalizations, as in the following example (Tsunoda 1978:113):

(19)   *Ngaju nga-rna jaru-marn-u-waji*
       I-nom aux-I   Djaru-speak-nominal-agent
       'I am a Djaru speaker'.

Djaru thus presents evidence analogous to Diyari, showing that cognate objects are like direct objects, yet cooccur with intransitive subject NPs.

2.5. Guugu Yimidhirr

Guugu Yimidhirr is spoken in northern Queensland; data are from Haviland (1979). In his description of Guugu Yimidhirr, Haviland (1979) draws a contrast between transitive verbs and intransitive verbs but is faced with a problem in describing the category of the verb 'to speak'. He notes: "the verb *yirrgaa* 'speak' is somewhat indeterminate between transitive and intransitive; it normally has an ABSolutive (or NOMinative) subject, but also allows an apparent object (usually a word like *guugu* 'language' or *milbi* 'story') [p. 83]." Note here Haviland's phrase "an apparent object"—he provides some slight evidence that the complement of *yirrgaa* does function syntactically like a transitive object. In Guugu Yimidhirr transitive verbs can be detransitivized and made "reflexive" by suffixing a derivational affix to the root; intransitive verbs do not take this affix. The verb *yirrgaa* does occur in the "reflexive," as in the following example:[4]

(20)   *Yurra   yirrga-ayi.*
       you all-nom speak-reflex-imper
       'You all have a talk'.

It seems then that *yirrgaa* has characteristics of both transitive and intransitive verb types.

2.6. Yidiny

Yidiny, described in Dixon (1977), was formerly spoken in northern Queensland, just south of Guugu Yimidhirr. Regarding transitivity in this

---

[4] The morpheme sequence "reflexive" plus imperative inflection is realized as -V*yi*, where V is a vowel identical to the last vowel of the verb root.

language, Dixon (1977) states categorically that "every Yidiny verb is inherently transitive or intransitive, and its transitivity is of the utmost importance for the syntactic operations that can be applied to it [p. 273]." Yet there are some verbs whose syntactic behavior does not fit this rigid pattern, and as a result they produce problems for the analysis, one of which Dixon (1977) briefly alludes to in a note:

> There are two kinds of construction in Yidiny that it is difficult to know how to classify. With a verb such as *nyanggaaji-n* 'talk' the noun describing the language that is being used can occur in absolutive case, apparently within the S NP. . . . And the noun *wabar* 'a walk' commonly functions in the same way with verbs like *gali-n* 'go':
>
> [787]   *ngayu wabar galing*   'I'm going for a walk'
>
> In the absence of any reason for treating them in any other way, it seems simplest to suggest that these may be a type of 'inalienable possession', with 'language' and 'walk' being regarded as 'part' of the actor in those cases! It would probably need a native speaker trained as a linguist to decide whether in fact this is a valid assignment [p. 364].

Clearly there are a number of problems raised by this quotation, not the least of which is the provision of semantic interpretation so that 'I' and 'walk' in (787) can refer to one individual. A search of the grammar shows that there are at least two other verbs that function in a way similar to those mentioned in the passage cited here.[5] In a note on page 472, Dixon states that *wugu burrgi-n* 'go working' (where *wugu* is a noun 'work' and *burrgi-n* is an intransitive verb 'go') is syntactically identical to *wabar gali-n* 'go walking' [cf. Example (787), cited here]. Also, in example (989) on page 471 we find:

[989]   *Ngayu wurrmba   wunaany.*
          I-nom asleep-abs lie-past
          'I lay asleep'.

In the vocabulary at the end of the grammar (pp. 546–549) *wuna-n* is given as an intransitive verb and *wurrmba* as an adjective meaning 'asleep', followed by the parenthetical note "& N a sleep?". I suggest that *wurrmba* does function as a noun in (989) and that all these verbs are intransitive, taking an objectlike complement. Dixon does not provide any syntactic evidence that these nouns have properties shared with transitive object NPs (other than absolutive case marking) but they are clearly parallel to constructions involving the same semantic concepts in the other languages described in this paper.

---

[5] Dixon (personal communication) also notes that the verb *nyamba* 'to dance' takes an intransitive subject plus a noun denoting the dance style, as in *ngayu warrma nyambaany* 'I danced Warrma-style'.

3. CONCLUSIONS

Disregarding Bandjalang for the moment, we find that the following verbs occur with objectlike complements in the languages surveyed:

	Verb	Complement
In all languages	'talk'	'language'
		'story'
In all except Djaru and Guugu Yimidhirr(?)	'lie'	'sleep'
In Yidiny, Djaru, and Diyari[6]	'dance'	'ceremony'
In Djaru and Diyari	'play'	'game'
In Yidiny	'go'	'walk'
		'work'
In Diyari	'wear'	'clothing'
	'be painted'	'pattern'

These verbs all belong to the semantic class of "cognate object" verbs; they take highly specific objects which can be understood as closely connected semantically with the meaning of the verb.

Syntactically, clauses containing these verbs and their complements have characteristics of both transitive and intransitive clauses:

1. The clause contains two NPs, one of which has some or all of the morphosyntactic properties of a transitive object.
2. The other NP is case marked as if it were an intransitive subject. These clauses are thus part way between fully transitive clauses and fully intransitive clauses, as the following table shows.

Sentence type		Verb class	
1. NP noun:ergative pronoun:nominative	NP noun:absolutive pronoun:accusative	V	transitive verb
2. NP noun:absolutive pronoun:nominative		V	intransitive verb
3. NP noun:absolutive pronoun:nominative	NP noun:absolutive pronoun:accusative	V	cognate object verb

These facts can be straightforwardly explained in terms of the theory of transitivity proposed by Hopper and Thompson (1980). In their paper, Hopper and Thompson propose that transitivity is a continuum defined

[6] See Note 5.

by a set of components: Clauses with more highly transitive components are more likely to be coded as transitive than those with fewer transitive components. One of these transitivity components is "individuation" of the object NP, that is, the degree of distinctness of the object from the subject and from the background (which will be a function of other parameters such as animacy, number, definiteness, and referentiality—see Hopper and Thompson, 1980). Cognate objects are low in individuation, they are not distinct from the situation described by the verb, and hence we might expect clauses containing them to be lower in transitivity than canonical transitives. This is clearly the case in the languages described here; they have subjects case marked as if they were INTRANSITIVE subjects.

Bandjalang also reflects this lower transitivity of cognate object constructions, not in having subjects case marked like intransitive subjects, but in *never* allowing an object, just as fully intransitive clauses do not have objects. Thus, cognate object constructions are part way between transitive and intransitive constructions in Bandjalang also (although it reflects the fact in a way different from the other languages surveyed).

An examination of cognate object constructions in six Australian languages has shown that the claim that transitivity is a simple dichotomy is untenable. Linguists working on these languages must be prepared to accept that some clauses will be neither fully transitive nor fully intransitive but show features which place them between these two poles on the transitivity continuum.

ACKNOWLEDGMENTS

This paper was written while I was a postdoctoral fellow at the University of California, Los Angeles and the Massachusetts Institute of Technology; I am grateful to the Commonwealth Fund of New York for its generous support through the Harkness Fellowships program. For data and comments I thank R.M.W. Dixon, Ken Hale, David Nash, and Sandra Thompson, none of whom can be held responsible for any errors herein.

REFERENCES

Austin, P. (1978) *Fieldnotes on the Kanyara Languages: Bayungu, Dhalandji and Burduna*, unpublished material.
Austin, P. (1981) *A Grammar of Diyari, South Australia*, Cambridge University Press, Cambridge.
Blake, B. J. (1977) *Case Marking in Australian Languages*, Australian Institute of Aboriginal Studies, Canberra.
Blake, B. J. and R. M. W. Dixon, eds. (1979) *The Handbook of Australian Languages*, Vol. 1, Australian National University Press, Canberra.

Crowley, T. (1978) *The Middle Clarence Dialects of Bandjalang,* Australian Institute of Aboriginal Studies, Canberra.

Dixon, R. M. W., ed. (1976) *Grammatical Categories in Australian Languages,* Australian Institute of Aboriginal Studies, Canberra.

Dixon, R. M. W. (1977) *A Grammar of Yidiny,* Cambridge University Press, Cambridge.

Dixon, R. M. W. (1979) "Ergativity," *Language* 55, 59–133.

Dixon, R. M. W. (1980) *The Languages of Australia.* Cambridge University Press, Cambridge.

Haviland, J. (1979) "Guugu Yimidhirr," in B. J. Blake and R. M. W. Dixon, eds., *The Handbook of Australian Languages,* Vol. 1, Australian National University Press, Canberra.

Hopper, P. and S. Thompson (1980) "Transitivity in Grammar and Discourse," *Language* 56, 251–299.

Silverstein, M. (1976) "Hierarchy of Features and Ergativity," in R. M. W. Dixon, ed., *Grammatical Categories in Australian Languages,* Australian Institute of Aboriginal Studies, Canberra.

Tsunoda, T. (1978) *The Djaru Language of Kimberley Western Australia,* unpublished doctoral dissertation, Monash University, Melbourne, Australia.

THE INTERACTION OF SEMANTIC AND SYNTACTIC FUNCTIONS AND FRENCH CLITIC CASE MARKING IN CAUSATIVE SENTENCES

JOËLLE BAILARD

A number of analyses have been proposed that try to account for the form of causative sentences with *faire* + infinitive. For the most part these analyses have been based on data which is in agreement with the normative rules inherited from the seventeenth century prescriptivist grammarians rather than on actual current usage. No systematic account has been given for the use which is made of the *le–lui* opposition before *faire* in active causative sentences.

Typically, analyses of French causatives have either focused uniquely on structural factors or uniquely on interpretation. In this paper, I would like to show that, although it is possible to give a consistent explanation of the use of the dative and accusative clitics before *faire* + infinitive in semantic terms, the syntactic rules necessary to capture the relation between simple active sentences and corresponding causative sentences must make reference both to semantic and to syntactic functions.[1]

---

[1] Given the recent emphasis in French linguistics on trying to account for language acquisition, it should, perhaps, be specified here that my intention is not to provide rules

49

1. THE PASSIVE–ACTIVE DISTINCTION
IN *FAIRE* + INFINITIVE SENTENCES

It is a rather widely held assumption that French causative sentences may receive either an active or a passive interpretation. Thus it is said by many linguists that sentences like (1) are passive sentences whereas sentences like (2) are active sentences:

(1)   *J'ai fait préparer la mayonnaise **par** Marcel.*
        'I had the mayonnaise prepared by Marcel'.

(2)   *J'ai fait préparer la mayonnaise **à** Marcel.*
        'I had Marcel prepare the mayonnaise'.

In transformational analyses, that assumption has been reflected, for instance, by having two distinct causative transformations (e.g., Kayne 1975) or one causative transformation operating on either an active or a passive embedded sentence (e.g., Hyman and Zimmer 1976).

Recently, this interpretation of the construction has been challenged on diachronic grounds by Saltarelli and Chamberlain (Saltarelli 1980; Chamberlain and Saltarelli 1982), who have argued that *faire* + infinitive sentences cannot be interpreted as passive. Consider, however, the following example:

(3)   a–b.   *Au dîner, les chefs ont décidé de faire manger le*
                missionaire.
        a.   'At dinner, the chiefs decided to make the missionary
                eat'.
        b.   'At dinner, the chiefs decided to have the missionary
                eaten'.

In Example (3), *le missionaire* may be understood as having either the semantic function of agent in relation to the embedded verb (a) or that of patient, the embedded agent being in the second case unexpressed (b).

It is to such sentences as (2) and (3a), where the topical NP in the lower clause has the function of agent, or sometimes of experiencer, that the label "active causative sentence" will refer, in opposition to "passive

---

which might be useful to describe a particular idiolect, but rather to describe what might be called "normal usage," based on descriptions provided by traditional grammars, such as Grevisse (1968) and Harmer (1979). As much as possible I shall be using actual data rather than constructed examples, because the impact of prescriptive grammar on the form of causative sentences in careful French is such as to make rather dubious the value of self-reports from linguists or their consultants.

causative sentence'' which will be used to refer to sentences such as
(1) and (3b).

2. THE RELATIONAL APPROACH TO FRENCH CAUSATIVES

Among the forms which the active causative construction may take
are the following, where the arguments are full NPs:

(4)   *Elle a fait marcher **Jean**/***à Jean**/***par Jean**.*
       'She made John walk'.

(5)   *Elle a fait nettoyer les toilettes **au général**/***le général**/***par le**
       général.*
       'She had the general clean the toilet'.

(6)   *Elle a fait envoyer une lettre au client **par la secrétaire**/***la**
       secrétaire/***a la secrétaire**.*
       'She had the secretary send a letter to the client'.

(I shall be using the term "transitive direct" to refer to verbs subcategorized for and occurring with a direct object, "transitive indirect" to
refer to verbs subcategorized for and occurring with an indirect object,
and "pseudointransitive" to refer to verbs which are subcategorized for
an optional direct object and are being used without one. The term
"intransitive" will be reserved for those verbs which are not subcategorized for object.)

Sentences (4)–(6) are typical in that, when the verb introduced by
faire is a verb of action, it is generally the case that with full NPs the
arguments of the embedded verb may take only the forms illustrated
here. If the embedded verb is intransitive, as in (4), the "embedded
subject" may take only the form of a direct object. If the embedded verb
is transitive direct, as in (5), the "embedded subject" will take the form
of an indirect object. If the embedded verb occurs with both a direct
and an indirect object, as in (6), then the embedded subject may take
only the form of an adverbial phrase.

It is the existence of such restrictions which led Comrie (1976) to claim
that the form of the arguments in French causative sentences provides
support for relational grammar and for the Relational Accessibility Hierarchy. Similarly, Radford (1976, 1978) argued that these restrictions
are evidence that relational grammar is superior to transformational grammar for French.

With respect to clitics, there is one fact that may be construed as
evidence for the concept of a hierarchy of syntactic functions. When

both the subject and the direct object of the lower verb take the form of clitics, the clitic referring to the object may be placed immediately before the lower verb or it may be placed before the causative verb with the clitic referring to the embedded subject. Thus, corresponding to Sentence (2), we may have either (7) or (8):

(7)   *Elle l'/*lui a fait la préparer.*
        'She made him prepare it'.

(8)   a. *Elle la lui/*l' a fait préparer.*
            b. **Elle l'a fait préparer par lui.*
        a–b. 'She made him prepare it'.

When the clitic referring to the embedded object is not "raised," as in (7), it and the clitic referring to the embedded subject will be in the accusative, whereas if the embedded object of the same two-argument verb is placed before *faire,* the clitic corresponding to the embedded subject must be in the dative. This case difference may be interpreted as evidence that the form of the lower subject is determined by the Relational Accessibility Hierarchy, in the sense that the case in which the embedded subject may appear must be the one corresponding to the highest available position in the hierarchy, the assumption being that one verb can have only one argument taking the form of subject, and of direct or indirect object, with the "terms" being organized hierarchically as follows: Su > DO > IO. To use the terms of Comrie (1976), we might conclude on the basis of (7) and (8) that French does not allow doubling on subject or on direct object.

However, not all causative sentences containing clitics appear so obviously compatible with a relational analysis. Among the sentences we would like to be able to account for here are the following (these sentences and most of the literary examples given in what follows were collected by Harmer 1979):

(9)   . . . *la lueur d'angoisse qui réveille le tigre et le fait dévorer le dompteur.*   (R. Massip)
        '. . . the glimmer of anxiety which awakens the tiger and makes him devour the trainer'.

(10)   *Elle restait jolie. Qu'on le lui dise la faisait hausser les épaules.*   (A. Perrin)
        'She remained pretty. To be told that she was made her shrug her shoulders'.

(11)   *Il se rappelait . . . ce que, le souffle coupé, la joie **la** faisant*
         rejeter la tête en arrière, elle avait répété dans son
         bonheur.   (P. Vialar)
         'He remembered . . . what, out of breath, joy making her
         throw back her head, she had repeated in her happiness'.

(12)   *De penser à Talleyrand **lui** fit songer au père de Noël*
         Schoudler.   (M. Druon)
         'Thinking of Talleyrand made him think about Noël
         Schoudler's father'.

(13)   *Ma façon de dessiner **leur** fit, toutefois, douter du jugement*
         de Cassegrain qui m'avait engagé.   (J. Faizant)
         'My way of drawing made them question the judgment of
         Cassegrain who had hired me'.

(14)   *D'autres joies . . . **lui** feront profiter heureusement de ses*
         dernières années.   (Nouvelles Literaires)
         'Other joys . . . will make him happily take advantage of his
         later years'.

(15)   *Un craquement **lui** fit regarder du côté du lit.*   (L. Estang)
         'A snapping noise made him look in the direction of the bed'.

(16)   *Surtout ne pas dresser les élèves en perroquets: **leur** faire*
         *comprendre, avant de **leur** faire apprendre.*   (Dauzat)
         'Especially one should not train students like parrots: make
         them understand, before making them learn'.

I am not aware of any analysis where the only functions of nominals taken into account are relational ones, and in which sentences like (9)–(16) are considered. Such sentences will constitute a marked case for any theory, and they are in contradiction with the predictions of the Relational Accessibility Hierarchy.

Examples (9)–(11) are problematic for proponents of the hierarchy because, according to the hierarchy, the clitic preceding *faire* + infinitive should be in the dative instead of the accusative, as the position of the clitic may be taken as evidence that *faire dévorer*, for instance, forms a unit and that the full NP following the lower verb is functioning as the direct object of the entire verbal unit, which should preclude the possibility of our finding a second nominal in the accusative associated with *faire* + infinitive. Conversely, in Examples (12)–(16), the hierarchy would lead us to expect that the clitic would be in the accusative, since the highest term position available is that of direct object.

To understand how the dative and accusative clitics are used before
faire + infinitive, one must take into consideration the meaning of the
verb and the function of the accusative–dative opposition.

3. THE FUNCTION OF THE DATIVE CLITIC
   IN SIMPLE SENTENCES

Before we try to make generalizations as to the use of the dative clitic
in causative sentences, it may be useful to consider first how that clitic
is used elsewhere in French syntax. Consider the following examples:

(17)   *Il va à Paris.*
         'He is going to Paris'.

(18)   *Il y/*lui va.*
         'He is going there'.

(19)   *Il vint à eux.*
         'He came to them'.

(20)   **Il leur vint.*
         'He came to them'.

(21)   *Il a répondu à Jean.*
         'He answered John'.

(22)   *Il lui/*y a répondu.*
         'He answered him'.

(23)   *Il a donné un coup de pied à Jean sans le faire exprès.*
         'He accidentally kicked John'.

(24)   *Il lui/*y a donné un coup de pied sans le faire exprès.*
         'He accidentally kicked him'.

Whereas *à* + NP may be used in all the cases where the dative clitic
is used, the converse is not true. The dative clitic may be used instead
of *à* + NP only in reference to a noun which is animate and which has
the semantic function of experiencer or beneficiary.

In their semantic analysis of French causatives, Cannings and Moody
(1978) argued that the dative clitic *lui* has the same basic meaning as the
preposition *à*, a meaning which they defined in terms of "thematic relations," following Gruber (1965) and Jackendoff (1972). Their assumption was that the meaning of *à* was based on its opposition with *par,*
the two prepositions differing essentially in terms of orientation.

Cannings and Moody themselves noted that it is by no means clear that the theory of thematic relations in its present formulation can provide the optimal characterization of the semantic relations holding between elements in causative sentences, and that the precise delineation of notions such as goal and theme becomes highly problematic as soon as one goes beyond the domain of simple verbs of movement.

The characterization they gave of goal and theme, two of the thematic relations they considered central, was as follows:

> Our interpretation of "Goal" is a deictic orientation of the "Theme" (which may be an object or a situation) toward a given object or person which may be translated in spatial or more abstract terms. Thus, with verbs of movement, the spatial progression is towards the object of A. . . .
> With verbs involving a transaction, the Goal is the recipient, the Theme "moving" to him/her. . . .
> With verbs of informing, the Goal is the addressee, the Theme, the information conveyed [p. 334].

The notion of goal was extended to include what in Fillmore's terms would be an experiencer or beneficiary, as for instance with verbs conveying punishment or reward.

As for the notion of source, we are told that "the deictic opposite of A is DE, which generally signals what Gruber calls Source, and this preposition shares with PAR the deictic property of orientation away from its object [p. 334]."

For theme, Cannings and Moody suggested that in the *faire à* construction "the Theme is a kind of generic change of which the object of A is the Goal [p. 335]." They assumed also that the subjects of intransitive verbs are always themes.

To return to the use of *lui* in simple sentences, Cannings and Moody argued that the thematic explanation they proposed for causative constructions was supported by the unacceptability of sentences such as (26) occurring after (25):

(25)   *C'est moi qui ait dû **lui** faire tailler les buissons #aux/par les jardiniers, puisque lui s'obstinait à laisser trainer les choses.*
   'I am the one who had to get the gardeners to cut the bushes for him, since he persisted in letting things go'.

(26)   *#Les jardiniers **lui** ont taillé les buissons.*
   'The gardeners cut the bushes for him'.

It is not clear to me, however, how their analysis would lead us to expect (26) to be unacceptable, to preclude that *lui* might be interpretable as goal by their definition. Furthermore, it is not obvious that the unacceptability of (26) is due to semantic rather than to stylistic factors. Consider the following examples:

(27)   *Il aura intérêt à **me** tailler ces rosiers un peu plus*
         soigneusement la prochaine fois.
         'He'd better trim these rose bushes for me a little more
         carefully next time'.

(28)   *Surveille-**moi** ça de très près.*
         'You watch that for me very carefully'.

(29)   *Allez-**moi** mettre votre blouse.*   (Courteline)
         'Go and put on your blouse for me'.

Sentences (27)–(29) are all perfectly ordinary sentences. They differ from (26) in that they are characteristic of a more casual style and the choice of a first person pronoun suggests a personal involvement which is difficult to associate with the tone of (26) possibly because of the use of a verb and determiner low in affectivity. This difference in personal involvement might well be responsible for the difference illustrated here in the acceptability of the so-called "dative of interest." Certainly, Sentence (26) is also quite questionable even outside of the context in which it was presented, whereas (30), which is grammatically similar to it, is perfectly acceptable:

(30)   *Ils **lui** ont massacré ses rosiers.*
         'They ruined his rosebushes'.

The dative clitic here may receive exactly the same interpretation as in the other simple sentences where we found it to be acceptable. It can be taken to refer either to a beneficiary or experiencer. Where the dative clitic may not be used instead of *à* + NP, as shown by Examples (17)–(20), is precisely where that phrase has the function of goal in the usual sense of the word.

Cannings and Moody were thus mistaken in their assumption that *à* has exactly the same semantic function as the dative case on clitics. Although the notion of goal that they proposed might be roughly appropriate in relation to *à*, it is inaccurate to claim that it corresponds to the basic meaning of the dative clitic.

There is no reason to assume that the dative clitic has a different function in causative sentences than it has elsewhere in the grammar, and we shall see that it is possible to give a unified semantic explanation for the use of the dative clitic before *faire* + infinitive in active sentences by making use of semantic functions more specific than thematic relations, such as the semantic roles proposed by Fillmore (1968), particularly those of agent and experiencer.

4. THE FUNCTION OF THE DATIVE CLITIC IN ACTIVE CAUSATIVE SENTENCES

One of the facts that Cannings and Moody's thematic analysis did not allow them to explain is the deviance of sentences such as (31):

(31)   *Il **lui** à fait boire.
        'He made him drink'.

Cannings and Moody noted that this was one aspect of the problem which Kayne's transformational analysis (Kayne 1975) in terms of the Specified Subject Condition could account for whereas their analysis could not. Given their interpretation of à and lui, there is no reason why we should expect lui to be unacceptable here when there is no other argument present in the sentence that might qualify as goal by their definition.

The V̄-preposing analysis in Quicoli (1980) is another structural analysis that can capture the unacceptability of sentences such as (31). For Quicoli, the accusative–dative alternation before faire + infinitive is dependent on the interaction between his V̄-Preposing rule and his Case Marking rule. If V̄-Preposing does not apply, Case Marking makes the embedded subject accusative, whereas if V̄-Preposing applies first, it moves the infinitive with its object(s) to the left of the embedded subject in such a way that when Case Marking applies, it marks that subject as dative. This interaction allows Quicoli to capture the case difference between sentences such as (9)–(11) and (32)–(34), by the same three authors:

(32)   Je me multipliais pour **lui** faire apprécier la rue
            provinciale.   (R. Massip)
        'I spared no efforts to make him appreciate the provincial street'.

(33)   Il rêvait et elle n'avait pas le moyen de **lui** faire prendre
            conscience de la totale absurdité de son entreprise.
            (A. Perrin)
        'He was dreaming and she had no way of making him realize the total absurdity of his endeavor'.

(34)   . . . *une adresse que rien ne **lui** ferait oublier et qui était celle*
           de Frida.   (P. Vialar)
           '. . . an address that nothing would cause him to forget and
           which was Frida's'.

   Bordelois (1974) had suggested that to account for sentences such as
those in (9)–(11), in addition to her phrase structure and Equi NP Deletion
analysis, there could be an optional rule of case changing, which would
change the dative into an accusative. As noted by Quicoli (1980), however, no evidence has been given which would justify the existence of
such a rule.
   Kayne (1975) considered sentences such as (9)–(11) marginal, and
stated that they could not be derived from the deep structure he pos-
tulated for active causative sentences. This is because, in his analysis,
both the *A*-Insertion rule, which moves the embedded subject to the
right of the embedded direct object and inserts the preposition (an operation that feeds Clitic Placement), and the *Faire*-Infinitive rule which
raises the verb are obligatory transformations.
   With respect to embedded pseudointransitives, the adoption by Kayne
of the Specified Subject Condition correctly leads him to predict that a
sentence like (31) will be unacceptable, as Clitic Placement would not
be allowed to move a pro-form out of an embedded sentence if in doing
so it would move across the underlying subject.
   Similarly, Quicoli's analysis rules out sentences such as (31) because,
for him, as only the verb is dominated by $\bar{V}$ in such a construction,
whether $\bar{V}$-Preposing were to apply or not, the subject would always be
immediately to the right of the verb, which, given his formulation of the
Case Marking rule, would make the application of that rule always result
in an accusative.
   In fact, Quicoli claimed that his analysis revealed a significant generalization about the language, namely that when an embedded verb is
a pseudointransitive (in his terms an "intransitive"), the embedded subject may only be in the accusative. We saw, though, with (15) and (16)
that the dative also may be acceptable in that construction.
   The lack of an explanation for the unacceptability of Sentence (31)
within their analysis led Cannings and Moody (1978) to conclude that
"one can merely note the plausability of a semantic account."
   We saw, however, that although Sentence (31) with pseudointransitive
boire is unacceptable with the dative clitic, that clitic may occur before
other pseudointransitive verbs embedded after *faire*. Recall also Sentences (12)–(14), where the only object the embedded verbs are sub-

categorized for is an indirect object introduced by either *à* or *de*. These verbs might thus be called intransitive just as *boire* was by Quicoli with respect to (31), with the result that under his analysis the three sentences should be unacceptable, in agreement with the prescriptive norm (cf., e.g., Girault-Duvivier (1856); Damourette and Pichon (1935–1938), but contrary to actual usage.

In sentences such as (12)–(14), the embedded subject may always take the form of an accusative clitic instead of a dative:

(35)   *De penser à Talleyrand le fit songer au père de Noël Schoudler.*
         'Thinking of Talleyrand made him think of Noël Schoudler's father'.

(36)   *Ma façon de dessiner toutefois les fit douter du jugement de Cassegrain qui m'avait engagé.*
         'My way of drawing, however, made them question the judgment of Cassegrain who had hired me'.

We saw also that embedded transitive direct verbs may be preceded by either a dative or an accusative clitic referring to the embedded subject, again contrary to the prescriptive norm which requires the dative.

What all these facts suggest is that structural factors can only be a subpart of the factors that determine the possible case marking of the clitic before *faire* + infinitive. To understand how those clitics are used, it is necessary to consider first the meaning of the embedded verb in question.

If an embedded transitive direct verb is a true verb of action, then either the accusative or the dative is acceptable. Thus, corresponding to (9)–(11), we may have:

(37)   *. . . et lui fit dévorer le dompteur.*
         '. . . and made him devour the trainer'.

(38)   *Qu'on le lui dit lui faisait hausser les épaules.*
         'To be told that made her shrug her shoulders'.

(39)   *. . . la joie lui faisant rejeter la tête en arrière.*
         '. . . joy making her throw back her head'.

If, by contrast, the embedded transitive direct verb is a verb of experiencing, then only the dative is acceptable, hence the consistent use of the dative before, for example, *apprécier, prendre conscience,* and *oublier*. Thus Sentence (32) would be quite odd with an accusative:

(40)   ??*Je me multipliais pour le faire apprécier la rue provinciale.*
          'I spared no efforts to make him appreciate the provincial
          street'.

With a verb of action, the language user may choose to encode the
agentiveness of the embedded subject, or, alternatively, to represent that
argument in terms of the effects on it of its own action or of some other
event, that is, treat it as experiencer. With a verb of experiencing, on
the other hand, one does not have such a choice, hence the regular
presence of the dative clitic, which, as we saw, functions to mark either
the beneficiary or experiencer.

The contrast noted here is consistent with the Transitivity Hypothesis
proposed by Hopper and Thompson (1980). For Hopper and Thompson,
transitivity is seen as a global property of an entire clause such that an
activity is "carried" or "transferred" from an agent to a patient. Their
claim is that, if two clauses in a language differ in that the first of the
two is higher in transitivity according to any of the ten components of
transitivity which they identify, and if a grammatical or semantical difference shows up elsewhere in the clause, that difference will also show
the first clause to be higher in transitivity. Among the ten components
are kinesis (i.e., activity) and potency of the agent.

In the data we have just been discussing, we indeed find that the
presence of the accusative correlates with higher kinesis, and for French
the accusative is the case associated with a typical patient.

This fact is at odds with another claim made by Hopper and Thompson—
that universally datives are the canonical objects, that they are more
likely to be animate and/or referential. However, one other criterion
which according to Hopper and Thompson contributes to high transitivity
is the affectedness of the object, and in that respect we saw that, in
French, the use of the dative clitic is quite consistently associated with
an object that has the function of experiencer or of beneficiary, not of
patient. When the object of a verb is truly functioning as patient, in the
sense that it is presented as the entity undergoing the change due to the
realization of the action described by the verb, then that object in French
(as in many languages) will typically take the form of a direct object,
not of an indirect one:

(41)   *Il l'/*lui à tué/blessé/frappé.*
          'He killed/wounded/hit him'.

The interpretation of the dative clitic as a marker of the experiencer
in opposition to the accusative clitic before *faire* + infinitive is consistent
with certain observations by Kayne (1975) and by Cannings and Moody

(1978) about some semantic contrasts associated with a difference in clitic case. Kayne noted that for the speakers who use the accusative as well as the dative clitic before an embedded transitive direct verb, there are semantic restrictions on the use of these clitic forms having to do with the antecedent of the pronouns, that for the speakers who accept *les/leur* in Sentences (42)–(43), *les* can refer to children, but not to articles of clothing, whereas in the "normal" sentence with the dative, *leur* can refer to either:

(42)   *Je **les** ai faits prendre l'air.*
        'I made them get some air'.

(43)   *Je **leur** ai fait prendre l'air.*
        { 'I made them get some air'. }
        { 'I aired them out.' }

With the accusative clitic the sentence may be interpreted to mean either that some person got exposed to some air or was caused to undertake some activity, since "prendre l'air" is often associated with some form of exercise such as walking. With the *leur* sentence, on the other hand, no dynamic interpretation is possible when the clitic has an inanimate antecedent, and even when the dative is referring to an animate noun the most likely interpretation, for this speaker at least, is the less kinetic one, namely that the embedded subject got exposed to some air rather than made to engage in some form of activity.

Similarly, one of the contrasts which Cannings and Moody noted that their analysis could not account for involved the following sentences:

(44)   *Ça **lui** a fait gagner Paris en un temps record.*
        'That made him win Paris in record time'.

(45)   *Ça **l'**a fait gagner Paris en un temps record.*
        'That made him reach Paris in record time'.

According to Cannings and Moody, given their analysis, Sentence (44) should be ambiguous between 'winning Paris' and 'reaching Paris', but it is felt by many speakers to have only the former reading, although the same speakers prefer (45) on the movement reading.

Given that one of the functions of the dative clitic in and outside of causative sentences is to mark the experiencer as opposed to the patient, it is then quite natural that, when a case opposition is associated with a difference in the interpretation of the verb, the occurrence of the dative clitic should be associated with the less kinetic reading (e.g., 'win' rather than 'reach') and the occurrence of the accusative clitic with the more kinetic one.

An alternative explanation of the case contrast before *faire* + infinitive was proposed by Hyman and Zimmer (1976), which involved directness of causation. Hyman and Zimmer suggested that the case difference reflected a difference between direct (i.e., 'make') and indirect (i.e., 'have') causation, with the accusative implying direct causation and possibly the use of force or pressure, and the dative, indirect causation.

That this cannot be the general explanation for the use of the dative and accusative clitics before *faire* can be seen by comparing Sentences (9)–(11) with Sentences (32)–(34). Sentences (9)–(11) with Sentences (33)–(39). Sentence (9), where Massip uses the accusative, can only be understood as meaning 'to make', but Sentence (32), where the writer uses the dative instead, may be interpreted as implying either 'to make' or 'to have'. Similarly, Sentences (10) and (11), with the accusative like (9) can only be interpreted as meaning 'to make'; but 'to make' is also the only possible meaning of Sentence (33), and that is also a possible meaning of Sentence (34).

On the basis of sentences such as these, then, we might say that the accusative clitic in opposition to the dative is consistently associated with direct causation but that the latter may be interpreted as indeterminate with respect to directness of causation.

Hyman and Zimmer did take into account the notion of affectedness, which is relevant to the experiencer–patient contrast, in their analysis of passive causative sentences with full NPs. They noted the suggestion by Pinkham (1974) that the embedding of a passive sentence after *faire* cannot occur (or not so readily) when the embedded verb is a verb of experiencing as opposed to a verb of action, because with a verb of experiencing, the object of the embedded verb is not affected by the realization of the clause, thus:

(46)   *J'ai fait voir le film à Maurice.*
        'I had Maurice see the film'.

(47)   ??*J'ai fait voir le film **par** Maurice.*
        'I had the film seen by Maurice'.

They noted also the following contrast:

(48)   *J'ai fait lire la lettre à Maurice.*
        'I had Maurice read the letter (to himself)'.

(49)   *J'ai fait lire la lettre **par** Maurice.*
        'I had the letter read by Maurice (to others)'.

Hyman and Zimmer suggested that here also there is a difference in affectedness, the letter being affected in (49) but not in (48). They did not, however, make use of this notion in trying to explain clitic case opposition.

The same semantic distinction agent–experiencer allows us to explain the use of the clitics before embedded transitive direct and before embedded pseudointransitive verbs. We saw with Examples (12)–(14) that, in contradiction with the prescriptive rule, the dative clitic may be used before embedded transitive indirect verbs, but it is not found before all such verbs. All the examples reported have in common that the lower verb is one of experiencing, not of action. We do not find examples such as:

(50)   *Il **lui** a fait parler à Jean.
        'He made him talk to John'.[2]

Similarly, the only cases where the dative clitics may occur before an embedded pseudointransitive is when the verbs are verbs of experiencing, hence the contrast in acceptability between (15) and (16) on the one hand and (31) on the other.

To summarize, although the conditions under which the dative clitic may be used to represent an embedded subject differ depending on the subcategorization of the verb for object, a consistent semantic explanation can be given for the usage of the le–lui opposition when we take into consideration the meaning of the lower verb and the distinction between agent and experiencer.

5. TOWARD A DESCRIPTION OF CLITIC USAGE WITH *FAIRE* + INFINITIVE

We considered here several analyses that attempted to give a consistent description of causative sentences by taking into account solely syntactic factors, and we saw that these analyses were not compatible with the full range of facts to be described. It was also noted that Cannings and Moody had doubt as to the possibility of giving a thorough explanation of the form of the causative sentences by referring only to semantic factors, more precisely to thematic relations, and that their analyses also led to some false predictions as to the acceptability of the dative clitic.

We found, however, that it is possible to give a consistent semantic explanation of the case opposition found before *faire* + infinitive in active sentences if we recognize that the dative clitic does not have

---

[2] Some speakers accept such sentences as

Il lui a fait télégraphier à ses parents.

'He made him send a telegram to his parents'.

though. For these, it will be necessary to mark as exceptional the few relevant verbs of communication.

exactly the same function as *à* + NP and serves to mark an experiencer or a beneficiary. In active causative sentences, the crucial semantic contrast with respect to case marking of the embedded subject proved to be that between agent and experiencer.

This does not mean that the function of the dative clitic is more restricted in causative sentences than in simple sentences. Space limitations prevent us from exploring in detail the use of the accusative and dative clitics in passive causative sentences, but the following example should suffice to show that the dative clitic may be used to mark a beneficiary before *faire* + infinitive as well as an experiencer:

(51)   *Je **le lui** ai fait envoyer.*
$\left\{ \begin{array}{l} \text{'I had him send it'.} \\ \text{'I had it sent to him'.} \end{array} \right\}$

When the sentence is interpreted as active, *le* refers to the embedded patient and *lui* to the embedded subject. When the sentence is interpreted as passive, *le* again refers to the embedded patient but *lui* then refers to the beneficiary.

The dative clitic before *faire* + infinitive thus can be used to refer to a beneficiary, but only when the clause is interpreted as passive:

(52)   **Je **lui** ai fait envoyer un télégramme à Marie.*
'I had Marie send him a telegram'.

What remains to be done here is to try to give the syntactic rules which would allow us to describe and predict accurately current usage of the dative–accusative opposition before *faire* + infinitive in active causative sentences.

In the case of embedded intransitives, for instance, the absence of a case opposition might quite plausibly be explained in terms of the fact that all such verbs are verbs of action, hence there is no semantic motivation for having a contrast in case marking:

(53)   *Elle *lui/le fera partir.*
'She will make him leave'.

At the level of description, however, we need a rule that allows us to capture the difference between (53) and (16), for instance, where the clitic also occurs before *faire* and an infinitive not followed by any NP.

We saw earlier that when only embedded verbs of action are considered, the generalization that emerges about the form of the arguments is readily statable in relational terms and is in agreement with the Relational Accessibility Hierarchy. In addition, the crucial syntactic differences that we saw affect the constraints on the use of the dative clitic in reference to an experiencer have to do with subcategorization of the verb for object. Consequently, we would like to have for French some syntactic rules that would allow us to state the interaction of semantic and syntactic functions, and syntactic redundancy rules would seem quite appropriate for this.

In his reply to Wasow (1977), Anderson (1977) argued that the redundancy rules found necessary for English need not make reference to syntactic functions and should instead be stated in terms of thematic relations, following Jackendoff's (1972) proposal for English passive. We saw here, though, that, for causative sentences, using the thematic relation of goal as Cannings and Moody tried to do did not allow us to give a consistent explanation of certain occurrences and interpretations of dative and accusative clitics.

It was noted also that Cannings and Moody felt that no exact definition of the notion of theme had been given. Anderson (1977) proposed the following characterization: "The Theme is 'the logical topic' of the clause: the element that the clause is about, in a purely logical sense divorced from any particular use of the clause in discourse [p. 367]." To this he added the general rule that themes are to be found in the position of intransitive subjects or of transitive direct objects but can never correspond to an indirect object.

If Anderson's theme rule were valid for French and if it were the case that the theme function were always assigned to the constituent "that the clause is about," then we should expect overall a great stability in the subcategorization of individual verbs for objects in the absence of some perceptible change in the meaning of these verbs.

However, in Bailard (1982), I have shown that there have been numerous instances of verbs that have undergone a change in their subcategorization for object without at the same time undergoing any shift in meaning, a fact with which historical grammarians have long been familiar (see, e.g., Brunot 1905; Nyrop 1930). Compare, for instance, two Classical French sentences, (54)–(55), with their contemporary French equivalents, (56)–(57):

(54)   *Qu'a-t-il soupé? Luy? **Rien.***
       'What did he eat for supper? Him? Nothing'.

(55)   *Biron **lui** contredisant tout exprès.*   (Astrée, 17th C.)
       'Biron contradicting him on purpose'.

(56)   *De **quoi** a-t-il soupé? Lui? **De rien.***
       'What did he eat for supper? Him? Nothing'.

(57)   *Biron **le** contredisant tout exprès.*
       'Biron contradicting him on purpose'.

On the basis of such evidence, I suggested that syntactic redundancy rules for French must be allowed to refer to syntactic functions, and in Bailard (1982a). I proposed to describe the relation between simple transitive direct sentences and the corresponding *faire* sentences with clitics with a redundancy rule referring both to symlactic and to semantic functions. The rule is reformulated in Bailard (1982b) as follows:

(58)   CAUSATIVE RULE 1

$$
\left[\begin{array}{ccc} \overset{x}{\left[\begin{array}{c} +\text{NP} \\ +\text{Su} \\ \langle +\text{Agt}\rangle_1 \\ \langle +\text{Exp}^{\text{cer}}\rangle_2 \end{array} \right]_S} & \overset{X}{\left[+\text{V} \right]} & \overset{y}{\left[\begin{array}{c} +\text{NP} \\ +\text{DO} \end{array} \right]} \end{array} \right] \rightarrow \left[\begin{array}{cccc} \overset{w}{\left[\begin{array}{c} +\text{NP} \\ +\text{Su} \end{array} \right]} & \overset{v}{\left[\begin{array}{c} +\text{cl} \\ \langle +\text{DO}\rangle_1 \\ \langle +\text{IO}\rangle_2 \end{array} \right]} & \overset{FAIRE\ X'}{\left[\begin{array}{c} +\text{V} \\ +\text{Inf} \end{array} \right]} & \overset{y}{\left[\begin{array}{c} +\text{NP} \\ +\text{DO} \end{array} \right]} \end{array} \right]_S
$$

where X and X' represent the finite form and the infinitive of a verbs respectively.[3]

One might argue that syntactic functions need not be mentioned in the redundancy rules because that information might be recoverable on the basis of structural description. Kayne (1975), for instance, had argued that clitics should be transformationally generated, in which case the feature specifications [+ DO] and [+ IO] might not be necessary for the clitics, because clitics are supposedly in complementary distribution with full NPs.

Although this is true for one type of sentence that we might like to consider basic in the sense that it is associated with the fewest presuppositions (e.g., *Je vois Paul–Je le vois*, 'I see Paul'–'I see him'), this is certainly not the case in the other basic type of sentence that we encounter in everyday French:

(59)   *Il est parti **Paul.***
        'Paul has left'.

(60)   *Il₁ l₂a fini l'article₂ Maurice₁.*
        'Maurice has finished the article'.

Such sentences may be interpreted as involving topicalization, but need not be, and it is doubtful if there are many speakers who will not use some such sentences at least occasionally. It is the generalization of this pattern which had led Sauvageot (1962) to compare contemporary French to the Bantu languages.

---

[3] Arguments for the use of a unidirectional arrow instead of the bidirectional one made popular by Jackendoff (1975) are given in Bailard (1982a).

Sentences (59) and (60) raise questions as to the justification for treating at least some occurrences of clitics as arising by transformation; and, in the absence of strong arguments against the possible alternative which is to provide a unified treatment by generating all clitics by means of phrase structure rules, it would appear desirable to do just that. And this would entail that at least the syntactic features [+DO] and [+IO] would have to be treated as primitives, given that DO and IO may occupy the same position, and, for the redundancy rules at issue, that the syntactic functions of direct and indirect object must be referred to concurrently with semantic functions.[4]

Other syntactic redundancy rules which will be necessary to capture the relation between simple active transitive indirect, pseudointransitive, and intransitive sentences and the corresponding causative sentences are as follows:

(61)   CAUSATIVE RULE 2

$$
\begin{bmatrix} \begin{bmatrix} x \\ \mathrm{I\,NP} \\ +\,\mathrm{Su} \\ \langle +\,\mathrm{Exp}\rangle \end{bmatrix} \begin{bmatrix} X \\ +\,\mathrm{V} \\ \langle +\,\mathrm{Pseudointransitive}\rangle \end{bmatrix} \end{bmatrix}_{\mathrm{S}} \rightarrow \begin{bmatrix} \begin{bmatrix} W \\ +\,\mathrm{NP} \\ +\,\mathrm{Su} \end{bmatrix} \begin{bmatrix} V \\ +\,\mathrm{cl} \\ \begin{Bmatrix} +\,\mathrm{DO} \\ \langle +\,\mathrm{IO}\rangle \end{Bmatrix} \end{bmatrix} \end{bmatrix}_{\mathrm{S}} \begin{bmatrix} FAIRE\ X' \\ +\,\mathrm{V} \\ +\,\mathrm{Inf} \end{bmatrix}
$$

(62)   CAUSATIVE RULE 3

$$
\begin{bmatrix} \begin{bmatrix} x \\ +\,\mathrm{NP} \\ +\,\mathrm{Su} \\ \langle +\,\mathrm{Exp}\rangle \end{bmatrix} \begin{bmatrix} X \\ +\,\mathrm{V} \end{bmatrix} \begin{Bmatrix} \dot{a} \\ de \end{Bmatrix} \begin{bmatrix} y \\ +\,\mathrm{NP} \\ +\,\mathrm{IO} \end{bmatrix} \end{bmatrix}_{\mathrm{S}} \rightarrow \begin{bmatrix} \begin{bmatrix} W \\ +\,\mathrm{NP} \\ +\,\mathrm{Su} \end{bmatrix} \begin{bmatrix} V \\ +\,\mathrm{cl} \\ \begin{Bmatrix} +\,\mathrm{DO} \\ \langle +\,\mathrm{IO}\rangle \end{Bmatrix} \end{bmatrix} \end{bmatrix}_{\mathrm{S}} \begin{bmatrix} FAIRE\ X' \\ +\,\mathrm{V} \\ +\,\mathrm{Inf} \end{bmatrix} \begin{Bmatrix} \dot{a} \\ de \end{Bmatrix} \begin{bmatrix} y \\ +\,\mathrm{NP} \\ +\,\mathrm{IO} \end{bmatrix}
$$

Causative Rule 1 will account for sentences such as (9), (32), (37), and (40); Causative Rule 2 for sentences such as (15) and (31) and (53); Causative Rule 3 for (12), (35), and (50).

6. CONCLUSION

In this paper, it was shown that the use of the dative and accusative clitics before *faire* + infinitive can be given a consistent semantic ex-

---

[4] A fuller discussion of the necessity for referring to the syntactic functions of subject, direct object, and indirect object may be found in Bailard (1982b).

planation if we make use of some of the semantic functions proposed by Fillmore (1968) and that, when one wishes to describe and predict under which specific conditions these clitics can be used, the syntactic rules necessary to capture the relation between simple active sentences and corresponding causative sentences must refer simultaneously to the semantic functions of agent and experiencer and to syntactic functions such as direct object and indirect object.

ACKNOWLEDGMENTS

I am indebted to Sandy Thompson, Paul Schachter, Joe Emonds, and Ed Keenan, who all have contributed substantially to this paper, and also to Philippe Barbaud, Paul Hirschbuhler, and Carlos Quicoli for some very useful suggestions and discussions. But I particularly wish to thank here George Bedell.

REFERENCES

Anderson, S. R. (1977) "Comments on the Paper by Wasow," in P. Culicover, T. Wasow, and A. Akmajian, eds., *Formal Syntax*, Academic Press, New York.

Bailard, J. (1982a) "The Form of Redundancy Rules," in *Proceedings of the Tenth Anniversary Linguistic Symposium on Romance Languages*, University of Washington, Seattle.

Bailard, J. (1982b) "Diachronic Evidence and the Form of French Grammar."

Bordelois, I. (1974) *The Grammar of Spanish Causative Complements*, unpublished doctoral dissertation, Massachusetts Institute of Technology, Cambridge, Massachusetts.

Brunot, F. (1905) *Histoire de la Langue Française*, Collin, Paris.

Cannings, P. and M. D. Moody (1978) "A Semantic Approach to Causation in French," *Lingvisticae Investigationes* 2, 331–362.

Chamberlain, J. and M. Saltarelli (1982) "Latin Origins of Romance Causative Constructions. The Rise of Raising," in *Proceedings of the Tenth Anniversary Symposium on Romance Languages*, University of Washington, Seattle.

Comrie, B. (1976) "The Syntax of Causative Constructions: Cross-Linguistic Similarities and Divergences," in M. Shibatani, ed., *The Grammar of Causative Constructions*, Academic Press, New York.

Damourette, J. and E. Pichon (1911–1950) *Des mots à la pensée. Essai de grammaire de la langue française*, D'Artney, Paris.

Fillmore, C. J. (1968) "The Case for Case," in E. Bach and R. Harms, eds., *Universals in Linguistic Theory*, Holt, Rinehart and Winston, New York.

Girault-Duvivier, C. P. (1856) *Grammaire des Grammaires, ou Analyse Raisonnée des Meilleurs Traités sur la Langue Française*, 16th ed., Cotelle, Paris.

Grevisse, M. (1968) *Le Bon Usage*, 9th ed., Duculot, Gembloux.

Gruber, J. (1965) *Studies in Lexical Relations*, unpublished doctoral dissertation, Massachusetts Institute of Technology, Cambridge, Massachusetts.

Harmer, L. C. (1979) *Uncertainties in French Grammar*, P. Rickard and T. Combe, eds., Cambridge University Press, Cambridge.

Hopper, P. and S. Thompson (1980) "Transitivity in Grammar and Discourse," *Language* 56, 251–299.

Hyman, L. and K. Zimmer (1976) "Imbedded Topics in French," in C. Li, ed., *Subject and Topic,* Academic Press, New York.

Jackendoff, R. (1972) *Semantic Interpretation in Generative Grammar,* MIT Press, Cambridge, Massachusetts.

Jackendoff, R. S. (1975) "Morphological and Semantic Regularities in the Lexicon," *Language* 51, 639–671.

Kayne, R. (1975) *French Syntax: The Transformational Cycle,* MIT Press, Cambridge, Massachusetts.

Keenan, E. L. and B. Comrie (1972) "Noun-phrase Accessibility and Universal Grammar," *Linguistic Inquiry* 8, 63–99.

Nyrop, K. (1930) *Etudes de Grammaire Française,* Hovedkomissionaer A. G. Host, Copenhagen.

Pinkham, J. (1974) Passive and *Faire-par* Causative Construction in French, senior essay, Harvard University, Cambridge, Massachusetts.

Quicoli, C. A. (1980) "Clitic Movement in French Causatives," *Linguistic Analysis* 6, 131–185.

Radford, A. (1976) "On the Non-transformational Nature of Syntax: Synchronic and Diachronic Evidence from Romance Causatives," in M. Harris, ed., *Romance Syntax,* University of Salford, Salford, England.

Radford, A. (1978) *Italian Syntax: Transformational and Relational Grammar,* Cambridge University Press, Cambridge.

Saltarelli, M. (1980) "Syntactic Diffusion," in *Proceedings of the International Conference on Historical Linguistics IV,* Stanford University. Benjamin, Amsterdam.

Sauvageot, A. (1962) *Français Écrit et Français Parlé,* Larousse, Paris.

Wasow, T. (1977) "Transformations and the Lexicon," in P. Culicover, T. Wasow, and A. Akmajian, eds., *Formal Syntax,* Academic Press, New York.

THE ABSOLUTIVE: ITS SCOPE IN ENGLISH AND KALKATUNGU

BARRY J. BLAKE

The absolutive, a grammatical relation embracing intransitive subject and direct object, has received some attention in recent years, principally but not exclusively in relation to ergative languages. In relational grammar, the absolutive and the ergative (transitive subject) are recognized as defined relations alongside subject, object, and indirect object (Postal 1977:276). This paper deals with evidence for the absolutive in English, a language normally described in terms of subject and object, and in Kalkatungu, a language with an ergative–absolutive system of case marking and some signs of deep or syntactic ergativity.

1. GRAMMATICAL RELATIONS IN ENGLISH

1.1. Justification for Object

If one considers the diversity of the intuitively determined semantic roles of the participants that follow the verb in the following sentences,

71

one might be prompted to conclude that the common morphosyntactic treatment afforded to them justifies the notion of a cover term like direct object.

(1)   *John hit the dog.*
       agent   affected patient

(2)   *John built a boat.*
       agent   effected patient

(3)   *John saw a boat.*
       perceiver neutral patient

(4)   *John liked the new car.*
       experiencer neutral patient

(5)   *John had a nice car.*
       possessor neutral patient

However, many linguists (e.g., Fillmore 1968:25; J. Anderson 1977:38; Starosta 1978:472–478) go a long way toward obviating the need for a grammatical relation such as direct object by defining one semantic role, which we shall call *patient,* so broadly that it encompasses the affected, effected, and neutral varieties illustrated in Sentences (1)–(5).

The existence of sentences like (6) would seem to demand that a grammatical direct object be established, as the participant immediately following the verb seems to contrast with a participant that surely falls within the scope of a broadly defined patient.

(6)   *John gave the little girl a book.*
       recipient   patient

However, the *girl* in (6) does not share many morphosyntactic properties with the postverbal participants of (1)–(5). Although the recipient in (6) can appear as the subject of a corresponding passive, it differs from the patients of (1)–(5) in that in most varieties of English it cannot be *wh*-questioned or relativized and, furthermore, it cannot appear as the subject of a "*tough* construction." The passive of (6) could be handled by a hierarchical rule that gives precedence to nonpatient obliques over patient obliques or by a rule based directly on semantic roles. In any case the passive must be made sensitive to roles. Sentence (5), for example, does not have a corresponding passive because of the role of the subject; similarly, in Sentence (5) the patient defies "*tough* movement."

With verbs like *weigh* and *cost,* the postverbal entity seems to bear the role of extent, and with *leave* (in the sense of 'exit' not in the sense of 'relinquish' or 'abandon') the complement seems to bear the relation of location, or more precisely, source. Whether one agrees with these role labels or not, the point is that the complements contrast with a subject that seems to be patient. However, these complements do not seem to provide grounds for setting up a grammatical relation *object*. They seem to be adverbial, as is revealed by the *wh*-forms and pro-forms that correspond to them, and it is not clear that one would want to frame any rules embracing these complements and those in (1)–(5).

(7)   *How much did the book weigh/cost?*

(8)   *It weighed/cost that much/so much.*

(9)   *John left there.*

Another sentence pattern that might seem to demand the establishment of an object is the one that includes a verb like *believe, expect,* or *think* with a noun phrase complement followed by an infinitival complement.

(10)   *Everyone expected the old man to pay for the dinner.*

(11)   *Everyone thought the New Australian to have been the culprit.*

The NP immediately following the verb is grammatically part of the main clause, as is demonstrated by passivizing the main clause or by relativizing or pronominalizing the NP in question.

(12)   a. *The old man was expected by everyone to pay for the dinner.*
         b. *I saw the old man everyone expected to pay for the dinner.*
         c. *Everyone expected him to pay for the dinner.*

One could say that semantically the NP in question belongs in the infinitival complement, as it is sensitive to the selectional restrictions of the verb of the complement and not to those of the main verb. In light of this I have been tempted to say that the NP following *believe, think,* and *expect* in these constructions bears no semantic role to these verbs. However, if one defines patient so broadly that it is the complement of the positively defined roles such as agent, instrument, etc., it is possible to label as patient virtually any participant that cannot be ascribed to agent, instrument, location, etc. Many who have considered semantic roles have come to the conclusion that every clause must have a patient. I have never seen any justification for this dogma, but if one accepts it, then the NP following *believe*, etc., will have to be considered patient. I suppose it is not too unreasonable to consider these NPs patients if we take the complement of verbs such as *see* or *like* to be patients, as these entities play no positive part in any activity or process. If one does consider these NPs patients, then it seems the need for the grammatical relation of object is entirely obviated. Stephen Anderson (1977) claims that "NPs from a lower clause bear no thematic [=semantic] relation in a higher one [p. 371]" and sees pairs of sentences such as (10) and (12a) as evidence for the need for a passive based on grammatical as opposed to semantic relations. Certainly the position one adopts on this matter is critical for the notion of object, and if one has to rely on "NPs from a lower clause" to support the existence of object, its status seems marginal at best.

1.2. Justification for Subject

If we can eliminate the need for object by framing rules in terms of roles, one might wonder if it were possible to define a role such as actor in such a way as to embrace the agent of (1) and (2), the perceiver of (3), the experiencer of (4), and perhaps even the possessor of (5). The difficulty with such a proposal would be that the common morphosyntactic treatment afforded to the preverbal participants of (1)–(5) extends to the preverbal participants that occur with intransitive verbs. The role of actor might be appropriate in the case of verbs like *shoot* and *spit* in their intransitive usage, perhaps even with *hop, jump* and *gallop,* but with the majority of intransitive verbs the preverbal participant is certainly not actor-like but rather patient-like. Consider, for example, *fall, grow, be, drip, melt, trickle, ooze, disappear,* and *evaporate.* It seems that the existence of such verbs is crucial to the notion of subject because they rule out the possibility of treating the morphosyntactic similarity of the preverbal participants in terms of a role.

A number of linguists consider all instances of intransitive subject (S_i) to be [+patient] (I will assume without argument that semantic roles can be represented as features; see J. Anderson, 1977:85; Starosta 1978). Jackendoff (1972:29) following Gruber (1965) takes all instances of S_i to be [+patient] (he uses Gruber's term "theme"), as does John Anderson (1977) (he uses the term "absolutive"), though both of them allow [+agent] to cooccur with [+patient] for verbs where S_i can be said to initiate the activity as well as undergo it (e.g., with *walk* or *gallop*). Starosta (1978) takes all instances of S_i to be [+patient] without qualification and does not allow a participant to bear more than one role.

1.3. Absolutive

The fact that S_i and the direct object (O) are characteristically [+patient] has not gone unnoticed; there are a number of references in the literature to properties shared by S_i and O. We review these in what follows, paying some attention to whether they are properties of [+patient] or whether they are properties of a syntactic conjunction of S_i and O, which I refer to as the absolutive.

Only S_i and O correspond to the *of*-phrase of a gerundive nominalization.

(13)   a.   *The wind howls.*
        b.   *the howling of the wind*

(14)   a.   *The groom cuts the cake.*
        b.   *the cutting of the cake*
        c.   **the cutting of the groom*

Chomsky (1957:88–89) considered the phrase *the shooting of the hunters* to be ambiguous, as it could be derived either from the O of transitive *shoot* or from the S_i of the intransitive *shoot*. However, the reading related to the S_i agent, as well as such forms as *the hopping/running/skipping of John,* where the verb is of the type characterized by Jackendoff (1972:34) as being both [+agent] and [+patient], are not only highly unnatural, but virtually nonexistent in texts (S. Thompson, personal communication, reports, for example, that in a count of 100 nominalizations, none involved an agent). In short, these nominalizations seem to be based on roles, specifically on $[^{+\text{patient}}_{-\text{agent}}]$, not on syntactic relations. Note that the dubious contender for the title of O, the recipient in a sentence like (6), cannot be the basis for a gerundive nominalization:

(15)   **the giving of the little girl (a book)*

Note that S_i and O control the subject of the infinitival complement of verbs of wishing and commanding.

(16)   *John$_i$ wants (John$_i$) to go.*

(17)   *John wants Bill (Bill) to go.*

(18)   *John told Bill (Bill) to go.*

The generalization appropriate here seems to be compatible with [+patient].

Furthermore, S_i and O are the sole repositories for "raised participants," participants that are constrained by the selectional restrictions of the verb of a lower clause rather than of the verb to which they bear a grammatical relation.

(19)   **John** *seems to like lamingtons.*

(20)   *Everyone expected* **Landy** *to win the mile.*

John Anderson (1977:63) sees this restriction on raising as being compatible with [+patient] (his "absolutive"), since the target of raising can be specified as the patient of the raising verb—either the patient of transitive verbs like *believe* or *want* or the intransitive patient of verbs like *happen*. If one adopts Stephen Anderson's view—referred to earlier—that the raised participants bear no semantic relation in their clause, then one can take the behavior of verbs like *believe, expect, want, happen* and *seem* to provide evidence for an absolutive target for raising.

Case grammarians usually recognize a distinction between inner and outer locatives. An inner locative specifies the position or direction or source of a participant and an outer locative specifies the location or setting of the action or event as a whole. Starosta (1978:493) claims that the inner locative, which he calls locus, has the [+ patient] as its scope. This seems to raise the possibility that the scope of inner locatives is the absolutive, and indeed it is easy to find examples that appear to support this.

(21)   *John lives in Koo-Wee-Rup.*

(22)   *John put Mary on the 'Spirit'.*

In (21) *John* (S_i) is in *Koo-Wee-Rup* and in (22) *Mary* (O) gets to ride in the illustrious express. However, this does not hold true for a number of intransitive verbs.

(23)   *The marksman shot at the target.*

(24)   *The punk rocker spat on the fans in the front row.*

(25)   *The baby weed on the new Axminster.*

(26)   *The activist punched at the prime minister.*

(27)   *The Ayatollah wrote to Xaviera.*

(28)   *Bazza bet on the Sydney Cup.*

In these examples S_i seems to be semantically $\left[\begin{smallmatrix} -\text{patient} \\ +\text{agent} \end{smallmatrix}\right]$, and a patient is understood in the meaning of the verb (*bullets, spittle, urine, punches, a letter, a wager*). In each example the understood patient, not S_i, is the scope of the inner locative.

Locatives referring to body parts seem to be of the inner type and to refer only to [+ patient] participants.

(29)   *John was sick in the stomach.*

(30)   *Bill punched John in the ribs.*

(31)   *Bill struck Harry in the face.*

(32)   **Bill struck at Harry in the face.*

Note that in (32) where the intended victim is himself an inner locative the body part locative cannot be used.

The fact that the scope of the inner locative is a patient rather than the absolutive is supported by examples of the following type where the inner locative refers to a nonabsolutive patient.

(33)   *John gave Mary the Ben Ean on a silver tray.*

It seems that Starosta's claim about the scope of inner locatives needs some modification. The inner locative does not refer to S_i if S_i is an agent and not a patient. Where an intransitive is created by object incorporation, a common process in some languages, or by object deletion, as could be considered the case with *shoot* as in (23), *spit* in (24) or *write* as in (27), the derived S_i appears to be $[^{+\,\text{agent}}_{-\,\text{patient}}]$. There are also verbs like *urinate* and *defecate* where a patient is understood as separate from an agent S_i, but where there is no clear case for deriving the intransitive from a corresponding transitive. A generalization that does hold up is that if a sentence constituent locative refers to an NP (as opposed to referring to the setting for the action as a whole), that NP must be [+ patient].

In sum, it seems that there is no clear evidence for a syntactic relation embracing S_i and O in English, and that any properties these two appear to share is simply a reflection of the fact that they are characteristically [+ patient]. As I pointed out earlier, the evidence for object is weak anyway. In contrast, subject is a well-founded entity which shows up in rules of word order, agreement, case assignment, and in certain rules of deletion, for example, with infinitival complements. Subject is obviously semantically heterogeneous, embracing as it does the patient of intransitive verbs and the agent of transitive verbs, to say nothing of the roles of experiencer, possessor, and location with some transitive verbs.

John Anderson (1977:243–267, 1979:4–16) sees ergative languages as lacking subject formation and as having grammars organized in terms of case relations (semantic roles) including the absolutive relation (patient role). Similarly Kibrik (1979) says that "pure ergative languages use only the Situational Component for actant coding [p. 62]" where the "Situational Component" is the semantic structure corresponding to some extralinguistic situation and is described in terms of a verb and the semantic roles of its arguments. One might expect that if a language lacked the subject relation, then the patient might be more overt and that there might be an absolutive relation in lieu of subject. With this in mind, I turn to the ergative language, Kalkatungu. Kalkatungu is a particularly suitable language in which to explore the possibility of an absolutive, as not only does it have an ergative–absolutive system of case marking, it also appears to have something akin to the celebrated "ergative syntax" that distinguishes Dyirbal and a number of other Australian languages.

2. KALKATUNGU

2.1. Basic System of Kalkatungu

Kalkatungu, an Australian language of the Pama–Nymgan family (Blake, 1979) employs an ergative–absolutive system of case marking, with the ergative marking the agent (A) of transitive verbs and the absolutive marking S_i and O. There are also bound pronouns, but these operate in a nominative–accusative system. The two systems between them yield a three-way distinction in case forms—one for S_i, one for A, and one for O.

	Case markings		
	free	bound	Case forms
S_i	—	—	Nominative
A	erg.	—	Ergative
O	—	acc.	Accusative

A is pretty much a semantic agent.[1] It embraces the agent of verbs like la 'hit' and iṭiti 'throw' and the perceiver of nanʸi 'see'. Verbs with what we might want to call experiencer subjects in English (e.g., want and fear) come up as intransitive verbs in Kalkatungu, and there are no locative subjects as in The first chapter contains the definitions. In Kalkatungu, O is basically the patient of a transitive verb, but there seem to be derived instances of O that are semantically dative (explained in what follows) rather than patient.

The following examples illustrate the system of case marking (the absolutive is ∅ and has not been glossed).

(34)   Maṛapai maḷta iŋka-ṇa-na.
        woman   mob come-past-they
        'The women came'.

---

[1] Some examples of inanimate A occur. Lightning, fire and flood I take to be agents, but where we find the falling limb hit him on the head, we have a good candidate for an instrumental A. Interestingly enough Kalkatungu usually marks the verb in such cases with -nti, the causative/advancement marker.

(35)   *Maṛapai-ṭu maḻta-yi ŋai ḻayi-ṇa-ŋi-na   makaṭi-ṭu.*
        woman-erg mob-erg me hit-past-me-they hand-instr
        'The women hit me with their hands'.

In (35) *ŋai* is in its basic form but the cross-referencing *-ŋi* is marked
suppletively as accusative. The operation of the free and bound systems
of marking the first and second singular pronouns is given in the following
table.

		1		2	
S_i		*ŋai*	-∅	*n'ini*	-n
A		*ŋaṭu*	-∅	*n'inti*	-n
O		*ŋai*	-ŋi	*n'ini*	-kin (~ -yin)

The bound pronouns may cross-reference an NP, as in (35), or stand in
lieu of one. Their use is optional in independent clauses except with the
imperfect aspect marker, *-miṇa,* or the perfect, *-mpa.*

   Word order in independent clauses is free with a good deal of fronting
for topicalization and focusing. In subordinate clauses the verb is almost
always in final position.

   Kalkatungu has a number of productive mechanisms that affect transitivity. First of all, there is the familiar type of causativization in which
a transitive verb is derived from an intransitive one with O of the derived
verb corresponding to S_i. There is also an advancement mechanism
whereby a locative, instrumental or causal participant can be advanced
to O. Locative advancement usually occurs with intransitive verbs, and
the effect of advancing the locative is to produce an O and thus a
transitive verb. The marker *-(ma)nti* is used to signal both causativization and advancement.

   Kalkatungu has two mechanisms that involve detransitivization. Any
transitive verb may be intransitivized by putting the agent in the nominative and the patient in the dative. This antipassive derivation is marked
on the verb by the form *-yi* at least in subordinate clauses. In independent
clauses nonfuture verbs seem to be regularly marked by *-yi* whether
antipassive or not. The following example, however, contains a verb
from a small conjugation class where antipassive is registered by a form
distinct from *-yi.*

(36)   a. *Ḍa-ṭu wakaṛi ŋkaayi-ṇa yuku-ŋku.*
           I-erg fish   spear-past spear-inst
           'I speared a fish with a spear'.

b.   *Ḍai wakaṛi-i ŋkaa-ḷi   yuku-ŋku.*
I   fish-dat spear-a/p spear-inst
'I spear fish with a spear'.

Note in passing that A and instrumental participants are marked by the
same ergative–instrumental case marking (*-ṭu, -tu, -ṭu, -(ŋ)ku, -yi* being
allomorphs), but instrumental participants cannot be cross-referenced
and remain unaffected by intransitivization.

The other intransitivization mechanism is reflexive–reciprocal formation. Reflexive–reciprocal verbs are derived intransitives with the verb
marked by *-ti*.

(37)   *Matʸumpa-ṭu kupaŋuru ḷayi-ṇa ṭapantu-ṭu.*
kangaroo-erg old-man   hit-past foot-inst
'The kangaroo kicked (lit., hit with foot) the old man'.

(38)   *Pa-watikaya matʸumpa ḷa-ti   ṭapantu-ṭu.*
that-dual   kangaroo hit-re foot-inst
'Those two kangaroos are kicking one another'.

In these and other examples I will leave unglossed the *-yi* that marks
most independent transitive verbs.

The reflexive–reciprocal verb form normally expresses identity of
agent and patient, but with one or two verbs it is used simply to
intransitivize.

2.2. Ergative Syntax

Kalkatungu has some coreference rules that are ergative in the sense
that they single out A or the absolutive (i.e., S_i–O). For example, a
participial phrase may be used to qualify an NP but the coreferent NP
in the participial phrase must be in S_i or O function. Where the agent
of a transitive verb is coreferent, the participial clause must be intransitivized so that the agent appears in S_i function. Compare (39), where
the coreferent NP is in S_i function, and (40), where it is in O function,
with (41), where the agent of the transitive verb is the coreferent NP.
Here the antipassive has been used. This is evident from the dative
marking for the patient and from the suffix *-yi* on the verb (although in
independent clauses, nonfuture transitive verbs are marked regularly
with *-yi* whether antipassivized or not, in dependent clauses *-yi* signals
antipassive).

(39)   *Piḷapiḷa ḷuŋa-ṇa iŋka-tʸin.*
child   cry-past walk-participle
'The child cried walking along (as he walked along)'.

(40)   *Piḷapiḷa ḷuŋa-ṇa ŋa-ṭu ḷa-n^{y}in.*
         child   cry-past I-erg hit-participle
         'The child cried when I hit him (I hitting)'.

(41)   *Piḷapiḷa unuani-ṇa   ṭuku-u   ḷa-yi-n^{y}in.*
         child   rejoice-past dog-dat hit-a/p-participle
         'The child was happy hitting the dog'.

   In finite complements expressing purpose, indirect commands, etc., the antipassive is used if A is coreferent with the absolutive, or at least so it seems (as we shall see later in the paper, this requires some important modification. These complements are marked by the presence of a complementizer *a-* to which clitic pronouns are suffixed. In a transitive complement the only combinations of clitic pronouns that have been observed are those of first singular (A or O) with third nonsingular (A or O). In other cases, a hierarchical principle operates and only the higher person may be encoded as a clitic. The hierarchy is $1 > 2 > 3$. If the sole clitic represents A and if it coreferences the absolutive in the governing clause, the antipassive must be used in the complement.
   The most common pattern is the following.

(42)   *Daḷi iŋka kalpin-ku a-ḷi   ḷa-yi.*
         we–2 go   man-dat comp-we-2 kill-a/p
         'We two are going to hit/kill the young man'.

   In (42) the clitic pronoun is *-ḷi; kalpin* is not represented by a clitic since *-ḷi* is higher on the person hierarchy and combinations of first dual and third are not allowed (the clitic for third singular O is zero anyway). Now since *-ḷi* represents A and there is no clitic for O and since *ḷi* coreferences S$_i$, the antipassive must be used in the complement. The marking on *-ḷi* is unaffected since clitic pronouns operate in a nominative–accusative system. Note, however, the presence of *-yi* on the verb and the dative marking on *kalpin*. The word order is interesting too. The complementizer–clitic combination appears regularly in second position within the complement (Wackernagel's law in a complement) with the verb usually in final position. In intransitive complements the complementizer–clitic comes first and the verb last.
   Another common pattern is one in which A coreferences O. Note the word order in the complement of (43). *Kuntu,* the negative, which shows a not unexpected affinity for clause-initial position, precedes the complementizer–clitic but the patient appears after the verb.

(43)   *Da-ṭu n^{y}ini pati-ṇa   kuntu a-   ni aṛi-li yaun-ku maa-t^{y}i.*
         I- erg you tell- past not   comp-you eat-a/p big- dat food-dat
         'I told you not to eat a lot of food'.

In (43) the antipassive is used because *-ni* coreferences *n^{y}ini*. This contrasts with the following sentence, in which the antipassive is not used since A coreferences A (*ḻaa* is suppletive for complementizer–first singular subject, and *awa* is the nonantipassive of the verb for 'give' contrasting paradigmatically with *an^{y}i-yi*, the antipassive):

(44)   *Ḏa-ṯu ṉaa kuṯu unpi ŋa-t^{y}i kuḻa-aṉa ḻaa   awa.*
        I-erg this egg bring me-dat father-to comp-I give
        'I brought these eggs to give to my father'.

In (44) *ŋat^{y}i* is proclitic to *kuḻaaṉa* and hence does not exhibit concordial case marking.

2.3. Advancements

Besides the nominative, ergative, and accusative, Kalkatungu has case forms for dative, locative, allative, ablative, instrumental, and causal ('because of'). In Relational Grammar terms, an inner locative, instrumental, and causal can be advanced to O. A dative complement to S_i can advance and become O and a dative adnominal to O may ascend and become O. The recipient of *an^{y}i* 'to give' may appear in the allative or as O, as will be discussed in what follows.

ADVANCEMENT OF RECIPIENT

The recipient of *an^{y}i* 'to give' can be expressed in the allative as in (45) or in the accusative as in (46). The word order in the examples is a common one but not the only one possible.

(45)   *Maṟapai-ṯu an^{y}a piipa kalpin-kuṉa.*
        woman-erg gave paper man-allative
        'The woman gave the paper to the man'.

(46)   *Maṟapai-ṯu an^{y}a kalpin piipa.*
        woman-erg gave man   paper
        'The woman gave the man the paper'.

It is convenient to consider that (46) contains an advancee, but whereas other constructions containing nonpatient objects are formally and functionally marked with respect to their counterparts with patient objects, in the case of *an^{y}i* the pattern illustrated in (46) is not formally marked, not functionally restricted, and is much more common than the pattern in (45).

It appears that *kalpin* in (46) is O. Certainly the NP corresponding to *kalpin* is the one that can be cross-referenced as in (47).

(47)   *Maṟapai-ṯu anʸa-ŋi (ŋai) piipa.*
         woman-erg gave-me (me) paper
         'The woman gave me paper'.

However, the recipient advancee is not clearly O any more than its
counterpart in English [see comments on (6)]. It has not proven possible,
for example, to get an example with the putative O recipient as the head
of a participial clause as in (39)–(41). A sentence like (46) or (47) can
be detransitivized by the antipassive but both the accusative NPs go into
the dative, so this does not distinguish as O one NP rather than another.

Intuitively, it would seem that this advancement of the recipient does
not affect semantic roles. One would assume that *kalpin* is as much
recipient in (46) as in (45) and *piipa* patient in both (46) and (45). Certainly
the case marking on *piipa* remains unchanged across the two constructions and gives no sign of any reinterpretation.

It is interesting to note the part the advancee plays in the coreference
system. Earlier it was pointed out that in purpose-type complements the
antipassive was used where A coreferenced the absolutive. Note, however, that where A coreferences an advancee with the verb *anʸi*, the
antipassive is not used.[2]

(48)   *Ṯumpaki awa-ŋi ḻaa   itʸa.*
         tobacco give-me comp-I bite
         'Give me some tobacco to chew'.

(49)   *Ati   tʸaa ŋa-ṯu anʸa yuru a-i   ṉuwa ŋurku.*
         meat here I-erg gave man comp-he see   for-nothing
         'I gave the man the meat just to look at'.

It seems that either we have to deny that the recipient has become O
or we have to modify the claim that the antipassive is used in complements of this type when A coreferences the absolutive. The latter seems
preferable. Let us consider the possibility that the antipassive is used
when A coreferences the patient, in other words, that it is semantically
triggered. This is supported by other examples to be given in what
follows.

Advancement of Dative

The dative in Kalkatungu appears to cover the roles of possessor,
beneficiary, purpose, and goal. It is used adnominally and in this usage

---

[2] This is incorrectly reported in Blake (1979:65) where I state that where A coreferences
the recipient the antipassive is used "in some instances." I had mistaken some datives
arising from instrumental advancement for antipassive datives. On checking I now find
only one example of a recipient triggering antipassive against many examples that work
like (48) and (49).

it indicates Possessor ('my meat') or beneficiary ('meat for me'). It is
used to mark the complement of a few two-place verbs that take in-
transitive-type marking (*waira ṉu* 'to like', *miḻṯiṉanʸi* 'to wait for', etc.)
where we could perhaps say it marked goal, and it is used to mark the
purpose adjunct of an intransitive verb ('I am going for fish'). Where the
dative occurs in Kalkatungu as a constituent of a sentence it is always
a complement to S_i, in fact to a participant that is $[^{+\text{agent}}_{-\text{patient}}]$. Where it is
adnominal, the noun on which it is dependent must be understood to be
in a [+patient] relation to it irrespective of the role this noun bears to
its verb.

First of all let us illustrate the ascension of a dative adnominal to O.
If we compare (50a) and (50b) we see that *nʸini,* which is dative in (50a)
(in the form *nʸunku*), is accusative in (50b) and cross-referenced by an
accusative clitic, and that the verb is marked in (50b) by *-nʸtʸama,* which
loses its *nʸ* by a dissimilation rule when it is suffixed to a stem containing
a nasal–stop cluster.

(50)   a.   *Ḏa-ṯu inʸtʸi-mi utʸan nʸun-ku.*
              I-erg chop-fut wood you-fut
              'I will chop your wood (or wood for you)'.

        b.   *Ḏa-ṯu inʸtʸi-tʸama-mi-kin   nʸini utʸan.*
              I-erg chop-dat/adv-fut-you you wood
              'I will chop you the wood'.

The advancement of a dative complement or adjunct in an intransitive
clause occurs only for the purposes of rendering the verb transitive so
that it can then be made reflexive–reciprocal. As noted earlier, reflexive–reciprocal verbs are derived intransitives marked by *-ti.* Consider,
for example, *ŋkuma* 'to look for'. It is a two-place verb taking intran-
sitive-type marking, nominative S_i, and dative complement. To express
the notion 'looking for one another' the verb must be transitivized by
-nʸtʸama so that it can then be intransitivized by *-ti.*

(51)   *Kalpin ŋkuma-tʸama-ti-muyu.*
        man   look-for-dat/adv-re-dual subject
        'The two men are looking for one another'.

The same sort of thing can be observed with an intransitive verb taking
a dative adjunct: *ṉanti* means 'to bark' and the entity barked at can be
expressed in the dative; 'barking at one another' is *ṉanti-tʸama-ti,* parallel
to *ŋkuma-tʸama-ti.*

The usefulness of *-nʸtʸama* can be seen if we consider the case where
a semantic dative is coreferent with a participant in a governing clause.

Consider the verb *ṉiṯa* 'to steal'. It occurs in the construction illustrated in (52) with the person who is stolen from appearing as an adnominal dative.

(52) *Iti-yi   ṉiṯayi ŋa-ṯʸi   ṉṯia.*
      man-erg steal me-dat money
      'The man stole my money'.

If *-nʸtʸama* is suffixed to the verb it enables the person stolen from to appear as O as with the English verb 'to rob'.

(53) *Iti-yi   ṉiṯa-nʸtʸamayi ŋai ṉṯia.*
      man-erg steal-dat/adv me money
      'The man robbed me of my money'.

This derived O can then play a part in the coreference system. In (54) the derived O of the participial clause is coreferent with S_i in the governing clause. Without the *-nʸtʸama* mechanism, one would have to have made the participial clause adverbial by the addition of the locative *-ta*. This would have been no great problem, but there would have been no way to avoid repeating *kalpin* as an adnominal dative.

(54) *Kalpin arkunaan-ati-ṉa   ŋa-ṯu ṉiṯa-nʸtʸama-ṯʸin.*
      man   wild-become-past I-erg steal-dat/adv-participle
      'The man got wild (at) being robbed by me'.

The fact that the derived accusative with *-nʸtʸama* verbs can be cross-referenced and the fact that it can be the coreferent participant in the participial construction the head of which must be absolutive indicates that it is O. As far as I can see, the derived accusative is still semantically dative. The [+patient] of the verb in the basic construction, as in (50a) and (52), does not receive any new case marking in the derived construction, and it is difficult to see how it can be anything but [+patient]. If this is so, then presumably the derived accusative cannot be [+patient], at least insofar as the principle of there being only one instance of each role per clause holds. Now I believe there can be two instances of a number of roles providing only one is an inner participant. However, here both participants are inner in the sense that they are in the case frame of the verb as opposed to being optional peripheral constituents.

Example (54) may give the impression that the participant ousted from the O function can be deleted. It is not clear that this is possible. A third person participant is regularly represented by zero in Kalkatungu.

It is interesting to observe the part the derived O plays in coreference where purpose-type complements are involved. In (55), A of the complement is coreferent with the derived O, but there is no antipassive.

This is similar to what we observed in (48) and (49) with reference to [+recipient] in O function.

(55)   Ati   t'aa   tuyi-n^{y}t'amia   a-i   ala.
        meat here cut-dat/adv-imp comp-he eat
        'Cut him the meat to eat'.

This suggests that the derived O is still semantically dative and that the coreference rule operates not with respect to absolutives but with respect to patient. This is confirmed by the following example where the antipassive is used in a purpose complement where A coreferences the demoted (non-O) patient.

(56)   Kuntu t'ipa-yi kut'ukut'u ŋulurmi-n^{y}t'amayi-ɳa a-i
        not   this-erg pup   keep-dat/adv-past   comp-he
        piṭimpi-yi.
        suck-a/p
        'He didn't keep her a pup to drink the milk'.

In (56) -n^{y}t'ama indicates that a 'dative' is O and this must be the bitch, which is given from the context. The bitch is represented by zero.

2.4. Antipassive

As noted earlier, Kalkatungu has an antipassive construction as an alternative to the normal transitive construction. In this construction a nominative corresponds to the ergative of the transitive construction and a dative to the accusative.

(57)   a.   Ṭuku-yu ṭuar   it'ayi.
              dog-erg snake bite
              'The dog bites/bit the snake'.

        b.   Ṭuku ṭuar-ku   it'ayi.
              dog snake-dat bite
              'The dog is biting the snake'.

In the future tense and in subordinate clauses the antipassive is registered on the verb by -yi (with some verbs exhibiting suppletive alternation). In nonfuture tenses and aspects, independent verbs take a -yi suffix in both the transitive and antipassive constructions.

In independent clauses the antipassive has a semantic function. It indicates ongoing, uncompleted activity [note the translation of (57b) as opposed to that of (57a)] or it refers to indulgence in an activity rather than to a particular instantiation of the activity. It is also correlated with indefinite, nonspecific patients. In terms of the Hopper–Thompson characterization of transitivity (Hopper and Thompson 1980:268–270), the use of the antipassive in independent clauses correlates with low transitivity on a number of different parameters. A good instance of the function of the antipassive is found in (58) where the verb is stative, A weakly agentive, and the patient generic.

(58)   *Kuntu ŋata ŋiṯi   mani-n^{y}t^{y}aŋu maḻta-a   kuu*
        not   we   here get-habitual   much-dat rain-dat
        pirinaŋu manamana-ṯiŋu.
        up-from sky-from
        'We don't get much rain here "from longa top" '.

The antipassive is used in subordinate clauses as noted earlier. Here it has a syntactic function, signaling that A is coreferent with a participant in a governing clause.

The case marking used in the antipassive is the same as that used for intransitive verbs with a dative adjunct and for semitransitive or middle verbs such as *waira ṉu* 'to like' or 'to want'. The antipassive should probably be considered syntactically intransitive as the case marking suggests. However, confirmation for this proves somewhat elusive; one finds sentence patterns like that of (59) and like that of (60).

(59)   *Ṯuku it^{y}ayi.*
        dog   bite
        'The dog bites'.

(60)   *Ṯuku-yu it^{y}ayi.*
        dog-erg bite
        'The dog bit him/her/it'.

The translations suggest that (59) is intransitive and (60) transitive. However, since a third person singular object is normally represented by zero [as in (60)], then (59) could be interpreted as having a zero representing a nonspecific patient. Against this it can be argued that there is no evidence that zero can represent a nonaccusative complement unless one were to ascribe zero complements to intransitives generally. It seems that the complement of an antipassive verb can be omitted, but not the complement of a normal transitive verb.

Whereas it is possible to represent the object by a clitic of the accusative series, no instance has ever been observed of the complement of an antipassive verb being represented by this series of clitics.

It seems, then, that an antipassive clause is indeed intransitive, but this leaves open the question of whether antipassivization affects semantic roles. I think there are reasons to believe that the antipassive represents a morphosyntactically different construction from the transitive, but not one involving any change in the semantic relationships of the participants to the verb. Of course, the use of the antipassive in an independent clause is semantically significant, but only in an aspectual way.

One piece of evidence to suggest that the dative complement of an antipassive verb remains [+patient] is provided by inner locatives. In Kalkatungu the restriction of inner locatives to referring to patients shows up in an obvious way. If the location of a nonabsolutive participant is to be specified, it must be done by putting that location in a participial phrase modifying the participant in question. The locative then has the covert S_i head of the participial phrase as its scope and indirectly by coreference the qualified constituent of the superordinate clause. In the following examples the verb of the participial phrase is *ini* which means 'be located, exist, remain'.

(61)   *Piḷapiḷa ŋuyi-ṉa kuu-ŋka.*
        child   fall-past water-loc
        'The child fell in the water'.

(62)   *Maṛapai-ṯu piḷapiḷa ara-ntiyi   kuu-ŋka.*
        woman-erg baby   enter-cause water-loc
        'The woman put the baby in the water'.

(63)   *Maṛapai-ṯu kuu-ŋka ini-n^yin-ṯu   ŋai ṉan^ya.*
        woman-erg water-loc sit-part-erg me saw
        'The woman (sitting) in the water saw me'.

(64)   *Maṛapai-ṯu iŋka-ṉa piḷapiḷa-aṉa kuu-ŋka   ini-n^yin-kuṉa.*
        woman-erg go-past child-all   water-loc sit-part-all
        'The woman went to the kid (sitting) in the water'.

Now the one exception to this rule is that an inner locative can refer to the dative complement of an antipassive verb. I suggest that an inner locative must refer to a [+patient] participant on semantic grounds and that the fact that the inner locative can refer to the dative complement indicates that this complement is [+patient] [cf. (32)].

(65)   *Maṯu   maa-t^yi ṯuyi   ut^yan-ta.*
        mother food-dat cook-a/p fire-loc
        'Mother is cooking the meal on the fire'.

We noted earlier that Kalkatungu appeared to use the antipassive in purpose-type complements when A coreferenced the absolutive in the governing clause. We also noted that coreference with an O derived by a "dative movement" advancement or -*n^yt^yama* ascension did not trigger antipassive. Now it can happen that a clause governing a purpose complement can itself be antipassivized because of its coreference relations with a yet higher clause. Consider, for example, (66) where the second clause has been antipassivized because the A of this clause is coreferent with *kanimain^{y}t^{y}ir* in the first clause, and then consider the coreference relations between the third clause and the second.

(66)   *Da-tu ṇan^{y}a kanimain^{y}t^{y}ir yuṇtu-u ṇulurma-yi-n^{y}in*
       I-erg saw   policeman   arm-dat grab-a/p-participle
       a-i   iti-nti   a-i   aṇtakata.
       comp-he return-caus comp-he lock-up
       'I saw the policeman grab his arm and bring him back and lock him up'.

Note that the antipassive is not used in the third clause even though A appears to coreference S$_i$ in the second clause. This S$_i$ is of course a derived one. We could account for the absence of the antipassive in the third clause by assuming the antipassive is triggered by coreference between A and a [+patient] participant in the higher clause. We can then attribute the absence of the antipassive in the third clause to the presence of a [+agent] participant in the second clause. This analysis would be in line with that suggested in conjunction with dative movement advancement and *-n^{y}t^{y}ama* ascension.

Similarly in (67) we find that the antipassive is not used in the third clause though A coreferences S$_i$. This S$_i$ is a derived one, the antipassive being used in the second clause because A coreferences (a basic) S$_i$ in the first clause.

(67)   *Iŋka ṇaḷi yuku-yan   a-ḷi   ŋkaa-ḷi   ṇun^{y}t^{y}aani-t^{y}in*
       go   we-2 spear-having comp-we-2 spear-a/p lie-participle
       a-ḷi   ṇuwa.
       comp-we-2 see
       'We go with spears to spear him, to see him when he's lying down'.

If it is correct that the antipassive is used to signal coreference between A of a purpose clause and a [+patient] participant in the governing clause, we could try to test this principle against verbs meaning *spit*, *shoot*, etc., that is, against intransitives that I characterized as [$^{+\text{agent}}_{-\text{patient}}$]. However, the only verbs with meanings like these in Kalkatungu are transitive. One verb, however, which is interesting in this respect is *ŋkuma* 'to look for', which takes a nominative S$_i$ and a dative complement. When A of a purpose complement is coreferent with this S$_i$, no antipassive is used in the complement.

(68)   *Dai ŋkumayi paa ṯuku-u ḻaa   kanimi.*
        I   look-for there dog- dat comp-I tie
        'I'm looking there for the dog to tie it up'.

I interpret this as evidence that *ŋkuma* has a [+agent] subject. Independent corroboration of this can be found in the behavior of *ŋkuma* in
complements. It alternates between *ŋkumi* (nonantipassive) and *ŋkumayi*
(antipassive) according to whether the 'seeker' is coreferential with a
higher patient or not.

3. CONCLUSION

As I am sympathetic to the view that ergative–absolutive case marking
is semantically based, I am suspicious of claims that there are ergative
and absolutive grammatical relations. There may be, but before one can
posit new grammatical relations one has to check that the evidence is
not in fact based on semantic relations. Postal (1977:280) claims that
ergatives (transitive subjects) behave differently from intransitive subjects with respect to causativization in French. Whereas intransitive
subjects become direct objects, ergatives become objects marked by *à*
('to'). He does not mention that the preposition can be *par* rather than
à with most verbs. He does not appear to have any means of describing
how one expresses the generalization that verbs of perception do not
allow *par*. A plausible account of causativization can be given in terms
of roles (see Starosta, 1978). Until this possibility is dismissed, the
"ergative" basis of the process remains dubious.

The existence of roles is inevitable, but grammatical relations are not,
and one can easily imagine a language without them. I suspect that direct
object is not as firmly established as the frequent use of the term suggests,
and that subject is certainly not universal, at least in the sense of an
entity subsuming S_i and A and manifested in noncontingent properties.

The absolutive does not seem to be warranted in English; the evidence
that could be adduced in support of it can be handled in terms of a
broadly defined patient. The best piece of evidence comes from "raising," but even if we do take the view that the "target" of "raising"
should not be described in terms of [+patient], we still only have evidence for an absolutive target, not for the absolutive as the basis for a
rule.

The absolutive shows up in Kalkatungu in the case marking on nouns
but not in the case forms. I use "case form" in the traditional sense of
case, a case form being determined by distinctions made in any one

paradigm. If one treats the bound pronouns as being nominal constituents that are obligatorily unstressed, then a comparison of the free and bound paradigms reveals three case forms—nominative, ergative, and accusative. Even if one deals in rules of case marking, one finds that no rule need refer to the absolutive as S_i and O simply remain unmarked in contradistinction to A.

It is sometimes pointed out that the absolutive is the essential grammatical relation in an ergative language. This is not so in Kalkatungu. A is a nuclear constituent and can be cross-referenced. Indeed A contrasts with a kind of indirect agent that is represented by a peripheral constituent with intransitive verbs.

(69)   *Kaṯir muṟi (ununkaṯi-ṯunu).*
        grass wave wind-causal
        'The grass waves (in—because of—the wind)'.

I do not think A can be deleted any more than O can.

It has been claimed that the absolutive in an ergative language represents a grammaticalized topic (Wierzbicka 1980; Mallinson & Blake 1981). This is not clearly true in Kalkatungu, though I believe it is true of some ergative languages. The absolutive tends to be the zero case form in ergative languages and is often cross-referenced, sometimes to the exclusion of A. Both these features are suggestive of topic status. Moreover, in many ergative languages the first and second person pronouns tend to operate in a nominative–accusative system. A likely interpretation of this is that because they are inherently highly topic-worthy, they tend to eschew the relatively peripheral ergative position and occupy the more central, more topical absolutive position. In Kalkatungu, as we noted earlier, first and second bound pronouns but not free ones operate in a nominative–accusative paradigm. To the extent that an absolutive represents a topic we can expect to find evidence of an absolutive grammatical relation, as the basis of grammatical relations is ultimately topic.

The absolutive does show up where a -n^yin participial clause, or a relative clause, qualifies an NP. As explained above, the coreferent participant in a participial clause must be absolutive. The absolutive shows up in much the same way in a number of ergative languages, in Chukchee, for instance (Comrie 1979:229), and in Quiche (Larsen and Norman 1979:358). The absolutive involved here is a derived one. It could be an S_i derived by antipassivization or it could be an advancee derived by advancement. It seems to me that what is involved is clearly a syntactic conjunction of S_i and O. The requirement that a coreferent participant in a participial clause be absolutive is doubtless related to the topic status that the absolutive holds (or held in the past). The coreferent participant is maximally presupposed by virtue of its being given in the main clause and is thus the best candidate in the participial clause for topic.

The most interesting aspect of Kalkatungu is the coreferencing system employed with the purpose complement with *a-*, illustrated in (42)–(44), and also with the purpose complement with *-n^{y}t^{y}aaya* and *ana* complements (not illustrated here; see Blake 1979:68–75). As noted at various points in the text, the antipassive is used if A coreferences the Patient of a governing clause.[3] As far as I know such a coreferencing principle has not been claimed for any other language although something of this kind is not too unexpected in Australia in light of the fact that Dyirbal (Dixon 1972, 1979) and a number of other Queensland languages are described as having coreference rules based on the absolute, more specifically, surface absolutive (Dixon 1979:62–65).

Some will probably want to describe the coreference principle in another way. On the evidence I have presented one could argue that it is not the patient that is significant in the coreference system but the underlying absolutive. The antipassive is used in complements if A coreferences the patient rather than the recipient with *an^{y}i* 'to give', and the patient of the basic construction where *-n^{y}t^{y}ama* is concerned, and the antipassive is not used when A coreferences an S$_i$ that is derived from an underlying A. If one takes the view that the underlying absolutive is the determinant one must accept that 'A gives B to C' is basic in relation to 'A gave C B' and as *ŋkuma* 'to look for' behaves as if it contained an A despite its case marking (68), one would have to assume it is underlyingly transitive. Whether the coreference principle is sensitive to [+patient] or the underlying absolutive, it must be a matter of [+patient], given that the underlying absolutive will always be [+patient].

Kalkatungu does not have constructions with "raised" participants as in (19)–(20) nor gerundive nominalization, so there is no scope for the absolutive in these areas. With verbs of wishing and commanding there are no constructions with an infinitival complement, so that one cannot talk about control of the subject (or indeed of the absolutive) of the complement. Inner locatives refer to patients as in English, but this is clearly semantic and presumably universal. Kalkatungu does have an ergative–absolutive character, however, because of the pervasiveness of the case marking and of the alternations between the transitive and antipassive constructions in subordinate clauses.

The part the absolutive plays in language can only be determined from the study of a large number of languages. The data presented here indicate

---

[3] On the basis of a few examples it appears that the antipassive can be used in a governing clause where A coreferences a subordinate patient.

that in Kalkatungu the absolutive shows up only in a constraint on clauses qualifying NPs, a constraint to the effect that the coreferent NP in the qualifying clause must be absolutive. This type of constraint has been reported from a number of other ergative languages. On the other hand, there are a number of phenomena that appear to link S_i and O, but these seem to be based on the role of patient. It may be that the ergative–absolutive case marking in many languages may be based on the agent–patient semantic distinction. Certainly all S_i–O links should be examined to see if in fact they are based on patient rather than manifesting a syntactic relation.

ACKNOWLEDGMENTS

The Kalkatungu data in this paper were collected on field trips financed by the Australian Institute of Aboriginal Studies and Monash University. I would like to thank Gavan Breen for collecting some of the material for me, and Stephen Paterson for his comments on the draft of the paper.

REFERENCES

Anderson, J. M. (1977) *On Case Grammar*, Croom Helm, London.
Anderson, J. M. (1979) "On Being without a Subject," distributed through the Indiana University Linguistics Club, Indiana University, Bloomington, Indiana.
Anderson, S. (1977) "Comments on the Paper by Wasow," in P. W. Culicover, T. Wasow, and A. Akmajian, eds., *Formal Syntax*, Academic Press, New York.
Blake, B. J. (1979) *A Kalkatungu Grammar*, Pacific Linguistics, Canberra.
Chomsky, N. (1957) *Syntactic Structures*, Mouton, The Hague.
Comrie, B. (1979) "Degrees of Ergativity: Some Chukchee Evidence," in F. Plank, ed., *Ergativity*, Academic Press, London.
Dixon, R. M. W. (1972) *The Dyirbal Language of North Queensland*, Cambridge University Press, Cambridge.
Dixon, R. M. W. (1979) "Ergativity," *Language* 55, 59–138.
Fillmore, C. (1968) "The Case for Case," in E. Bach and R. Harms, eds., *Universals in Linguistic Theory*, Holt, Rinehart and Winston, New York.
Gruber, J. S. (1965) *Studies in Lexical Relations*, unpublished doctoral dissertation, Massachusetts Institute of Technology, Cambridge, Massachusetts.
Hopper, P. and S. Thompson (1980) "Transitivity in Grammar and Discourse," *Language* 56, 251–299.
Jackendoff, R. (1972) *Semantic Interpretation in Generative Grammar*, MIT Press, Cambridge, Massachusetts.
Kibrik, A. E. (1979) "Canonical Ergativity and Daghestan Languages," in F. Plank, ed., *Ergativity*, Academic Press, London.
Larsen, T. W. and W. M. Norman (1979) "Correlates of Ergativity in Mayan Grammar," in F. Plank, ed., *Ergativity*, Academic Press, London.

Mallinson, G. and B. J. Blake (1981) *Language Typology,* North-Holland, Amsterdam, The Netherlands.

Postal, P. (1977) "Antipassive in French," in J. A. Kegal, D. Nash, and A. Zaenen, eds., *Proceedings of the Seventh Annual Meeting of the North Eastern Linguistic Society,* Department of Linguistics, MIT, Cambridge, Massachusetts.

Starosta, S. (1978) "The One Per Cent Solution," in W. Abraham, ed., *Valence, Semantic Case and Grammatical Relations,* John Benjamins, Amsterdam, The Netherlands.

Wierzbicka, A. (1980) *The Case for Surface Case.* Karoma, Ann Arbor.

GRAMMATICAL RELATIONS IN HUICHOL

BERNARD COMRIE

0. INTRODUCTION

0.1. The Huichol Language

Huichol, one of the most viable of the surviving Uto-Aztecan languages, is spoken in West–Central Mexico. To date, there is relatively
little work on Huichol, perhaps reflecting the geographical isolation of
the area inhabited by the Huichol. The most significant work is that by
Joseph E. Grimes and his associates; see, in particular, Grimes (1959,
1964), McIntosh and Grimes (1954), and also the discussion of Huichol
in various parts of Grimes (1974). These works deal with the Central
dialect of Huichol. The present article is based on material in the Santa
Catarina dialect, the most divergent dialect of Huichol from the Central
dialect, although dialect differentiation is relatively small—my consultant
was usually able to interpret sentences read to him from the publications
cited above, even in isolation, but recognized several of the forms therein
as being from a different dialect.

For the purposes of comparison between the Central dialect and the
Santa Catarina dialect, I would note the following salient differences:
A few of the pronominal affixes are different, in particular the third

95

person plural subject prefix *me-* (Central *we-*) and the second person singular object prefix *me(ci)-* (Central *ma(ci)-*) (Grimes 1964:13). The occurrence of the third person singular object prefix *i-* differs from that given for the Central dialect by Grimes (1964:26–27): In the Central dialect, this prefix is omitted if and only if the verb is immediately preceded by its object; in the Santa Catarina dialect, the prefix is required if the object noun phrase is omitted, but seems otherwise to be optional (the criteria governing this optionality have not yet been worked out). In the Central dialect, most main clause verbs in assertions require the prefix *p(i)-*, otherwise the sentence is most naturally interpreted pragmatically as a yes–no question; my consultant associates this frequent use of *p-* with other dialects of Huichol, and in his own speech I have not uncovered any instances of contrast between verbal forms with and without *p-*: The occurrence of this prefix seems to be fully predictable in terms of the phonological and morphological structure of the verb, although further detailed work is required on this topic.

0.2. Theoretical Framework

The main theoretical point of this article is to exemplify, through the use of Huichol material, a methodology for establishing grammatical relations in a language. As such, the article can be viewed alongside the recent development of relational grammar, an offshoot of transformational grammar, in which a wide range of syntactic processes are stated in terms of grammatical relations, in particular subject, direct object, and indirect object (in addition to other noun phrase arguments of a predicate, often called nonterms or impure terms). Relational grammar is most closely associated with the pioneering work of David M. Perlmutter and Paul M. Postal. However, the present article is not conceived within relational grammar in the narrow sense. In particular, much of the detailed argumentation stems from my misgivings over some of the assumptions, to my mind unjustified, that are frequently made within relational grammar.

More specifically, within the paper I make only minimal assumptions about what grammatical relations exist in Huichol and try to establish, solely on the basis of evidence provided by Huichol, what grammatical relations this language requires for an adequate description of its syntax. This may be contrasted with the usual relational grammar methodology, where a certain set of grammatical relations is taken for granted and the investigator's task is viewed as uncovering how these grammatical relations can be used in describing the syntax of the language in question.

In the body of this article, I demonstrate a number of logically independent grammatical processes that allow us to isolate two grammatical relations in Huichol, in addition to a residual set of noun phrase arguments that are, essentially, syntactically inert (i.e., that do not participate in any of the major syntactic processes of Huichol). Because the methodology advocated gives only language-specific results, it does not in itself permit identification of these two grammatical relations with those established for any other language. However, a comparison of the noun phrases that bear these two grammatical relations in Huichol with their correspondents in translation-equivalent sentences in other languages would permit us to make the following identifications:

1. The grammatical relation defined internally to Huichol by control of subject case marking, subject–verb agreement, reflexive possessive, and switch reference, corresponds to that called subject in other languages.

2. The grammatical relation defined internally in Huichol by control of verb–object agreement and correspondence to the subject of a passive sentence corresponds in part to what are called direct objects and in part to what are called indirect objects in other languages; for this second grammatical relation I shall use the neutral term "prime object."

The fact that cross-language comparability emerges from the application of our methodology to Huichol is significant, as such comparability was not built into the model a priori. Universals and typological generalizations that are established are more significant than those that are presupposed.[1]

The assignment of grammatical relations that is argued for in this paper is essentially an assignment of surface structure (or final) grammatical relations. The following would seem to me to be the most cogent reasons for establishing, in addition, more abstract (underlying, deep structure, initial) grammatical relations—again using the methodology of language-specific criteria:

1. Different criteria fail to identify the same set of grammatical relations, so that one could argue that a given noun phrase bears different grammatical relations in different strata, that is, the different criteria define grammatical relations in different strata.

2. In order to account for sentence relatedness (e.g., that between actives and passives), one might assign different grammatical relations in different strata (e.g., such that active and passive correspondents

---

[1] There is also some degree of cross-language comparability among criteria (e.g., control of reflexivization and switch reference by subjects only is frequent across languages).

would share the same grammatical relations in one stratum but different grammatical relations in another stratum).

I emphasize that I consider these the *most* cogent reasons—this does not imply that I consider them necessarily cogent.

As regards Point (1) of the previous paragraph, the Huichol constructions I have examined provide no evidence of "diffuseness" of grammatical relations, so this particular kind of evidence for different levels or strata is not available.[2] As regards Point (2), Huichol does have (closely) corresponding active and passive pairs, though it is again far from clear that this justifies postulating different levels or strata in the derivation of the passive sentence, rather than simply stating a relation directly between the surface/final grammatical relations of the passive sentence and those of the corresponding active sentence. As far as I can tell, the only grammatical relations that Huichol requires are subject and prime object, as surface/final grammatical relations; the onus of proof is on those who would multiply these entities.

1. MORPHOLOGY AND GRAMMATICAL RELATIONS

In Huichol, there are two aspects of morphology that give prima facie tests for grammatical relations: case marking of noun phrases, and verb agreement. As noted in detail in what follows, case marking distinguishes grammatical relations in only a very few instances, whereas distinction by verb agreement is much more widespread. Word order does not provide any strong means of distinguishing grammatical relations, so that where case marking and verb agreement are both ambivalent the resultant sentence is ambiguous, as is the case in Sentence (5).

1.1. Case Marking

The majority of Huichol noun phrases, pronominal and nonpronominal, have no case marking to distinguish subject from object(s); as indicated

---

[2] With this one might contrast the passive in Ute (Givón, this volume), where the notion of "subject" does seem somewhat diffuse—see also Note 9. Even where such diffuseness does exist, it is far from clear that this is sufficient justification for positing different levels/ strata, rather than having different networks of relations within a single level/stratum (or, conceivably, the postulation of different levels/strata is just one way of formalizing the notion of diffuseness of grammatical relations, i.e., of accounting for the fact that different criteria give contradictory assignments of grammatical relations).

below, various oblique objects (instrumentals, etc.) do have postpositional case marking. In the following sentences, the noun phrases are
not case marked. In (1)–(4), the verb agreement in fact serves to identify
the person and number of both subject and object, and the pronouns can
be omitted. In (5), where the verb agreement does not uniquely identify
subject and object, both being third person plural, the resultant sentence
is ambiguous:[3]

(1)   *(nee) ne- nua.*
        I   1sg arrive
        'I arrived'.

(2)   *(eeki) pe- nua.*
        you   2sg arrive
        'You arrived'.

(3)   *(taame) (eeki) te- meci-zeiya.*
        we   you   1pl 2sg   see
        'We see you'.

(4)   *(eeki) (taame) pe- taci-zeiya.*
        you   we   2sg 1pl see
        'You see us'.

(5)   *Uukaraawiciizi tiiri   me- wa- zeiya.*
        women   children 3pl 3pl see
        'The women see the children' or
        'The children see the women'.

In (3)–(4), the order of words may be changed without changing the
cognitive meaning; in (5), changing the word order does not disambiguate
the sentence.

A small number of noun phrases do, however, show a case distinction
between subject and nonsubject. Noun phrases including a numeral take
the ending *-ti* on the numeral if the noun phrase is subject, but *-me*
otherwise [i.e., for objects, including oblique objects that already have
a postposition of their own, as with the instrumental in (8)]:

(6)   *Tiiri yi- huuta-ti   me- niu?aziani.*
        children two   subj 3pl arrive
        'Two children arrived'.

---

[3] The following abbreviations are used: ant–anterior; benef–benefactive; instr–instrumental;
pass–passive; pl–plural; refl–reflexive; sa–same reference; sg–singular; simul–simultaneous;
subj–subject; sw–switch reference.

(7)   *Tɨɨri yɨ- nauka-tɨ   me- wa- zeiya uukaraawiciizɨ yɨ-*
        children four   subj 3pl 3pl see   women
          huuta-me.
          two   nonsubj
        'Four children see two women'.

(8)   *Taame cɨɨkɨ te- paukuuwaazɨ kɨyezɨ nauka-me   -kɨ.*
        we   dog 1pl beat   sticks four   nonsubj instr
        'We beat the dog with four sticks'.

A similar case distinction is shown in coordinate noun phrases, where the coordinator *maa-* 'and' takes the ending *-tɨ* if part of the subject noun phrase, *-me* otherwise:

(9)   *Wan maria maa-tɨ   me- nekɨɨne.*
        Juan Maria and   subj 3pl leave
        'Juan and Maria left'.

(10)   *Wan maria maa-tɨ   tuizu me- niunaneeni.*
        Juan Maria and   subj pig   3pl buy
        'Juan and Maria bought a pig'.

(11)   *Nee wan maria maa-me   ne- wa- ruzei.*
        I   Juan Maria and nonsubj 1pl 3pl see
        'I saw Juan and Maria'.

In place of *maa-me, maa-ka* is also possible.[4]

Case marking of noun phrases thus enables us, in certain instances, to distinguish between subjects and nonsubjects, but does not provide any finer subcategorization within the latter.

1.2. Verb Agreement

In Huichol, intransitive verbs agree in person and number with their subject. Transitive verbs take the same prefixes as intransitive verbs to indicate subject agreement, plus another set, usually formally distinct, to indicate object agreement. The prefixes for the Santa Catarina dialect are set out in Table 1. Some person and number combinations have identical or potentially identical prefixes for both subject and object, and

---

[4] The case suffixes seem related to the verb suffixes used in the switch-reference system (discussed in what follows), and to suffixes used in certain other constructions to relate predicates to either a subject or a nonsubject (Grimes 1974:144–145). The full details of this relationship, in both a synchronic and diachronic (including comparative Uto-Aztecan) perspective, remain to be worked out.

TABLE 1
PRONOMINAL AFFIXES IN HUICHOL (SANTA CATARINA DIALECT)

Independent	Subject	Object	Reflexive object	Possessive	Reflexive possessive
nee 'I'	*ne-*	*ne(ci)-*	*ne-*	*ne-*	*ne-*
eeki 'you'	*pe-*	*me(ci)-*	*ʔa-*	*ʔa-*	*ʔa-*
——[5]	——	*(i)-*	*yi-*	*-ya*	*yu-*
taame 'we'	*te-*	*ta(ci)-*	*ta-*	*ta-*	*ta-*
zeemi 'you-all'	*ze-*	*ze-*	*yi-*	*ze-*	*yu-*
——[5]	*me-*	*wa-*	*yi-*	*wa-*	*yu-*

we shall therefore concentrate on those that show an overt distinction. The subject prefix always precedes the object prefix, and may be separated from it by other prefixes. In the third person singular, the subject prefix is always, and the object prefix often, null. For the moment, we shall not specify what kind of object triggers verb–object agreement. Examples (12)–(15), which are the same as (1)–(4), provide simple illustration using an intransitive verb [(12)–(13)] and a transitive verb that takes only one object [(14)–(15)]:

(12)   *Nee ne- nua.*
       I   1sg arrive
       'I arrived'.

(13)   *Eeki pe- nua.*
       you 2sg arrive
       'You arrived'.

(14)   *Taame eeki te- meci-zeiya.*
       we   you 1pl 2sg   see
       'We see you'.

(15)   *Eeki taame pe- taci-zeiya.*
       you we   2sg 1pl see
       'You see us'.

Where a verb takes more than one object (or, more generally, more than one nonsubject argument), only one of these can trigger verb agreement. Thus object agreement does distinguish among different kinds of nonsubjects, unlike case marking. We shall return to this crucial property

---

[5] Huichol has no specifically third person pronouns, demonstratives being used instead—for example, *iya* (the most neutral) and *miiki*. Some of these demonstratives are neutral for number.

in what follows. At least provisionally, we shall use the term PRIME OBJECT to refer to those objects that trigger object agreement.

2. SYNTACTIC TESTS FOR GRAMMATICAL RELATIONS

In addition to morphological correlates of grammatical relatiòns, Huichol syntax provides us with a number of syntactic tests, in particular the reflexive possessive prefix and the existence of a same reference–switch reference distinction with certain subordinate verbs. In this section, I will examine the behavior of these constructions in active sentences, showing that they provide a means of distinguishing between subject and nonsubject on syntactic grounds in addition to the morphological differences already discussed.

2.1. Reflexive Possessives

In Huichol, one of the essential components of the possessive construction is the possessive affix on the possessed noun. Most of these affixes are prefixes, similar to the prefixes on verbs and indeed to the independent pronouns, although the third person singular possessive affix is a suffix -ya; for the forms, see Table 1. In the third person (singular and plural) and in the second person plural, Huichol distinguishes nonreflexive from reflexive possessive prefixes, the reflexive prefix being yu- for all three combinations of person and number.[6] For the other combinations, the ordinary possessive prefix is used, and these therefore provide no crucial evidence here.

The basic rule governing the occurrence of the reflexive possessive prefixes is that they occur if and only if the possessor is coreferential with the subject of the sentence. Even where other coreference possibilities would make perfect, or even better, sense, they are excluded:

(16)   *Iya yu- niwe kuuwaayaa.*
        he refl son beat
        'He$_i$ is beating his$_i$ son'.

(17)   *Iya nuʔaa-ya kuuwaayaa.*[7]
        he son   3sg beat
        'He$_i$ is beating his$_j$ son'.

---

[6] My consultant uses only *yu-* as the second person plural–third person reflexive possessive prefix; as the reflexive object prefix he prefers *yi-* (see Table 1), but also accepts *yu-*.

[7] In the Santa Catarina dialect, the third person singular possessed form of *niwe* 'son' is suppletive; my consultant recognized the expected form *niwee-ya* as occurring in other dialects, but not his own.

(18)   *Miiki yu- kiye -ki   me- pe-i-   kuuwaazi.*
        they refl stick instr 3pl   3sg beat
        'They$_i$ beat him$_j$ with their$_i$/*his$_j$ stick'.

(19)   *Zeeme yu- kiye -ki   ze- pe-i-   kuuwaazi.*
        you-all refl stick instr 2pl   3sg beat
        'You-all$_i$ beat him$_j$ with your$_i$/*his$_j$ stick'.

(20)   *Zeeme kiyee-ya -ki   ze- pe-i-   kuuwaazi.*
        you-all stick 3sg instr 2pl   3sg beat
        'You-all$_i$ beat him$_j$ with his$_{j/k}$ stick'.

In Sentence (20), there is no way of showing whether the stick belongs to the person beaten or to some other person not mentioned in the sentence, as the only distinction possible with the reflexive versus non-reflexive possessive affixes is coreference with the subject versus all other possibilities.

2.2. Switch-Reference

Like many other Uto-Aztecan languages, Huichol has a distinction between same reference and switch reference with certain subordinate verb forms; the forms are discussed by Grimes (1964:64–65), who uses the terms "proximate" and "obviative" for same reference and switch reference, respectively. In Huichol, this opposition is restricted to a small set of subordinate verb forms, rather than being a general phenomenon throughout the syntax of clause combining. Where the opposition exists, the same-reference (sa) form is used when the subject of the subordinate clause is the same as that of the main clause, and the switch-reference (sw) form elsewhere, that is, where the subject of one clause is coreferential with a nonsubject of the other clause, or where the clauses have coreferential nonsubjects, or where the clauses have no noun phrase in common. In Huichol, the verb form that is marked for same or switch reference retains its full set of verb agreement prefixes, so that there is a certain amount of redundancy, at least at first sight: In (21), for instance, the prefix *ne-* on *ne-nua-ka* indicates first person singular, but so does the same-reference suffix *-ka*, given that the subject of the main clause is first person singular:

(21)   *Nee ne- nua   -ka,   paapaa ne- p-ii- ʔiiti.*
        I   1sg arrive sa-ant tortilla 1sg 3sg give
        'When I arrived, I gave him a tortilla'.

(22)   *Nee ne- nua   -ku,   iya paapaa nec-uʔiiti.*
        I   1sg arrive sw-ant he tortilla 1sg give
        'When I arrived, he gave me a tortilla'.

(23)   *Uuka nua - ku,   nee ne- petia.*
        girl   arrive sw-ant I   1sg leave
        'When the girl arrived, I left'.

As third person pronouns can have several possible referents, the same-reference versus switch-reference system can here serve to distinguish different entities referred to by third person pronouns or verb affixes (including the null affix):

(24)   *Kuuyeika-ti,   nec-uzei.*
        walk   sa-simul 1sg see
        'While he$_i$ was walking, he$_i$ saw me'.

(25)   *Uuki kuuyeikaa-kaku,   uuka nec-uzei.*
        man walk   sw-simul girl 1sg see
        'While the man was walking, the girl saw me'.

Switch reference versus same reference thus gives another test distinguishing subject from nonsubject (but not discriminating within the latter). In fact, it allows us to test for subjecthood in two clauses simultaneously, provided the two noun phrases we want to test are coreferential.[8]

3. GRAMMATICAL RELATIONS IN THE PASSIVE

In this section, we will be concerned with the passive of sentences that in the active contain a single object, that is, sentences of the type

---

[8] Though not relevant to the establishment of grammatical relations, a further interesting question that arises is the behavior of the same–switch-reference system when the two subjects are neither coreferential nor disjoint, that is, when the relation between them is of proper inclusion (e.g., 'I'–'we', 'you'–'we' [interpreted inclusively], 'you' (singular)–'you-all', 'he'–'they' [where the referent of 'he' is a member of the referent of 'they'], 'he'–'you-all' [interpreted inclusively]). In such instances, my consultant rather consistently treated instances of proper inclusion as equivalent to coreference, for example:

(i)   *Nee ne- haataʔa-ka,   tanaiti te- pekii.*
       I   1sg arrive   sa-ant together 1pl leave
       'When I arrived, we left together'.

(ii)   *Taame te- haataʔazia-ka,   nee ne- petia.*
       we   1pl arrive   sa-ant I   1sg arrive
       'When we arrived, I left'.

Sometimes, however, switch-reference markers were allowed. I suspect that analysis of natural text/discourse will be required to elucidate the relevant parameters.

'My father beat me'. In Huichol, incidentally, passives of intransitive sentences are not possible. A representative active–passive pair is given in (26)–(27):

(26)   *Ne- yau   nee neci-haukuuwaazɨ.*
         1sg father I   1sg beat
         'My father beat me'.

(27)   *Nee ne- paukuuweiyaazɨ.*
         I   1sg beat-pass
         'I was beaten'.

In Huichol, there are several morphological means of forming passive verbs (Grimes 1964:97), and I shall not attempt any finer segmentation of passive verb forms into morphemes. In the Huichol passive, it is impossible to include the agent; thus, for example, there is no literal translation of *I was beaten by my father*, which would have to be expressed as an active sentence, that is, as (26). When really pressed, my consultant volunteered as the equivalent of *I was beaten by my father* the compound sentence 'I was beaten, my father did it'.

Our concern in this section will be with the grammatical relation of the noun phrase that cooccurs with the passive verb in sentences like (27)—the noun phrase *nee* 'I' in this particular example. A priori, this noun phrase could be either an object (as in the corresponding active), or a subject, since the relation object-of-active–subject-of-passive holds in the passive of many languages, including English. Within Uto-Aztecan languages, both the personal (English-type) passive and impersonal type (retention of the object as an object) are found (Langacker 1976).[9] My consultant prefers to translate Huichol passives into Spanish not as personal passives [i.e., *yo fue pegado* for (27)], but rather as active sentences with unspecified third person plural subject [i.e., *me pegaron*, literally

---

[9] The latter, impersonal, type essentially characterizes the passive in the (distantly) genetically related language Ute, discussed in Givón's contribution to this volume. About the only formal syntactic property the Huichol and Ute passives have in common is the impossibility of expressing the agent. In Huichol, the only passive sentences are those corresponding to an active sentence with a prime object; the noun phrase in the passive sentence corresponding to the prime object of the active sentence has the full range of subject properties and no prime object properties, as illustrated in detail in this section. In Ute, there is a passive corresponding to any active sentence with at least one nonsubject argument. Although the nonsubject argument (or one of the nonsubject arguments) of the active corresponds to the topic of the passive, this topic does not have any formal syntactic subject properties (except, perhaps, for some speakers, control of number agreement in the nominal–habitual aspect). In contrast, the agent, even though it cannot be expressed, does still have at least one formal syntactic property—namely, control of number agreement in the verb.

'(they) beat me']. However, all of these comparisons are purely circum-stantial, and fortunately there is clear evidence internal to Huichol that the noun phrase *nee* in (27) is subject, on the basis of the tests discussed earlier.

First, we can consider case marking with those noun phrases (numeral and coordinate noun phrases) that show a case-marking distinction be-tween subject and nonsubject. In passive sentences, the relevant argu-ment takes the subject suffix *-ti:*

(28)   *Türi yi- huuta-ti   me- puutiweiya.*
         children two   subj 3pl beat-pass
         'Two children were beaten'.

(29)   *Wan maria maa-ti   me- puutiweiya.*
         Juan Maria and subj 3pl beat-pass
         'Juan and Maria were beaten'.

Second, the verb agreement with this noun phrase is always subject agreement and never object agreement, where the two are distinct, as can be seen in (28)–(29), and more straightforwardly in (30):

(30)   *Türi   me- puutiweiya.*
         children 3pl beat-pass
         'The children were beaten'.

Third, the noun phrase that cooccurs with the passive verb in sentences like (27) can control possessive reflexivization, which was shown earlier to be a subject property:

(31)   *Iya yu- kiye -ki   paukuuweiyaazi.*
         he refl stick instr beat-pass
         'He$_i$ was beaten with his$_i$ stick'.

Sentence (31) cannot be interpreted to mean that some unspecified per-son(s) beat him with that unspecified person's/those unspecified persons' stick, although (32) could be given this interpretation (in addition to one where none of agent, patient, and possessor of the stick are coreferential):

(32)   *Iya kiyee-ya -ki   paukuuweiyaazi.*
         he stick 3sg instr beat-pass
         'He$_i$ was beaten with his$_j$ stick'.

In Huichol, possessive reflexivization is an obligatory process, so (32) can only be interpreted to mean that the person beaten is not the one who owned the stick.

Finally, the distribution of same-reference and switch-reference suf-fixes provides further evidence that the noun phrase in question is a subject, given the data in what follows and the observation made earlier that the same-reference suffixes require that the subjects of both clauses be coreferential:

(33)   *Nunuuci nua   -ka,   paukuuweiyaazɨ.*
        child   arrive sa-ant beat-pass
        'When the child₍ᵢ₎ arrived, he₍ᵢ₎ was beaten'.

(34)   *Nunuuci nua   -ku,   uuki paukuuweiyaazɨ.*
        child   arrive sw-ant man beat-pass
        'When the child arrived, the man was beaten'.

In (34), the person beaten cannot be the child. Sentence (35) shows that the order of the clauses is not relevant:

(35)   *Nee ne-haukuuweiyaazɨa-ka,   ne- petɨa.*
        I   1sgbeat-pass   sa-ant 1sg leave
        'When I was beaten, I left'.

(36)   *Nee ne-haukuuweiyaazɨa-ku,   wan nec-upareewi.*
        I   1sgbeat-pass   sw-ant Juan 1sg help
        'When I was beaten, Juan helped me'.

4. VERBS WITH MORE THAN ONE OBJECT

4.1. Recipient Noun Phrases

In this section, we will consider verbs that take more than one object (ditransitive verbs), such as 'give' and 'show', considering in particular tests to distinguish between the two objects that such verbs can take. So far, we have noted only one test that discriminates among objects, namely verb–object agreement, which functions as a test in that a verb can agree with only one of its objects. The following examples show that with verbs such as 'give', object agreement is always with the recipient— I use this as a hopefully neutral term to indicate the noun phrase that occurs in the Z slot in English X *gave/showed/etc.* Y *to* Z:

(37)   *Nee waakanaari ne- meci-tɨkiitɨ eeki.*
        I   chickens   1sg 2sg give you
        'I gave the chickens to you'.

From Sentence (37), we note several things. First, neither the recipient nor the patient ('chickens') is case marked in any way, nor is there any possibility of differential case marking (i.e., other than the general non-subject suffixes on numeral and coordinate noun phrases) with other kinds of noun phrases in these syntactic positions. Efforts to elicit any alternative syntactic pattern proved fruitless, other than paraphrases involving a sequence of clauses. Second, the object agreement prefix refers to the recipient, and cannot refer to the patient. This is true even where the recipient is also third person, as in (38), and, crucially, even in sentences where both recipient and patient are human, as in (39)–(40):

(38)   *Nee tumiini uukari ne- wa- ruzeiyastia.*
         I   money girls   1sg 3pl show
         'I showed the money to the girls'.

(39)   *Nee uukari uuki ne- puuzeiyastia.*
         I   girls   man 1sg show
         'I showed the girls to the man'.

(40)   *Nee uuki uukari ne- wa- puuzeiyastia.*
         I   man girls   1sg 3pl show
         'I showed the man to the girls'.

In (39), the null prefix in the object agreement slot means that the object must be third person singular (i.e., of the noun phrases in the sentence it must be the third person singular noun phrase *uuki* 'man'); by the rule, this noun phrase must be recipient, so the sentence means 'I showed the girls to the man', and not 'I showed the man to the girls'. Conversely, in (40) the third person plural object prefix *wa-* refers to the third person plural noun phrase *uukari* 'girls', which by the rule must be the recipient; that is, the sentence means 'I showed the man to the girls'. Note that the word order is not decisive. My consultant, incidentally, had no hesitation in distinguishing (39) and (40) precisely as indicated here.

As far as verb agreement is concerned, then, we seem to have one grammatical relation that unites the patient of monotransitive verbs with the recipient of ditransitive verbs. Morphologically, patients of ditransitive verbs behave quite differently from those of monotransitive verbs, thus suggesting a grammatical relation, to which we give the neutral name "prime object," including all and only those noun phrase positions that trigger verb–object agreement.[10]

---

[10] I say "noun phrase positions" rather than "noun phrases" because third person singular noun phrases in these positions only optionally trigger verb–object agreement. This construction for ditransitive verbs is very common cross-linguistically (Faltz 1978). For further illustration, from Bantu languages, see Hyman and Duranti (in this volume); most of the points made in this section apply equally to objects in most Bantu languages, in that a recipient or benefactive is prime object in preference to a patient. Compare the claim in Hopper and Thompson (1980) that animacy—which is more characteristic of recipients and benefactives than of patients—is a special case of individuation, which in turn is a major component of the object in transitivity.

A final note on person and number agreement with ditransitive verbs in Huichol: It seems to be impossible to construct a sentence where the patient of a ditransitive verb is nonthird person, that is, a sentence of the type *He showed me to you.* Huichol sentences that I constructed on this model were judged ungrammatical, irrespective of which object I let control object agreement, and my attempts to elicit such sentences produced constructions translating literally as 'He told you to see me', 'He told me to go to you'. Human patients are not absolutely excluded, however, as can be seen from (39)–(40).

In addition to the morphological test of object agreement, our earlier discussion of the passive provides a further test for prime objects, in that the passive too distinguishes between different objects. We observed that the passive has a subject corresponding to the object of the active. If an active verb has more than one object, then only one of these objects can be subject of the corresponding passive. It transpires that the noun phrase in question is the one we earlier termed prime object, that is, the recipient with a ditransitive verb:

(41)   *Eeki tumiini pe- puuzeiyastɨari.*
         you money 2sg show-pass
         'You were shown the money'.

In (41), the pronominal prefix *pe-* is unambiguously a second person singular subject prefix, so it is clear that *eeki,* the recipient, functions as subject. This can be further tested by considering case marking with numeral or coordinate noun phrases and same–switch-reference:

(42)   *Tɨɨri yɨ -nauka-tɨ   tumiini me- puuzeiyastɨari.*
         children four   subj money 3pl show-pass
         'Four children were shown the money'.

(43)   *Eeki pe- nua- -ka,   tumiini pe- puuzeiyastɨari.*
         you 2sg arrive sa-ant money 2sg show-pass
         'When you arrived, you were shown the money'.

4.2. Benefactive Noun Phrases

In Huichol, the behavior of benefactive noun phrases is almost exactly the same as that of recipients. If we compare Sentences (44), without a benefactive, and (45), with a benefactive, then we note that all the objects lack special case marking to indicate that they are or are not benefactives. Where a benefactive is present, the verb takes an extra suffix, which can thus be regarded as the verbal benefactive suffix:

(44)   *Zeeme nawazɨ ze- puunanai.*
         you-all knife   2pl buy
         'You-all bought a knife'.

(45)   *Zeeme nawazɨ ze- ne- teʔunanairi.*
         you-all knife   2pl 1sg buy-benef
         'You-all bought a knife for me'.

As is shown by the verb agreement prefix *ne-*, first person singular, in
(45), agreement is with the benefactive, not with the patient. That is,
benefactives, just like recipients, take precedence over patients in being
deemed prime objects. This can be seen even more clearly in (46), where
the prefix *wa-* is quite unambiguously an object prefix referring to 'the
children':

(46)   *Eekɨ nawazɨ tɨɨri   pe- wa- rutinanairi.*
         you   knife   children 2sg 3pl buy-benef
         'You bought the knife for the children'.

In the passive of benefactive constructions, it is again the benefactive,
as prime object, that becomes the subject of the passive, as can be seen
from its case marking where relevant [as in (47)], its verb agreement
[as in all of (47)–(49)], and same–switch-reference [as in (49)]:

(47)   *Eeki nawazi pe- puunanairiyeri.*
         you   knife   2sg buy-benef-pass
         'You were bought the knife'.

(48)   *Tɨɨri yɨ-nauka-tɨ   nawazɨ me- puutinanairiyeri.*
         children four   subj knife   3pl buy-benef-pass
         'Four children were bought a knife'.

(49)   *Nee ne- nua   -ka,   nawazɨ ne- puunanairiyeri.*
         I   1sg arrive sa-ant knife   1sg buy-benef-pass
         'When I arrived, I was bought a knife'.

As with recipients, there is no other straightforward way of construct-
ing benefactives, for instance with one of the postpositions that exist in
Huichol. When pressed to find an alternative means of expression, the
only possibility allowed by my consultant was an involved paraphrase
of the type 'you bought the knife, you gave it to the children', with two
separate clauses.[11]

---

[11] Joseph E. Grimes has pointed out to me that, in some dialects at least, new benefactive
postpositions seem to be developing out of such two-clause constructions, with reinterpretation of the second clause as a postpositional phrase.

To summarize the discussion so far: Grammatical properties of noun phrases in Huichol suggest the identification of two grammatical relations: "subject," characterized by subject–verb agreement, subject case marking on certain noun phrases, triggering of possessive reflexivization, and control of same-reference suffixes; and "prime object," characterized by verb–object agreement, and the possibility of appearing as subject of the corresponding passive. In addition, there are noun phrases that are neither subject nor prime object. In the present state of my knowledge of Huichol, there is no justification for recognizing any other grammatical relations, in particular none for distinguishing "direct object" from "indirect object" from other nonsubjects. In view of the range of similarities between "prime object" and "direct object" in other languages, it would be justifiable to use the term "direct object" in place of my "prime object." The only reason I did not do this was to avoid confusion in speaking of ditransitive verbs, where in many languages the direct object is the patient, rather than the recipient or benefactive as in Huichol.

The most important point here is the treatment of ditransitive verbs. Within relational grammar, the standard analysis of English pairs like (50)–(51) is that in the initial stratum *the knife* is direct object and *Francis* indirect object for both sentences. In (50) the final grammatical relations are the same, whereas in (51) the indirect object is advanced to become final direct object, with concomitant demotion of the initial direct object:

(50)   *I gave*   *the knife*   *to Francis.*
       initial subject   initial direct object   initial indirect object
       final subject   final direct object   final indirect object

(51)   *I gave*   *Francis*   *the knife.*
       initial subject   initial indirect object initial direct object
       final subject   final direct object   final nonterm

In Huichol, one could construct a similar analysis, except that the advancement to direct object would be obligatory, rather than optional, as Huichol sentence (37), repeated as (52), parallels (51) rather than (50):

(52)   *Nee waakanaari ne- meci-tɨkiitɨ eekɨ.*
       I   chickens   1sg 2sg give you
       'I gave you the chickens'.

However, within Huichol this analysis would have no motivation, as there is no way in which the noun phrase *waakanaari,* which would be initial direct object, behaves like other direct objects rather than like noun phrases that are neither subject nor direct object. In the absence of any reasonable paraphrase where the patient of a ditransitive verb shows up as a direct (prime) object, and in the absence of any properties that would treat such patients like clear instances of direct objects, the inescapable conclusion for Huichol is that they are not direct objects.

4.3. Verb Stem Suppletion

Of course, the strongest claim I can make with respect to the treatment of patients of ditransitive verbs in Huichol is that, as I am unaware of any way in which they behave like direct objects, they should not be treated as direct objects. It is always possible that future work may uncover some property according to which these noun phrases do behave like direct objects, thus forcing revision of my original claim. But unless and until such evidence is forthcoming, the claim stands that there is no justification for any assignment of grammatical relations to a sentence like (52) other than one where 'I' is subject, 'you' is prime (direct) object, and 'chickens' belongs to the general class of noun phrases that are neither subject nor prime (direct) object.

There is one phenomenon in Huichol that might seem to provide evidence for treating patients of ditransitive verbs as direct objects at some level of derivation, namely the behavior of verb stem suppletion. In this last expository section, I shall try to show that this is certainly not a necessary conclusion to draw from the behavior of such suppletion, and that there is actually evidence against this solution.

In Huichol, as quite generally in Uto-Aztecan languages, certain verbs have different stems depending on the number (singular versus plural) of one of their arguments. This phenomenon is in addition to the regular person and number agreement by means of prefixes on the verb; it is in fact more widespread, as it applies equally to inanimate noun phrases, whereas for purposes of verb agreement inanimate noun phrases are treated as singular, whatever their real world number. Sometimes the singular and plural stems share morphological material in common, but often they are simply suppletive. With transitive verbs, it is always the number of the patient that is relevant, never that of the subject or non-patient prime object, irrespective of the final (derived) grammatical relations. Thus the verb 'kill' has a singular stem -*mie* and a plural stem -*qii* (Grimes 1964:98):

(53)   *Wan maria maa-ti   me- neci-mieni.*
        Juan Maria and subj 3pl 1sg kill-sg
        'Juan and Maria are killing me'.

(54)   *Nee wan maria maa-me   ne- wa- qiini.*
        I   Juan Maria and nonsubj 1sg 3pl kill-pl
        'I am killing Juan and Maria'.

(55)   *Nee waakana ne- mec-umiʔiiri   eekɨ.*
        I   chicken 1sg 2sg kill-sg-benef you
        'I killed the chicken for you'.

(56)   *Nee waakanaari ne- mec-uqiʔiiri   eekɨ.*
        I   chickens   1sg 3pl kill-pl-benef you
        'I killed the chickens for you'.

(57)   *Eekɨ waakana pe- peumiʔiyeri.*
        you chicken 2sg kill-sg-benef-pass
        'You were killed a chicken'.

(58)   *Eekɨ waakanaari pe- peuqiʔiyeri.*
        you chickens   2sg kill-pl-benef-pass
        'You were killed chickens'.

In each of these examples, the relevant factor determining the correct
alternant for the verb stem is the number of entities being killed. Thus
we have a property that seems to link together all patients, irrespective
of their final grammatical relation, which could be interpreted as a test
for initial direct objects. In all these sentences, then, the entity/entities
being killed would be initial direct object, and in (55)–(58) the advancement of the initial indirect object to direct object would cause the demotion of the initial direct object to a nonterm.

First, we should note that this is far from a necessary conclusion to
draw from these data. The initial generalization we gave was in fact in
semantic, rather than syntactic, terms (i.e., in terms of the number of
the patient). One could therefore state the rule directly in terms of the
semantic roles of noun phrases, rather than in terms of putative initial
grammatical relations. The stem *-mie* would *mean* 'kill one entity',
whereas the stem *-qii* would *mean* 'kill more than one entity', and this
meaning would remain constant under changes of grammatical relation.

Moreover, the suppletion of verb stems that one finds in Huichol and
other Uto-Aztecan languages is not restricted to patients of transitive
verbs. One finds the same kind of suppletion with many intransitive
verbs, in which case it is the number of the subject that is relevant, as
in (59)–(60):

(59)   *Nee tuapɨrie   ne- hantia.*
        I   Santa-Catarina 1sg go-sg
        'I go to Santa Catarina'.

(60)   *Taame tuapɨrie   te- pekɨɨ.*
        we   Santa-Catarina 1pl go-pl
        'We go to Santa Catarina'.

Given this stem suppletion dependent on the number of the subject, it is clearly inaccurate to say that verb stem suppletion in Huichol is conditioned by the number of the initial direct object. One possibility would be to have a disjunctive characterization: The conditioning factor is the initial direct object, if there is one, or the initial subject otherwise. However, this disjunction destroys the original motivation for stating the conditioning factor in terms of initial grammatical relations, which was to avoid a disjunction of the type "direct object if there is only one object and the other object if there is more than one." The statement could be simplified slightly by saying that the verb stem suppletion is controlled by the number of the initial absolutive of the ergative–absolutive system, but in the absence of any other evidence in Huichol for setting up grammatical relations on an ergative–absolutive basis, it is not clear that this is really different from the disjunctive characterization; and if it is, then the argument for initial direct objects is destroyed, as "initial absolutive" includes many things other than initial direct objects.

Conceivably, the semantic characterization suggested earlier is the best solution to verb stem alternation in Huichol, provided this characterization is generalized along the following lines: Verb stem alternation in Huichol is controlled by the number of the entity most directly affected by the situation described by the verb. With transitive verbs, this is the patient; with intransitive verbs, this is the single argument thereof, irrespective of the extent to which this has agent or patient properties. With respect to our examples, just as -*mie* means 'kill one thing' and -*qii* 'kill more than one thing', so -*tia* means 'for one thing to go' and -*kɨɨ* means 'for more than one thing to go'. This distinction would then be quite independent of grammatical relations.

5. CONCLUSIONS

In this article, I have tried to establish that Huichol syntax requires recognition of two grammatical relations: subject and prime (direct) object. The latter, in distinction to many other languages, unites patients of monotransitive verbs with recipients/benefactives of ditransitive verbs, on the basis of shared morphological and syntactic properties. There are no such properties uniting patients of both monotransitive and ditransitive verbs. Because of the way in which the data were collected—working with a single native speaker, away from the natural environment of his language, primarily through elicitation in Spanish—a number of questions remained unanswered, especially regarding the functions of these various constructions in natural discourse. The investigation of these remaining questions is to be the task of future research.

ACKNOWLEDGMENTS

The material included in this article is based on work with a single speaker of the Santa Catarina dialect of Huichol, Mariano Valadez, to whom my deepest appreciation is due. The emphasis of the article is on syntax, and several details of the phonemic transcription require further checking. The material was obtained primarily through elicitation in Spanish; it remains a task for the future to test the generalizations made on this basis against parallel constructions occurring in natural discourse.

My work on Huichol has been greatly facilitated by the pioneering work on this language by Joseph E. Grimes. I have utilized the transcription system of Grimes (1964), except that I use *i* rather than ∧, and have not indicated tone or word-internal phonological juncture. The morphological structure of Huichol verbs is rather complex, including a fair amount of suppletion; as the emphasis of the present article is on syntax, I have often not commented on morphological idiosyncrasies that are not germane to the points at issue.

Versions of this paper were read to audiences at the University of Arizona (Tucson), the University of Newcastle (New South Wales), the University of Western Australia (Nedlands/Perth), and Auckland University (New Zealand), and at seminar meetings of Los Angeles Americanists, the Australian National University (Department of Linguistics, School of General Studies; Canberra), and the Summer Institute of Linguistics (Papua New Guinea branch, Ukarumpa). I am grateful for all the comments received at these presentations, and also for comments by Joseph E. Grimes, Paul J. Hopper, and Sandra A. Thompson.

REFERENCES

Faltz, L. (1978) "On Indirect Objects in Universal Syntax," in D. Farkas, W. Jacobsen, and K. Todrys, eds., *Papers from the Fourteenth Regional Meeting,* Chicago Linguistic Society, University of Chicago.

Grimes, J. (1959) "Huichol Tone and Intonation," *International Journal of American Linguistics* 25, 221–232.

Grimes, J. (1964) *Huichol Syntax,* Mouton, The Hague.

Grimes, J. (1974) *The Thread of Discourse,* Mouton, The Hague.

Hopper, P. and S. Thompson (1980) "Transitivity in Grammar and Discourse," *Language* 56, 251–299.

Langacker, R. (1976) *Nondistinct Arguments in Uto-Aztecan,* University of California Press, Berkeley and Los Angeles.

McIntosh, J. B. and J. Grimes (1954) *Niuqui 'iquisicayari: Vocabulario Huichol–Castellano Castellano–Huichol,* Instituto Lingüístico de Verano, Mexico City.

CASE MARKING, PHONOLOGICAL SIZE, AND LINEAR ORDER

DAVID GIL

It is generally taken for granted that the role of case-marking systems in language is semantic by nature. Traditionally, the purpose of case markings has been assumed to be the indication of thematic or grammatical relations between NPs and their governing verbs. More recent work—for example, Comrie 1978; Moravcsik 1978b, 1978c; and Hopper and Thompson 1980—has shown that case markings reflect a more variegated array of semantic properties; among these properties are nominal features such as definiteness, animacy, concreteness, and affectedness, as well as clausal features such as aspect, punctuality, volitionality, and mode.

In this paper, evidence is provided to support the claim that case-marking systems may function in a way that is radically different from that hitherto supposed. It is argued that in addition to their semantic role, case-marking systems reflect the organization of linguistic material at a somewhat more superficial level of structure. In particular, it is shown that the assignment of case is sensitive to the phonological size of constituents, and to their linear order in the clause.

117

The first part of this paper contains an analysis of the Hebrew case-marking preposition *et;* the claim is made that in addition to its role as definite direct object marker, *et* functions to increase the phonological size of constituents occurring toward the ends of phrases and clauses. In the second part, the facts concerning *et* are shown to fall out of a more general principle whereby phonologically small constituents precede phonologically large ones. In addition to accounting for patterns of case marking in Hebrew and other languages, this principle may also provide an explanation for a variety of seemingly unrelated syntactic phenomena.

1. HEBREW *ET*[1]

The traditional analysis of Hebrew *et* as a definite direct object marker—presented in what follows—fails to provide an adequate account of its distribution. The problems are evidenced by constructions in which *et* fails to occur before a preverbal object, or, conversely, those in which it occurs before a postverbal subject. It will be argued here that, in fact, *et* tends to mark the first nonoblique NP to follow the verb, especially if this NP is phonologically small. The distribution of *et* is thus sensitive to the phonological size of constituents and their linear order, in addition to their semantic properties. Independent support for this analysis will be provided in the form of data from a dialect of Classical Hebrew in which *et* has been bleached of its usual semantic functions.

1.1. The Semantic Functions of *Et*

In almost all dialects of Modern Hebrew, *et* is obligatory before definite direct objects. These are generally of one of the following categories:

[1] Unless otherwise noted, the Hebrew data are drawn from a dialect of Modern Hebrew which may conveniently be characterized as Standard Hebrew. Standard Hebrew lies midway on the cline (or pecking order) between Prescriptive Hebrew, taught and generally forgotten in elementary and secondary schools, and Substandard Hebrew, used by some speakers in colloquial contexts, and differing even further from Prescriptive Hebrew. Although these dialects represent idealized points on a continuum, they probably also reflect diachronic trends in the evolution of Modern Hebrew. The data from Modern Hebrew are supplemented with data from two sources of Classical Hebrew: Biblical Hebrew, a heterogeneous set of dialects in which most of the Old Testament was written during the first millenium B.C., and the little-known dialect of the Samaritan Chronicles—see Footnote 11.

proper nouns, pronouns, NPs preceded by the cliticized definite article *ha*, and genitival constructions—for example:[2]

(1) *Dan ra?a et   david.*
   Dan saw-3sgm David
   'Dan saw David'.

Evidence for the semantic role of *et* is provided by the fact that the constituents *dan, ra?a*, and *et david* in (1) can occur in all six possible permutations, and the result is a grammatical sentence in which *david* is marked as being the direct object of the verb. Much the same is true for *?εθ*, the cognate of *et* in Biblical Hebrew—see Gesenius (1813 §117) and Hoftijzer (1965:29–33).

In some instances, however, *et* may precede a direct object that is an interrogative or indefinite pronoun, or otherwise indefinite; in such cases, *et* typically occurs before an NP that is highly individuated. The preposition *et* thus functions as a marker of high transitivity, in the sense defined by Hopper and Thompson (1980). That is to say, *et* marks those clauses which are high on the transitivity scale, according to the set of features provided by Hopper and Thompson, and in particular, those features listed under the heading of individuation. One such feature, definiteness, has already been noted to account for most occurrences of *et* before direct objects; three other features of individuation governing the occurrence of *et* before indefinite NPs are referentiality, animacy, and concreteness—these are discussed in more detail in Gil (1981).

1.2. Phonological Size and Linear Order

The distribution of *et*, however, cannot be completely accounted for in semantic terms. As is shown in this section, its occurrence is governed also by the phonological size of constituents and their linear order.

PREVERBAL OBJECTS WITHOUT *ET*

As noted earlier, *et* is optional before direct object interrogative pronouns. Consider now the following questions:

[2] Data from Modern Hebrew are provided in a phonemic transcription, which also corresponds to the Sephardi pronunciation (though not to the more commonly cited Ashkenazi pronunciation); *h* and *ʕ* represent unvoiced and voiced pharyngeal fricatives respectively, and the glottal stop is indicated only word medially. For Classical Hebrew dialects, a standard Biblical Hebrew transcription is employed.

(2) $\left\{ \begin{matrix} \emptyset \\ et \end{matrix} \right\}$ *mi   hayeled ohev.*
     who the-boy love-sgm
     'Whom does the boy love?'

(3)   a. $\left\{ \begin{matrix} \emptyset \\ et \end{matrix} \right\}$ **mi** *hayeled ohev.*
         who the-boy love-sgm
         '*Whom* does the boy love?'

    b.   *hayeled ohev* $\left\{ \begin{matrix} ?\emptyset \\ et \end{matrix} \right\}$ **mi.**
         the-boy love-sgm   who
         'The boy loves *whom?*

(4)   *mi   ohev* $\left\{ \begin{matrix} *\emptyset \\ et \end{matrix} \right\}$ *mi.*
     who love-sgm   who
     'Who loves whom?'

Example (2) is an ordinary question with fronted interrogative pronoun. Example (3a) is an echo question with fronted interrogative, and (3b) is an echo question with interrogative pronoun in nonfronted position. Example (4) is a question containing two interrogative pronouns.

The examples show that whereas in preverbal position the direct object *mi* 'who' can occur either with or without *et*, in postverbal position, *et* is preferred: Without *et* the question is either of questionable acceptability, as in (3b), or entirely unacceptable, as in (4). No semantic explanation of these facts is evident; in particular, (3a) and (3b) come close to being synonymous. We must conclude, then, that the occurrence of *et* before the direct object *mi* is governed by the position of the direct object in relation to the verb.

Similar behavior with respect to *et* is exhibited by the semantically dissimilar demonstrative pronoun *ze* 'this'—see Example (16) in what follows—though, apparently, not by any other direct object NPs. In particular, the occurrence of *et* before *eyze anašim* 'which people' (synonymous with *mi*), is not sensitive to the linear order of the direct object in relation to the verb.[3] Thus the unique behavior of direct objects *mi*

---

[3] See Gil (1981) for the relevant examples. Note, also, that unlike *mi*, the interrogative pronoun *ma* 'what' may occur postverbally in echo questions without *et*. The reason is that in echo questions, *ma*, like English *what*, may stand for an arbitrary sequence of morphemes, or even syllables: Thus, from 'I quoted Sibawayhi' are derivable 'You quoted *what?*', 'You quoted Siba*what*hi?', 'You *what*ed Sibawayhi?', 'You *what?*', etc.

and *ze* cannot be accounted for in terms of any common semantic properties. Instead, it will be argued, the common property responsible for the distinctive behavior of *mi* and *ze* with respect to *et* is their short monosyllabic form.

POSTVERBAL SUBJECTS WITH *ET*

A much larger class of constructions in which the occurrence of *et* cannot be accounted for in semantic terms is that of postverbal subjects, which—contrary to expectations—may be marked with *et*. Such constructions are of the canonical form:

(5)   V (Prep NP$_2$) *et* NP$_1$

Typically, these constructions alternate with constructions in which the subject NP$_1$ precedes the verb, and *et* is optional or unacceptable:

(6)   (*et*) NP$_1$ V (Prep NP$_2$)

Examples of constructions of the form (5) include the following:[4]

(7) a. *Haya   li   et hasfarim šeracita.*
         was-3sgm to-me   the-books that-wanted-2sgm
         'I had the books that you wanted'.
     b. *Haya   po   et hasfarim šeracita.*
         was-3sgm here   the-books that-wanted-2sgm
         'The books that you wanted were here'.

(8) a. *Zaxur   li   et ze.*
         remembered-sgm to-me   it
         'I remember it'.
     b. *Daruš   li   et ze.*
         demanded-sgm to-me   it
         'It is needed by me'.
     c. *Katuv   li   et ze.*
         written-sgm to-me   it
         'It is written here with me./I have it written'.
     d. *Ḥašuv   li   et ze.*
         important-sgm to-me   it
         'It is important to me'.

---

[4] For further examples of "intrusive" *et* before subjects in Modern Hebrew, see Berman (1978:219), Gil (1981), Givón (1976:176–178) and Ziv (1976a, 1976b). Bar-Adon (1959:396–400) also cites examples from children's speech in Israel. Sentences of the form (5) were also common in Biblical Hebrew—see Hoftijzer (1965:14–17) for an exhaustive listing. Examples from Biblical Hebrew are cited in Longacre (1960:71) and Keenan (1976:325,331).

(9)   *Štey   hakvucot hit ʔamnu   et oto   mispar   hpaʕamim.*
        two-of the-teams practiced-3pl   the-same number-of the-times
        'The two teams have practiced the same number of times'.

(10)   *Wayyiwwɔleð laḥanox ʔɛθ ʕirɔð.*
        and-born-3sgm to-Enoch   Irad
        'And unto Enoch was born Irad'.   (Genesis 4 18)

Constructions such as (7)–(9) are ungrammatical in Prescriptive Hebrew, though accepted by speakers of Standard or Substandard Hebrew.
Their acceptability appears to be governed by the following hierarchy:
possessives > existentials > other intransitive clauses; in other words,
the use of *et* before subject NPs is in the process of spreading from
possessives through existentials to other intransitive clauses. Thus, possessive constructions in which *et* marks the subject possessee phrase—
as in (7a)—are used by all but the die-hard purists, and existentials/
locatives with *et*—such as (7b)—are also quite widespread. Sentences
such as (8) and (9), however, have a distinctive substandard flavor, in
spite of the fact that parallel constructions—for example, (10)—are attested in Biblical Hebrew.

Various syntactic and semantic properties of these constructions are
discussed in detail by Gil (1981) for Modern Hebrew, and by Hoftijzer
(1965), Kaddari (1976:93–97), Saydon (1964), and Wilson (1890a, 1890b),
among others, for Biblical Hebrew. These properties may be summarized
as follows:

(11)   a.   The verb is almost always intransitive. In most instances,
              it is in a conjugation one of whose primary functions is that
              of the passive. It is typically nonprogressive, and of an ex-
              periential nature. In some cases, however, the verb may be
              replaced by a predicative adjective.
        b. NP_1, that which is preceded by *et,* is never agentive, is
              typically inanimate, and is often affected by the verb. Never-
              theless, it usually emerges as the most subject-like of the
              two NPs, according to the subjecthood criteria proposed by
              Keenan (1976). [Sentence (9) provides an obvious exception
              to this generalization.] Clearly, NP_1 is not a direct object—
              although it is preceded by the supposedly accusative marker
              et.
        c.   The optional oblique NP_2 differs from NP_1 in that it is typ-
              ically animate. However, like NP_1, it is not agentive, and
              it is typically affected by the verb, generally as a benefactee
              or malefactee.

      d. The clause as a whole is of low transitivity, in the sense defined by Hopper and Thompson (1980). Such clauses contrast with those in which *et* functions as a marker of highly transitive clauses, as noted earlier.

The properties in (11a)–(11d) indicate that the preposition *et* is fulfilling a very different role in (7)–(10) than that traditionally assumed: It is clearly not a marker of definite (or otherwise highly individuated) direct objects. What this different function of *et* may be is the prime concern of the remainder of this paper.

A Nonsemantic Analysis

Diverse accounts of the occurrence of *et* before subject NPs in Classical and Modern Hebrew have been proposed in the linguistic and philological literature.[5] Explanations have also been suggested for similar facts obtaining in other languages.[6] Practically all of these accounts, however, have been semantically motivated.[7] In this section, data will be presented to show that in Hebrew the occurrence of *et* is governed not only by semantic factors, but also by the phonological size of constituents and their linear order.

In Examples (12)–(15), constructions with postverbal subjects of the canonical form (5)—(12) and (14)—are contrasted with the corresponding constructions with preverbal subjects of the canonical form (6)—(13) and

---

[5] For example, Gesenius (1813 §121) and Sadka (1978) suggest a passivization analysis for Biblical Hebrew, and Shoshany (1979) proposes a similar account for Modern Hebrew possessives. Kaddari (1976:93–97) views the occurrence of ʔeθ before subject-like NPs in Biblical Hebrew as resulting from a process of "demotion," whereas Albrecht (1929) and Blau (1954) consider such constructions to be "blends" of passive and active sentences. Finally, Walker (1955) and Saydon (1964) argue for the function of ʔeθ as an emphatic particle. Arguments against each of these analyses are provided in Gil (1981).

[6] Formally, the occurrence of *et* before direct objects and subjects of intransitive verbs renders it an absolutive case marker in a split-ergative case-marking system. Such systems have been the subject of much recent interest—see Comrie (1978), Dixon (1979), and Moravcsik (1978c), among others. As is shown in Gil (1981), however, the distribution of *et* in Hebrew conforms to none of the known hierarchies that have been proposed to govern either split-ergative case-marking systems across the world's languages or the occurrence of an accusative marker in construction with subjects of intransitive verbs.

[7] A notable, albeit isolated, exception to this generalization is Bar-Daroma (1962), who suggests a nonsemantic account of the occurrence of ʔeθ in Biblical Hebrew. By examining the cantillation marks of the Biblical text, Bar-Daroma concludes that ʔeθ typically occurs during a pause in speech. Although different in substance from the analysis presented in what follows, Bar-Daroma's prosodic account of the distribution of ʔeθ foreshadows the prosodic explanation suggested in the second section of this paper for the dependence of case-marking systems on phonological size and linear order.

(15). Within each construction, subject NPs of different phonological sizes are contrasted:[8]

(12)   a.   *Haya*   *li* $\left\{\begin{matrix}*\emptyset \\ et\end{matrix}\right\}$ *ze.*
             was-3sgm to-me   it
             'I had it'.

       b.   *Haya*   *li* $\left\{\begin{matrix}??\emptyset \\ et\end{matrix}\right\}$ *hasefer.*
             was-3sgm to-me   the-book
             'I had the book'.

       c.   *Haya*   *li* $\left\{\begin{matrix}?\emptyset \\ et\end{matrix}\right\}$ *hasefer šeracita.*
             was-3sgm to-me   the-book that-wanted-2sgm
             'I had the book that you wanted'.

(13)   a. $\left\{\begin{matrix}?\emptyset \\ et\end{matrix}\right\}$ *ze haya   li.*
             it   was-3sgm to-me
             'I had it'.

       b. $\left\{\begin{matrix}?\emptyset \\ et\end{matrix}\right\}$ *hasefer   haya   li.*
             the-book was-3sgm to-me
             'I had the book'.

       c. $\left\{\begin{matrix}?\emptyset \\ et\end{matrix}\right\}$ *hasefer   šeracita   haya li.*
             the-book that-wanted-2sgm was to-me
             'I had the book that you wanted'.

(14)   a.   *Katuv*   *po* $\left\{\begin{matrix}*\emptyset \\ et\end{matrix}\right\}$ *ze.*
             written-sgm here   it
             'It is written here'.

       b.   *Katuv*   *po* $\left\{\begin{matrix}??\emptyset \\ et\end{matrix}\right\}$ *hamišpat   haze.*
             written-sgm here   the-sentence the-this
             'This sentence is written here'.

---

[8] Judgments represented by question marks should be compared "horizontally" (i.e., examples of same number but different letter) or "vertically" (i.e., examples of different number but same letter), but not "diagonally" (i.e., examples of different numbers and letters). For example, the "??" preceding "$\emptyset$" in (14b) may be contrasted with the "?" preceding "$\emptyset$" in (14c) or with the acceptable judgment of "$\emptyset$" in (15b), but not with the "?" preceding "$\emptyset$" in (13c).

c. *Katuv*   *po* $\left\{\begin{array}{c} ?ø \\ et \end{array}\right\}$ *hamišpat*   *haxi*   *arox*

    written-3sgm here   the-sentence the-most long

    šenixnas   *lašura.*

    that-enters to-the-line

    'The longest sentence that fits into the

    line is written here'.

(15)   a. $\left\{\begin{array}{c} ø \\ ?et \end{array}\right\}$ *ze katuv po.*

         it written here

      'It is written-3sgm here'.

   b. $\left\{\begin{array}{c} ø \\ ??et \end{array}\right\}$ *hamišpat*   *haze*   *katuv*   *po.*

         the-sentence the-this written-3sgm here

      'This sentence is written here'.

   c. $\left\{\begin{array}{c} ø \\ ???et \end{array}\right\}$ *hamišpat*   *haxi*   *arox šenixnas*   *lašura*

         the-sentence the-most long that-enters to-the-line

    katuv   *po.*

    written-3sgm here

    'The longest sentence that fits into the line is written

    here'.

The first generalization that is evident from this data is that a given subject NP is more likely to be marked with *et* in postverbal position than in preverbal position. Thus, contrasting (14a)–(14c) with (15a)–(15c), we see that the subject with *et* is better postverbally, in (14), whereas the subject without *et* is preferred preverbally, in (15). Comparing (12a)–(12b) with (13a)–(13b), we find that the subject with *et* is judged similarly in both postverbal and preverbal positions, but the subject without *et* is preferred in preverbal position, in (13a)–(13b). Only between (12c) and (13c) does there appear to be no effect of the subject NPs position on the judgment with respect to *et*. We may conclude, then, that the case marking of the subject NPs is governed, at least in part, by the position of the NP in relation to the verb, the marker *et* being preferred when the subject NP follows the verb. This is the same result as was seen to obtain for the object NP *mi* in the discussion of preverbal objects without *et*.[9]

---

[9] Ziv (1976a:346, 1976b:140–141) raises the possibility of a postverbal *et*-insertion rule, but rejects it out of hand. She provides no alternative account of these constructions.

A second generalization is that postverbal subject NPs are more likely to be marked with *et* if they are small than if they are large. Within each of the two sets of constructions (12) and (14), *et* is obligatory for the smallest subject NP, but the acceptability of "∅" case marking increases with the size of the NP.[10] Once again, the evidence here ties in nicely with that presented earlier: The case marking of the small subject NPs in (12a)–(15a) bears a strong resemblance to that of the small direct object *mi* in (2)–(4).

In fact, for small NPs, the occurrence of *et* appears to be completely insensitive to the grammatical role of the NP as subject or direct object. Consider, for example, the distribution of *et* before the monosyllabic demonstrative pronoun *ze* 'it'. In (16) *ze* is the direct object, in (17) it is the subject; despite this grammatical difference, the distribution of *et* is identical in both constructions—and is sensitive only to the linear order of *ze* with respect to the predicate:

(16)   a. $\left\{ \begin{matrix} \emptyset \\ et \end{matrix} \right\}$ *ze ra ʔiti.*

            it   I-saw-1sg

        b.   *ra ʔiti* $\left\{ \begin{matrix} *\emptyset \\ et \end{matrix} \right\}$ *ze.*

            I-saw-1sg   it

            'I saw it'.

(17)   a. $\left\{ \begin{matrix} \emptyset \\ et \end{matrix} \right\}$ *ze ḥaser.*

            it   missing-sgm

        b.   *ḥaser* $\left\{ \begin{matrix} *\emptyset \\ et \end{matrix} \right\}$ *ze.*

            missing-sgm   it

            'It is missing'.

To summarize, we have seen that the occurrence of *et* is conditioned in a variety of constructions by the position of the NP in relation to the verb, *et* being preferred in postverbal position. Moreover, we found that for postverbal subject NPs, the likelihood of the occurrence of *et* is inversely related to the phonological size of the constituent: Small NPs are more sensitive than large NPs to their position in relation to the

---

[10] For preverbal NPs, the effect of phonological size on the occurrence of *et* is less clear. In the possessive construction (13), there appears to be no effect; however, the word order in (13) is pragmatically and intonationally marked. Further work must be done to determine if in fact the acceptability of *et* decreases as the subject increases in size, as would seem to be the case in (15).

verb. In order to account for the distribution of *et* in Hebrew, we need recourse to the phonological size of constituents and their linear order; the semantic facts alone do not suffice. As we shall see, the two parameters governing the occurrence of *et* are related by means of a more general principle.

THE SAMARITAN CHRONICLES

In a remarkable dialect of Classical Hebrew described by Macdonald (1964),[11] the case marker *ʔɛθ* appears to have been bleached of its semantic function as definite direct object marker. Although the data provided by Macdonald are too fragmentary to enable any conclusive generalizations to be drawn, it would appear to be the case that in the Samaritan Chronicles *ʔɛθ* is a semantically empty particle whose only function is to (optionally) mark the second of two sister constituents (or the second and subsequent constituents in a series of sister constituents) within a clause or phrase.

In (18) *ʔɛθ* precedes the subject of a transitive verb, the direct object having been deleted, whereas in (19) it precedes both the subject and the direct object of the transitive verb. Both sentences are potentially ambiguous, subjects and objects presumably being identifiable by context.

(18)   *Waššɔmʕu   ʔɛθ yošvey   hɔʔɔrɛṣ.*
        and-heard-3pl   dwellers-of the-land
        'And the inhabitants of the land heard'.

(19)   *Hišlimu   ʔɛθ yošvey   givʕon ʔɛθ yiśrɔʔel.*
        surrendered-3pl dwellers-of Gibeon   Israel
        'The inhabitants of Gibeon have surrendered to Israel'.

In (20), *ʔɛθ* occurs in a passive clause reminiscent of Biblical Hebrew, but in the case at hand, it precedes an adverb, rather than an NP [cf. Standard Hebrew example (9)]:

(20)   *Wayyuggað   lammɛlɛx ʔiskander ʔɛθ ken.*
        and-was-told-3sgm to-the-king Alexander   so
        'And king Alexander was told accordingly'.

---

[11] The era to which the Samaritan Chronicles are attributable is the subject of a lively debate. According to Macdonald (1964, 1969), many of the texts are contemporary to Biblical Hebrew, written in a Samaritan dialect of Biblical Hebrew (rather than the local dialect known simply as "Samaritan Hebrew"), whereas others are later additions. Ben-Hayim (1971) takes issue with Macdonald's chronology, arguing that all the texts were written in the late nineteenth or early twentieth century. This two millenia difference in the dating of the texts is of course irrelevant to the present discussion. All the Samaritan Chronicle examples cited in this paper are from Macdonald (1964).

Assuming that the basic word order in the Samaritan Chronicles is VSO, ʔɛθ may apparently precede any postverbal constituent, regardless of the transitivity of the verb, the grammatical role of the constituent, and possibly even its syntactic category. The Hebrew of the Samaritan Chronicles has thus generalized the Biblical Hebrew rule whereby the occurrence of ʔɛθ was governed in part by the linear order of constituents: The semantic constraints on the form of the verb and the role of the NP holding for Biblical Hebrew have been lifted, and the occurrence of ʔɛθ would appear to be governed by linear order alone. The appropriate rule in the Samaritan Chronicles stipulates that for any sequence of clause-mates, all but the first may be marked with the preposition ʔɛθ.

An even more remarkable generalization of this rule appears to have taken place in the Samaritan Chronicles, whereby it has been downgraded from the clausal to the phrasal level—to wit, ʔɛθ also marks all but the first of a sequence of constituents within a phrase.[12] In (21), ʔɛθ marks the second of two conjuncts within the subject NP (as well as the direct object NP later in the sentence).

(21)   *Wayyirḥoṣu   yohošuaʕ wɛʔɛθ kol ʔɔšɛr ʕimmo   ʔɛθ kol*
        and-washed-3pl Joshua   and- all that with-him all-of
        bśɔrɔm.
        their-flesh
        'And Joshua and all who accompanied him washed the whole of their body'.

Macdonald also cites a passage in Biblical Hebrew displaying similar properties:

(22)   *Uvɔʔ   hɔʔari wɛʔɛθ haddov wanɔśɔʔ   śɛh*
        and-came-3sgm the-lion and- the-bear and-bore-3sgm lamb
        mɛhɔʕeðɛr
        from-the-flock
        'And there came a lion, and a bear, and took a lamb out of the flock'.   (Samuel I 17 34)

---

[12] In fact, *et* also functions at the phrasal level in Modern Hebrew nominalizations (see Berman 1973 for a detailed discussion). For example, the following NP is derivable from Sentence (1):

(1')   *reʔiyat   dan et david*
        seeing-of Dan   David
        'Dan's seeing of David'

Nominalizations in Hebrew present a complex picture which is beyond the scope of this paper; nevertheless, they would appear to provide further support for the claims being made here. Note that in (1')—as opposed to (1)—word order is fixed, and hence *et* obligatorily marks the last NP in the phrase, in accordance with the generalization concerning *et* and the linear order of constituents.

Loss of the semantic constraints governing the occurrence of ʔεθ appears to have set the stage for the linear order rule to percolate downward, applying to arbitrary sequences of sister constituents, be they dominated by a clausal or a phrasal constituent. The rule governing ʔεθ in the Samaritan Chronicles is thus of the form:

(23)   [$_C$ X A B Y] $\xrightarrow[\text{opt.}]{}$ [$_C$ X A ʔεθ B Y]

In rule (23) A, B, and C are arbitrary constituents such that C immediately dominates both A and B. The rule is subject to no semantic conditions or constraints.

The data thus support the claim that the occurrence of ʔεθ in the Samaritan Chronicles is governed by linear order alone.[13] Given the close relationship between the Samaritan Chronicles and other Hebrew dialects, the data provide independent evidence for a rule sensitive to linear order in the better known dialects of Hebrew, where it interacts in complex and variegated ways with rules of a semantic nature.

2. TOWARD A MORE GENERAL PRINCIPLE

Having provided evidence that the distribution of *et* in Hebrew is sensitive to the linear order of constituents and their phonological size, we would be well justified in taking a closer look at the significance of this possibly somewhat surprising result. Traditional wisdom has it that case-marking systems serve to distinguish between thematic relations of NPs, following in effect the Duchess's advice to Alice: "Take care of the sense, and the sounds will take care of themselves." But of what use, then, is a rule marking NPs with respect to linear order—a property that is in any case eminently visible? And why should a language be intolerant of phonologically small constituents in postverbal position, marking them with the accusative regardless of their semantic role?

In order to answer such questions, we must reassess the roles of case-marking systems in language. We shall argue that an important role of case marking is to effect an organization of linguistic material at a superficial level of structure, one that includes, among other features, the

---

[13] Due to the paucity of the data, this claim must of necessity remain tentative. Macdonald, who has examined the texts in detail, provides no indication of any semantic role played by ʔεθ in the Samaritan Chronicles. He does, however, note another function of ʔεθ—substitution for a preposition, about which we have nothing to say in this paper. With respect to phonological size, it is impossible to reach any conclusion from the data provided, though the surprising occurrence of ʔεθ before a small postverbal adverb in (20) is suggestive.

linear order of constituents and their phonological representations, but not necessarily their semantic properties. This organizational principle stipulates that, all other things being equal, an order in which small constituents precede large ones is preferable to an opposite order, in which large constituents precede small ones. Up to a point, then, case-marking systems take care of the sounds, leaving the senses to take care of themselves.

2.1. The Roles of Case-Marking Systems

The view that case-marking systems function to distinguish among thematic or grammatical relations of NPs in a clause has been the dominant if not the only view, from antiquity through to current linguistic literature such as Comrie (1978:379) and Dixon (1979:68–69).[14] With respect to definite direct object markers, Comrie (1976) attributes the relative frequency with which these occur across languages to the fact that definite direct objects are more similar to subjects than are indefinite direct objects, and hence are in greater need of being formally distinguished from them. In fact, Andersen (1971:14) suggests exactly this reason for the use of ʔεθ in Biblical Hebrew.[15]

Although, as we have observed, *et* provides the only means of distinguishing subject from direct object in sentences such as (1), the fact remains that Hebrew tolerates many constructions exhibiting subject–object ambiguity, as in the following sentences:

(24)   *Bederex klal lo oxlim   po anašim.*
        in-way-of rule neg eat-3plm here people
        a. 'People don't usually eat here'.
        b. 'One doesn't usually eat people here'.

(25)   *Namer ze lo pacaʕ   af   cayad.*
        tiger   this neg injured-3sgm even hunter
        a. 'This tiger has not injured any hunters'.
        b. 'No hunters have injured this tiger'.

---

[14] Dixon (1979:130–131) elaborates on this score, suggesting five factors determining case marking in languages: reflecting the syntactic pivot, reflecting the universal category "subject," reflecting underlying semantic tendencies, diachronic reasons, and internal grammatical reasons. Whereas the first two factors pertain to grammatical relations at underlying and surface stages of derivation, the third factor relates to the properties discussed by Moravcsik and by Hopper and Thompson—see what follows. The fourth and fifth factors are sufficiently broad as to encompass any form of explanation whatsoever.

[15] In support of this argument, Andersen cites the situation in Moabite, an ancient Semitic language closely related to Biblical Hebrew, in which ʔεθ was used to mark direct objects in V–N–N but not in N–V–N word order. In Moabite, ʔεθ thus distinguishes between arguments in those instances where they are not already separated by an intervening verb.

Thus, although *et* clearly serves to mark grammatical relations in (1), it fails to do so in all cases: In (24) and (25) it is not used where it could have prevented ambiguity. Moreover, in the intransitive sentences discussed earlier it occurs in a manner that, with respect to the disambiguation of grammatical relations, can only be characterized as redundant.[16] As a marker of grammatical relations, *et* is thus very inefficient.

A related approach to case marking—one that has been elaborated in, for example, Moravcsik (1978b, 1978c) and Hopper and Thompson (1980)—is to account for patterns of case marking in terms of semantic properties of a somewhat subtler nature than grammatical or thematic relations. As pointed out earlier, Hopper and Thompson's notion of transitivity provides an excellent characterization of a large class of constructions in which *et* precedes a direct object in Hebrew; however, it fails to account for those instances in which *et* precedes a subject NP in typically intransitive sentences. These latter constructions appear to display a split-ergative case-marking system, yet they violate most of the generalizations suggested for such systems, by Comrie (1978), Dixon (1979), Moravcsik (1978c), and others.

The occurrence of *et* in this latter class of constructions is, in fact, at least partially independent of semantic properties, reflecting instead the phonological size of constituents and their linear order. Such a conclusion is not as unusual as it may seem—suggestions to the effect that case marking may be determined by the linear order of constituents have persisted stubbornly in the linguistic literature alongside the more usual semantically based accounts. Anderson (1976) presents evidence from languages whose syntax follows a nominative–accusative pattern, but whose morphology patterns in an ergative–absolutive manner, in order to argue for the relative superficiality of case-marking processes. He then suggests that the case marking of an NP is determined by its linear order in relation to the other NPs in the clause. In support of this claim, he cites constructions in ergative case-marking languages in which the absolutive direct object has been deleted; in such instances, the case marking of the remaining NP typically changes from ergative to absolutive. Anderson notes that the case marking of the subject NP cannot be determined by its thematic relation to the verb, which remains constant under deletion of the object NP, but, rather, is sensitive to the presence or absence of another NP in the surface structure of the clause.

Perhaps more instances across languages of case marking being determined by linear order would be known if the plausibility of such systems were more generally acknowledged. One striking example of a

---

[16] And, of course, in Sentences (18) and (19) $ʔe\theta$ both fails to prevent ambiguity and occurs redundantly.

language in which case marking is determined by linear order is offered by Tzeltal. According to Keenan (1978:290), the discontinuous case marker *te -e* is carried by the *last* NP of the clause. In simple sentences, Tzeltal's basic VOS word order entails that it is the subject of the clause that is marked with *te -e*. In example (26), however, one NP is preposed out of the relative clause, and the remaining NP *te ziak-e,* with last NP marking, is ambiguous according to whether *ziak* is understood to be the subject or the direct object of the verb 'hit':

(26)   *Te winik-e macʔa la   smah te ziak-e.*
            man   that   past hit-3
         a.   'the man who hit Ziak'
         b.   'the man whom Ziak hit'

The occurrence of *te -e* in Tzeltal is thus governed by linear order, rather than by grammatical relations.

   A not too dissimilar account of the effect of linear order on case marking has often been proposed for English pronouns. Sapir (1921: 166–167) remarks that "at least part of the case feeling in *he* and *him* is to be credited to their position before or after the verb," further suggesting that "*he* and *him, we* and *us,* are not so much subjective and objective forms as pre-verbal and post-verbal forms." This view can be traced back at least as far as Cooper (1685), who characterizes the English pronominal forms as "verbis anteponuntur" and "postponuntur verbis & praepositionibus." Other sources arguing in favor of a rule sensitive to linear order rather than grammatical relations include Poutsma (1916:721) and Bloomfield (1933:192).

   The effect of linear order on the form of English pronouns is not limited to those constructions in which the order is determined in direct relationship to the verb. In the following example, adapted from Onions (1904:105), the pronoun is in both instances governed by the conjunction *but*—yet its form depends on whether it appears near the beginning or at the end of the sentence:

(27)   a.   *No one but* $\begin{Bmatrix} he \\ him \end{Bmatrix}$ *would have thought of it.*
         b.   *No one would have thought of it but* $\begin{Bmatrix} ʔhe \\ him \end{Bmatrix}$.

Another well-known source of variation in the form of English pronouns is provided by conjunctions. Gorbet and Woodall (1979) suggest a generalization whereby for conjunctions in subject position, nominative tends to precede accusative, as in the following:

(28)   *She and them left.*

This is exactly the situation that obtains in Sentences (21) and (22) in Classical Hebrew, in which the second of two conjoined NPs in subject position is marked with the supposedly accusative ʔεθ.

The possibility must be acknowledged that linear order plays an important role in determining case markings in a variety of languages. That the linear order of constituents should affect a language's morphology is hardly surprising: This has long been known to be the case for agreement, which typically applies in a unidirectional left-to-right manner.[17] Less expected, perhaps, is the dependence of case marking on the phonological size of constituents, shown in this paper to hold for Hebrew.[18] In this regard, it is extremely suggestive that the effect of linear order on case marking in English shows up in the pronominal system, consisting of typically monosyllabic words. Thus, in English, as in Hebrew, small constituents are more sensitive to linear order than are large constituents. And, in fact, this state of affairs is reflected by Greenberg's (1963) universal 43, whereby pronouns (small) exhibit case markings more often than do full NPs (large). Why this should be the case is suggested in the concluding section of this paper.

2.2. The Iambicity of Ordinary Language

We are now in a position to integrate the observations concerning the effect of phonological size and linear order on case marking, in the form of a general principle governing the organization of linguistic material. Note that in Hebrew, Tzeltal, and English, when the case marking of a constituent is determined (at least in part) by linear order, a phonologically nonzero element is added to the *second* of two constituents, or to a given constituent if it occurs in a *later* serial position in the clause or phrase. In Standard Hebrew, *et* before a subject or direct object NP is better in postverbal than in preverbal position; in the Hebrew of the Samaritan Chronicles, ʔεθ occurs before the second of two constituents in the clause or phrase; in Tzeltal, *te -e* applies to the last NP in a clause; and, in English, the somewhat larger accusative forms of the pronouns typically occur postverbally, and in later positions within clauses and

---

[17] The effect of linear order on agreement paradigms has been noted, among others, by Crockett (1976) for Russian, England (1976) for Old Spanish, Gesenius (1813) for Biblical Hebrew, and Moravcsik (1978a) for Arabic, French, Latin, and Temne—as well as by Greenberg (1963) in his universal 33.

[18] The closest I have found in the literature to such a claim is Poutsma (1916:715) and Jespersen (1949:262–273), who suggest that phonological shape (but not size) may affect the case of English pronouns. Jespersen refers to this possibility as the "influence of sound upon sense."

phrases. The effect of each of these case-marking rules is thus to increase the size of constituents occurring toward the ends of clauses and phrases.[19] Put differently, a function of case marking in each of these instances is to contribute to an organization of linguistic material in which smaller constituents precede larger ones.[20]

Viewed in this light, the reason why small constituents are more sensitive than large ones to case-marking rules becomes obvious. The scale of phonological size is not linear: The difference between a monosyllabic and a bisyllabic constituent is greater than that between a constituent with five syllables and a constituent with six. Hence, a rule whose function is to create a syllabic end-heaviness between pairs of constituents is more likely to apply to monosyllabic constituents than it is to five-syllable constituents.

The effect case marking has of increasing the phonological size of constituents occurring toward the ends of clauses is not limited to those instances discussed thus far, in which case marking is determined directly by linear order. A large number of the world's languages exhibit nominative–accusative case-marking systems: In almost all of these languages, the nominative marker is phonologically zero whereas the accusative is nonzero, and in almost all of these languages, the subject

[19] I am aware of several other languages in which case marking is determined by linear order; these languages, although not supporting this generalization, do not provide evidence against it either. In Samoan, the subject of a transitive clause may be preceded by a monosyllabic case marker only if it is postverbal (cf. *et* before subjects in Hebrew); however, if the subject precedes the verb, it is in turn preceded by a different monosyllabic marker indicating topic. The case marking of transitive subjects in Samoan is thus determined by linear order, but does not support the principle that small precedes large. A similar state of affairs holds in Kaluli, a Papuan language described by Schieffelin (1979): The ergative suffix $+\varepsilon$ applies only in OSV order; in SOV order the subject is marked with the absolutive suffix $+\mathrm{o}$. In Nandi, a Nilotic language described by Creider (1976), the first of a sequence of conjoined NPs is nominative, whereas subsequent NPs are in the accusative (cf. conjunction in the Samaritan Chronicles and for English pronouns). In Nandi, however, case is marked by tonal modifications of the noun, hence nominative and accusative NPs do not differ in phonological size. The Samoan, Kaluli, and Nandi facts, although providing further support for the claim that case marking may be determined by linear order, are thus neutral with respect to the generalization that when case marking is determined by linear order, the function of case marking is to effect an arrangement of small before large. We predict that in no language in which case marking is determined by linear order will the effect of case marking be the opposite of that suggested here, namely, to increase the size of constituents occurring toward the beginnings of clauses or phrases.

[20] This organizational principle is what is referred to here as the *iambicity* of ordinary language. This somewhat novel use of the term "iambicity" is justified later in this section, where it is suggested that this organizational principle may best be characterized in prosodic terms.

precedes the direct object in basic word order. As a result, the second NP of a transitive clause is typically the one that receives the nonzero case marker—the accusative morpheme contributing in such a way to the organizational principle whereby small constituents precede large ones.[21]

Languages with ergative case-marking systems appear to violate this principle, in that what is often the first NP in a transitive clause receives the typically nonzero ergative case marking. But in fact, according to the hierarchy suggested by Dixon (1979) and Moravcsik (1978c), full NPs are more likely to pattern ergatively than pronouns. Thus, in many ergative languages (e.g., Dyirbal) at least one important class of NPs which are phonologically small and hence more sensitive to the effects of an added nonzero case marker—namely, the pronouns—continue to pattern in a nominative–accusative manner. And in fact, it is often the case that the nominative pronoun is phonologically smaller than the corresponding accusative pronoun which follows it.

Case-marking systems thus instantiate an organization of linguistic material according to which small constituents precede large ones; moreover, they do so in two distinct but closely related ways. These two ways are formulated in principles (29) and (30). In these principles, A and B denote constituents, X and Y syntactic categories, S and S' sentences, m and m' morphemes, and c and c' grammatical constructions into which these morphemes may enter.

(29)   *Iambic Marking Principle*
    a. For any A and B and for any S:
       if A precedes B in S,
       then i. there may exist an m and a c such that B contains m in c but A cannot (contain m in c).
            ii. There does not exist an m' and a c' such that A contains m' in c' but B cannot.
    b. For any A and for any S and S':
       if S' is identical to S except that A occurs further to the right in S' than it does in S,
       then i. there may exist an m and a c such that A contains m in c in S' but not in S;
            ii. there does not exist an m' and a c' such that A contains m' in c' in S but not in S'.

---

[21] Interestingly, in at least one of the languages in which object precedes subject in basic word order—namely, Fijian—the nominative case marker is the one that is nonzero; Fijian thus also upholds the above principle.

(30)   *Categorial Iambic Marking Principle*
         For any X and Y:
         if X precedes Y in basic grammatical order,
         then i. there may exist an m and a c such that Y contains m
                    in c but X cannot.
                ii. there does not exist an m' and a c' such that X
                    contains m' in c' but Y cannot.

The Iambic Marking Principle (IMP), in its two related versions, is exemplified by those instances discussed in this paper of case marking being directly determined by the order of constituents. For example, Rule (23) governing the occurrence of ʔɛθ in the Samaritan Chronicles provides an instantiation of the IMPa, as do examples such as (28) in English. Case marking in Standard Hebrew and Tzeltal, as well as examples such as (27) in English, reflect the IMPb. The Categorial Iambic Marking Principle (CIMP) is exemplified by the more commonplace state of affairs in which case marking is determined by grammatical relations, coinciding with basic word order. It accounts for the cross-linguistic predominance of nominative–accusative case-marking systems by stipulating that if subjects generally precede direct objects, the latter syntactic category will receive a nonzero case marking.

Both versions of the IMP reflect the tendency for languages to increase the size of constituents occurring further to the right. The CIMP may be viewed as representing the result of a language having institutionalized the IMP into its grammar. Alternatively, the CIMP may be said to refer to the basic or underlying order of constituents, and the IMP to their surface order. In many languages, case marking is probably governed by the CIMP alone, whereas in Tzeltal, the occurrence of at least one case marker is apparently governed by the IMP alone. In Hebrew, case marking appears to be governed by both principles, interacting in a complex way.[22] Consideration of such interaction may shed light on diachronic properties of case-marking systems.[23]

[22] Consider, for example, Sentences (12)–(15). In these sentences, postverbal *et* is evidence for the IMP, and postverbal ∅ evidence for the CIMP; preverbal ∅ is predicted by both principles. In order to derive preverbal *et*, however, it is necessary to assume underlying VS order and the CIMP, with subsequent fronting of the subject NP—a somewhat less attractive analysis. It is worth noting, however, that (13) and (15) with preverbal *et* exhibit a more distinctive intonation contour than their *et*-less variants, possibly supporting such a more complex derivation.

[23] Anderson (1976), for example, suggests that historical processes may be accountable for in terms of the reanalysis of a case-marking rule sensitive to linear order as one sensitive to grammatical relations—essentially from the IMP to the CIMP. An example of reanalysis in the opposite direction might be the rise of *et* as a postverbal subject marker in Modern Hebrew.

The IMP and CIMP are formulated in a general way, making no specific reference to case marking. In fact, a variety of seemingly unrelated phenomena may be viewed as attesting to the pervasiveness of these principles throughout language. Consider, for example, the way in which three or more constituents of the same syntactic category may be conjoined. Many languages (e.g., English, Estonian, Circassian, Turkish, Thai, Tagalog, and Biblical and Modern Hebrew) permit the construction indicated in (31a), where a single conjunction occurs between the penultimate and last conjuncts; presumably no language allows a construction as in (31b), where a single conjunction occurs between the first two conjuncts. In (31a), the last of a series of constituents contains an additional morpheme, in accordance with the IMPa; rather than a case marker, this additional morpheme is a conjunction:

(31)   a.   A, B, C, *and* D
         b.   *A *and*, B, C, D

Note how the conjunction in (31a) functions analogously to the accusative marker *ʔεθ* in conjoined NPs in the Samaritan Chronicles, and to the accusative form in conjoined pronouns in English.

Another instantiation of the IMP is provided by the somewhat literary adverbial construction in English, in which an adjective modifies the second (never the first) occurrence of a noun, resulting in a phrase of the form N_i Prep A N_i. In this construction, the adjective occurring in the second NP provides for the greater phonological size of the second constituent, as stipulated by the IMPa. In the following passage from *The Naked Civil Servant* by Quentin Crisp, this construction is illustrated twice; the passage also contains an example of the conjunction rule discussed in the previous paragraph:

(32)   *Day after **uneventful** day, night after **loveless** night, we sat in*
         this café, buying each other cups of tea, combing each
         *other's hair, **and** trying on each other's lipsticks.*

Agreement paradigms provide further support for the IMP and CIMP. As was pointed out in Note 17, agreement typically proceeds from left to right. Let us now consider the case where constituent B agrees with constituent A if A precedes B, as in (33a), but where agreement is suspended if A follows B, as in (33b):

(33)   a.   A B + agreement
         b.   B A

The effect of agreement in (33a) is to increase the size of the second of two constituents, in accordance with the IMPa; when constituent order is reversed, in (33b), agreement is suspended, in order to prevent the first rather than the second constituent from increasing in size.

In Hebrew, agreement functions in concert with case marking, in order to uphold the IMP in subject–verb constructions. In Standard Hebrew, verbal agreement may be suspended in VS order. In Example (34a), the verb agrees with its preceding subject and is marked with the plural suffix + *im*. In (34b)—adapted from Bar-Adon (1959:398)—verbal agreement is suspended, and the postverbal subject is marked with *et:*

(34)   a.   [*otam   hadvarim*]   [*mesuparim*]
                same-plm the-things-plm are-told-plm
        b.   [*mesupar*] [*et otam   hadvarim*]
                is-told-sgm   same-plm the-things-plm
                'The same things are told'.

In both sentences, an extra syllable is added to the *second* of the two major constituents, agreement and case-marking paradigms working in unison to support the IMP.

More generally, it is the case that when agreement is not sensitive to scrambling, it applies most often from left to right in basic word order, in accordance with the CIMP. Thus, subject–verb agreement is left to right for the large majority of the world's languages with subject-initial basic word order, as is noun–adjective agreement for a somewhat smaller majority of the world's languages with noun–adjective order. Head–relative clause agreement (by means of a resumptive pronoun) is attested only in postnominal relative clauses. In all these cases, agreement functions in such a way as to increase the size of the second of two constituents, in either surface or basic word order.

The IMP and CIMP provide one way in which languages may uphold the general organizational principle whereby phonologically small constituents precede phonologically large ones, namely, by increasing the size of a constituent occurring toward the right of a clause or phrase, once its linear order is determined. Work in progress suggests that a wide variety of constituent order universals result from the same principle applied in the opposite direction—that is to say, given that one constituent is larger than the other, the two constituents will then be ordered in such a way that the smaller one precedes the larger one. One obvious example of this is Pāṇini's rule for compounds, discussed in Cooper and Ross (1975); other examples include clitic order in Tagalog, order of direct and indirect object in Hebrew, and Heavy NP Shift in English. A much larger range of facts results from the grammaticalization of this tendency, in the same way as the CIMP is derived from the IMP. For example, pronouns are usually smaller than full NPs; in language after language, there are rules stipulating that pronouns occur to the left of full NPs—even if particular pronouns are actually larger than particular full NPs. Other generalizations resulting from the ordering of small syntactic categories before large ones include the tendency for subjects and topics to occur sentence initially, and the tendency for sentential NPs to occur sentence finally. By extending this same principle cross-categorically, it is possible to account for a number of implicational universals: for example, articles (small) precede their nominal heads more frequently than do adjectives (larger), which in turn precede their nominal heads more easily than do relative clauses (even larger).

In this paper, evidence has been brought to bear in support of the claim that linguistic forms embody two orthogonal systems of organization. The first system, that which pertains more directly to the mapping of meanings onto sounds effected by the grammar, is reflected by—among other things—the semantic functions of case-marking systems. The second system of organization prescribes, inter alia, an arrangement of linguistic material whereby phonologically small constituents precede phonologically large ones; this system is reflected by those aspects of case-marking systems sensitive to the phonological size of constituents and to their linear order—as well as by a variety of other properties of language.

In order to represent these two orthogonal systems of organization a theory of language must contain a pair of essentially autonomous grammars, assigning each sentence two independent structures. Such a theory is in fact commonplace in the realm of metered verse, where a line of verse is generally assumed to have independent "grammatical" and "prosodic" structures. In Stein and Gil (1980:234), it is speculated that such a "two-grammar" theory may be appropriate for ordinary as well as for stylized language. To wit, just as a unit of verse is considered *iambic* if, say, its second part contains more syllables than its first, so a syntactic constituent may be considered *iambic* if its second daughter contains more syllables than its first. As we have shown in this paper, a variety of morphosyntactic rules conspire to create iambic constituents in language. This paper, accordingly, has provided some support for the relevance of the notion of "iambicity" to a theory of ordinary language.

ACKNOWLEDGMENTS

This paper is an abridged and modified version of Gil (1981) "Hebrew *et:* a Non-Semantic Analysis of a Case Marker." I would like to thank the following people for constructive comments on that earlier paper and/or other helpful suggestions: Ruth Berman, Ed Keenan, Elinor Ochs, Paul Schachter, Ronit Shoshany, and Sandy Thompson.

REFERENCES

Albrecht, K. (1929) *ʔt* vor dem Nominativ und beim Passiv," *Zeitschrift für die Alttes-tamentliche Wissenschaft* 47, 274–283.
Andersen, F. I. (1971) "Passive and Ergative in Hebrew," in H. Goedicke, ed., *Near Eastern Studies in Honor of W. F. Albright,* John Hopkins Press, Baltimore.
Anderson, S. R. (1976) "On the Notion of Subject in Ergative Languages," in C. N. Li, ed., *Subject and Topic,* Academic Press, New York.
Bar-Adon, A. (1959) [*Children's Hebrew in Israel*], unpublished doctoral dissertation, Hebrew University, Jerusalem (in Hebrew).
Bar-Daroma, Y. (1962) "Tafkid Hamila 'et' Bamikra," *Hachinuch* 34, 425–427.
Ben-Ḥayim, Z. (1971) "Neviʔim Rišonim Nusaḥ Šomron?" *Leshonenu* 35, 292–307.
Berman, R. (1973) [*Verbal Nouns in Modern Hebrew*], unpublished doctoral dissertation, Hebrew University, Jerusalem (in Hebrew).
Berman, R. (1978) *Modern Hebrew Structure,* University Publishing Projects, Tel Aviv.
Blau, J. (1954) "Zum Angeblichen Gebrauch von *ʔt* vor dem Nominativ," *Vetus Testamentum* 4, 7–19.
Bloomfield, L. (1933) *Language,* Holt, Rinehart and Winston, New York.
Comrie, B. (1976) *Aspect,* Cambridge University Press, Cambridge.
Comrie, B. (1978) "Ergativity," in W. P. Lehmann, ed., *Syntactic Typology: Studies in the Phenomenology of Language,* University of Texas Press, Austin.
Cooper, C. (1685) *Grammatica Linguae Anglicannae,* Menston, Yorkshire (reprinted by Scholar Press, 1968).
Cooper, W. E. and J. R. Ross (1975) "World Order," in R. E. Grossman, L. J. Sam, and T. J. Vance, eds., *Papers from the Parasession on Functionalism,* Chicago Linguistic Society, University of Chicago.
Creider, C. A. (1976) *A Syntactic Sketch of Nandi,* unpublished paper, University of Western Ontario.
Crockett, D. B. (1976) *Agreement in Contemporary Standard Russian,* Slavica, Cambridge, Massachusetts.
Dixon, R. M. W. (1979) "Ergativity," *Language* 55, 57–133.
England, J. (1976) "Dixo Raihel e Vidas: Subject–Verb Agreement in Old Spanish," *Modern Language Review* 71, 812–826.
Gesenius, W. (1813) *Gesenius' Hebrew Grammar,* E. Kautzsch and A. E. Cowley, eds. (2nd English ed., 1909, Clarendon Press, Oxford).
Gil, D. (1981) "Hebrew *et*: A Non-Semantic Analysis of a Case Marker," paper presented at the North American Conference on Afroasiatic Linguistics. Boston, Mass., 14 March 1981.
Givón, T. (1976) "Topic, Pronoun, and Grammatical Agreement," in C. N. Li, ed., *Subject and Topic,* Academic Press, New York.
Gorbet, L. and C. Woodall (1979) *The Form of English Pronominal Conjunctions,* paper presented at the annual meeting of the Linguistic Society of America, December 1979, Los Angeles.
Greenberg, J. H. (1963) "Some Universals of Grammar with Particular Reference to the Order of Meaningful Elements," in J. H. Greenberg, ed., *Universals of Language,* MIT Press, Cambridge, Massachusetts.
Hoftijzer, J. (1965) "Remarks Concerning the Use of the Particle *ʔt* in Classical Hebrew," *Oudtestamentische Studien* 14, 1–99.
Hopper, P. and S. Thompson (1980) "Transitivity in Grammar and Discourse," *Language* 56, 251–299.

Jespersen, O. (1949) *A Modern English Grammar, Part VII: Syntax,* Allen & Unwin, London.

Kaddari, M. Z. (1976) [*Studies in Biblical Hebrew Syntax*], Bar Ilan University, Ramat Gan (in Hebrew).

Keenan, E. L. (1976) "Towards a Universal Definition of 'Subject'," in C. N. Li, ed., *Subject and Topic,* Academic Press, New York.

Keenan, E. L. (1978) "The Syntax of Subject-Final Languages," in W. P. Lehmann, ed., *Syntactic Typology: Studies in the Phenomenology of Language,* University of Texas Press, Austin.

Longacre, R. E. (1960) "String Constituent Analysis," *Language* 36, 63–88.

Macdonald, J. (1964) "The Particle ʔt in Classical Hebrew: Some New Data on Its Use with the Nominative," *Vetus Testamentum* 14, 264–275.

Macdonald, J. (1969) *The Samaritan Chronicle II (Or Sepher Ha-Yamim) from Joshua to Nebuchadnezzar,* Walter de Gruyter & Co., Berlin.

Moravcsik, E. (1978a) "Agreement," in J. H. Greenberg, ed., *Universals of Human Language* 4, Stanford University Press, Stanford, California.

Moravcsik, E. (1978b) "On the Case Marking of Objects," in J. H. Greenberg, ed., *Universals of Human Language* 4, Stanford University Press, Stanford, California.

Moravcsik, E. (1978c) "On the Distribution of Ergative and Accusative Patterns," *Lingua* 45, 233–279.

Onions, C. T. (1904) *An Advanced English Syntax,* Macmillan, New York.

Poutsma, H. (1916) *A Grammar of Late Modern English, Part II, The Parts of Speech, Section I,B, Pronouns and Numerals,* P. Noordhoff, Groningen.

Sadka, Y. (1978) *Taḥbir Hamišpat,* Academon, Jerusalem.

Sapir, E. (1921) *Language: An Introduction to the Study of Speech,* Harcourt, Brace and World, New York.

Saydon, P. P. (1964) "Meanings and Uses of the Particle ʔt," *Vetus Testamentum* 14, 192–210.

Schieffelin, B. B. (1979) "A Developmental Study of Word Order and Case Marking in an Ergative Language," *Papers and Reports in Child Language Development* 17, Department of Linguistics, Stanford University, Stanford, California.

Shoshany, R. (1979) *Passives and Possessives in Hebrew,* unpublished paper, Tel Aviv University.

Stein, D. and D. Gil (1980) "Prosodic Structures and Prosodic Markers," *Theoretical Linguistics* 7, 173–240.

Walker, N. (1955) "Concerning the function of '*eth*" *Vetus Testamentum* 5, 314–315.

Wilson, A. M. (1890a) "The Particle ʔt in Hebrew, I," *Hebraica* 6, 139–150.

Wilson, A. M. (1890b) "The Particle ʔt in Hebrew, II," *Hebraica* 6, 212–224.

Ziv, Y. (1976a) "On the Diachronic Relevance of the Promotion to Subject Hierarchy," in S. B. Steever et al., eds., *Papers from the Parasession on Diachronic Syntax,* Chicago Linguistic Society, Department of Linguistics, University of Chicago.

Ziv, Y. (1976b) "On the Reanalysis of Grammatical Terms in Hebrew Possessive Constructions," in P. Cole, ed., *Studies in Modern Hebrew Syntax and Semantics,* North-Holland Linguistic Series 32, 129–152.

TRANSITIVITY, TOPICALITY, AND THE UTE IMPERSONAL PASSIVE

T. GIVÓN

1. INTRODUCTION: THE TYPOLOGY OF PASSIVIZATION

Cross-language comparison makes it clear that passive constructions involve a conflation of three distinct FUNCTIONAL DOMAINS:[1]

(1)   a.   CLAUSAL TOPIC ASSIGNMENT: The subject/agent of the active clause ceases to be the topic, and a nonagent argument assumes, by whatever means, the topic function in the passive clause.
   b.   IMPERSONALIZATION: The identity of the subject/agent of the active clause is suppressed in the passive, by whatever means.
   c.   DETRANSITIVIZATION: The passive clause is semantically less active, less transitive, more stative than the active clause.

Each one of these three functional domains is by itself complex and has other MEMBERS covering various sections of the domain. Thus, for example, the topic assignment domain straddles a large continuum begin-

---

[1] For a discussion of functional domains in typology, see Givón (1981b).

143

ning with zero anaphora, verb agreement and unstressed pronouns and going on to definitization, right- and left-dislocation, Y-movement, etc.[2] The domain of impersonalization may involve impersonal constructions other than the passive, such as *one does . . .* constructions, *you don't do that, they shoot horses don't they,* etc. Finally, the detransitivization domain commonly involves constructions such as adjectives, perfective/completive verbs, stative and middle-voice verbs, etc. As I have suggested elsewhere,[3] there is a wealth of both synchronic and diachronic evidence supporting this complex view of the passive functional domain.

When one moves to study the syntactic typology of passive constructions cross-linguistically (as well as intralinguistically, in that a language may have more than one construction that may be appropriately called "passive"), four *syntactic coding properties* turn out to be most valuable in characterizing passive clauses:

(2) a. The degree to which the new (nonagent) topic of the passive assumes the characteristic CASE-CODING PROPERTIES typical of the subject/agent of the active clause.
     b. The degree to which the IDENTITY of the subject/agent of the active clause is SUPPRESSED in the passive clause.
     c. The degree to which the passive clause retains semantic and syntactic characteristics of "activeness" or "transitivity."
     d. The degree to which various nonsubject/nonagent arguments of the active clause are free to become topics of the passive clause.

That these coding properties are graded rather than binary/discrete has been obvious for quite a while. Thus, Keenan (1975) has noted that the assumption of subject properties by the passive clause topic may be a matter of degree. The suppression of the agent of the active may be full—by obligatory DELETION—or partial—by DEMOTION to various other cases. Transitivity and activeness involve several semantic and syntactic properties that, when combined together, may produce a scale.[4] And restrictions on the case roles that may become topic of the passive range from most stringent to quite lax.[5]

The passive coding properties in (2) are not entirely arbitrary, and at the appropriate level[6] exhibit a certain degree of ICONICITY vis-à-vis the

---

[2] For a discussion of this scalar domain, see Givón (1981a, 1981b).

[3] Givón (1981b).

[4] See Hopper and Thompson (1980).

[5] See Givón (1979, Chapter 4).

[6] Our traditional notions of iconicity are quite primitive, considering only the most "pictorial," concrete level. But iconicity—or *nonarbitrariness*—of the coding level exists

three functional domains of the passive. Thus, Property (2a), the one relevant to the relational grammar concept of "promotion,"[7] is a coding expression of Functional Domain (1a). Property (2b), reminiscent of the relational grammar concept of "demotion,"[8] is a coding expression of Functional Domain (1b). And Property (2c) is a coding expression of Functional Domain (1c). Property (2d), on the other hand, arises from the need to preserve/recover the SEMANTIC ROLE of the new topic of the passive clause, and thus involves considerations of the case-marking system in both active and passive clauses.[9]

Given four explicitly scalar typological dimensions, one would expect the typology of passive clauses to be expressed in terms of multidimensional clustering. But in fact one finds that this is not the case. Rather, there seems to be only one major continuum along a single dimension in passivization, with the two extremes on the scale exemplified by the English type on one end and the Ute type on the other. There is only one way in which such a fact could be compatible with the typological properties outlined in (2a)–(2d): Namely, if those typological dimensions do *not* vary independently, but rather exhibit DEPENDENCIES among themselves. Such dependencies indeed exist, and they may be expressed in terms of dependencies of Properties (2b), (2c), and (2d) upon Property (2a):

(3)   The less the topic of the passive is coded by the subject/agent marking characteristic of the active clause, the MORE is the passive clause likely to obligatorily delete/suppress the subject/agent of the active.

(4)   The less the topic of the passive is coded by the subject/agent marking characteristic of the active clause, the MORE is the passive clause likely to retain vestiges of "transitivity" or "activeness."

(5)   The less the topic of the passive is coded by the subject/agent marking characteristic of the active clause, the MORE is the

at other, more abstract levels as well. After all, what better expression can one give to the topic assignment function than to mark the topic of the passive clause by all the syntactic and morphological trimmings of the *nominative* case of the active? Similarly, what better expression can one give to the suppression of the identity of the active subject/agent than obligatory deletion?

[7] See Perlmutter and Postal (1974), who, of course, make no allowance for the scalar, nondiscrete nature of "assuming subject properties."

[8] Perlmutter and Postal (1974) consider only "demotion to a *chômeur* case," thus not considering the vast majority of passives in natural languages where the subject/agent of the active must be obligatorily deleted.

[9] For an extensive discussion and cross-language comparative data, see Givón (1979, Chapter 4).

passive clause likely to tolerate a wider range of nonagent
case arguments as topic of the passive clause.

These three typological correlations are neither obvious nor logically
necessary, which makes them all the more valuable.[10] In fact, (3) and
(4) are on the face of it almost contradictory, suggesting that the passive-
type in which the subject/agent is most likely to be deleted/suppressed
is also the type where the agent may retain more vestiges of grammatical
control and the clause may remain "more transitive." In spite of the
nonobviousness of these correlations, they indeed represent the typological facts. Further, one could suggest coherent FUNCTIONAL motiva-
tions for all three:

Correlation (3): In the "nonpromotional" passive, as I shall subsequently illustrate with Ute data, no adjustment is made in the case
marking of any of the arguments in the clause. Although the verb itself
may be marked by an affix specific to the passive, all other marking
properties of the clause remain those characteristic of the ACTIVE. If the
underlying agent were NOT deleted obligatorily, a high potential would
exist for a massive role-and-transitivity confusion in the passive clause.

Correlation (4): Given Correlation (3), (4) seems almost contradictory,
as it suggests that obligatory agent deletion and active/transitive properties are necessarily coupled together in the passive clause, even though
one of the strongest features of transitivity/activeness here turns out to
be residual control, by the ABSENT agent, of grammatical processes in
the passive clause. The contradiction is only superficial, however, if one
bears in mind that "nonpromotional" passives retain the case-marking
characteristics—excepting the missing agent—of the active/transitive
clause. What transpires here is the surprising generalization concerning
the overt/syntactic marking of transitivity/activeness of clauses:

(6)   *Principle of syntactic coding of transitivity:* To the extent that
        the transitivity of a clause is coded by its case marking,[11] the
        case marking of the Agent plays a LESS important role in the
        coding of transitivity than the case marking of non-Agent
        arguments.

Principle (6) again seems to fly in the face of what we would logically
expect, given the normal assumption that activity/transitivity is an *Agent*-
correlated phenomenon. And, in fact, one could just as easily formulate

---

[10] Facts that are logically derivable from other facts are tautological, cf. Wittgenstein
(1918).

[11] The transitivity/activeness of clauses may also be coded by the form of the verb (i.e.
adjectival, perfective, stative, nominalized, 'be'-auxiliary, etc.) as noted by Keenan (1975).
In many "impersonal" passives, however, the verb may remain morphologically unmarked.

a converse coding principle such as (7):

(7)   The case marking of the agent plays a MORE important role in coding the transitivity/activeness of clauses than the case marking of the nonagent arguments.

But in fact, (6) is factually correct and (7)—although logically attractive—is counterfactual.[12] The contradictory nature of (6) is again only superficial, given two universal facts concerning agents:

(8)   *Nominative/topic case marking:* In nonergative languages, which are the vast majority of languages, the agent is case marked NOT for its semantic role of agent but rather for its PRAGMATIC role of subject/topic. Such marking is NEUTRAL with respect to the transitivity of the clause.

(9)   *Deletion:* Agents of active clauses are the most likely argument to be anaphorically deleted, as they tend to be the subject/topic of the clause and thus predictable. Agents of passive clauses—even of the "promotional" type—are also most commonly deleted,[13] given the IMPERSONAL function of passive. Thus, one way or another, the agent is the LEAST PRESENT argument in the clause in actual discourse.[14] It would obviously be a self-defeating communicative strategy then to code the transitivity/activeness status of the clause via the case marking of its agent.

Let us now turn to our last correlation:

Correlation (5): As I have shown elsewhere, the restriction on the type of arguments that can become the subject/topic of the passive clause is motivated by the need for case recoverability. In "promotional" passives, the new nonagent topic must lose its semantic case marking via such promotion and assume the PRAGMATIC marking of subject/topic. If only the direct object/accusative is accessible to passivization in such a typology, its semantic role is still "recoverable." But if other nonagent case roles were similarly "accessible," the semantic role of all nonagents becoming subject/topic of the passive would become nonrecoverable, unless special provisions are made.[15]

---

[12] See Hopper and Thompson (1980).

[13] See text counts from English in Givón (1979, Chapter 2).

[14] Keenan (1976) claims that subjects are "the most present" argument in clauses, but this is obviously a *semantic* generalization in the abstract. In actual discourse, subjects are the "least present" of all major arguments.

[15] For details see Givón (1979, Chapter 4). The Philippine, Indonesian, and Bantu exceptions to this generalization make a special provision for coding the semantic role of the newly promoted nonagent topic of the passive *on the verb,* thereby insuring recoverability.

If the Correlations (3), (4), and (5) hold, then one expects one major dimension in the typology of passivization. The English passive would represent one extreme of the continuum, scaling on coding properties (2a)–(2d) in the followying way:

(10)   a.   High coding of the promoted nonagent as subject of the
             passive
        b.   Less suppression of the identity of the agent
        c.   Highly stative/intransitive passive clause, semantically
        d.   Strong restrictions on arguments that are allowed to
             become the subject/topic of the passive clause.

The Ute extreme of the scale would have just the opposite properties. And the reason why one insists on talking about a *scale* rather than two categorical types is because each one of the properties (2a)–(2d) can be shown to be scalar.[16]

2. THE UTE PASSIVE

2.1. Morphological Preliminaries

As noted earlier, the agent/subject is obligatorily deleted from the Ute passive clause. The other arguments, whatever they be, retain their active clause case marking. The verb is marked by the passive infix *-ta-*. Thus consider:

(11)   Active: *Ta'wá-ci̱ 'u   sivá̱a̱tu-ci 'uwáy pa̱xá-qa.*
                  man-subj the-subj goat-obj   the-obj kill-ant
                  'The man killed the goat'.

(12)   Passive: *Sivá̱a̱tu-ci 'uwáy pa̱xá-ta-x̂a.*
                  goat-obj   the-obj kill-pass-ant
                  { 'Someone killed the goat'. }
                  { 'The goat was killed'.   }

2.2. Case Roles and Verb Types That Can Passivize

Ute conforms well to Correlation (5) in allowing, in addition to the direct object [see (11) and (12)], all other case roles to become the topic

---

[16] Keenan (1975) notes that promotion to subjecthood involves assumption of word order position, case marking and grammatical agreement, and that a topic-of-passive may be only *partially* promoted to subjecthood. The other coding properties of passives may also be scalar, see discussion above.

of the passive impersonal clause, albeit by default.[17] Thus consider:

LOCATIVE:

(13) Active: *Tuá-ci̱ 'u tɨká'na-pɨ-vwa-n 'aví-kya.*
child-subj the-subj table-obj-on-loc lie-ant
'The child lay on the table'.

(14) Passive: *Tɨká'na-pɨ-vwa-n 'aví-ta-x̂a.*
table-obj-on-loc lie-pass-ant
'Someone lay on the table'.

INSTRUMENTAL:

(15) Active: *Ta'wá-ci̱ 'u wií-ci-m wɨ́ɨka-x̂a.*
man-subj the-subj knife-obj-with work-ant
'The man worked with a/the knife'.

(16) Passive: *Wií-ci-m wɨ́ɨka-ta-x̂a.*
knife-obj-with work-pass-ant
⎰'Someone worked with a/the knife'.⎱
⎱'The knife was used for work'. ⎰

BENEFACTIVE:

(17) Active: *Ta'wá-ci̱ 'u múay-av tɨká-'iní-kɨ-xa.*
man-subj the-subj father-obj-own eat-make-ben-ant
'The man made food for his father'.

(18) Passive: *Múay-av tɨká-'iní-kɨ-ta-x̂a.*
father-obj-own eat-make-ben-pass-ant
'Someone made food for his own father'.

ASSOCIATIVE:

(19) Active: *Mamá-ci̱ 'u na'áci-ci-wa 'uwáy wɨ́ɨka-x̂a.*
woman-subj the-subj girl-obj-with the-obj work-ant
'The woman worked with the girl'.

(20) Passive: *Na'áci-ci-wa 'uwáy wɨ́ɨka-ta-x̂a.*
girl-obj-with the-obj work-pass-ant
'Someone worked with the girl'.

DATIVE:

(21) Active: *Ta'wá-ci̱ 'u mamá-ci-vɑ̱ɑ̱-cɨ 'apáĝa-qa.*
man-subj the-subj woman-obj-at-dat talk-ant
'The man talked about the woman'.

---

[17] Perlmutter and Postal (1974) assume only "promotion by full coding as subject." But as we shall see in what follows, when the active subject/agent is obligatorily deleted, *some* surviving argument can assume clausal topic function "by default," without any syntactic or morphological adjustment in the subject-coding properties.

(22)   Passive: *Mamá-ci-vǫǫ-cǫ 'apáǧa-ta-x̂a.*
         woman-obj-at-dat talk-pass-ant
         'Someone talked about the woman'.

When both a direct and indirect object are present, the one coming first is *more topical* within the active clause,[18] and in the passive clause that argument remains as the main clausal topic. Thus consider:

DIR–INDIR:
(23)   Active: *Mamá-ci̱   tǫkúa-vi wií-ci-m   cikáǫvi'ná-x̂a.*
         woman-subj meat-obj knife-obj-with cut-ant
         'The woman cut the meat with a knife'.

(24)   Passive: *Tǫkúa-vi wií-ci-m   cikáǫvi'ná-ta-x̂a.*
         meat-obj knife-obj-with cut-pass-ant
         { 'The meat was cut with a knife'.   }
         { 'Someone cut the meat with a knife'.   }

INDIR–DIR:
(25)   Active: *Mamá-ci̱   wií-ci-m   'urú   tǫkúa-vi*
         woman-subj knife-obj-with the-obj meat-obj
                  cikáǫvi'ná-x̂a.
         cut-ant
         'The woman used the knife to cut meat'.

(26)   Passive: *Wií-ci-m   'urú   tǫkúa-vi cikáǫvi'ná-ta-x̂a.*
         knife-obj-with the-obj meat-obj cut-pass-ant
         { 'The knife was used to cut meat'.   }
         { 'Someone used the knife to cut meat'.   }

The most intransitive or stative verbs can undergo passivization in Ute so long as they have *any* argument at all. And that argument could even be an incorporated *manner adverb*.[19] Thus consider:

(27)   Active: *Mamá-ci̱   'u   pǫká-wǫ́ǫ̱ka-x̂a.*
         woman-subj the-subj hard-work-ant
         'The woman worked hard'.

(28)   Passive: *Pǫ́ka-wǫ́ǫ̱ka-ta-x̂a.*
         hard-work-pass-ant
         'Someone worked hard'.

---

[18] Dative-shifting is involved here and, as in other languages, the argument coming first is "more topical," more definite, and more "accessible" to be promoted to main clause topic. For details see Givón (1979, Chapter 4).

[19] Most manner adverbs in Ute are adjectival, nominal, or verbal stems incorporated into the following verb stem. Word level phonology, stress rules and morphophonemic rules clearly establish the status of the Adv–V compound as single word.

(29)   Active: *Ta'wá-ci̱ tayúci-gyq̱y   'apáğa-qa.*
                  man-subj eloquence-have speak-ant
                  'The man spoke eloquently'.

(30)   Passive: *Tayúci-gyq̱y   'apáğa-ta-x̂a.*
                 eloquence-have speak-pass-ant
                 ⎰ 'Someone spoke eloquently'.   ⎱
                 ⎱ 'There was (some) eloquent speaking'.   ⎰

(31)   Active: *Tuá-ci̱   'u   tṵvṵ́ci̱ sṵpíyawi-kya.*
                  child-subj the-subj very   lazy-ant
                  'The child has been very lazy'.

(32)   Passive: *tṵvṵ́ci̱ sṵpíyawi-ta-x̂a.*
                 very   lazy-pass-ant
                 'Someone has been very lazy'.

But no verb can be passivized in Ute if it has *no* argument at all. Thus compare (33), (34), and (35) to (28), (30), and (32), respectively:

(33)   **wṵ́ṵka-ta-x̂a*
        work-pass-ant

(34)   **'apáğa-ta-x̂a*
        speak-pass-ant

(35)   **Sṵpíyawi-ta-x̂a*
        lazy-pass-ant

This type of data in Ute suggests that at least for this language Keenan (1975) could not be right in asserting that passivization involves ONLY the demotion of the subject/agent, in that here unless SOME argument exists to take over as *topic* of the passive clause, passivization cannot take place. And although this is promotion BY DEFAULT, it nevertheless is "promotion." As we shall see in what follows, other pieces of evidence also suggest that the surviving argument is indeed the clausal topic.

Sentential-verbal complements of verbs can also qualify for passivization/promotion-to-topic in Ute. Thus consider:

(36)   Active: *Ta'wá-ci̱ 'u   tṵká-vaaci̱ 'ásti-kya.*
                  man-subj the-subj eat-subord want-ant
                  'The man wanted to eat'.

(37)   Passive: *Tṵká-vaaci̱ 'ásti-ta-x̂a.*
                 eat-subord want-pass-ant
                 'Someone wanted to eat'.

(38)   Active: *Mamá-cị   'áapa-ci sivą́ą̇tu-ci pax̂á-vaaku̲ máy-kya.*
woman-subj boy-obj goat-obj   kill-subord tell-ant
'The woman told the boy to kill the goat'.

(39)   Passive: *Sivą́ą̇tu-ci pax̂á-vaaku̲ ('áapa-ci) máy-ta-x̂a.*
goat-obj   kill-subord (boy-obj) tell-pass-ant
'Someone ordered the killing of the goat (upon the
boy)'.

(40)   Active: *Ta'wá-cị pu̲cúcugwa-qa mamá-ci   'uwáy*
man-subj know-ant   woman-pos the-pos
pịcų́-kaa-na̲-'ǫy.
come-ant-rel-subord
'The man knew that the woman had arrived'.

(41)   Passive: *Pu̲cúcugwa-ta-x̂a mamá-ci   'uwáy*
know-pass-ant   woman-pos the-pos
pịcų́-kaa-na̲-'ǫy.
come-ant-rel-subord
{ 'Someone knew that the woman had arrived'. }
{ 'It was known that the woman had arrived'. }

2.3. Subject Agreement versus Topic Agreement: Promotion, Demotion and Transitivity

In this section, I will demonstrate how by the criterion of control over grammatical and semantic processes in the passive clause by the *subject/agent* of the active, the Ute passive is indeed highly transitive. On the other hand, the control over pronoun suffix agreement, a topic-related process, is ceded in the passive clause to the new nonagent *topic*.

PLURAL AGREEMENT OF THE VERB STEM

In active sentences in Ute, the subject controls the number agreement on the verb. Singular and dual subjects use the basic (unmarked) stem of the verb; plural subjects use the verb with the plural suffix or a corresponding plural suppletive form. Thus consider:

(42)   Singular: *Ta'wá-cị 'u   wų́ų̇ka-y.*
man-subj the-subj work-imm
'The man is working'.

(43)   Plural: *Táa-ta'wá-ci-u 'umu̲   wų́ų̇ka-x̂a-y.*
red-man-subj-pl those-subj work-pl-imm
'The men are working'.

(44)   Singular: *Mamá-ci̱   'u   'aví-y.*
          woman-subj the-subj lie-imm
          'The woman is lying down'.

(45)   Plural: *Máama̱-ci-u   'umy̱   kwaví-y.*
          red-woman-subj-pl those̱-subj lie-pl-imm
          'The women are lying down'.

Although the subject/agent is obligatorily deleted in Ute passivization, it retains control of verb pluralization, and does *not* cede it to the new topic in the passive clause. Thus, Ute passives may appear with either a singular or plural verb, and this remains a signal as to whether the subject/agent was singular or plural. Thus consider:

(46)   Singular: *Siv$q̱$qtu-ci 'uwáy pa̱x̂á-ta-x̂a.*
          goat-obj   the-obj kill-pass-ant
          $\left\{\begin{array}{l}\text{'Someone (sg) killed the goat'.}\\\text{'The goat was killed (by a sg agent)'.}\end{array}\right\}$

(47)   Plural: *Siv$q̱$qtu-ci 'uwáy pa̱x̂á-x̂a̱-ta-x̂a.*
          goat-obj   the-obj kill-pl-pass-ant
          $\left\{\begin{array}{l}\text{'Some people (pl) killed the goat'.}\\\text{'The goat was killed (by a pl subject/agent)'.}\end{array}\right\}$

The obligatorily deleted agent, it seems, retains important control over a grammatical/semantic process in the passive clause. And this is indeed one of the features of the high transitivity/activeness of the Ute passive.

TOPIC CONTROL OF PRONOMINAL AGREEMENT

The agreement of the verb with the singular/plural feature of the grammatical subject in Ute is, as we have seen, an obligatory process. Pronominal agreement, on the other hand, is neither "grammatical" nor obligatory in Ute. Rather, it is controlled by discourse–pragmatic considerations that are complex and subtle, roughly involving whatever argument is designated, at any point in the discourse, as the clausal *topic*. Further, the suffix pronoun need not appear on the verb, but most commonly is attached to the *first word* in the sentence/clause.

In active sentences, *any* argument of the verb—subject as well as nonsubject—may be the clausal topic, and thus may be coreferential with the suffix pronoun. And because the topic normally gets established in a preceding clause, in the relevant clause it appears *only* as a suffix pronoun.[20] Thus consider:

[20] For further detail on pronouns, anaphora, and discourse structure in Ute, see Givón (1980, Chapter 17).

(48)   Context: 'What did **the man** do?'
         Reply: *Tʉkúa-vi-'u sa'á-qa.*
                    meat-obj-he boil-ant
                    '**He** boiled some meat'.

(49)   Context: 'What happened to **the meat**?'
         Reply: *Ta'wá-ci-ux sa'á-qa.*
                    man-subj-it boil-ant
                    'The man boiled **it**'.

(50)   Context: 'What did the man do with the meat?'
         Reply: *Sa'á-qa-ux.*
                    boil-ant-it
                    'He boiled **it**'.

In (50), and in Ute discourse in general, if both the subject and object are made topical in the previous discourse, most commonly the subject is represented as zero, and the object controls the suffix pronoun. But this is a pragmatic tendency which may be reversed by subtle manipulation of the discourse context.

In passive clauses, on the other hand, only the nonagent topic can control the reference of suffix pronouns—never the deleted subject/agent. Thus consider:

(51)   Dative object topic:
         'Áavʉ̧ámʉ̧ (máama̲-ci-u)   tʉkúa-vi 'umʉ́-rugwá-ta̲-'ay.
         now-them (red-woman-obj-pl) meat-obj them-give-pass-imm
         'Now someone is giving them/the women meat'.

(52)   Direct object topic:
         'Áavʉ-ax̂ (tʉkúa-vi) máama̲ci-u   'umʉ́-rugwá-ta̲-'ay.
         now-it   (meat-obj) red-woman-obj-pl them-give-pass-imm
         'Now someone is giving it/the meat to the women'.

(53)   Subject/agent topic:
         *'áavʉ-'u   máama̲-ci-u   tʉkúa-vi 'umʉ́-rugwá-ta̲-'ay.
         now-he/she red-woman-obj-pl meat-obj them-give-pass-imm

As one finds in other languages with an altogether different passive type, the active retains WIDER PRAGMATIC OPTIONS as to topic assignment, whereas the passive is more LIMITED, most commonly to only ONE "promoted" nonagent topic.[21]

---

[21] I owe Tim Shopen (p.c.) the following observation:
Active: When **the farmer** wanted, **he** fed the cows. (Agent topic)
               When **the cows** were hungry, the farmer fed **them**. (object topic)
Passive:? When **the farmer** wanted, the cows were fed by him. (?Agent topic)
               When **the cows** were hungry, **they** were fed by the farmer. (object topic)

In sum, then, although the newly "promoted" nonagent topic of the passive clause in Ute does NOT acquire the grammatical ("unmarked") subject case marking and does NOT assume control over the grammatical process of subject–verb plural agreement, it does acquire the main PRAGMATIC property of the unmarked/grammatical subject, namely of being the clausal topic.

2.4. Other Active/Transitive Properties of the Ute Passive

As we have already seen, one feature of the active clause in Ute that is retained in the passive is the subject/agent's control over the singular–plural agreement of the verb. In this section I will investigate another active/transitive property of Ute passive clauses, that of embedding under MANIPULATIVE MODALITIES/VERBS.

As noted in the typological correlation (4), languages with the Indo-European–Bantu passivization type (i.e., full promotion of the nonagent topic to grammatical subjecthood and no obligatory deletion of the subject/agent) exhibit passive clauses that are rather STATIVE or "nontransitive" in their semantic properties. Most commonly, they describe A STATE RESULTING FROM AN ACTION rather than an action. This can be tested by embedding passive clauses under the scope of manipulative verbs, as typically such embeddings admit only active/agentive/control clauses.[22] Thus, consider the following examples from English:

(54)   Active: *The committee ordered Mary **to write the exam.***

(55)   Passive: *?The committee ordered the exam **to be written by Mary.***

As pointed out elsewhere (Givón, 1975), this restriction is not "grammatical" per se but rather hinges upon the semantic property of *control*. That is, if the person ordered/manipulated has control over the action, embedding under manipulative verbs/modalities is possible. Thus compare:

(56)   Active: *The committee ordered Joe **to bring coffee into the room.***

(57)   Passive: *The committee ordered coffee **to be brought into the room.***

So long as one can construct a semantic interpretation by which *some* agent has control over the desired action, Sentence (57) is felicitous.

The embedding of impersonal passive clauses under verbs of manipulation in Ute is routinely possible:

[22] See Givón (1975).

(58)   Active: *Mamá-ci*   *'áapa-ci máy-kya sivą́ątu-ci paxá-vaaku.*
                   woman-subj boy-obj tell-ant goat-obj kill-subord
                   'The woman told the boy to kill the goat'.

(59)   Passive: *Mamá-ci*   *'áapa-ci máy-kya sivą́ątu-ci*
                   woman-subj boy-obj tell-ant goat-obj
                   paxá-ta-vaaku.
                   kill-pass-subord

$$\left\{ \begin{array}{l} \text{'The woman told the boy that the goat should be killed'.} \\ \text{'The woman told the boy that \textbf{someone} should kill the goat'.} \end{array} \right\}$$

                   but not:
                   *'The woman told the boy that the goat should be
                   killed **by him**'.

Thus, as long as the identity of the subject/agent of the embedded clause
remains suppressed—and is not given away by coreferential identity with
the object of the manipulative verb—passive clauses can be embedded
in such active-designating environments.

Given the foregoing discussion, one would expect that Ute passive
clauses are "active enough" in their semantic properties to be embed-
dable under the imperative mode. But in fact that is not possible:

(60)   Active: *Sivą́ątu-ci paxá-nų!*
                   goat-obj   kill-imp
                   'Kill the goat!' (you-sg)

(61)   Passive: **Sivą́ątu-ci paxá-ta-nų!*
                   goat-obj   kill-pass-imp

The same prohibition is observed with the self-hortative ('let's . . . .')
mode:

(62)   Active: *'áavų-rami sivą́ątu-ci paxá-vaa!*
                   now-we-II goat-obj   kill-mod
                   'Let's (you and I) kill the goat!'

(63)   Passive: **'áavų-ramų sivą́ątu-ci paxá-ta-vaa!*
                   now-we-II goat-obj   kill-pass-mod

There is, however, a way of showing that this prohibition has nothing
whatever to do with the active-like properties (or lack of) of the Ute
passive clause, but rather with the absolute requirement of subject/agent
deletion ("identity suppression"). This is evident when one proceeds to

embed passive clauses under another exhortative modality of Ute, one which refers neither to speaker nor hearer. Thus consider:

(64)   Active: *Táa-sapa 'áapa-ci 'u   siváátu-ci paxá-vaa!*
                 exh-mod boy-subj the-subj goat-obj   kill-mod
                 'Let the boy kill a/the goat!'

(65)   Passive: *Táa-sapa siváátu-ci 'uwáy paxá-ta-vaa-tu!* (sg agent)
                 exh-mod goat-obj   the-obj kill-pass-mod-nom
                 ⎰'Let someone (sg) kill the goat!'   ⎱
                 ⎱'Let the goat be killed!' (by a sg-agent)⎰

(66)   Passive: *Táa-sapa siváátu-ci 'uwáy paxá-xa-ta-vaa-tu!*   (pl agent)
                 exh-mod goat-obj   the-obj kill-pl-pass-mod-nom
                 ⎰'Let someones (pl) kill the goat!'   ⎱
                 ⎱'Let the goat be killed!' (by a pl agent)⎰

And the same is also possible with the obligative mode, which again refers to third person agents:

(67)   Active: *Ta'wá-ci 'u   tuvúci-sapa siváátu-ci*
                 man-subj the-subj very-mod   goat-obj
                       paxá-vaaku.
                       kill-subord
                 'The man must/should kill the goat'.

(68)   Passive-sg: *Tuvúci-sapa siváátu-ci paxá-ta-vaaku.*
                     very-mod   goat-obj kill-pass-subord
                     'Someone must/should kill the goat!'

(69)   Passive-pl: *Tuvúci-sapa siváátu-ci paxá-xa-ta-vaaku.*
                     very-mod   goat-obj kill-pl-pass-subord
                     'Some people must/should kill the goat!'

What makes the imperative and first exhortative mode impervious to such an embedding is one simple fact: In both, the agent is clearly identifiable, being either 'you' or 'I and you'. But the Ute passive requires an obligatory suppression of the agent's identity, not only on the syntactic surface, but semantically. Hence this incompatibility.

3. DISCUSSION

3.1. Why Is the Ute Impersonal Passive a "Passive"?

At this point, one could play dumb and suggest that the Ute impersonal passive construction is really not a "passive" at all, given that, of the

three functional domains of the passive, it exhibits clearly only (1b)
AGENT IDENTITY SUPPRESSION; it exhibits (1a) TOPIC ASSIGNMENT only "by
default" and does not exhibit (1c) DETRANSITIVIZATION at all. However,
it is not clear that all "passives" exhibit all three properties to the same
degree. Thus, the "classical" Indo-European passive of English does
allow the agent to be present, although at the text count level the agent
is mostly suppressed.[23] Further, diachronic studies of the rise of passive
constructions reveal that they most commonly arise from a NONPASSIVE
member of one of the three functional domains of passivization, then
slowly get reanalyzed and gradually acquire properties of the two other
domains.[24] Thus, for example, in Kimbundu and Indonesian, "classical"-
looking passives—essentially of the English behavior-type, synchronically—arose diachronically from left-dislocated constructions, members
of the topic assignment domain.[25] In Spanish currently the impersonal
se construction is being further extended toward a more "classical"
passive, with the agent phrase added, at least in some dialects.[26] The
same is probably true for Italian and Romanian. Finally, in Romance,
Slavic, Finnish, Uto-Aztecan, and Semitic, "passives" of one type or
another are historically connected with other detransitivizing constructions such as the reflexive and reciprocal. And the "classical" passive
construction of English and Spanish arose historically from a stative/
adjectival/perfective form of the verb, together with the auxiliary 'be'.
The gradual assumption of properties relevant to the other domains of
the passive is thus the rule rather than the exception, as in all likelihood
ALL passive constructions shift into being "passive" via the historical
processes noted here. For a typological study of the passive, then, it is
important not to delimit our notion of what is a "passive" too stringently
and thus, in effect, throw the sweet passive baby out with the undesirable
bath water. When a passive construction arises historically from the
impersonalization functional domain, it may retain more transitive/active
properties. But by itself this should not make it less of a passive
construction.

3.2. Why Three Functional Domains Conflate in the Passive Construction

The diachronic facts raise the questions even more urgently than the
synchronic survey of cross-language data: Why do three seemingly

[23] See text count in Givón (1979, Chapter 2).
[24] See Givón (1981b, Section 5.).
[25] See Givón (1976, 1981b).
[26] See Givón (1981b, Section 5).

disparate functional domains—detransitivization–stativization, agent identity–suppression, and the promotion of a nonagent to clausal topic—conflate so often and so persistently, both synchronically and diachronically, in a single syntactic construction? It seems to me that the answer lies in the following three pragmatic/abductive inferences:[27]

(70)   If the identity of the agent—the most likely/unmarked clausal topic—is suppressed, then presumably another argument is meant to be the topic of the clause. Hence the conflation between the impersonalization and topic-assignment functional domains.

(71)   If the perfective/stative/resultative aspect of an event is focused upon, presumably the status of the agent is less important; hence the conflation between the detransitivization and impersonalization functional domains.

(72)   Finally, if the clause topic is a nonagent, it is likely then that the patient-related aspects of the event (i.e., resulting state) are being focused upon. Hence the conflation between the topic-assignment and detransitivization functional domains.

What these three inferences suggest is that not only the entire grammar but also single constructions within it behave like complex organisms, where mutual dependencies are not accidental but rather are predictable from a functional-typological investigation. Detransitivization, in this particular case, is thus not an atomic property of passive constructions, but rather is inferentially linked—in a motivated, nonarbitrary way—to the other functional domains of passivization. But this link of INTRANSITIVITY with agent suppression and nonagent topics is in fact part and parcel of Hopper and Thompson's (1980) observations. Inferences (70), (71), and (72) merely make it clear that the correlations are far from accidental.

3.3. The Overt Coding of Transitivity

Our coding principle (6) states that to the extent that transitivity is coded on the arguments (in addition to being coded on the verb), the case marking of the patient is more relevant to coding the transitivity of a clause than the case marking of the agent. This is further corrob-

---

[27] For an extensive discussion of pragmatic/abductive inference in syntax and semantics, see Givón (1981a). The original formulation of abduction is due to Peirce (1955), and its first systematic use in linguistics is due to Andersen (1973).

orated by some facts of Chukchee (B. Comrie, p.c.): Transitive clauses in the perfective are marked with ergative structure. However, if the object is incorporated into the verb, presumably being then generic, the clause loses its ergative marking and both active subject and verb are marked the way they are in intransitive clause. In other words, although the agent has not lost its agentivity, removing the patient is enough to downgrade the transitivity of the clause.

REFERENCES

Andersen, H. (1973) "Abductive and Deductive Change," *Language* 49, 765–793.

Givón, T. (1975) "Cause and Control: On the Semantics of Interpersonal Manipulation," in J. Kimball, ed., *Syntax and Semantics 4,* Academic Press, New York.

Givón, T. (1976) "Topic, Pronoun and Grammatical Agreement," in C. Li, ed., *Subject and Topic,* Academic Press, New York.

Givón, T. (1979) *On Understanding Grammar,* Academic Press, New York.

Givón, T. (1980) *Ute Reference Grammar,* Ute Press, Ignacio, Colorado.

Givón, T. (1981a) "Logic vs. Pragmatics, with Human Language as the Referee: Toward an Empirically Viable Epistemology," *Journal of Pragmatics* 6, 2.

Givón, T. (1981b) "Typology and Functional Domains," *Studies in Language.*

Hopper, P. and S. Thompson (1980) "Transitivity in Grammar and Discourse," *Language* 56, 251–299.

Keenan, E. L. (1975) "Some Universals of Passive in Relational Grammar," in R. E. Grassman, L. J. Sam, and T. J. Vance, eds., *Papers from the Eleventh Regional Meeting of the Chicago Linguistic Society,* University of Chicago.

Keenan, E. L. (1976) "Toward a Universal Definition of 'Subject'," in C. Li, ed., *Subject and Topic,* Academic Press, New York.

Peirce, C. S. (1955) *Philosophical Writings,* J. Buchler, ed., New York, Dover.

Perlmutter, D. and P. Postal (1974) "Relational Grammar," lecture notes, Summer Institute of the Linguistic Society of America, University of Massachusetts, Amherst.

Wittgenstein, L. (1918) *Tractatus Logico Philosophicus,* trans. by D. F. Pears and B. F. McGuinness (1960), Humanities Press, New York.

PASSIVIZATION IN MODERN WESTERN ARMENIAN

HELEN A. HAIG

1. INTRODUCTION

This study will propose a reanalysis of the morpheme *-v-* in Modern Western Armenian (MWA). The first part of the study will show that the morpheme *-v-* appears to have a dual function: It marks not only the passive voice but also the intransitive use of inherently transitive verbs—reduced valency. The question then arises as to what those two functions have in common that allows such a morphological correlation. The second part of this study will suggest an answer to the question by arguing that the morpheme *-v-*, in signaling both intransitivity and passivization, functions as a general detransitivizing marker. The detransitivizing function of marking for reduced valency is self-evident and will not be further explored. The detransitivizing function of passivization will be examined, however. It will be argued that passives in MWA are low in transitivity by virtue of the fact that a greater percentage of passives than actives occur in low transitivity verb forms. In defining transitivity, this paper will follow the hypothesis of Hopper and Thompson (1980), who propose that transitivity is a global property of an entire clause, and that a given clause may be evaluated as relatively high or low in transitivity on the basis of several parameters. Accordingly, low transitivity verb forms are

161

those that tend to be distributed in clauses that are low in transitivity, and that contribute to the low transitivity of that clause by themselves conveying a feature of low transitivity.

2. PASSIVE AND DETRANSITIVIZED VERBS

It is generally agreed that the verb system of MWA formally signals two voices: active and passive. The two voices are distinguished in that the passive is formed by insertion of the morpheme -v- between the verb stem and inflections for mood, tense, aspect, person, and number. Furthermore, those inflections for verbs and -v- follow the conjugational pattern of verbs with the -il infinitival ending, regardless of the infinitival ending (-el, -al, or -il) and the inflectional paradigm of the verb without the -v-. Most of the examples of the passive formation given by traditional grammars of MWA are stative expressions such as the following:[1,2]

(1)   *Hayr -er-ə   gə   hark   -v   -in.*
      father-pl-the i:imp respect-psv-un:3pl
      'The fathers are respected'.

(2)   *Naxakah-ə   g   əntər-v   -i.*
      president-the i:imp elect- psv-un:3s
      'The president is elected'.

(3)   *Namag-ə   kər   -v   -ets -av.*
      letter   -the write-psv-aor-3s
      'The letter was written'.

(4)   *Hartsum-ner-ə   gə   harts-v   -in   u   gə*
      question -pl -the i:imp ask   -psv -un:3pl and i:imp
         badasxan-v   -in.
      answer   -psv-un:3pl
      'The questions are asked and are answered'.

The traditional analysis of passivization seems to be accurate as far as it goes. There appears to be no other systematic means for forming passives in MWA. However, the analysis is problematical in that it cannot explain the following constructions:

[1] Sentences (1)–(4) are drawn from Andonian (1966).

[2] For a discussion of the morphological analysis of the verb system of MWA that is assumed in this study, see Kogian (1949) and Haig (1980). For gloss abbreviations, see the Appendix to this chapter.

(5)   *Hovanes-ə   badrast-v-ets-av tsutsahantes-i   -n   hamar.*
       John   -the prepare-v-aor-3s exhibit   -gen-the for
       'John prepared for the exhibit'.
       *'John was prepared for the exhibit'.

(6)   *Vartan-ə   hak -v-ets-av.*
       Vartan-the wear-v-aor-3s
       'Vartan dressed'.
       *'Vartan was dressed'.

(7)   *Hovanes-ə   ləvats-v-ets-av.*
       John   -the wash -v-aor-3s
       'John washed'.
       *'John was washed'.

(8)   *Hermine -n   pox   -v-ets-av.*
       'Hermine-the change-v-aor-3s
       'Hermine changed'.
       *'Hermine was changed'.

(9)   *Gə   hampur-v-ein.*
       i:imp kiss   -v-pst:3pl
       'They were kissing'.
       *'They were being kissed'.

(10)   *Gə   voγtšakur-v-ein.*
       i:imp embrace -v-pst:3pl
       'They were embracing'.
       *'They were being embraced'.

In Examples (5)–(10), the morpheme -*v*- occurs in active, not passive, sentences. The subject is agentive, with no accompanying object, in contrast to the canonical passive where the subject has patient status.

The question remains as to what the -*v*- morpheme signals in such cases. The data suggest that the morpheme -*v*- is an intransitive marker in that it occurs on verbs that have only one argument. However, not all intransitive verbs take such overt intransitive marking. Whether a given verb that is used intransitively can take the morpheme -*v*- depends upon the inherent meaning of the verb stem. It is when a verb stem is inherently transitive—semantically requiring a direct object as complement—that it takes the morpheme -*v*- when accompanied by only one argument. Such verb stems (given here with their infinitive endings) include the following:

(11)   *badrasdel*   'to prepare something'
         haknil   'to wear something'
         havakel   'to gather something'
         daradzel   'to spread something'
         kotsel   'to close something'
         poxel   'to change something'
         tsərel   'to scatter something'
         bahel   'to keep something'
         hašdel   'to reconcile something'
         hampurel   'to kiss someone/thing'
         voɣtšakurel   'to embrace someone/thing'

The examples of inherently transitive verbs used intransitively with -*v*- that have been illustrated so far—in (5)–(10)—all have agentive subjects. Such detransitivized verbs with -*v*-, however, can also take nonagentive subjects. In each of the following pairs of sentences, a verb stem is used transitively and then intransitively with a nonagentive subject. As is shown, the verb stem with -*v*- is unacceptable where there are two arguments, but it is obligatory where there is only one.[3]

(12)   *Takavor-ə   zəruyts-ə* $\begin{Bmatrix} *daradzvetsav \\ daradz\text{-}ets \end{Bmatrix}$

         king   -the rumor -the   spread-aor-3s
         'The king spread the rumor'.

(12′)   *Takavor-i   -n   zəruyts-ə* $\begin{Bmatrix} *daradzets \\ daradz\text{-}v\ \text{-}ets\text{-}av \end{Bmatrix}$

         king   -gen-the rumor -the   spread-intr-aor:3s
         'The king's rumor spread'.

(13)   *Azniv -ə   tur -ə* $\begin{Bmatrix} *kotsvetsav \\ kots\text{-}ets \end{Bmatrix}$.

         Aznive-the door-the   close-aor:3s
         'Aznive closed the door'.

---

[3] As can be seen from the following examples, the difference between a detransitivized verb and its transitive counterpart involves more than just the presence or absence of the morpheme -*v*-: the conjugational inflections also differ. As has already been pointed out, a verb with -*v*- is conjugated according to the -*il* paradigm even if the same verb without -*v*- is conjugated according to the -*el* or -*al* paradigm. Thus, a given verb can have two formal options by which to convey the same meaning with respect to mood, tense, person, and number. For example, the verb that occurs in (12), *daradzel* 'to spread', can convey 'past, perfective, third person, singular' with either -*etsav* (presence of -*v*-) or -*ets* (absence of -*v*-).

(13')   *Tur -ə* $\begin{Bmatrix} *kotsets \\ kots \text{ } \text{-}v \end{Bmatrix}$ *-ets-av* .
door-the   close-intr-aor-3s
'The door closed'.

(14)   *Giletsa-n   geragur-ə   yergu or   aveli* $\begin{Bmatrix} *g & bahvi \\ gə & bah & \text{-}e \end{Bmatrix}$
Grace -the food   -the two   days more   i:imp keep -un:3s
'Grace will keep the food for two more days'.

(14')   *Geragur-ə   yergu or   aveli* $\begin{Bmatrix} *gə & bahe \\ gə & bah & \text{-}v & \text{-}i \end{Bmatrix}$.
food   -the two   days more   i:imp keep -intr-un:3s
'The food will keep for two more days'.

(15)   *Vahe-n   šakar-ə   tšur -i   -n   metš* $\begin{Bmatrix} *ludzvetsav \\ ludz & \text{-}ets \end{Bmatrix}$.
Vahe-the sugar-the water-gen-the in   dissolve-aor:3s
'Vahe dissolved the sugar in the water'.

(15')   *Šakar-ə   tšur -i   -n   metš* $\begin{Bmatrix} *ludzets \\ ludz & \text{-}v & \text{-}ets\text{-}av \end{Bmatrix}$.
sugar -the water-gen-the in   dissolve-intr-aor-3s
'The sugar dissolved in the water'.

Thus, in constructions where an inherently transitive verb is used with only one argument, either the agent or patient may be missing. Conversely, the subject of such detransitivized verbs may be either an agent or patient.

The active status of (5)–(10) and (12')–(15') (even where the subject is a patient) is further demonstrated by the fact that such sentences cannot take oblique agentive phrases, in contrast with canonical passives which can take an agent in the ablative case. Thus, whereas the following canonical passive sentences take an agentive phrase:

(16)   *Namag-ə   kər -v -ets-av Mari-e -n.*
letter   -the write-v-aor-3s Mari-abl-the
'The letter was written by Mari'.

(17)   *Hartsum-ner-ə   gə   harts-v-in   u   gə*
question -pl -the i:imp ask   -v-un:3pl and i:imp
badasxan-v-in   usutsitš-ner-e   -n.
answer   -v-un:3pl teacher -pl -abl-the
'The questions are asked and are answered by the teachers'.

166 Helen A. Haig

sentences such as (5)–(10) and (12′)–(15′) do not:

(18) *Vartan-ə hak -v-ets -av ir hayr -e -n.
Vartan-the wear-v -aor-3s his father-abl-the
*'Vartran dressed by his father'.

(19) *Hovanes-ə ləvats-v-ets av hivantabah-e -n.
John -the wash -v-aor-3s nurse -abl-the
*'John washed by the nurse'.

(20) *gə hampur-v-ein zavag-ner-e -n.
i:imp kiss -v-pst:3pl child -pl -abl-the
*'They were kissing by the children'.

(21) *Šakar-ə tšur -i -n metš
sugar -the water-gen-the in
    ludz -v-ets-av Vahe-ye -n.
    dissolve-v-aor-3s Vahe-abl-the
*'The sugar dissolved in the water by Vahe'.

(22) *Geragur-ə yergu or aveli gə bah -v-i
food -the two days more i:imp keep-v-un:3s
    Giletsa-ye -n.
    Grace -abl-the
*'The food will keep for two more days by Grace'.

Evidence for the nontransitive status of active verbs marked with -v- lies in the fact that they cannot cooccur with formally distinct objects even when those objects are realized only as reflexive or reciprocal pronouns. Reflexive constructions are illustrated in the following two sentences (reflexive pronoun in boldface italic).

(23) Hovanes-ə iŋkziŋkə zarg -av.
John -the himself hit-aor-3s
'John hit himself'.
(24) Meŋk iŋkziŋknis bašdban-ets -iŋk.
we ourselves defend -aor-1pl
'We defended ourselves'.

The unacceptability of verb stems marked with -v- occurring with re- flexive objects is illustrated in (25)–(26):

(25) Hovanes-ə iŋkziŋkə {*ləvatsvetsav / ləv -ats}.
John -the himself wash-aor:3s
'John washed himself'.

(26)   *Hovanes-ə   iŋkziŋkə*   { *poxvetsav* } .
                                 { pox   -ets }
        John   -the himself   change-aor:3s
        'John changed himself'.

Similarly, reciprocal pronoun objects, as in:

(27)   ***Zirar***   *g*   *ampasdan-en*.
        each:other:acc i:imp accuse   -un:3pl
        'They accuse each other'.

(28)   ***Iraru***   *gə*   *naxants-in*.
        each:other:gen i:imp envy   -un:3pl
        'They envy each other'.

cooccur only with verb stems that are active and transitive in form, as
is illustrated in the following.

(29)   ***Zirar***   { *gə   hampurvein* } .
                        { gə   hampur-ein }
        each:other   i:imp kiss   -pst:3pl
        'They were kissing each other'.

(30)   ***Zirar***   { *gə   voɣtšakurvin* } .
                        { gə   voɣtšakur-en }
        each:other   i:imp embrace -un:3pl
        'They are embracing each other'.

3. PASSIVE AND VERB FORMS WITH LOW TRANSITIVITY

The morphological correlation between intransitivity and passivization
carries certain implications for passives. Given that -*v*- plays a detransitivizing function in terms of verbal valency, one might expect the -*v*-
to have a similar function in passive constructions. In fact, examination
of data shows that passive constructions tend to be lower in transitivity
than actives. This relative low transitivity of passives is evidenced by
several facts.

One such fact is that a greater percentage of passives than actives are
in low transitivity verb forms, as was borne out by a study of the distribution of verb forms in narrative texts (short stories, the combined
length of which was roughly 7000 words). High transitivity forms include
verbs marked for perfective aspect (aorists), volitional–manipulative
forms (imperatives), and verbs in the volitional–certainty mode. Low

transitivity forms include verbs overtly marked for imperfective aspect
(past imperfects and tense-unspecified forms), participle/'be' constructions that include resultative and stative verbs such as the perfect or past
perfect (which, as Hopper and Thompson indicate, are traditionally recognized as low transitivity forms), and participles that function as predicate adjectives in copular stative constructions. Also included with low
transitivity forms are participles in participial clauses, and verbs in the
irrealis mode (subjunctives).

   The specific results of the text count of the distribution of actives and
passives with respect to transitivity of verb forms are presented in what
follows. For each verbal construction the following two questions are
examined: What percentage of the total number of actives occur in that
verb form, and what percentage of the total number of passives? The
two percentages are then compared. As will be shown, 90% of the passives occur in low transitivity forms with 10% in high transitivity forms.
The situation differs significantly for the actives, which are evenly divided
between high and low transitivity forms.

   First, however, the following chart is presented to show the distribution
of the total number of verb forms counted. (Actives and passives occur
at a ratio of 18 actives for every 1 passive.)

(31)   TOTAL NUMBER OF VERB FORMS COUNTED: 1328[4]

High transitivity forms			Low transitivity forms		
	N	%		N	%
Imperatives	72	5	Imperfectives	464	35
Volitional–certainty	38	3	Perfects	50	4
Aorists	523	40	Copular constructions	32	2
			Participial clauses	19	1
			Participial adjectives	22	2
			Subjunctives	108	8
Total	633	48		695	52

   As has been mentioned, three high transitivity verb forms occur in the
narrative texts studied: imperatives, volitional–certainty forms, and
aorists. Imperatives in MWA are formally distinguished with unique
conjugational endings (and, in irregular verbs, special stem forms). In
the texts counted, there are 72 imperatives, all of which occur within
dialogue, none of which utilizes detransitivizing morphology. In fact, the

---

[4] No tokens in the text count were counted in the more than one category.

grammar of MWA does not allow imperatives to take a -v- at all. Examples of imperatives are given in (32)–(33):

(32) *Kən-a   gantš-e   z -anoŋk.*
      go -imprtv:2s call -imprtv:2s acc-they
      'Go call them'.

(33) *Yert-aŋk   uriš anasun-i   mə hartsən-eŋk.*
      go -imprtv:1pl other animal -dat a   ask   -imprtv:1pl
      'Let us go ask another animal'.

Another high transitivity form, volitional–certainty verbs, resemble imperatives in that they occur only with actives in the texts examined for this study. In contrast to imperatives, however, volitional–certainty forms *can* occur with the -v- morphology, in accordance with the grammar of MWA. Volitional–certainty forms constitute 3% (38 out of 1258) of the total number of actives. Examples include:

(34) *Hosgits bidi tš -ell -em.*
      from:here v:c neg-lcave-un:1s
      'I absolutely refuse to leave here'.

(35) *Yes polor harvadz-ner-ə   verin harg -i -n*
      I   all   blow   -pl -the above story-dat-the
      bidi de yavor-em.
      v:c place -un:1s
      'I intend to place all blows to the upper part (of your body)'.
      (one man speaking to another right before a fist fight)

Aorists, the third of the high transitivity forms, are unlike imperatives and volitional–certainty forms in that they do occur with passives in the texts examined, although the incidence of passive aorists is relatively low. Of the active forms, 41% (517 out of 1258) are aorist, whereas only 10% (7 out of 70) of the passives are. Even more striking, however, is the fact that 99% of all the aorists themselves are active. The following are examples of active aorists:

(36) *Džampa-n hantib-ets -av iži   mə.*
      road   -the meet -aor-3s viper a
      'On the road he came upon a viper'.

(37) *Kəlx-u -n metš ir tuyn -ə ver   -ats.*
      head-gen-the in its poison-the boil:aor-3s
      'Its poison boiled in its head'.

Examples of passive aorists include:

(38)   *Nepukotosor   kən   -ats Dadzar-ə   urge*
        Nebuchadnezzar go:aor-3s   temple -the from:where
        aratšnort-v-ets -av kahana-ner-u   -n   pənagaran-ə.
        directed -v-aor-3s priest   -pl -dat-the quarters   -the
        'N. went to the temple from where he was directed to the
        priests' quarters'.

(39)   *Kerezman-ə   pag -v-ets -av.*
        tomb   -the seal-v-aor-3s
        'The tomb was sealed'.

For one of the low transitivity forms listed earlier, namely the imperfectives, the percentage of actives occurring remains greater than the
percentage of passives. However, the discrepancy is not as great for
imperfectives as it is for aorists: 23% more of the total number of actives
than passives occur in imperfective forms, whereas 31% more of actives
than passives occur in aorists. In active forms, 36% (455 out of 1258)
are imperfective whereas in passive forms 13% (9 out of 70) are imperfective. Examples of active imperfectives are as follows:

(40)   *Nav-ə   gə   sur -ar   alik -ner-u   vəra-ye -n.*
        boat-the i:imp rush-pst:3s wave-pl -gen over-abl-the
        'The boat was rushing over the waves'.

(41)   *Dzov -ə hezahampur gə   mərmənts-er.*
        ocean the mildly   i:imp murmur -pst:3s
        'The ocean was murmuring mildly'.

Examples of passive imperfectives include:

(42)   *Uriš desag bašdonakər-er-ə   gə   kər -v-ein*
        other kinds document   -pl-the i:imp write-v-pst:3pl
            barsger-e -n.
            Persian-abl-the
        'Other documents {were/used to be} written in Persian'.

(43)   *Yegeyetsagan araroyutyun-ner-ə   gə   gadar -v-ein*
        church   service   -pl -the i:imp conduct-v-pst:3pl
            masnamp huyn masnamp asori   lezu   -ner-ov.
            partly   Greek partly   Assyrian language-pl -inst
        'Church services were conducted partly in Greek and partly in
        Assyrian'.

Low transitivity forms also include constructions that utilize a participle and the verb 'be' (inflected for person, mood, aspect, tense, number,
and person). As is traditionally recognized, participle + 'be' constructions have an indeterminate status as isolated forms in that they may be

interpreted in two ways: as either perfects or copular/predicate adjective constructions (with the adjective phrase realized as a participle).[5] This study will maintain the distinction between the two interpretations as they differ with respect to the distribution ratio of actives to passives.

Several criteria are used here to distinguish perfects from stative copular constructions. The criteria involve syntactic, semantic, and discourse factors. Under some circumstances, the interpretation of the 'be' construction is clear from word ordering. Perfect constructions can occur in certain word order patterns that are not acceptable for stative copular constructions, in which the adjective phrase must precede the verb 'be'. Thus, when a sentence has a participle following 'be', that construction is necessarily perfect, as in:

(44) *Mintšev aysor tš -e*   **han**   *-v-adz votš*
      until   today neg-be:i:imp:un:3s produce-v-pp not
      meg havanagan nəšan.
      one plausible   indication
      'Until today, not a single plausible indication {has been/*is} produced'.

(45) *Təšpaxtapar mintšev hima al   tš -e*
      Unfortunately until   now also neg-be:i:imp:un:3s
      pox   -v-adz.
      change-v-pp
      'Unfortunately, until now it also {has not been/*is not} changed'.

A second criterion for determining interpretation of constructions with 'be' involves the inherent meaning of the verb and the noun phrases in a given sentence. Thus, in Sentence (46) a perfect interpretation would be incoherent.

(46) *Derevazurg yev angentan pər   -v-adz en*
      leafless   and lifeless   spread-v-pp be:i:imp:un:3pl
      ayki-ner-ə   tašd -i   -n   yeres-ə.
      vine-pl -the field -gen-the face -the
      'Leafless and lifeless the vineyards {are/*had been} spread upon the plain'.

---

[5] The indeterminate status of participle + 'be' constructions can be illustrated by the examples of isolated sentences.
  (i) *Tur -ə   goγbə-v- adz er.*
       door-the lock   -v-pp be:i:imp:pst:3s
       'The door {had been/was} locked'.
  (ii) *Geragur-ə   yep -v-adz er.*
       food   -the cook-v-pp be:i:imp:pst:3s
       'The food {had been/was} cooked'.

In Sentence (47), a perfect reading is rendered unacceptable by the generic nature of the statement.

(47)   *Ask   mə daravor gyaŋk-i   -n   badmutyun-ə   **artsanakər***
       nation any century life   -gen-the history   -the record
       -v-adz e   *anor pənig lez*   *-vi -n   metš.*
       -v-pp be:i:imp:un:3s its   native language-gen-the in
       'The history of centuries of life of any nation {is/*has been}
       recorded in its native language'.

Discourse factors serve as an additional criterion for distinguishing between stative copular and perfect 'be' constructions. For example, the overall temporal structure of the discourse can imply a specific interpretation for a given clause. Thus, in (48) the temporal connective *mintšter* 'while' dictates a simultaneous reading between the main and subordinate clauses. A perfect interpretation would be inconsistent with a simultaneity reading. Therefore, the 'be' construction must be classified as stative copular.

(48)   *Yev mintšter gatoɣigosaran-i   senyag-i   -n   metš tər*
       and while   Catholicosate -gen room   -gen-the in   place
       -v-adz er   *ayd veratoɣ -i   -n   anšuntš*
       -v-pp be:i:imp:pst:3s that dignitary-gen-the breathless
       marmin-ə,   aŋge   kitš heru dak vidžapanutyun
       body   -the, from:there little far   hot discussion
       deɣi g   unen-ar.
       place i:imp have -pst:3s
       'And while the breathless body of that dignitary {was/*had
       been} placed in the room of the Catholicosate, a little
       distance away from it, a heated discussion was taking
       place'.

With the above criteria as a basis for distinguishing perfect and copular constructions, the discussion will now focus upon the distribution of actives and passives in those constructions. A greater proportion of the total number of passives than actives occur as perfect and copular adjective phrase constructions. In fact, passives tend to concentrate in those two constructions (42 out of 70). The texts counted reveal 17% (12 out of 70) of passives in perfect forms versus 3% (38 out of 1258) of actives in perfect forms. Even more striking is the discrepancy between passives and actives in copular constructions: The percentage of passives is 27 (19 out of 70), whereas that of actives is only 1 (13 out of 1258). (The reasons for the greater incidence of passives in copular constructions than perfects may lie in the greater stativity—and hence lower transitivity?—of the copular constructions relative to perfects. That explanation will not be pursued here.)

Among the low transitivity forms are found also nonfinite clauses with a participle as the main verb. Both active and passive participial clauses function as adverbial clauses or relative clauses. As text counts show, 10% (7 out of 70) of passives occur in participial clauses whereas only 1% (12 out of 1258) of actives do. Sentence (49) exemplifies active participial clauses, Sentence (50) passive participial clauses:

(49)   *Payts ter votk-ə   ners tšə -tər -adz, gaŋk*
         but   yet foot-the in   neg-put-pp, stop
         ar   -av sarsapahar.
         take:aor-3s in-terror
         'But before setting foot inside, he stopped in terror'.

(50)   *Dzov -ə   gardz   -es   medzadaradz vosgepayl aŋgoyin mən*
         ocean-the think:sb-un:2s large   shining   quilt   a
         er,   harkar -v-adz tsereg-van išxan -i   -n   hamar.
         be:i:imp:pst:3s arrange-v-pp day -gen prince-dat-the for
         'You would think that the ocean was a large shining quilt,
         arranged for the sovereign of day'.

Participles can also be used as adjectives, either with or without -*v*-morphology—although the percentage of passive participial adjectives is greater (13%, 9 out of 70) than the percentage of active participial adjectives (1%, 13 out of 1258). Examples of actives include:

(51)   *Dəxmar pan -ner mi   əs -er, badasxan-ets*
         stupid   thing-pl neg:imprtv say-2s, answer -aor:3s
         neyats -adz Kristos.
         offend-pp Christ
         ' "Don't say stupid things," answered Christ, offended'.

(52)   *Hokn-adz dəya-n   kəna -ts -av.*
         tire -pp boy -the sleep-aor-3s
         'The tired boy fell asleep'.

As can be seen, the adjective + participle typically precedes the noun phrase. Such is the case for passives as well:

(53)   *Porakər-v-adz pazmativ sebakərutyun   -ner ga-n.*
         engrave-v-pp numerous cuneiform writing-pl exist:i:imp-un:3pl
         'There are numerous engraved cuneiform writings'.

Finally, there are subjunctive low transitivity verb forms. The percentages of actives and passives in subjunctives differ by only 2%; that

is, 8% (101 out of 1258) for actives versus 10% (7 out of 70) for passives.
Examples of actives include the following:

(54)   *G   uz -es   vor **votšəntša**   **-tsən -em**   *polor*
        i:imp want-un:2s that annihilate:sb-caus-un:1s all
        hutayasdan-ə.
        Judea   -the
        ' "Do you want me to annihilate all Judea?" '

(55)   *Yete indzi xošor gədor mə banir **da**   -s   kez*
        if   to:me large piece a   cheese give:sb-un:2s you:acc
        g   azad-em.
        i:imp free -un:1s
        ' "If you give me a large piece of cheese, I will free you" '.

Examples of passives include:

(56)   *Vai   te   naxəntats mə əsdeɣdz-v-i.*
        shame that precedent a   set:sb -v-un:3s
        'For shame lest a precedent be set'.

(57)   *Xelatsi ayn e,*   *vor uriš -i   -n*
        wise   that be:i:imp:un:3s who other-gen-the
        *kordz-i   -n tšə -**xarnə**   -**v-i**   -r.*
        work -gen-the neg-mix:up:sb-v-un:3s-neg
        'Wise is he who does not get mixed up in someone else's
        business'.

The following chart summarizes the distribution of actives and passives.

(58)   DISTRIBUTION OF ACTIVES AND PASSIVES

	Total		Active		Passive	
	N	%	N	%	N	%
Imperatives	72	5	72	5		
Volitional–certainty	38	3	38	3		
Aorists	523	40	516	41	7	10
Imperfectives	464	35	455	36	9	13
Perfects	50	4	38	3	12	17
Copular constructions	32	2	13	1	19	27
Participial clauses	19	1	12	1	7	10
Participial adjectives	22	2	13	1	9	13
Subjunctives	108	8	101	8	7	10

4. CONCLUSION

As can be seen from the data presented in this paper, a greater percentage of passives than actives occur in verb forms that involve features of low transitivity such as imperfective aspect, stativity, and irrealis mode. Conversely, actives have a greater tendency than passives to occur in contexts having features of high transitivity such as volitionality and perfective aspect. The demonstrated low transitivity of passives is consistent with the morphological correlation between passivization and intransitive marking of verb stems. The consistency of this correlation is underscored by the fact that in all the passives counted, not one token had an expressed agent. Thus, the passive, like the intransitive, is essentially a one-argument construction in MWA.

Whether the correlation is one holding between two productive processes or between a productive process (passivization) and frozen derivational morphology is not entirely clear. It is not clear on the basis of present research whether the verbs that take intransitive marking are predictable. Nevertheless, certain conclusions are suggested by the correlation: The morpheme -v- in MWA is a detransitivizing marker and it reflects a relationship between intransitivity and passivization.

REFERENCES

Andonian, H. (1966) *Modern Armenian*, Armenian General Benevolent Union, New York.
Haig, H. (1980) "Verbal Morphology of Modern Western Armenian," unpublished paper, University of California, Los Angeles.
Hopper, P. and S. Thompson (1980) "Transitivity in Grammar and Discourse," *Language* 56, 251–299.
Kogian, Fr. S. L. (1949) *Armenian Grammar (West Dialect)*, Mechitarist Press, Vienna.

APPENDIX: ABBREVIATIONS

Abbreviation	Meaning	Introduced
abl	Ablative	p. 165
acc	Accusative	p. 167
aor	Aorist	p. 162
caus	Causative	p. 174
dat	Dative	p. 169
gen	Genitive	p. 163
i	Indicative	p. 162

APPENDIX *(continued)*

Abbreviation	Meaning	Introduced
imp	Imperfective	p. 162
imprtv	Imperative	p. 169
ins	Instrumental	p. 170
intr	Intransitive	p. 164
MWA	Modern Western Armenian	p. 161
neg	Negative	p. 169
pl	Plural	p. 162
pp	Past participle	p. 171
pst	Past	p. 163
psv	Passive voice	p. 162
s	Singular	p. 162
sb	Subjunctive mood	p. 173
un	Unmarked for tense	p. 162
v	The *-v-* morpheme	p. 163
v:c	Volitional/certainty mood	p. 169
1	First person	p. 166
2	Second person	p. 169
3	Third person	p. 162

HIGH TRANSITIVITY IN HUA

JOHN HAIMAN

This essay will focus on the meaning of an auxiliary verb in Hua, a Papuan language of the Eastern Highlands of New Guinea. The verb in question is *to-,* which occurs independently with the meanings 'leave, place, put'. Cognates with much the same distribution are attested in many of the neighboring languages—both of the East-Central family and of the Eastern family—of the New Guinea Highlands stock.[1] Move *to-* (Renck 1975:141–144), Fore *'ta-* (Scott 1978:112), Asaro *-d-* (Strange 1973:89), Gahuku *T ~ (m)* (Deibler 1976:19), Bena-bena *to-* (Young 1971:76), Gimi *ata-,* and Siane *edo-,* from the East-Central family, and Awa *-t-* (Loving and McKaughan 1973:47) and Tairora *-te-* (Vincent 1973:583), from the Eastern family, are the documented parallels.

With the exception of Renck, who identifies a number of functions for Move *to-,* and Deibler, who recognizes two for Gahuku *T,* the authorities I have cited agree that the lexeme under discussion is a "benefactive verb," its only function being to allow the expression of a beneficiary of the preceding conjoined "main verb." The beneficiary object in all

---

[1] Genetic affiliations of languages cited are as ascribed in Wurm (1975).

177

Syntax and Semantics, Volume 15

cases is expressed as a direct object pronominal prefix on the auxiliary TO verb.

Thus Scott (1978:112) for Fore:

(1)   *Nae-' -ti mae-wae-na   -'ta -ye*
        1sg -obl-to get -all -1sg-obj-TO-3sg-ind
        'He gets it all **for me**'.

Strange (1973:89), for Asaro:

(2)   *Nasu'-ma kele   ne   -d -ezo.*
        arrow -the extract 1sg-obj-TO-imp-sg
        'Pull out the arrow **for me**'.

Young (1971:16), for Bena-bena:

(3)   *Hu ke   -to -'ohube.*
        do 2sg-obj-TO-1sg-ind
        'I did it **for you**'.

Loving and McKaughan (1973:47) for Awa:

(4)   *Nene poedah wega kabada nin   -t -eh'.*
        my pig   he   seek 1sg-obj-TO-3sg-ind
        'He searched for my pig **for me**'.

Vincent (1973:583), for Tairora:

(5)   *Rumpa ti   -mi -te -ro*
        tie   1sg-obj-give-TO-3sg-ind
        'He tied it **for me**'.

My own fieldwork on Hua, Gimi, and Siane, together with the observations of Renck on Move and Deibler on Gahuku, suggest to me that *TO* is associated with a much greater variety of functions.

Nevertheless, the data assembled in what follows are all from Hua, and the claims that are made for Hua *to-* are made with total confidence for only two other cognate morphemes: Gimi *ata-* and Siane *edo-*.

My contention is that the *to-* auxiliary verb is employed under the following conditions, which define its meaning:

(6)   a.   The main verb involves at least two participants
        b.   The object of the verb is human
        c.   The object is distinct from the subject
        d.   The main verb without the *to-* auxiliary is either
             intransitive or, if transitive, occurs with nonhuman
             objects

The next section will provide the indispensable minimum information on the syntax of what I will call "*to*- support." The section following that will provide the data to substantiate the claim made in (6) about its function in Hua, and identify the common denominator of (6a)–(6d).

1. THE SYNTAX OF "*TO*- SUPPORT"

A verb complex in Hua consists of the following elements:

(7)   (negative) (object prefix) stem (personal desinences)

The stem, in turn, may consist of several elements:

(8)   root (aspectual auxiliaries) (future auxiliary)

When two clauses are conjoined, the verb of the first will occur in a "medial form" (Pilhofer 1933), distinct from the "final form" of the second. Medial clauses, like subordinate clauses in more familiar languages, are thus unable to stand as complete utterances. Final clauses, like principal clauses, are identical with complete utterances.

Where the subject of the medial verb is identical with that of the following verb, the medial verb will occur in one form, the "like-subject medial," or LSM. Otherwise, the medial verb will occur in another form, the "changed-subject medial," or CSM.

All medial verbs, whether LSM or CSM, will have as their final morpheme a personal desinence (actually a pronoun), which agrees in person and number with the subject of the following verb. This desinence, the "anticipatory ending," will be denoted by the letter A.

The major morphological difference between LSM and CSM relates to the presence or absence of the immediately preceding personal desinence, the "medial ending" M, which agrees in person and number with the subject of the medial verb itself. Predictably, CSMs include such a desinence, and LSMs do not:[2]

(9)   CSM = stem + M + A
        LSM = stem + $\emptyset$ + A

A further difference between LSM and CSM occurs in the stem itself. Although both LSM and CSM must agree in tense with the following verb, LSM may not carry any overt tense auxiliary at all; CSM, in

---

[2] This account, which I have elsewhere dubbed "the naive theory" (Haiman 1980b), disregards certain complications which are irrelevant to the present analysis.

contradistinction, must occur with the future auxiliary in future tense, and without this auxiliary in the nonfuture:

(10)   CSM stem = root (aspectual auxiliaries) (tense auxiliary)
       LSM stem = root (aspectual auxiliaries)

Now, the supporting verb *to-* in Hua is not an auxiliary verb in surface structure, but one that is conjoined, by the medial verb construction, with the preceding "main verb." This preceding main verb is an LSM which occurs with only one affix, the anticipatory desinence A. All other affixes, including the prefixes and suffixes on the stem enumerated in (7), and the auxiliary verbs which follow the root in (8), occur as prefixes and suffixes on the supporting verb *to-*.

If *to-* support is viewed as a transformation applying under as yet unspecified semantic conditions, then the structural description and structural change of the rule may be represented informally as follows:

(11)   prefixes root auxiliaries desinences $\Rightarrow [2 + A]_{LSM} 1 + to + 3 + 4$
          1   2   3   4

In Haiman (1980a), I claimed that a transformation like (11) actually existed. I am no longer sure of this, and (11) is repeated here as a convenient mnemonic device for representing the distribution of affixes on verbs with and without the supporting verb *to-*. By way of illustration, I offer several minimally contrasting pairs in what follows. The main verb is *vo-* 'lie down, sleep'; with *to-* support, *vo+A to-* means 'lay down, put to sleep'. Note that *vo-*, an intransitive verb, can occur with any verbal affixes but the object prefixes, while the corresponding transitive verb *vo+A to-* occurs with all possible verbal affixes. Note also that all the affixes occurring with the intransitive *vo-* occur (as does the object prefix) on the support verb of its transitive congener.[3]

(12)   a.   *Vo -e.*
            sleep-1sg-ind
            'I slept'.
       b.   *Vo -da   ∅   -to -e.*
            sleep-1sg-A 3sg-obj-TO-1sg-ind
            'I put him to sleep'.

(13)   a.   *ʔA'-vo -gu   -e.*
            neg-sleep-future-1sg-ind
            'I will not sleep'.

---

[3] It is uncertain whether the main verb [(2) in the structural description given in (11)] ever actually occurs with the pronoun object prefix that surfaces on the supporting verb *to-*.

(13)　b.　*Vo -da   ʔa' -∅   -to -gu   -e.*
　　　　　sleep-1sg-A neg-3sg-obj-TO-future-1sg-ind
　　　　　'I will not put him to sleep'.

(14)　a.　*Ve -su -ga   -ka*
　　　　　sleep-fut-1sg-M-2sg-A
　　　　　'I will sleep and you will . . .'
　　　b.　*Vo -da   k   -te -su -ga   -ka*
　　　　　sleep-1sg-A 2sg-obj-TO-fut-1sg-M-2sg-A
　　　　　'I will put you to sleep and you will . . .'

(15)　a.　*Vo -bai -su -mamo*
　　　　　sleep-prog-fut-1sg-conditional
　　　　　'If I will be sleeping . . .'
　　　b.　*Vo -da   ∅   -to -bai -su -mamo*
　　　　　sleep-1sg-A 3sg-obj-TO-prog-fut-1sg-conditional
　　　　　'If I will be putting him to sleep . . .'

There is no space nor need to review here the extensive morphological and syntactic evidence that the LSM (indeed, the entire medial clause) is a surface structure *nominalization,* nor the equally cogent, though less direct, evidence that at a deeper level medial clauses are *conjoined* with the clauses that they precede (see Haiman 1977, 1980a). But there is some interest in noting the propensity for coordination, where other more familiar languages use compounding or complementation.

It is clear from the immediately preceding examples that *to-* may function simply as a causative morpheme. We are accustomed to see such morphemes surface either as verbal affixes, perhaps auxiliary verbs, or as higher verbs with the intransitive clause as their object complement. Thus, in Comrie (1976:262), to cite but one familiar example, the latter structure is viewed as the underlying structure from which, in different languages, the former may be derived by a transformation of verb raising.

In expressing the causative morpheme as a conjoined verb, Hua is at variance with a very widespread pattern. In part, I believe that this divergence is very deep: Like many other Papuan languages with medial verb constructions, Hua seems to eschew complementation in subject or object position.[4] But in another respect, the divergence is comparatively superficial. As specified in (8) and exemplified in (13)–(15), Hua does have auxiliary verbs; and I contend that the difference between *to-*

---

[4] But not elsewhere—complements in oblique cases abound, as do complement clauses in the nominative and ergative absolute constructions. Nominative absolute constructions are conditionals; ergative absolute constructions are cause clauses whose results follow independently of human agency or volition.

and a surface structure auxiliary is generally minimal, and in some cases, nonexistent.

The only morphological distinction between Verb + A *to-* and Verb + Auxiliary in Hua are the following: (*a*) *to-*, unlike auxiliary verbs in general, may occur with prefixes; and (*b*) the preceding main verb, unlike verbs followed by a true auxiliary, may occur with a single personal desinence, the anticipatory pronoun A. Thus, for example, (16) contrasts, in the presence of the boldface morphemes, with (17).

(16)   *Vo* **-na** **d**   *-te -e.*
        sleep-3sg-A 1sg-obj-TO-3sg-ind
        'He put me to sleep'.

(17)   *Vo* ∅ ∅ *re -e.*
        sleep   perf-3sg-ind
        'He has slept'.

Note, however, that the verbal prefixes on *to-* need not occur, or are phonologically null, when the verb is not negated (i.e., the negative suffix *ʔa'-* does not appear) and the object is 3sg (i.e., the object prefix is ∅).

When there are no prefixes on *to-*, the anticipatory desinence on the preceding main verb is optional. Thus (18a) alternates with the apparently synonymous (18b).

(18)   a. *Vo* -na ∅   *-te -e.*
            sleep-3sg-A 3sg-obj-TO-3sg-ind
            'He put her to sleep'.

        b. *Vo* ∅ ∅   *-te -e.*
            sleep 3sg-obj-TO-3sg-ind
            'He put her to sleep'.

The latter is morphologically indistinguishable from (17), a Verb + Auxiliary construction.

I think it is likely that *to-* is on the way to becoming a true auxiliary in Hua—and I also think it possible that many of the presentday auxiliaries in Hua may have gone through a stage comparable to that exhibited now by *to-*.[5]

2. THE FUNCTION OF *"TO-* SUPPORT"

In our survey of the various meanings of the verb *to-* we will do well to begin with its most obvious, and already illustrated function—that of

[5] There is some syntactic evidence as well that no clause boundary exists in surface structure between V and *to-*. It should be noted in particular that the "NP ecology constraint" cited as (52) in what follows presupposes the absence of such a boundary.

converting intransitive verbs to the corresponding transitives or causatives.

Verbs in Hua are not generally marked for transitivity. There are, of course, transitive verbs like *do-* 'eat', *bro-* 'put', and *Ko-* 'look at, see', which have no intransitive congeners. There are also intransitive verbs like *fri-* 'die', whose causative counterparts are suppletive. But together with these there are a truly enormous number of verbs like English *break*, which can be interpreted as either transitive or intransitive depending on the way in which they are used. The following represents a small illustrative sample of such verbs (all in the third person singular form):

			Intransitive	Transitive
(19)	a.	*Aipahie.*	'It began'.	'He began it'.
	b.	*Bkaie.*	'He drowned'.	'He swallowed it'.
	c.	*Buhie.*	'It burst out'.	'He released it'.
	d.	*Frufie.*	'He came out'.	'He removed it'.
	e.	*Furete.*	'He was born'.	'He found it'.
	f.	*Hakrie.*	'He hid'.	'He hid it'.
	g.	*Hatgie.*	'It ended'.	'He ended it'.
	h.	*Hefie.*	'It broke'.	'He broke it'.
	i.	*Tgie.*	'It split'.	'He split it'.

My concern here is to show when these and other verbs take *to-* support to become transitive.

It is clear from (19) that *to-* support is not required merely when a verb has an object. It *is* required, however, when the object is human. Thus, the following contrasts:

(20)	a.	*Aipahie.*	'He made it begin'.
	b.	*Aipahuna te.*[6]	'He made her begin'.

(21)	a.	*Frufie.*	'He removed it'.
	b.	*Frufuna te.*	'He removed her'.

(22)	a.	*Hakrie.*	'He hid it'.
	b.	*Hakrina te.*	'He hid her'.

(23)	a.	*Buhie.*	'He released it'.
	b.	*Buhuna te.*	'He released him (from fasting obligations)'.

Similar contrasts can be observed in the case of verbs that are unambiguously transitive but allow either human or nonhuman objects:

---

[6] The interlinear glosses give underlying forms which differ from the phonemic representations in sentences like (20)–(26). For example, *te + e* surfaces as /te/, etc.

For that matter, the interlinears also disregard certain irrelevant complications, especially in the matter of verb agreement and object pronoun infixation in one class of verbs.

(24)   a.   *Iroe.*   'I left it'.
        b.   *Iroda toe.*   'I left him'.

(25)   a.   *Bi'aine.*   'You squashed it'.
        b.   *Bi'aika tane.*   'You put him down'. (metaphorically)

(26)   a.   *Broe.*   'I put it down'.
        b.   *Broda ktoe.*   'I put you down'. (physically)

Finally, there are a number of verbs which, if transitive, require human objects and thus invariably occur with *to-* support whenever they are used transitively. Among them are *vo-* 'sleep', familiar from Examples (12)–(18), and *ho-* 'get stuck', whose transitive congener means 'fuck'.

It may be appropriate to digress for a moment on the subject of verbs of motion—of all intransitive verbs, surely the most common. In a number of publications, it has been accepted that the causative corresponding to *come* is *bring* (cf. Binnick 1971). Yet there is a fundamental difference between the purely causative notion 'make come' and what I will call the pseudocausative notion 'bring': In the first case, the causer is himself unmoved, whereas in the second he not only causes someone else to come, but also comes himself. This difference is reflected in Hua (as, of course, it is in English), in the following way.

The pseudocausative verbs *bring, take* and their like are rendered in Hua by a verbal compound consisting of the transitive verb *ri-* 'hold, take' (which occurs as an LSM) and the appropriate verb of motion *o-* 'come', *vu-* 'go', *ormi-* 'come down', *ha + vu-* 'go up', etc. The true causative verbs are rendered, as are the other transitive verbs discussed in this section, by the use of *to-* supporting the preceding verb of motion. Thus the typical contrast:

(27)   a.   *Ri -na   havi -e.*
             take-3sg-A go up-3sg-ind
             'He took it up'.
        b.   *Hau -na   te -e.*
             go up-3sg-A TO-3sg-ind
             'He made him go up'.

Sentences like (27b), which suggest direct physical coercion, are rather infrequent. For less direct causation, and notions corresponding to English *send* and *summon,* Hua has the monolexemic (and suppletive) transitive verbs *havai-* 'send', and *vzguhu-* 'pull, invite, summon'.

A special class of intransitive verbs are those which correspond to English reflexives of a certain type. No distinction is made in much of the generative literature between reflexives exemplified by the following two sentences:

(28)   a. *I washed myself.*
        b. *I kicked myself.*

There is a significant basis even in English, however, for distinguishing
between them. In sentences like (28a), as is well known, the reflexive
pronoun is optional, and generally redundant. The basis for this distinction, I contend, is that for a class of predicates, including *wash* and many
others, the object, *in the unmarked case,* is identical with the subject.
The absence of the reflexive pronoun object in sentences like *I washed*
is thus motivated in the sense that an unmarked grammatical form corresponds to an unmarked state of affairs. The mild deviance of (28a)
derives from the fact that a marked grammatical form—the presence of
the reflexive pronoun—corresponds to an unmarked state of affairs.
Matters are different in sentences like (28b), where the reflexive pronoun
is indispensable. This is because for verbs like *kick,* the object, in the
unmarked case, is *distinct* from the subject. Here it is the presence of
the reflexive pronoun object which is grammatically iconic (cf. Haiman
1980b) insofar as the marked grammatical form corresponds to a marked
state of affairs.

Verbs like *wash,* whose objects are typically identical with their subjects, I will call introverted verbs; verbs like *kick,* whose objects in the
unmarked case are distinct from their subjects, I will call extroverted
verbs. It is of course possible that the class of verbs identifiable as
introverted or extroverted on the basis of language-specific operational
criteria (such as the optionality of a reflexive pronoun object in English)
may also be language specific. But I suspect that whatever the language-
specific criterion that allows a distinction to be made, the class of introverted verbs in all languages will have many of the same members:
verbs of grooming, motion, and change of posture. Thus, in English,
reflexive pronoun objects are redundant, or even deviant, with verbs of
grooming like *wash, shave,* and *dress,* and verbs of posture like *sit down*
and *stand up.* And in Hua, where the criterion for distinguishing between
introverted and extroverted verbs is entirely different, verbs will align
themselves in these two classes in much the same way as in English.

The possibility does not even exist in Hua of confusing sentences like
(28a) and (28b), the superficial syntax of introverted and extroverted
verbs being entirely distinct.

For extroverted verbs like *Ko-* 'see, look at' whose human objects are
typically not identical with their subjects, the reflexive object pronoun,
as in English, is identical with the emphatic pronoun, which is marked
by definition. A marked form of the object nominal expression thus
corresponds to the marked state of affairs. Compare the unmarked (29),

whose object pronoun *dgaimo*, like all unstressed pronouns, is generally dropped after verb–object agreement copies the prefix on to the transitive verb, with the marked (30), whose object pronoun *dgaidimo*, iconically emphasized by the simple repetition of the 1sg morpheme *d-*, can never be deleted.

(29)   *(Dgaimo) d   -ga -ne.*
        Me   1sg-obj-see-2sg-ind
        'You saw me'.

(30)   *Dgai -di   -mo d   -go -e.*
        Me -myself   1sg-obj-see-1sg-ind
        'I saw myself'.

For introverted verbs whose human objects are typically identical with their subjects, the only structure available in Hua is one in which they are treated as intransitives. It is possible to say, literally, 'I washed', but it is impossible to say 'I washed myself'. Verbs in this category include not only *auva zo-* 'wash body', but also *ható-* 'scratch', *mna-getagefu-* 'look for lice', *meso kki-* 'shave beard', *frava fro-* 'smear grease', *ku' vai-* 'put on clothes', *kai egi-* 'take off skirt', *ekeni vai-* 'bejewel, adorn', *rgino-* 'turn around', *fitobai-* 'sit down', *ehi-* 'stand up', and many others. Sentences like (31) are typical in that (as in English) an unmarked grammatical structure corresponds to an unmarked state of affairs.

(31)   *Ehi   -e.*
        stand-up-3sg-ind
        'He stood up'.

The marked state of affairs with introverted verbs is that in which the human object is distinct from the subject, and corresponding to this marked state of affairs is the marked construction with *to-*. It will be seen from a consideration of the following sentence pairs that *to-* support is available to mark transitive verbs *only when the objects of these verbs are distinct from their subjects:*

(32)   a. *Ehie.*   'He stood up'.
        b. *Ehina te.*   'He stood her up'.

(33)   a. *Ekenimo vaie.*   'He put jewelry on (himself)'.
        b. *Ekenimo vaina te.*   'He put jewelry on (another)'.

(34)   a. *Dmeso kkue.*   'I shaved my beard'.
        b. *Dmeso kkina dte.*   'He shaved my beard'.

(35)   a.   *Frava frone.*   'We smeared mud on (ourselves)'.
       b.   *Frava frota ptone.*   'We smeared mud on them'.

(36)   a.   *Auva ze.*   'She washed'.
       b.   *Auva zona te.*   'She washed him'.

(37)   a.   *Mnagetagefie.*   'He looked for lice (on himself)'.
       b.   *Mnagetagefuna te.*   'He looked for lice (on another)'.

To drive this point home, we should also note that Hua has a large class of impersonal transitive predicates (comparable to M.E. *(me)thinks,* German *(mich) ekelt* 'I am nauseated', or Russian *(mne)xolodno* 'I am cold'). The subject of such verbs does not exist, and is thus presumably a fortiori not distinguished from the object. The *to-* construction is impossible for the Hua analogs of such impersonal verbs, most of which are compounds of the form root + *hau-* 'affect'. The object surfaces as a pronominal object prefix on *hau-*, which very likely is an alternant of the prototypical transitive verb *hu-* 'do'. It is even possible to construct slightly odd but acceptable minimal contrast pairs that illustrate the distinction between *to-* transitives and impersonal transitives:

(38)   a.   *Zasi d   -hai -e.*
            cold 1sg-obj-affect-3sg-ind
            'I am cold'. (impersonal transitive)
       b.   *Zasi hu-na   d   -te -e.*
            cold do-3sg-A 1sg-obj-TO-3sg-ind
            'He made me cold'.

The latter sentence is somewhat odd, but interpretable inasmuch as the subject exposed or forced the patient to expose himself to the wind.

What is shown by (38) is the truth of Condition (6a), which requires that the main verb involve at least two (human) participants. Condition (6c), that the object be distinct from the subject, may be viewed as a special case of Condition (6a), and is illustrated in Sentences (32)–(37).

Up to this point, the examples of the transitivizing function of *to-* have been accounted for by one of two possible statements:

1. *To-* occurs on transitive verbs which otherwise have only nonhuman objects [e.g., (20)–(26)].
2. *To-* occurs on intransitive verbs which otherwise are interpreted as reflexive or middle verbs [e.g., (32)–(37)].

Actually, the transitivizing function of *to-* is somewhat broader, as can be seen from the following pairs:

(39)   a. *Kigihi-e.*
            laugh -3sg-ind
            'He laughed'.
        b. *Kigihu-na   ∅   -te -e.*
            laugh -3sg-A 3sg-obj-TO-3sg-ind
            'He laughed **at him**'.

(40)   a. *Kakorana hi -e.*
            initiation do-3sg-ind
            'He performed the initiation'.
        b. *Kakorana hu -na   p   -te -e.*
            initiation do-3sg-A 3p-obj-TO-3sg-ind
            'He initiated **them**'.

(41)   a. *Rusamo   hi -e.*
            white-magic do-3sg-ind
            'He performed white magic'.
        b. *Rusamo   hu-na   d   -te -e.*
            white-magic do-3sg-A 1sg-obj-TO-3sg-ind
            'He treated **me**'.

The three verbs *kigihu-* 'laugh', *kakorana hu-* 'perform initiation', and *rusamo hu-* 'perform white magic' are neither transitive with nonhuman objects, nor middle (with objects understood to be identical with their subjects). They are transitive verbs whose object must be human, but whose object need not be specified. Where the object is unspecified, they are "undirected transitives" and morphologically indistinguishable from intransitive verbs. When the object, which must be human, is specified, then *to-* support occurs.

The verbs *kakorana hu-* 'initiate', and *rusamo hu-* 'work white curative magic', require human objects. *Kigihu-* 'laugh' does not. It is worth pointing out, once again, that *to-* support occurs only when the object is *human*—as in (20)–(26), but the form of the nonhuman object is not the same as in these earlier sentences. For transitive verbs like *hefu-* 'break', the object occurs in the nominative, or unmarked, case. Pronouns in this case are dropped if object–verb agreement occurs. The verb *kigihu-*, on the other hand, takes objects in the benefactive case, marked by the case affix *-hi'* or *-si'*. Objects in the benefactive case, not normally subject to object–verb agreement, are not dropped:

(42)   *Mabo-si' kigihi -e.*
        that -ben laugh-3sg-ind
        'He laughed at that'.

Now, pronoun objects, including the object pronoun ∅ '3sg', occur only when these objects have human referents. At least in translation (42) is parallel with (39b), differing from it only in that the object in (39b) is human, whereas that of (42) is not. Is it not possible, then, that (39b) is derived by a process of benefactive object–verb agreement and a subsequent deletion of the unstressed benefactive object?

This question brings us finally to the allegedly basic and prototypical function of the *to-* auxiliary: to allow the expression of benefactive objects, as in (1)–(5). I hope by this time to have shown that such is certainly not the *only* function of *to-* in Hua. Nevertheless, it is one of the functions of this verb. In the brief discussion that follows I will show the conditions under which a pronominal prefix on *to-* corresponds to (*a*) a noun phrase in the benefactive case; and (*b*) (what is not the same thing) a noun phrase understood as the beneficiary of the action of the main verb.

To anticipate the conclusions of this discussion, the first correspondence is totally unsystematic, and the second only slightly less so: Whether used as a morphological or syntactico-semantic criterion, the category "benefactive" seems to be incidental, or irrelevant, to the distribution of the verb *to-*.

I shall begin with the possible claim that the object of *to-* represents an expression in the benefactive *case,* as this claim is the easiest to refute. Of the Hua examples considered up to this point, only one, Sentence (39b) is even possible as a candidate. In all other cases, the direct object of *to-* can be expressed only as a nominal expression in the nominative (or absolutive) case. Thus, it clearly cannot be maintained that nouns in the benefactive case represent the *only* possible source for pronominal objects on *to-*.

Nor is it true that all nouns in the benefactive case may surface as pronominal objects on *to-*. There are a number of verbs in Hua which take benefactive government. Among them are *kigihu-* 'laugh at', *korihu-* 'run away from, fear', the impersonal transitive *hau-* 'like', whose experiencer occurs in the absolutive as the direct object prefix, while the "likee" occurs in the benefactive, and a number of others. However, *kigihu-* is the only such verb whose benefactive object may be expressed as a pronominal prefix on a supporting verb *to-*. It is totally impossible, for example, to transform the grammatical sentence (43) into the conjectured sentence (44):

(43) *Kgai -si' korihu -e.*
       you -ben run-away-1sg-ind
       'I ran away from you; I fear you'.

(44)   *Korihu -da   k   -to -e.
         run-away-1sg-A 2sg-obj-TO-1sg-ind

The latter sentence is grammatical only as a causative 'I made you run away' parallel to the causatives with human causees exemplified in (20)–(26).

    Speaking generally, *to*- corresponds to the benefactive case only where the latter is used with benefactive *meaning,* as in sentence (45):

(45)   Kgai-si' zu'   ku -e.
         you -ben house build-1sg-ind
         'I built a house for you'.

This sentence corresponds to a grammatical, though perhaps not entirely synonymous, sentence (46):

(46)   Zu'   ki -da   k   -to -e.
         house build-1sg-A 2sg-obj-TO-1sg-ind
         'I built you a house'.

In (46), finally, we see a sentence parallel to Examples (1)–(5). In this sentence, the object of the verb *to*- *is* unambiguously the beneficiary of the main verb.

    It is the first sentence in which this is true; hence the (semantic) beneficiary is not the *only* category to be expressed in this way.

    It remains to be shown that the circumstances under which a beneficiary *may* be expressed as such an object [i.e., the circumstances under which a sentence like (45) may be transformed into one like (46)] are so limited that the semantic category of "benefactiveness" is at best of merely incidental relevance.

    Any action, whether transitive or intransitive, may be performed for a beneficiary. The normal way to express this beneficiary is by an object in the benefactive case:

(47)   a.   Kgai-si' ai'o   -e.
              you -ben come-up-1sg-ind
              'I came up for you'.   (verb is intransitive)
         b.   Kgai-si' fu ebgu-e.
              you -ben pig kill -1sg-ind
              'I killed the pig for you'.   (verb is intransitive)
         c.   Kgai-si' fu bzamo   mu -e.
              you -ben pig sweet-potato give-1sg-ind
              'I gave the pig sweet potatoes for you'.   (verb is
              ditransitive)

Now, given a verb V, what is the meaning of the corresponding construction V *to-?*

If the verb is intransitive, as in (47a), V *to-* invariably forms the corresponding transitive or causative:

(48)   *Ai'o   -da   k   -to -e.*
        come-up-1sg-A 2sg-obj-TO-1sg-ind
        'I made you come up'.
        *'I came up for you'.

If the verb is ditransitive, as in (47c), *to-* support creates something uninterpretable:

(49)   *Fu bzamo   mi -da   k   -to -e.*
        pig sweet-potato give-1sg-A 2sg-obj-TO-1sg-ind
        *'I gave the pig sweet potatoes for you'.
        *'I made you give sweet potatoes to the pig'.

Only if the verb is transitive does V *to-* correspond to a benefactive construction. Thus, corresponding to (47b), as (45) corresponds to (44), is the following sentence:

(50)   *Fu ebgi-da   k   -to -e.*
        pig kill -1sg-A 2sg-obj-TO-1sg-ind
        'I killed the pig for you'.
        *'I made you kill the pig'.

But even then, the correspondence is not a reliable one, as has already been demonstrated by (24)–(26), or, for that matter, by (32)–(37) or even (39)–(41). In the first class of cases, *to-* support on an unambiguously transitive verb specified merely that the object was human; in the second, that the object was identical with the subject; and in the third, where *to-* support increased the valency of the verb by admitting a third (human) argument, that the action was performed *on* (but not necessarily for the benefit of) someone.

How, then, are the indubitable correspondences (45) to (46), and (47b) to (50), to be explained? My own belief is that nothing more is required than the conditions outlined in (6). If a construction V *to-* must have a human object distinct from its subject, the first logical possibility is that this is the direct object of the verb. If, however, the verb in question already has a specified object, this possibility is not available and the human object will be assigned some other role. This other role, depending on the pragmatics of the verb in question, will frequently be that of the beneficiary of the action. The hierarchical relationship between direct

object and beneficiary roles may be illustrated with the following minimal
contrast pair:

(51)   a. *Iro -da   k   -to -e.*
             leave-1sg-A 2sg-obj-TO-1sg-ind
             'I left you'.
         b. *Bzamo   iro -da   k   -to -e.*
             sweet-potato leave-1sg-A 2sg-obj-TO-1sg-ind
             'I left sweet potatoes for you'.

The main verb *iro-* is unambiguously transitive. In (51a), where no nonhuman direct object is specified, the human object of *to-* is interpreted
as the direct object of *iro-*. In (51b), where the nonhuman direct object
bzamo 'sweet potatoes' is spelled out, the only possible interpretation
for the human object is that of beneficiary.

The fact that sentences like (49), where the V of V *to-* is ditransitive,
are ungrammatical, remains problematical: Why can the object of *to-* in
such cases not be interpreted as the beneficiary? I suggest that the answer
to this question lies in a language-specific "NP ecology constraint" in
Hua, stated as follows:

(52)   A clause may have only one object pronoun expressed as a
         verbal prefix.

The Hua ditransitive verbs *mi-* 'give', *veri-* 'show', and *hafro-* 'snatch
from' all have object prefixes. These correspond to what we would
identify in English as their indirect objects, as it is typically the indirect
object of a ditransitive verb which is human. If these verbs were to occur
with the auxiliary *to-,* which also ocurred with object prefixes, there
would be a violation of (52).

The same constraint rules out *to-* support on ordinary transitive verbs
with human objects expressed as prefixes on those verbs, like *Ko-* 'look
at', *Kovi-* 'carry on one's back', or *ni-* 'bite'. Thus, while it is possible
to say (53) it is not possible, per (52), to say (54):

(53)   *Kgai-si' d   -govi -e.*
         you -ben 1sg-obj-carry-3sg-ind
         'He carried me on his back for you'.

(54)   **D   -govi -na   k   -te -e.*
         1sg-obj-carry-3sg-A 2sg-obj-TO-3sg-ind
         'He carried me on his back for you'.

CONCLUSIONS

Where *to-* takes as its object the second of two arguments in a clause, this argument is invariably interpreted as the direct object of the transitive verb V *to-;* where its object is the third argument, the argument is characteristically, though not always, interpreted as the beneficiary of the transitive verb, if the direct object role is already occupied.

The hierarchical relationship between direct object and beneficiary roles is clearly reminiscent of the celebrated Keenan–Comrie hierarchy (Keenan and Comrie 1977; Comrie 1976). I find this hierarchy relevant, inasmuch as it would be most surprising if the order of preferred interpretations were reversed (benefactive first, direct object second), but it also seems to be of limited usefulness in predicting the meaning of V *to-* verbs, and of their objects.

If it were fully applicable to the present case, the Keenan–Comrie hierarchy would predict that the single argument of a V *to-* verb would be its *subject*. In fact, V *to-* verbs require at least two arguments.

It would also predict that the third argument of a V *to-* verb would be its *indirect object*. In fact, that is one role that the object of *to-* can never play. Where the human object of *to-* is the third argument of the clause in which it appears, this object is either the direct object or the benefactive object, the choice being determined by the pragmatics of the verb.

The properties of *to-* in Hua, and the identification of its object, seem to be most accurately predicted by the conditions enumerated in (6). If it is possible to argue that these conditions share some semantic unity, then the existence of *to-* support in Hua lends some justification to the argument that they are related, and to the more general proposition that where different categories are mapped on to the same linguistic form, then those categories share a common meaning.

In fact, the conditions listed under (6), together with others, are enumerated by Hopper and Thompson (1980) as contributing to "high transitivity," defined as a feature of entire clauses.[7] Transitivity is higher when (*a*) the number of participants is two or more, and (*b*) the object is individuated. The object, in turn, is individuated, when (*a*) it is human, and (*b*) it is distinct from the subject. It is these conditions which are satisfied by (6). I know of no other theory besides that of Hopper and Thompson which claims that they are in any way related. Yet the facts

---

[7] The components contributing to high transitivity are outlined in the Introduction of this volume.

of *to-* support, in suggesting that some relationship exists among them, insofar as isomorphism between form and content is the general rule (cf. Haiman 1980b) may be said to argue, in a small way, for the correctness of that theory.

REFERENCES

Binnick, R. (1971) "Bring and Come," *Linguistic Inquiry* 2, 260–265.

Comrie, B. (1976) "The Syntax of Causative Constructions: Cross-Language Similarities and Divergences," in M. Shibatani, ed., *Syntax and Semantics 6,* Academic Press, New York.

Deibler, E. (1976) *Semantic Relations of Gahuku Verbs,* Publications of the SIL in Linguistics and Related Fields, 48, Norman, Oklahoma.

Haiman, J. (1977) "Connective Particles in Hua: An Essay on the Parts of Speech," *Oceanic Linguistics* 16, 53–107.

Haiman, J. (1980a) *Hua: A Papuan Language of the Eastern Highlands of New Guinea,* Benjamins, Amsterdam, The Netherlands.

Haiman, J. (1980b) "The Iconicity of Grammar: Isomorphism and Motivation," *Language* 56, 515–540.

Hopper, P. and S. Thompson (1980) "Transitivity in Grammar and Discourse," *Language* 56, 251–299.

Keenan, E. and B. Comrie (1977) "Noun Phrase Accessibility and Universal Grammar," *Linguistic Inquiry* 8, 63–100.

Loving, R. and H. McKaughan (1973) "Aawa Verbs, I: The Internal Structure of Independent Verbs," in H. McKaughan, ed., *The Languages of the Eastern Family of the New Guinea Highlands Stock,* University of Washington Press, Seattle.

Pilhofer, G. (1933) "Grammatik der Kâte-Sprache in Neuguinea." Zeitschrift für eingeborenen Sprachen, *Beiheft* 14.

Renck, G. (1975) *A Grammar of Yagaria,* Pacific Linguistics B-40, Department of Linguistics, Research School of Pacific Studies, Australian National University, Canberra.

Scott, G. (1978) *The Fore Language of Papua New Guinea,* Pacific Linguistics B-47, Department of Linguistics, Research School of Pacific Studies, Australian National University, Canberra.

Strange, D. (1973) "Indicative and Subjunctive in Asaro," *Linguistics* 110, 82–98.

Vincent, A. (1973) "Tairora Verb Structure," in H. McKaughan, ed., *The Languages of the Eastern Family of the New Guinea Highlands Stock,* University of Washington Press, Seattle.

Wurm, S., ed. (1975) *Papuan Languages and the New Guinea Linguistic Scene,* Pacific Linguistics C-38, Department of Linguistics, Research School of Pacific Studies, Australian National University, Canberra.

Young, R. (1971) *The Verb in Bena-bena: Its Form and Function,* Pacific Linguistics B-18, Department of Linguistics, Research School of Pacific Studies, Australian National University, Canberra.

ASPECT AND TRANSITIVITY IN (NICOLA LAKE) OKANAGAN

YVONNE M. HÉBERT

This paper discusses the opposition between -*s* and -*n*, which occurs in Okanagan[1] constructions such as:

(1) *C-c'ka-s-t-ín*   *ʕi ʕin-skláw'*.
     perfect-count-*s*-*t*-1sg$_{trans}$ the my-money/beaver
     'I'm actually counting my money'.

(2) *C'ka-n-t -ín*   *ʕi ʕin-skláw'*.
     count-*n*-*t*-1sg$_{trans}$ the my-money/beaver
     'I counted my money'.

Examples such as (1) are felicitous when the speaker is engaged in the activity specified by the verbs, whereas examples such as (2) are felicitous only when the speaker has completed the activity.

Two hypotheses have already been advanced to account for this alternation:

---

[1] Most of the data is from the Nicola Lake dialect of Okanagan, an Interior Salishan language spoken in British Columbia.

Syntax and Semantics, Volume 15

(3)   THE CONTROL HYPOTHESIS (Thompson 1976, 1979, Thompson and
        Thompson, to appear): -n-t marks a control transitive,
        implying control by the subject, agent or implied agent,
        whereas the -s-t marks a causative.

(4)   THE CUSTOMARY INVOLVEMENT HYPOTHESIS (Mattina 1978a,
        1978b): -s-t predicates always imply either purposeful or
        customary involvement on the part of the actor whereas -n-t
        lacks this implication.

In this paper, I will examine these two hypotheses and show that they
are empirically inadequate. I will propose· and support the following
alternate hypothesis:

(5)   THE ASPECT HYPOTHESIS: the -s/-n markers reflect an aspectual
        distinction, indicating imperfective and perfective,
        respectively.

Evidence for the Aspect Hypothesis is based on (a) the distribution
of the prefix c-'present perfect' (PF); (b) the cooccurrence of adverbials
with verbals, which according to Friedrich (1974:S4) is the universal
criterion for aspect; (c) the restrictions on these markers when occurring
with punctual roots; (d) the tendency of passive constructions to be
associated with the completed aspect (i.e., perfect, perfective) (Chung
and Timberlake, to appear); and (e) the cooccurrence of the -n with the
-nú morpheme in constructions where the agentive subject has limited
control over the activity.

Both the Control Hypothesis and the Customary Involvement Hypothesis link their claims to transitivity, specifically to the -t morpheme,
traditionally termed "transitive" in Salishan studies. This link is not
made by the Aspect Hypothesis. Two definitions of transitivity will be
considered. With transitivity defined as the structure between a predicate
and its arguments, I will show that the -t morpheme occurs in constructions that are not transitive. With transitivity in its traditional understanding defined globally over a clause, I will show that this -t ranks
high in transitivity as a scalar value, following from the Transitivity
Hypothesis proposed by Hopper and Thompson (1980).

This paper adresses the following questions:

1. What is the criterion for the identification of aspect?
2. How is transitivity to be defined; is it marked in this language and,
   if so, at what level?
3. What link, if any, is there between aspect and transitivity?

A word about morphology and terminology is in order. There are three
sets of subject pronominals in Okanagan. In this paper, I will follow the

Salishan terminological practice with respect to them. One set, termed TRANSITIVE, which cooccurs with the -s/-n morphemes, is suffixed after -t, onto predicates in the active voice having at least two distinct surface arguments, regardless of whether or not a nominal subject is specified. A second set, subject pronominal clitics, occurs in reflexives, reciprocals, intransitives, and in the middle voice; this set has been termed INTRANSITIVE. The third set of pronominals is the genitive set, used as subject in clauses in the subjunctive mood.

1. THE ASPECT HYPOTHESIS

Before proceeding to the syntactic evidence to support this hypothesis, let us explore briefly the two aspectual categories of imperfective and perfective: their universality, their characteristics, and their definition.

That Okanagan may encode this distinction is not unusual when we consider languages more generally. These two aspect categories, along with a third, were proposed by Friedrich (1974:S36) for the analysis of aspect systems. The morphology of, for example, Russian, encodes the two basic aspect categories of imperfective–perfective, each of which includes a number of semantic features not otherwise distinctively marked (cf. Timberlake 1979 for a discussion). Hopper (1977–1978, 1979a) notes the universality of this aspectual distinction and its basis in discourse.

According to Comrie (1976), the concept of imperfectivity may be characterized as expressing a continuous or durative situation as well as a habitual or customary situation, occurring over an extended period of time, whereas perfectivity may be characterized as indicating completed action, as being a resultative, that is, indicating the successful completion of a situation. Perfectivity includes but is not limited to punctual or instantaneous situations, to situations of short as opposed to long duration, or to the termination or beginning of a situation, as the perfective denotes a complete situation, with beginning, middle, and end. Comrie makes the following distinction between these concepts, in addition to citing the characteristics listed above: "Perfectivity indicates the view of a situation as a single whole, without distinction of the various separate phases that make up that situation; while the imperfective pays essential attention to the internal structure of the situation (1976:16)." Both the lists of characteristic semantic features of these two aspectual categories and the distinction between an external view of a situation for perfectivity versus an internal view for imperfectivity are relevant to the discussion of the three hypotheses for -s/-n in Okanagan.

Let us now proceed to the syntactic evidence for the Aspect Hypothesis:
1. The prefix c-, 'present perfect' (PF), used to express a relation between a present state and a past event may cooccur with the $-s$ marker:[2]

(6)   *C-c'ka-s-t-ín   ʕi ʕin-skláw'.*
         PF-count-s-t-1sg$_{trans}$ the my-money/beaver
         'I'm actually counting my money'.

However, the cooccurrence of c- and $-n$ results in ungrammaticality:

(7)   **C-c'ka-n-t-ín   ʕi ʕin-skláw'.*
         PF-count-n-t-1sg$_{trans}$ the my-money/beaver

The tc- prefix has broader usage and may occur in the middle voice:

(8)   *Kn   c-c'k-ám   ʕapəna ʔ.*
         1sg$_{intr}$ PF-count-middle now/today
         'I actually count now'.

Examples such as (6), with the $-s$ marker, in the active voice, refer to activity that has been going on for a long time, whereas examples such as (8), in the middle voice, are interpreted as the subject acting upon itself, for its own benefit, or as having some particular skill at the act. For instance, (6) and (8) are felicitous when the speaker is actually engaged in counting—(6) to convey that the speaker has been counting for some time, (8) to convey that counting is a particular skill, for example, where the speaker is calculating or bookkeeping. Thus the cooccurrence with the c- prefix provides initial support for the identification of the $-s$ morpheme as marking imperfective aspect.

2. According to Friedrich (1974:S4), the universal criterion for aspect is the possibility of cooccurrence of adverbials and verbals, notably in the case of durational features. In (NL) Okanagan, the adverbial *pʕutíʔ* 'still' is attested with the $-s$ morpheme or with the middle construction, but not with the $-n$ morpheme:

(9)   a.   *Pʕutíʔ c-x^{w}ƛ'ʕ-s-t-ín.*
              still   PF-whittle-s-t-1sg$_{trans}$
              'I'm actually still whittling it'.
         b.   *Pʕutíʔ kn   (c-)x^{w}ƛ'ʕ-ám.*
              still   1sg$_{intr}$ (PF)whittle-middle
              'I actually still whittle'.

---

[2] Hébert (1982) provides additional discussion of the perfect in Okanagan, both present and past; of four uses of the perfect; of three parameters; and of interaction with subjunctive/irrealis mood.

    c. *$P\Omega ut\acute{\iota}{}^{?} x^{w} \acute{x}'\Omega$-*n-t-ín*.
        still   whittle-*n-t*-1sg$_{trans}$

Thus, the grammaticality of *pΩutí?* with the -*s* morpheme, but not with -*n*, provides clear support for the identification of -*s* as a marker of imperfective aspect.

    3. Additional evidence for the Aspect Hypothesis comes from the interplay of the two general types of aspect that can be distinguished. According to Chung and Timberlake (to appear),

> inherent aspect . . . is the view of the event inherent in the meaning of a lexical item or combination of lexical items (typically a predicate), and sentential aspect . . . characterizes the view of the event presented by the entire sentence or clause . . . and is usually coded morphologically, if a language makes any overt aspectual distinctions at all. . . . Inherent aspect is important in that it interacts with sentential aspect and can sometimes force the selection of one (sentential) aspectual category over another.

If the -*s*/-*n* morphemes encode aspectual distinctions, then there should be significant interaction between them and punctual predicates which specify events that cannot be continued or drawn out. Examples such as those in (10) show that predicates of punctual or instantaneous events accept the -*n* marker:

(10)   a.   *Trq'-n-t-ín* Ωi *p'Ωúk^{w}la?*.
           kick-*n-t*-1sg$_{trans}$ the ball
           'I kicked the ball'.
     b.   *T'ka-n-t-ín* Ωi *stΩúp*.
           downward-*n-t*-1sg$_{trans}$ the stove motion of hand and lower
              arm from elbow
           'I put my hand on the stove' (to see if it's warm).
     c.   *Xalít-n-t-$\emptyset$* $\Omega \partial$ *Ωan-stx^{w}ús!*
           call-*n-t*-1sg$_{trans\,imp}$ the your-sister
           'Call your sister!'
     d.   *MΩá?-n-$\emptyset$-n* Ωi *lpΩút*.
           break-*n-t*-1sg$_{trans}$ the cup
           'I broke a cup'.
     e.   *Wík-n-$\emptyset$-n* Ωi *cítx^{w}-t∂t*.
           see-*n-t*-1sg$_{trans}$ the house-our
           'I saw our house'.

However, examples such as those in (11) show that predicates that are inherently punctual or momentaneous do not accept the basic -*s* marker:

(11)   a. *Trq'-s-t-ín   ʕi p'ʕúkʷlaʔ.
           kick-s-t-1sg_{trans} the ball
        b. *T'ka-s-t-ín . . .
                   -s-t-1sg_{trans}
           downward motion of hand and lower arm-
        c. *Xalít-s-t-∅!
           call-s-t-1sg_{trans imp}
        d. *Mʕáʔ-s-t-n.
           break-s-t-1sg_{trans}
        e. *Wík-s-t-n.
           see-s-t-1sg_{trans}

It has already been shown that the c- 'present perfect' prefix, indicating
"actually occurring action" is restricted in cooccurrence to the -s marker
only. In isolated sentences, the c- does not of itself trigger the -s with
punctual predicates:

(12)   a. *C-trq'-s-t-ín.
              PF-kick-s-t-1sg_{trans}
        b. *C-t'ka-s-t-ín.
              PF-downward etc.-s-t-1sg_{trans}
        c. *C-wík-s-t-n.
              PF-see-s-t-1sg_{trans}

However, the combination of c- and -s is attested in dependent clauses
and provides the additional meaning that the activity has been occurring
before and still continues:

(13)   ʕincaʔ ʕə c-trq'-s-t-ín   ʕi p'ʕúkʷlaʔ.
        me   rel PF-kick-s-t-1sg_{trans} the ball
        'It's me who has been kicking the ball'.

   Chung and Timberlake (to appear) identify four uses of the perfect in
English; in one of these, "the perfect is used for events which began
at some preceding time and have continued up to the time in question
(this is labelled the UNIVERSAL PERFECT by McCawley 1971). In such cases,
the continuing relevance of the event consists exactly in the fact that
it is still occurring." The following sentence exemplifies this use of the
perfect:

(14)   *He's been trying to stop smoking for years.*

The combination of tc- and -s to indicate that the activity has occurred
before and is still occurring (i.e., perfect aspect) can also interact with
an adverbial of habitual, durational occurrence:

(15) a. *ʔaẋl-ásq't c-ẋalít-s-t-n.*
         every-day PF-call-*s-t*-1sg$_{trans}$
         'I used to call him every day'.
      b. *ʔaẋl-ásq't c-mʕáʔ-s-t-n.*
         every-day PF-break-*s-t*-1sg$_{trans}$
         'I used to break one a day'.

Noting that punctuality is a subcomponent of perfectivity, it has been shown that predicates that are inherently punctual require the *-n* marker and are ungrammatical with the *-s* marker only. However the *-s* marker can be triggered in context, in combination with the *ts-* prefix in dependent clauses or with adverbials of habitual occurrence, to indicate continuing recurrence of an event. These facts provide significant support for the identification of *-n* as marking perfective aspect and *-s* as marking imperfective aspect.

4. According to several sources (Chung and Timberlake, to appear, Delancey 1979, Langacker and Munro 1975, Hopper 1979a), passive tends to be associated with the completed aspect (e.g., perfect, perfective). The perfect differs from the perfective in characterizing events that have resulted from a state, and can thus be described as a relational aspect. The perfect resembles the perfective in often viewing events that have resulted from a state as complete; hence, the similarity between the perfect and a subcomponent of the perfective. For example, the passive shows perfective morphology in Russian:[3]

(16) *Ètot zavod byl postroen inostrannymi rabočimi.*
      this factory was pft-built foreign   workers$_{instrumental}$
      'This factory was built by foreign workers'.

In a passive construction in Okanagan, the predicate is marked with the *-tǝm* suffix whereas the agentive by-phrase, if present, takes the same combination of specifiers as does an instrumental noun phrase: *ʕi t*, consisting of *ʕi* 'specific' and *t* 'nonspecific.'

(17) *Cq'a-n-t-ín ʕi stúnx ʕi t xẋ'út.*
      hit-*n-t*-1sg$_{trans}$ the beaver instr rock
      'I hit the beaver with a rock'.

The following sentences illustrate that Okanagan passives show the *-n* marker, thus providing additional support for its identification as the marker of perfective aspect:

---

[3] From class notes, D. M. Perlmutter, Romance Linguistics, Spring 1979, University of California, San Diego.

(18)   a.   *Kíʕlus-n-təm ʕi sp'íc'ʕn.*
              coil-*n*-pass   the rope
              'The rope was coiled'.
        b.   *ʕi p-ptw'ínaxʷ k'ɬ-p'aʔcí-n-təm ʕi   t X'x̌-X'x̌áp*
              the dim-woman dir-choke-*n*-pass instr redup-grown up
              'The old lady was choked by the old man'.
        c.   *ʕi t səláxt-s   ɬʕác-n-təm.*
              instr friend-his bruise-*n*-pass
              'There was bruising by his friend'. (lit.: 'by his friend
              bruised')

Aspectual and voice distinctions manifest viewpoint of a situation.
DeLancey (1979) points out that in the passive which specifies the patient
from an agent → patient viewpoint, one is necessarily looking at the
termination viewpoint of a situation, hence perfective aspect which views
the event as a whole. That is to say, if one considers the activity specified
by the predicate in agent–patient constructions as a continuum along
which an agent may affect a patient, the passive voice which focuses
upon a patient is necessarily toward the end of this continuum, tending
to carry intrinsic perfective meaning and to show one of the completed
aspects. This termination viewpoint of a situation manifested in perfective
aspect is relevant to the next argument supporting the Aspect Hypothesis
and links the two arguments.

5. In Okanagan, the morpheme -*nú* appears on a predicate in an
agent–patient construction to indicate that the agentive subject was in
limited control of the activity specified. For instance, (19) was uttered
when the speaker had reached for the sugar bowl and hit the clock with
his elbow:

(19)   *Cq'aʔ-nú-n-∅-n.*
        hit-ltdc-*n*-*t*-1sg$_{trans}$
        'I managed to hit it'.

This -*nú* morpheme, 'limited control', does not specify whether the action
was intentional or not. When it cooccurs with second consonant reduplication which indicates accidental action with no intention on the part
of the subject, an unintentional reading results. For instance, in (20), the
speaker had slapped the addressee, without having meant to do so:

(20)   *T'qʷ-qʷ-nú-n-t-s-n.*
        slap-accid-ltdc-*n*-*t*-2sg$_{obj}$-1sg$_{trans}$
        'I slapped you unintentionally'.

This limited control morpheme -*nú* cooccurs only with the -*n* marker and is not attested with -*s*. Examples such as (19)–(21) are felicitous just after the completion of the activities specified by the predicates.

(21) a. *ʔʕuc   mip-nú-n-t-xʷ?*
          yes/no Q $\left\{\begin{array}{l}\text{feel}\\\text{know}\end{array}\right\}$-ltdc-*n*-*t*-2sg$_{trans}$
          'Did you manage to feel it?'

      b. *K-c'xʷ-xʷ-na ʔ-nú-n-t-s-n*   *t   ʕəltíʔ*
          distributive-pour-accid-loc-ltdc-*n*-*t*-2sg$_{obj}$-1sg$_{trans}$ some tea
          'I unintentionally spilled some tea on you'.

If one considers the activity specified by a predicate in agent–patient constructions as a continuum along which an agent may affect a patient, then in specifying that the agent performed the activity unintentionally or without full control, one is reaching for the patient end of the continuum and necessarily looking at the termination viewpoint of a situation, hence perfective aspect. Thus, this restricted cooccurrence of the limited control morpheme to the -*n* offers additional support for the Aspect Hypothesis which claims that -*n* marks perfective aspect and -*s* imperfective.

Reviewing the evidence—(1) from the distribution of the *c*- marking actually occurring action, (2,3) from the interplay of adverbials, punctual roots, and the morphology in question, and (4,5) from the appearance of -*n* in passive and limited control constructions, regarded from the termination viewpoint of a situation—the Aspect Hypothesis appears plausible. The terminology imperfective–perfective for -*s* and -*n* respectively is herewith adopted as these terms encode the semantic distinctions—of durative, continuative, and habitual as opposed to noncontinuing, punctual, and completed—which apply to describe the data that have been cited here.

This aspectual distinction must be marked in some basic sentences, but not in others. It is obligatory in the active voice with predicates having two nonoblique arguments only, regardless of whether these are or are not distinct:

(22) a. *Q'ʷʕ'a-n-t-ín   ʕi stəm'tím'.*
          wring-pft-*t*-1sg$_{trans}$ the clothes
          'I wrung the clothes'.

      b. *Q'ʷʕ'a-s-t-ín   ʕi stəm'tím'.*
          wring-impft-*t*-1sg$_{trans}$ the clothes
          'I'm wringing the clothes'.

    c.   *Kn   kʷukʷ-s-cút.*
        1sg$_{intr}$ thank-impft-refl
        'I'm thanking myself'.
    d.   *Kʷu kʷən-n(-t)-wíxʷ.*
        1pl$_{intr}$ catch-pft-(-*t*)recip
        'We caught each other'.

The appearance in a passive has already been noted. The markers do not occur, in the active voice, on predicates having two nonoblique arguments as well as an oblique indirective or benefactive argument:

(23)   a.   *ʕi x̓'x̌-x̓'x̌áp   naq'ʷ-m-ɫ-t-s   ʕi kwwʕáp*
        the REDUP-grownup steal-*m*-indir-*t*-3sg$_{trans}$ the horses
            ʕi pptw'ínaxʷ
            the old-lady
        'The old man steals the horses from the old lady'.
    b.   *ʕi x̓'x̌-x̓'x̌áp   naq'ʷ-x-t-s   t   snkɫc'ʕə́sqaxaʔ*
        the redup-grownup steal-bene-t-3sg$_{trans}$ some horses
            ʕi pptw'ínaxʷ
            the old lady
        'The old man steals a herd of horses for the old lady'.

Nor does it occur in the middle voice:

(24)   *ʕi ʕin-stəmtímaʔ q'c'-ám   t   yamxʷaʔ*
        the my-grandmother weave-middle some basket
        'My grandmother weaves a basket'.

The markers are optional, in the active voice, on predicates having two arguments, one consisting of a benefactive nondistinct from the other, a surface subject:

(25)   a.   *Kʷu k'ʷəl'-x-cút.*
        1pl$_{intr}$ work-bene-refl
        'We work for ourselves'.
    b.   *Kʷu k'ʷəl'-x-s-cút*
        1pl$_{intr}$ work-bene-impft-refl
        'We are working for ourselves'.

The markers are also optional in certain intransitives having a patient animate subject:

(26)   a.   *Kn   qʷə́l'-t.*
        1sg$_{intr}$ warm-*t*
        'I'm warm'.

b. *Kn   q^{w}ə́l'-s-t.*
1sg$_{intr}$ warm-impft-*t*
'I'm warming (myself)./I'm keeping warm'.

2. THE CUSTOMARY INVOLVEMENT HYPOTHESIS

The Customary Involvement Hypothesis (Mattina 1978a:91–93, 1978b:99) claims that the *-s/-n* occur in transitive constructions that obligatorily include reference to two and only two persons—an actor and a primary goal—and that they are distinguished by the fact that

(27)   *-s-t* predicates always imply either purposeful or customary involvement on the part of the actor and are characterized as transitives with implied reference to a third person, a secondary goal, coterminous with the actor; whereas *-n-t* predicates imply reference only to an actor and a primary goal.

Since these claims are ambiguous in some respects, the following will be assumed, based on the data in Mattina (1978b):

1. The customary involvement referred to in *-s-t* constructions is usually purposeful, but there is no specifiable criteria to determine when it is one and not the other.
2. *-n-t* constructions are, then, necessarily without purposeful or customary involvement.
3. A primary goal is a patient (surface direct object) and a secondary goal is a recipient, here presumably coreferential with, and non-distinct from, the actor.
4. The term actor refers to an agentive subject.

The Customary Involvement Hypothesis, with respect to the *-s-t* marking, states that the primary reference is to an actor who is customarily or purposefully involved. This notion of customary involvement is indeed compatible with the Aspect Hypothesis as imperfective aspect includes reference to a customary, habitual situation or event. Furthermore, by shifting the analysis to event or action rather than to an actor, an undefined term, we avoid including in the grammar explanations referring to secondary versus primary goal in constructions that have previously been stated to be only two-place transitives. That *-n-t* does not have reference to a customarily or habitually involved actor follows from the statement for *-s-t* and is equally compatible with the Aspect Hypothesis.

Additionally, the Customary Involvement Hypothesis claims that the markings in question occur only with transitive constructions, that is, only with two-place predicates. I take this to mean constructions with only two distinct nominals, one of which is a subject and the other a direct object, again based on the data presented in Mattina (1978b). Examples (22a) and (22b) were cited earlier to show that the aspectual distinctions must be marked in such constructions. From this claim it follows that the markings are not expected to cooccur with a subject pronoun that has been identified as intransitive. Yet examples (25b), (22c), and (22d) illustrate that these aspectual morphemes do indeed cooccur with the set of subject pronominals termed intransitive. Hence, the traditional labeling practice leads to inconsistencies, which argues against the Customary Involvement Hypothesis.

In Mattina (1978b), reflexive and reciprocal constructions are labeled as pseudointransitive, as they are transitive in logical form and intransitive in their choice of subject pronominals in basic sentences. The appearance of $-s/-n$ in these constructions is noted there as parallel to the $-s-t$ and $-n-t$ of the Customary Involvement Hypothesis. These $-s/-n$ are in fact identical in meaning and identical in occurrence, appearing obligatorily in the active voice, in constructions which are transitive in logical form, as exemplified in (22a)–(22d), (23a)–(23b), and (24). The explicit realization that these $-s/-n$ are identical eliminates the necessity of setting up duplicate morphemes such as $-scút/-ncút$ and $-s(t)wíx^w/-n(t)wíx^w$.[4]

Thus, although the Customary Involvement Hypothesis is compatible with the Aspect Hypothesis with respect to the habitual reference associated with the $-s$ marking and the lack of this association with $-n$, a strictly interpreted Customary Involvement Hypothesis which rests on transitivity as characterized by Mattina is not supported by the data. The claim made by the Customary Involvement Hypothesis that $-s-t$ predicates may also imply reference to purposeful involvement on the part of the actor will be discussed in conjunction with the claims made by the Control Hypothesis.

---

[4] More specifically, Mattina (1978b) sets up $-s-t-sút/-n-t-sút$ and $-s-t-wíx^w/-n-t-wíx^w$. There is no clearcut phonological evidence that the $-t$ is indeed present in these constructions. The one example given of $-stwíx^w$ in (Colville) Okanagan probably consists of the $-st(u)$ causative, a frozen morphological form, from Proto-Salish $*-stax^w$, with the reciprocal $-wíx^w$:

(i) *Nixəl'-m-n-təm 1x   q^{w}ʕəl-stu-wíx^w*
    hear-m-pft-pass 3pl$_{intr}$ talk-cause-recip
'They were heard arguing with each other'.

This is the only instance of $-s$ or of $-t$ before $-wíx^w$ in my data.

3. THE CONTROL HYPOTHESIS

The Control Hypothesis (Thompson 1976, 1979; Thompson and Thompson, to appear) has been proposed for the contiguous Interior Salishan language, Thompson:

(28)   -*s-t* marks a causative, implying that the action or state results from the activity of some agent who is not in full control; -*n-t* marks a control transitive, implying control by the subject (Thompson and Thompson, to appear).

In Thompson (1979), the statements are weakened: (*a*) with respect to -*n-t,* to control by the agent, and in passive forms, by the implied agent; and (*b*) with respect to -*s-t,* to not apparently affecting the control status of the stems to which it is attached.

This is part of an important broader hypothesis which claims that control distinctions comprise an independent system in Salishan grammatical structure (Thompson 1976, 1979). This broader hypothesis seems to consist of two parts:

1. An indication of control achieved by the marking of lexical items, with the two features [±control] and [+limited control] having been proposed to classify all predicative roots.
2. The identification of affixes that mark the control status of a construction, specifically, -*n* marking a control transitive and the Proto-Salish form *-*nəxʷ* and its progeny marking limited control, whereas other affixes do not appear to affect the control status of the predicative stems to which they are attached, for example, the -*s-t* causative.

Since a control system has been suggested as permeating Salishan grammatical structure, it is appropriate to consider a Control Hypothesis in light of Okanagan data. However, the discussion herein will be confined to the productive -*s*/-*n* alternation, with "transitive" -*t* as a separate issue.

To support an analysis of -*s-t* as a causative, one must first decide which type of causative is involved. According to Shibatani (1976), a large number of languages distinguish two types of causative forms: morphologically regular and productive forms and morphologically irregular, nonproductive forms, termed productive causatives and lexical causatives, respectively. The productive causatives can be illustrated in English by the following sentences:

(29)   a.   *John caused the door to open.*

   b.   *Grannie had the child drink the chicken broth.*
   c.   *Sharon made Norman shave off his mustache.*

Okanagan does not have a productive causative construction. Sentences such as (29b) and (29c) with three nominals are ungrammatical in Okanagan:

(30)   a.   *Sharon páẋ-s-s-t-s*   *Norman ʕi*
                  shave-face-impft-*t*-3sg$_{trans}$ the
                              cause?

              sʕùpcín-s
              mustache-3sg$_{gen}$

        b.   **Yaya? síw's-* . . .   *ʕi sk'^{w}k'$^{'w}$ímǝlt ʕi cíkn*
              Grannie drink- ?   the baby   the chicken
              ʕi st'xítk^w-s
              the broth-3sg$_{gen}$

Thus the *-s-t* does not mark a productive causative in Okanagan.

   A lexical causative relates the two forms of verbs such as *open, thaw, melt, harden, kill/cause to die, close,* and *thicken* in sentences such as:

(31)   a.   *John opened the door.*
        b.   *The door opened.*

It can be seen that in Sentences (31a) and (31b) the noun *door* bears the same semantic relation to the verb but not the same surface grammatical relation. The same pattern can be seen with examples from Turkish:[5]

(32)   a.   *John buz-u eri-t-ti.*
                  ice-acc melt-cause-pst
              'John melted the ice'.
        b.   *Buz eri-di.*
              ice melt-pst
              'The ice melted'.

(33)   a.   *Hasan çorbayï koyulaş-tïr-di.*
                  soup-acc thicken-cause-pst
              'Hasan thickened the soup'.
        b.   *Çorba koyulaş-tï.*
              soup   thicken-pst
              'The soup thickened'.

If the *-s* marks a lexical causative in (NL) Okanagan, then one should

---

[5] This Turkish data and explanations were provided by İnci Özkaragöz (University of California, San Diego).

be able to predict its appearance in pairs of sentences such as (28)–(33) where a nominal bears the same semantic relation to its predicate in each member of the pair. However, the prediction is not borne out:

(34)   a.   *Kn   s-c-ʕáym'-x   t   stíq.*
            1sg_intr *s*-PF-thaw-prog some meat
            'I'm actually thawing out some meat'.
       b.   *ʕi stiq s-c-ʕáym'-x.*
            the meat *s*-PF-melt-prog.
            'The meat is actually thawing'.

Moreover, according to Shibatani (1976), a lexical causative is an irregular and nonproductive form. It has already amply been shown that the -*s* morpheme, like the -*n,* is regular, productive, and obligatory in some constructions and optional in others [cf. (22)–(24)]. Hence a lexical causative analysis cannot be supported for (NL) Okanagan.

In constructions where a causative analysis of some type is tempting, other translations more readily reveal the imperfective aspect consistently encoded in the event:

(35)   *Kʼʷúlʼ-m-s-t-n.*
       work-*m*-impft-*t*-1sg_trans
       'I'm making him work./I'm working him'.[6]

Shibatani (1976:1–2) gives two conditions which two events must satisfy to be said to constitute a causative situation:

1. The relation between the two events is such that the speaker believes that the occurrence of the caused event occurred after the occurrence of the causing event.
2. The relation between the causing event and the caused event is such that the speaker believes that the occurrence of the caused event is wholly dependent on the occurrence of the causing event.

Proponents of an analysis of -*s-t* as a causative morpheme have not shown that this morpheme characterizes causative situations, meeting the two conditions cited here, nor that two events are involved. A causative analysis of -*s* is not supported for (NL) Okanagan, regardless of the type of causative, lexical or productive.

The Control Hypothesis claims that -*n-t* marks a control transitive,

---

[6] See Hébert (1982), regarding the relational construction, Class C, for an analysis of the -*m(i)* morpheme as marking an advancement of an instrumental object to direct object, obligatory with animate instrumental objects. This class of constructions may receive a weak causative interpretation.

implying control by a subject; this is its strongest version (Thompson and Thompson, to appear). It is subsequently weakened to control by an agent or by an implied agent (Thompson 1979). The following arguments show that the -n does not specifically indicate control, for either version.

1. The limited control morpheme -nú, which indicates that the agentive subject has limited control over the activity specified by the predicate, cooccurs with -n, as has already been discussed.

(36)   C'q'-n-t-ín   ʕe c-rʕíp   ʕi t xX'út ʔʕuɫ
        hit/throw-pft-t-1sg_trans the PF-upright instr rock and
        xíq'-n-∅-n;   cq'-q'-nú-n-∅-n   ʕi naqs ʕə
        miss-pft-t-1sg_trans; hit-accid-ltdc-pft-t-1sg_trans the other the
        c-rʕíp
        PF-upright
        'I threw at the tree with a rock and I missed; I
        unintentionally hit the other tree'.

Example (36) shows that the -n cannot possibly imply control by the subject, as it cooccurs not only with the limited control morpheme -nú but also with the second consonant reduplication which marks accidental action.

2. The passive constructions are problematic for the strong version of the Control Hypothesis. The -n occurs as part of the verbal morphology in passives; however, in impersonal passives, such as (18c), there is no specified final subject to act as controller. In (18a) the final subject is an unlikely candidate for controller as it is an inanimate rope, and in (18b) it is semantically an animate patient undergoing the action. Thus the strong version of the Control Hypothesis cannot be supported.

3. When we turn to the weaker versions of the hypothesis, passives again provide counterarguments. There is in Okanagan an animacy constraint which renders ungrammatical a passive with a final inanimate subject and an animate agentive oblique:

(37)   a. Tr'q-n-tə́m ʕi sqəl'tmíxʷ ʕi t səxʷwʕlq'ám.
            kick-pft-pass the man   instr policeman
            'The man was kicked by the policeman'.
        b. *Tr'q-n-tə́m ʕi p'ʕúkʷlaʔʕi t ttw'ít.
            kick-pft-pass the ball   instr boy

Also of interest to the Control Hypothesis is the Langacker and Munro (1975) hypothesis for passives and their meaning which states, in part, that agentive phrases, when they occur, are derived from an external source and are not considered an intrinsic part of the passive construction. Given the animacy constraint on the passive in Okanagan and given the Langacker and Munro proposal, if one is to support a Control Hypothesis for passive constructions with an unspecified agentive phrase (such as 18a), one needs to show, first of all, that an agentive phrase is intrinsically present at some underlying level and that it is subsequently deleted, and second, how a deleted agent retains control of the activity specified by the predicate. This has not been shown. Therefore neither version of the Control Hypothesis can be supported for the (NL) Okanagan data presented here.

It can further be observed that the Control Hypothesis and the Customary Involvement Hypothesis contradict each other. The former states that the subject or agent of the -n construction is in control. The latter states that the actor is in control in an -s construction; by extension, the actor is not in control in an -n construction. Impersonal passives such as (18c) do not support the strong version of the Control Hypothesis as they contain no specified subject to be in control. Nor does (18c) support the Customary Involvement Hypothesis as it was identified as a purposeful action which is supposed to be associated with -s marking. Thus, if either -s or -n can be purposeful, the distinction between these morphemes cannot be that of control.

It has been shown that neither the Customary Involvement Hypothesis nor the Control Hypothesis can be stretched to account for all the data. In contrast, the Aspect Hypothesis (a) offers an explanation for the "causative" of the Control Hypothesis, (b) includes the assignment of customary reference to -s of the other hypothesis, (c) accounts for the data presented here, without depending crucially on transitivity, and (d) allows an explanatory statement of the viewpoint in common to passive and limited control constructions.

4. TWO DEFINITIONS OF TRANSITIVITY

Two definitions of transitivity—"structural transitivity" and "traditional transitivity"—will be discussed with respect to the -t morpheme, which appears frequently in this paper and which is traditionally termed "transitive" in Salishan studies. Both the Control Hypothesis and the Customary Involvement Hypothesis crucially involve the identification of the -t morpheme with transitivity. In what follows it will be shown that this -t does not mark transitivity at either an underlying level or a surface level, where transitivity is defined structurally.

(38)   STRUCTURAL TRANSITIVITY: Transitivity is defined as the
          structure relating a predicate and two nonoblique

arguments, a subject and direct object, at a specifiable
level.

This -*t* occurs in the active voice in agent–patient constructions, consisting of a predicate with two nonoblique arguments, as exemplified in
(22a)–(22b). If -*t* marks transitivity at an initial or underlying level, then
(*a*) it should not appear in an intransitive benefactive, for example, in
(39); (*b*) it should appear in reflexives and reciprocals, for example, (40);
and (*c*) it should appear as well in the middle voice in a two-argument
construction where the second argument bears the same semantic and
grammatical relation to the predicate as it does in the corresponding
active, as in (41):

(39)   *T'-t'ʕúm'-t'ʕm'-s-x-t-∅*   *ʕi   ƛ'x̌-x̌-ƛ'x̌áp.*
         dim-smile-redup-face-bene-*t*-sg$_{tr\ imp}$ the redup-pl-grownup
         'Smile for the elders!'   (T-shirt motto)

(40)   *Kn   k'ł-qx^w-n-cút.*
         1sg$_{intr}$ dir-protect-pft-refl
         'I protected myself'.

(41) a. *ƛ'ʕək'^{w}-p-n-t-ín   ʕi paták.*
         pierce-*p*-pft-*t*-1sg$_{trans}$ the potato
         'I pierced the potato (in the pot to see if it was cooked)'.
      b. *Kn   ƛ'ʕək'^{w}-p-ám   t paták.*
         1sg$_{intr}$ pierce-*p*-middle a potato
         'I pierce a potato (to serve myself)'.

Thus Sentences (39)–(41) establish that -*t* does not mark transitivity at
the initial or underlying level.

If this -*t* marks transitivity at the final or surface level, then it should
not appear in a passive which may have one nonoblique argument (18a),
or one oblique argument as in an impersonal passive (18c). Thus this
morpheme does not mark final or surface transitivity. Hence the integrity
of -*t* as a marker of transitivity, as defined in (38), cannot be maintained
at either underlying or surface level.

Additionally a -*t* occurs in certain intransitive constructions which
have an ultimate patient subject at the surface level [cf. (26a)–(26b)]. If
this is the same -*t* as above, then it is obviously not a marker of transitivity, as defined in (38).[7]

---

[7] Mattina (1973, 1978) identifies this -*t* as "stative." This -*t* may appear with the imperfective marker as in (26b), but not with inchoatives, or progressives as in (34), or with
inceptives. Thus "stative" is a plausible analysis. The status of this -*t* and its relationship
with the 'transitive' -*t*, with which it does not cooccur, is discussed in Hébert (1982) on
the clausal structure of (NL) Okanagan.

Also relevant to the Okanagan data is the traditional understanding of transitivity.

(42)   TRADITIONAL TRANSITIVITY: Transitivity is defined globally over
        an entire clause, referring to the carrying over or
        transferring of an action from the agent to the patient.

According to the Transitivity Hypothesis advanced by Hopper and Thompson (1980), (a) this traditional notion of transitivity involves a number of components, each associated with some aspect of the effectiveness with which the transitive event takes place; and (b) transitivity is a crucial parameter in language use, with these components clustering to play a significant role in discourse. (See the Introduction to this volume for a listing of the transitivity components.) This paper will address only part of this hypothesis: transitivity as a scalar value. A clustering of the high-transitivity components would rank high on the transitivity scale, whereas a clustering of their opposites would rank low. Given the facts presented previously with respect to -t 'transitive' of Okanagan, clauses marked with this morpheme, cluster with most, if not all, of the component parts of transitivity and thus rank high in transitivity.

The Transitivity Hypothesis also permits us to see a link between perfectivity, control, and transitivity. The semantic notion of control by the subject and/or agent is not necessarily violated by the supported identification of -n as a marker of perfectivity. Significantly, we have seen that perfectivity is associated with a termination viewpoint of a situation. A control analysis necessarily implies a focus upon the termination viewpoint of an action or event, thus the likelihood of perfective marking of an action or event within the full control of the agent and the successful carrying over or transferring of the action to the patient. As has already been noted, both the Okanagan limited control and passive constructions which focus on the patient are associated with the termination viewpoint and take the -n marker of perfectivity. Hence, perfective clauses rank high on the transitivity scale in that they correlate with several components: object totally affected, agent high in potency, realis, affirmative, volitional, action, and two or more participants. Thus, the link between aspect and transitivity becomes apparent.

5. CONCLUSIONS

The following conclusions may be drawn:

1. An Aspect Hypothesis is plausible for (NL) Okanagan, with -s marking imperfectivity and -n marking perfectivity.

2. Part of the Customary Involvement Hypothesis, with respect to customary or habitual reference of -s, can be subsumed into the Aspect Hypothesis, but the remainder of the Customary Involvement Hypothesis is inadequate for the facts of (NL) Okanagan.
3. The Control Hypothesis cannot fully account for the data presented here, although the notion of control shares a termination viewpoint of the situation with perfectivity.
4. The -t is not a marker of transitivity at either an underlying or surface level with transitivity defined structurally, but it ranks high in transitivity as a scalar value, with transitivity defined traditionally.

Much remains to be discovered about aspect in Okanagan. The syntactic behavior of the aspectual system in complex and compound constructions, especially with respect to sequential or simultaneous action, has not been examined. The interaction of mood and aspect has not been mentioned nor has the discourse function of imperfective versus perfective aspect been considered. For Malay, Hopper (1979a) discusses the foregrounding function of the perfective—for example, signaling serial events and relating the main story line—and the backgrounding function of the imperfective—for example, narrating ongoing events, commenting on the main events, and drawing the descriptive background for these chief occurrences. These will be productive areas for future work in Okanagan.

ACKNOWLEDGMENTS

This work has been supported by an Isaac Walton Killam Predoctoral Fellowship, 1977–1980, held at the University of British Columbia, and also in part by the British Columbia Provincial Museum, in the summers of 1978 and 1979.

Many thanks to Sandra A. Thompson and to Paul J. Hopper for their valuable suggestions, and also to Jessica L. Roberts, Sandra Chung, Anthony Mattina, Terry J. Klokeid, Germán Westphal, and especially to Alan Timberlake. The responsibility for this analysis of Okanagan remains mine alone.

Many thanks are given to the native speakers who patiently teach me of their language: Joe Pete Saddleman of Quilchena, Herman Edwards of Keremeos, Bernice Baptiste of Penticton, all in British Columbia, Tillie George of Colville, Washington, Sharon Lindley, and especially Joe Albert Michel, of Quilchena, on Nicola Lake, my main teacher. It is they who first alerted me to the possibility of an aspectual distinction for -s and -n by insisting and persisting in explaining that -s meant that the action was continuing and that -n meant that the action was completed. The first four were in training at the University of Victoria, during 1978–1979, to become language instructors. Importantly, these speakers represent the geographical spread of the language, from the northwesternmost area (Quilchena) to the southeasternmost (Colville).

An earlier version of this paper entitled "A Note on Aspect in (NL) Okanagan" was presented at the 14th International Conference on Salishan Languages, Western Washington

University, Bellingham, August 9–11, 1979. The present version was presented in a colloquium at Simon Fraser University, June 25, 1980.

REFERENCES

Chung, S. and A. Timberlake (to appear) "Tense, Aspect and Mood," in T. Shopen et al., eds., *Language Typology and Syntactic Field Work,* volume 3: *Grammatical Categories and the Lexicon,* chapter 2.
Comrie, B. (1976) *Aspect: An Introduction to the Study of Verbal Aspect and Related Problems,* Cambridge University Press, Cambridge.
DeLancey, S. (1979) "Aspect, Transitivity and Viewpoint," presented at the UCLA Symposium on Tense/Aspect: Between Semantics and Pragmatics, May 4–6.
Friedrich, P. (1974) "On Aspect Theory and Homeric Aspect," *International Journal of American Linguistics* 40.4, Part 2, Memoir #28.
Hébert, Y. M. (1982) *Clausal Structure of (Nicola Lake) Okanagan.* Unpublished doctoral dissertation, University of British Columbia.
Hopper, P. (1977–1978) "Some Observations on the Typology of Focus and Aspect in Narrative Language," *NUSA: Linguistic Studies in Indonesian and Languages of Indonesia* 4, 14–25.
Hopper, P. (1979a) "Aspect and Foregrounding in Discourse," in T. Givón, ed., *Discourse and Syntax,* Academic Press, New York.
Hopper, P. (1979b) "On Perfectivity and Possession," presented at the UCLA Symposium on Tense/Aspect: Between Semantics and Pragmatics, May 4–6.
Hopper, P. and S. Thompson (1980) "Transitivity in Grammar and Discourse," *Language* 56, 251–299.
Langacker, R. and P. Munro (1975) "Passives and Their Meaning," *Language* 51, 789–830.
Mattina, A. (1973) "Colville Grammatical Structure," *University of Hawaii Working Papers in Linguistics* 5.3.
Mattina, A. (1978a) "The Colville Transitive System," presented at the 13th International Conference on Salishan Languages, University of Victoria, August 17–19.
Mattina, A. (1978b) "Parallels between the Colville Transitives and Pseudo-Intransitives," in D. Malsch, J. Hoard, and C. Sloat, eds., *Proceedings of the 8th Annual Meeting of the Western Conference on Linguistics,* Linguistics Research Inc., Edmonton, Alberta.
McCawley, J. (1971) "Tense and Time Reference in English," in C. Fillmore and D. Langendoen, eds., *Studies in Linguistic Semantics,* Holt, Rinehart and Winston, New York.
McCawley, J. (1976) "Remarks on What Can Cause What," in M. Shibatani, ed., *The Grammar of Causative Constructions,* Academic Press, New York.
Shibatani, M. (1976) "The Grammar of Causative Constructions: A Conspectus," in M. Shibatani, ed., *The Grammar of Causative Constructions,* Academic Press, New York.
Thompson, L. (1976) "The Control System: A Major Category in the Grammar of Salishan Languages," in B. Efrat, ed., *The Victoria Conference on Northwestern Languages,* Publications of the British Columbia Provincial Museum, Victoria, B.C.
Thompson, L. (1979) "Control in Salish Grammar," *University of Hawaii Working Papers in Linguistics* 11, 133–150.
Thompson, L. and M. Thompson (to appear) "Thompson," in *The Handbook of American Indians,* The Smithsonian Institution, Washington, D.C.
Timberlake, A. (1979) "Invariance and the Syntax of Russian Aspect," presented at the UCLA Symposium on Tense/Aspect: Between Semantics and Pragmatics, May 4–6.

ON THE OBJECT RELATION IN BANTU

LARRY M. HYMAN
ALESSANDRO DURANTI

The object relation in Bantu has been the subject of a number of excellent papers (see references). Whether descriptive or theoretical in orientation, these studies have revealed an intricate network of (direct) object properties which, although varying from language to language, expose a general Bantu character. In the present study an initial attempt is made to synthesize these findings on the basis of the Bantu languages studied thus far.[1] We begin by addressing the nature of grammatical relations in Bantu. We then discuss the grammatical properties characteristic of objects in Bantu, and the factors that determine which arguments of a verb have access to these properties. Finally, we consider some tentative conclusions concerning the typology and the history of the object relation in these Bantu languages.

[1] These include Haya, Sesotho, Logooli, Shona, Nyakyusa, Kimbundu, Shambala, and parts of Sukuma, Ciluba, Chaga, Punu, and Basaa, in addition to the published sources represented in the references.

217

1. GRAMMATICAL RELATIONS IN BANTU

In Bantu we can establish without controversy the following grammatical relations: (*a*) subject, (*b*) (direct) object, and (*c*) oblique. These
three relations are illustrated in the following sentence from Haya:[2]

(1)   *Kat' á-ka-téél' ómwáána n'énkoni.*
        Kato he-P_3-beat child   with stick
        'Kato beat the child with a stick'. (P_3 = before yesterday past)

Here *Kató* is the subject, *ómwáána* the object, and *énkoni* the oblique.
In a "neutral" or "unmarked" sentence, the subject precedes and conditions agreement on the verb, which is in turn directly followed by the
object. An oblique then follows an object (if present) and is normally,
but not always, preceded by a preposition (here by *na* 'with'). Except
in the imperative, each verb must have an explicit subject (either nominal
or pronominal) and can have, the sense permitting, an oblique (preposition + noun or pronoun). Only transitive verbs can support an object
when there is no verbal extension present, as will be discussed in what
follows.

The major difficulty arises as soon as the notion of an "indirect" object
is considered. In each Bantu language there exist a small number of
simplex (monomorphemic) verbs which, in addition to the subject, can
take two nominal complements without marking either one with a preposition. Among the verbs frequently found in this category are 'to give',
'to steal', 'to smear', 'to hide', 'to ask', and 'to teach'. Two Haya
examples are seen in (2) and (3).

(2)   *A-ka-h'   ómwáán' ébitooke.*
        he-P_3-give child   bananas
        'He gave the child bananas'.

(3)   *A-ka-siig'   ómwáán' ámajûta.*
        he-P_3-smear child   oil
        'He smeared the child with oil' or 'He smeared oil on the
        child'.

In these examples we observe two nouns in succession which follow the
verb without being preceded by a preposition. In a typical European
language one might identify these nouns as an indirect followed by a

---

[2] For further discussion of the Haya in this and later sections, see Duranti and Byarushengo (1977), Hyman (1977), and Duranti (1979).

direct object. The same would be said about the examples in (4) and (5).

(4)   *A -ka-túm -il' ómwáán' ébitooke.*
      he-P$_3$-send-app child   bananas
      'He sent the child bananas'.

(5)   *A-ka-cumb-il' ómwáán' ébitooke.*
      he-P$_3$-cook-app child   bananas
      'He cooked the child bananas'.

In these examples, *ómwáána* 'child' would be the indirect object (sometimes called the "applied" or "prepositional" object in Bantu) and *ébitooke* 'bananas' the direct object. These examples differ from (2) and (3) by the presence of the applied (app) extension *-il-* which marks the imminence of an applied object, either a recipient as in (4) or a beneficiary as in (5). (In other cases the applied extension introduces a locative, and in other Bantu languages it introduces an instrument.) Other extensions that make possible a sequence of nouns without prepositions are the causative/instrument *-is-* and the locative enclitics which "objectivize" the locatives of classes 16, 17 and 18 (cf. Trithart 1975; Dalgish 1976a, 1976b; Stucky 1976).

In a final situation which we shall consider here, two nouns are possible in sequence when the first represents a possessor "affected" by the action of the verb. Thus, instead of the construction in (6), we find that in (7).

(6)   ?*A-ka-hénd' ómukono gw' ómwáána.*
      he-P$_3$-break arm   of child
      'He broke the child's arm'.

(7)   *A-ka-hénd' ómwáán' ómukôno.*
      he-P$_3$-break child   arm
      'He broke the child's arm'.

In (6) the associative construction is used only if the possessor ('child') is not affected by the action of the verb ('to break'). In this context this would mean that the arm was not part of the child—that is, the arm had already been severed from the body (of someone, not necessarily the child) before being broken in (6).[3] In (7) we have two successive nouns since the affected possessor is treated as an object.

---

[3] For discussion of this construction, see Voeltz (1976), Hyman (1977), Morolong and Hyman (1977), Hinnebusch and Kirsner (1980), and Fox (1981).

2. OBJECT PROPERTIES

We have seen in the preceding section three circumstances where two postverbal nouns follow each other without a preposition: (*a*) certain rare verbs like 'to give' can take two nouns without a preposition; (*b*) certain extensions such as the applied extension introduce a second object; and (*c*) an affected possessor can be realized as an object. In the foregoing we have avoided the term "indirect object," which we feel is not appropriate for Bantu. (For further discussion of the nonuniversality of "indirect object," see Faltz 1978.)

In each of the above three cases we must ask what the grammatical relations are between each noun and the verb. In order to determine this we shall consider the three most frequently used tests, namely: (*a*) word order, (*b*) subjectivization, and (*c*) cliticization. As has always been assumed by Bantuists, a true object should (*a*) have access to the position immediately following the verb; (*b*) be capable of assuming the subject role through passivization; and (*c*) be expressable as a clitic object marker (OM) within the verbal complex. Although other tests are applied in the literature,[4] we will content ourselves with these three, which already provide enough variation in Bantu languages to draw certain conclusions about the status of objects. Let us apply these tests, then, to Sentences (2), (5), and (7).

As we can see from (8), the two nouns in (2) can be placed in either order in Haya [cf. (2)]:

(8)   *A-ka-h'   ébitook' ómwáana.*
        he-P₃-give bananas child
        'He gave bananas to the child'.

Similarly, in (9) it is observed that either 'child' or 'bananas' can be subject of the corresponding passive construction:

(9)   a.   *Omwáán' a-ka-háá-bw'   ébitooke.*
             child   he-P₃-give-pass bananas
             'The child was given bananas'.
        b.   *Ebitooke bí-ka-háá-bw'   ómwáana.*
             bananas they-P₃-give-pass child
             'The bananas were given to the child'.

Finally, in (10) the two nouns occur as pronouns in the OM clitic position:

---

[4] Other tests are discussed and illustrated in Kimenyi (1979), Trithart (1976), Duranti and Byarushengo (1977), and Gary and Keenan (1977).

(10)   a. *A-ka-mú-h' ébitooke.*
            he-P₃-him-give bananas
            'He gave him bananas'.
        b. *A-ka-bí-h' ómwáana.*
            he-P₃-them-give child
            'He gave them to the child'.

In fact, in Haya (but not always in other Bantu languages), both nouns can be cliticized and cooccupy the OM slot:

(11)   *A-ka-bi-mú-h-a*
        he-P₃-them-him-give
        'He gave them to him'.

Thus, given the three criteria (word order, subjectivization, cliticization) we must conclude that both 'child' and 'bananas' are objects when following the verb 'to give'. Similarly, in the following examples involving the app extension and its benefactive referent in (5), both 'child' and 'bananas' are objects (cf. Gary and Keenan 1977 for KinyaRwanda):

(12)   *A-ka-cumb-il' ébitook' ómwáana.*
        he-P₃-cook-app bananas child
        'He cooked the bananas for the child'.

(13)   a. *Omwáán' a-ka-cumb-il-w' ébitooke.*
            child   he-P₃-cook-app-pass bananas
            'The child was cooked bananas'.
        b. *Ebitooke bí-ka-cumb-il-w' ómwáana.*
            bananas they-P₃-cook-app-pass child
            'The bananas were cooked for the child'.

(14)   a. *A-ka-mú-cumb-il' ébitooke.*
            he-P₃-him-cook-app bananas
            'He cooked bananas for him'.
        b. *A-ka-bí-cumb-il' ómwáana.*
            he-P₃-them-cook-app child
            'He cooked them for the child'.

However, when we attempt to apply the three tests to (7), quite different properties result. First, as seen in (15), 'arm' cannot appear after the verb with 'child' following it. Also, as seen in (16), 'child' can subjectivize, but 'arm' cannot.

(15)   **N-ka-hénd' ómukón' ómwáana.*
        I-P₃-break arm   child

(16)   a.   *Omwáán' a-ka-hénd-w'*   *ómukôno.*
            child   he-P$_3$-break-pass arm
            'The child's arm was broken' (Lit., 'the child was broken
                the arm').
       b.   **Omukóno gú-ka-hénd-w'*   *ómwáana.*
            arm   it-P$_3$-break-pass child
            Lit., 'the arm was broken the child'.

And, finally, we observe in (17) that 'child' can cliticize into the OM
position, but 'arm' cannot.

(17)   a.   *N-ka-mu-hénd'*   *ómukôno*
            I-P$_3$-him-break arm
            'I broke his arm' (Lit., 'I broke him the arm').
       b.   **N-ka-gu-hénd'*   *ómwáana*
            I-P$_3$-it-break   child
            Lit., 'I broke it the child'.

We therefore conclude that 'child' is an object in (7), but that 'arm' is
not an object, but rather a "prepositionless oblique." Thus, one cannot
determine solely from the absence of a preposition whether a postverbal
noun is an object.[5] As a final demonstration of this last point, it should
be noted that the agent of a passive sentence lacks a preposition in Haya,
as seen in (18).

(18)   *Ebitooke bí-ka-cumb-w'*   *ómukâzi.*
       bananas they-P$_3$-cook-pass woman
       'The bananas were cooked by the women'.

The passive agent cannot cliticize as a pronoun, as seen in (19).

(19)   **Ebitooke bí-ka-mú-cumb-w-a.*
       bananas they-P$_3$-her-cook-pass
       'The bananas were cooked by her'.

Since this nonobject passive agent can also appear with a (nonhuman)
object following it, as in (20), this constitutes another example of two

---

[5] Other constructions have been found which exhibit the same object properties as in
the affected possessor construction. For example, in the Haya sentence *A-ka-téél' ómwáán'
énkoni* (lit., 'he beat child stick'), which should be compared with Sentence (1), *ómwáána*
'child' is an object, whereas *énkoni* 'stick' is an oblique. The meaning is something like
'he stick-beated the child'. This oblique is reminiscent of the adverbial objects found in
Igbo and other West African Kwa languages and incorporated nouns such as the complex
English verb 'to pistolwhip'.

prepositionless nouns following the verb, where only one ('bananas') is a real object.[6]

(20)   *Omwáán' a-ka-cumb-il-w'   ómukázy' ébitooke.*
        child   he-P₃-cook-app-pass woman   bananas
        Lit., 'The child was cooked bananas by the woman'.

Sentences (2), (4), and (5) have the sequence object + object, whereas (7) has object + oblique and (20) has oblique + object. The fourth possibility, oblique + oblique, is provided in (21), where neither the passive agent 'woman' nor the possessed body part 'arm' can cliticize, as seen in (22).

(21)   *Omwáán' a-ka-hénd-w'   ómukázy' ómukôno.*
        child   he-P₃-break-pass woman   arm
        Lit., 'the child was broken the arm by the woman'.

(22)   a. **Omwáán' a-ka-mu-hénd-w'   ómukôno.*
           child   he-P₃-her-break-pass arm
           Lit., 'the child was broken the arm by her'.
        b. **Omwáán' a-ka-gu-hénd-w'   ómukâzi.*
           child   he-P₃-it-break-pass woman
           Lit., 'the child was broken it by the woman'.

3. ACCESS TO OBJECT PROPERTIES

In the preceding section we have determined that word order, subjectivization, and cliticization serve as three criteria for object status. We have seen, also, that a postverbal noun not preceded by a preposition can either be an object or a prepositionless oblique. In this section we examine the following factors which may influence the likelihood that an NP argument will exhibit object properties: (*a*) semantic case relations, (*b*) person–animacy, and (*c*) determinedness.[7]

The first two factors can be summarized in terms of the following semantic hierarchies in (23) and (24).

---

[6] Note that in (20) the passive agent *ómukázy'* 'woman' is in immediate postverbal position because of its human status. It is impossible to have two human nouns following a passivized verb in Haya. As the passive agent is an oblique rather than a true object, we conclude that word order is the weakest of the three criteria of object status.

[7] These three parameters were first pointed out for Bantu by Hawkinson and Hyman (1974) and have been further developed by Morolong and Hyman (1977), Duranti (1979), and Trithart (1979). For further discussion of animacy and determinedness in direct objects, see Comrie (1979) and Hopper and Thompson (1980).

(23)   Benefactive > Recipient > Patient > Instrument

(24)   1st > 2nd > 3rd human > 3rd animal > 3rd inanimate

The sign > stands for "more likely to undergo/trigger certain grammatical processes than." These hierarchies must be interpreted relatively as not every language in which they are at work draws all of the distinctions made in (23) and (24), and some languages may make finer distinctions (particularly in degrees of animacy within third person referents). As seen in (23), benefactives (ben) have greater access to object properties than recipients (rec), which in turn have greater access than patients (pat) and instruments (inst). Other case relations will ultimately have to be added, including causative agents and, in Bantu, locatives. In (24) we have collapsed two separate hierarchies into one general statement. The first is a personal hierarchy whereby first person is higher than second person which is higher than third person in attracting object properties. The second is an animacy hierarchy whereby 3rd human is greater than 3rd animal which is greater than 3rd inanimate. Again, there is room for further distinctions (e.g., man versus woman versus child versus slave, according to the culture). We shall refer to (26) as the person–animacy (PA) hierarchy.

Finally, we note that a more "determined" (or "individuated," according to Hopper and Thompson (1980)) referent will have greater access to object properties than a less determined one. Thus, presupposed, definite singulars are higher in this hierarchy than asserted, indefinite, or nonspecific plurals, etc.

Although all three hierarchies play some role in most Bantu languages, by far the most influential factor is the PA hierarchy. In many Bantu languages a noun low in the case hierarchy (23) can receive object properties for the simple reason that its referent is human [i.e., high in the PA hierarchy (24)]. In order to isolate the human factor in determining object properties, a study based on Sesotho was undertaken by Morolong and Hyman (1977). In this study the following test sentences provided all four logical combinations of human/nonhuman benefactive and patient noun objects:

(25)   A.   'I cooked food for the child'.
              Ben–human   Pat–nonhuman
         B.   'I cooked food for the feast'.
              Ben–nonhuman   Pat–nonhuman
         C.   'I called the children for the feast'.
              Ben–nonhuman   Pat–human
         D.   'I called the children for the chief'.
              Ben–human   Pat–human

Each of the two nouns in each test sentence was submitted to the three tests for object status (word order, subjectivization, and cliticization).

(26)   A.   *Ke-phehétsé ngoaná lijó.*   I-cooked/app child food[8]
             *Ke-phehétsé lijó ngoaná.   I-cooked/app food child
       B.   *Ke-phehétsé mokété lijó.*   I-cooked/app feast food
             Ke-phehétsé lijó mokéte.   I-cooked/app food feast
       C.   *Ke-bítselítsé baná mokéte.*   I-called/app children feast
             *Ke-bítselítsé mokété baná.   I-called/app feast children
       D.   *Ke-bítselítsé morena baná.*   I-called/app chief children [A]
             Ke-bítselítsé baná morena.   I-called/app children chief [A]

As seen in the Sesotho sentences in (26), the two nouns occurring after the verb can occur in either order PROVIDED THAT a nonhuman noun does not precede a human noun—as in the starred second sentences of A and C. As indicated by [A], it can be noted that both sentences in D are ambiguous, meaning either 'I called the children for the chief' or 'I called the chief for the children'.

In (27) we observe that except for *mokéte* 'feast' in C, both nouns in each test sentence can be subjectivized:

(27)   A.   *Ngoaná ó-phehétsoé lijó.*   child he-was-cooked/app food

             Lijó lí-phehétsoé ngoaná.   food it-was-cooked/app child

       B.   *Mokété ó-phehétsoé lijó.*   feast it-was-cooked/app food

             Lijó lí-phehétsoé mokéte.   food it-was-cooked/app feast

       C.   *Baná bá-bítselítsoé mokéte.*   children they-were-called/ app feast
             *Mokété ó-bítselítsoé baná.   feast it-was-called/app children

       D.   *Morena ó-bítselítsoé baná.*   chief he-was-called/app children [A]
             Baná bá-bítselítsoé morena.   children they-were-called/ app chief [A]

---

[8] As the intended meanings of the test sentences are given in (27), we shall not provide English translations for the Sesotho sentences. The abbreviation "app" stands for the applied extension which, because of fusion with the *-il-* past tense extension, will not be separated from the verb radical by hyphens.

And, finally, in (28), it is observed that except for *mokéte* 'feast' in the second sentence in C, either noun in each test sentence can be expressed through a corresponding pronoun in the clitic OM position:

(28)   A. *Ke-mó-phehétsé lijó.*   I-him-cooked/app food
            Ke-lí-phehétsé ngoaná.   I-it-cooked/app child
        B. *Ke-ó-phehétsé lijó.*   I-it[feast]-cooked/app food
            Ke-lí-phehétsé mokéte.   I-it[food]-cooked/app feast
        C. *Ke-ba-bítselítsé mokéte.*   I-them-called/app feast
            *Ke-o-bítselítsé baná.   I-it[feast]-called/app chief
        D. *Ke-mo-bítselítsé baná.*   I-him-called/app children [A]
            Ke-ba-bítselítsé morena.   I-them-called/app chief [A]

Sesotho, unlike Haya, does not allow more than one pronoun in the clitic OM position.

From the preceding it becomes clear that animacy is an important factor in determining object status in Sesotho. Although details vary from language to language,[9] we have found no Bantu language where animacy is irrelevant in determining which arguments will acquire object properties in such utterances. In Sesotho we have seen that a nonhuman noun cannot precede a human noun. In addition, in (27) and (28) we observe that when the benefactive is nonhuman and the patient is human, it is the patient that acquires *all* of the object properties—and at the expense of the benefactive, which is not an object at all, but a prepositionless oblique. This last fact comes as a surprise since in the A sentences we see that Sesotho can in fact accommodate a human and a nonhuman object in sequence after the verb—but only if the human is the benefactive and the nonhuman is the patient! In (29)–(31) we observe that the affected possessor construction lines up exactly with the properties of the preceding C sentences:

(29)   a. *Ke-robílé ngoaná letsóho.*   I-broke child arm
        b. **Ke-robílé letsóhó ngoaná.*   I-broke arm child

(30)   a. *Ngoaná ó-robíloé letsóho.*   child he-was-broken arm
        b. **Letsóhó lé-robíloé ngoaná.*   arm it-was-broken child

(31)   a. *Ke-mó-robílé letsóho.*   I-him-broke arm
        b. **Ke-lé-robílé ngoaná.*   I-it-broke child

---

[9] One has but to compare the Shona situation reported by Hawkinson and Hyman (1974) with that reported in Morolong and Hyman (1977) for Sesotho to see that two languages can be animacy-oriented in very different ways (cf. also Duranti 1979 for a comparison of Shambala and Haya).

In (29b) *letsóho* 'arm' cannot precede the affected possessor *ngoaná* 'child'.[10] In (30b) it cannot subjectivize, and in (31b) it cannot cliticize as a pronoun. Therefore, we conclude that in the affected possessor construction in Sesotho, as in Haya, the (body) part is not an object. It is in this sense parallel to the nonhuman benefactive in the C sentences in (26), (27), and (28). As has been argued by Hyman (1977) and Morolong and Hyman (1977), both the C sentences and the affected possessor construction involve an argument acquiring object properties because of its higher status along an "affectedness" scale. When one breaks a child's stick, the stick is affected; when one breaks a child's arm, the CHILD is affected. Thus, in Bantu languages, being an object MEANS being an important participant in an event (cf. Hinnebusch and Kirsner (1980).

4. TYPOLOGY OF OBJECT PROPERTIES

We have indicated that there are differences in the ways in which individual Bantu languages treat objects. In this necessarily programmatic statement, we shall consider the following parameters: (*a*) word order, (*b*) cliticization; and (*c*) the PA hierarchy.

In approaching the question of word order in the comparative study of the object relation in Bantu, we are concerned primarily with the following questions:

1. Is the order of objects fixed, variable, or free?
2. Is the order of objects determined by case, the PA hierarchy, and/ or determinedness?

Important related questions involve the role or relevance of ambiguity, the ability of an object to be left dislocated (in the presence of another object), and the number of object nouns permitted after the verb. In determining word order variability, it is necessary to consider potentially ambiguous versus potentially nonambiguous combinations (e.g., test sentences D versus A, respectively). In some Bantu languages, for example, Logooli,[11] the equivalents of the two sentences in (28D) unambiguously mean 'I called the children for the chief' and 'I called the chief for the

---

[10] This is not because the affected possessor is human, since it need not be, as seen in the following examples (cf. also Voeltz 1976):

  (i)   *Ke-robílé sefáté lekala* (I-broke tree branch);
  (ii) **Ke-robílé lekala sefáte* (I-broke branch tree).

[11] We are indebted to Rachel Angogo for all of the statements and examples concerning Logooli, a Luhya language spoken in Kenya.

children'. That is, the first human noun is always interpreted as the benefactive. In others, such as Sesotho, as we have seen, such sentences are ambiguous. Similarly to Logooli, in Shona (Hawkinson and Hyman 1974), nouns can be moved out of the benefactive–patient order if there is recoverability of the case relations from the previous discourse. This is related to the role of determinedness in word order. In general, a noun whose referent is presupposed (from discourse or otherwise) will tend to come earlier than one which is not so presupposed. An ultimate typology will not only consider the above factors (case, PA, determinedness), but also treat their interaction. At the moment it appears that some languages (e.g., Logooli) are case oriented, whereas others (e.g., Sesotho) are animacy oriented. Determinedness seems to play a lesser role in the languages we have intestigated, although the singular–plural distinction contributes potentially to the ordering of object clitics (Duranti 1979).

Turning to cliticization, it is important to ask the following questions:

1. What function or functions can the clitic fulfill?
2. How many clitics can occur in sequence (in what order, and under which cooccurrence constraints)?
3. What is the interaction between clitics and other grammatical processes?

In (1) we refer to the following four attested functions of clitic OM markers in Bantu: (*a*) pronominalization, (*b*) left dislocation, (*c*) relativization, and (*d*) object agreement. As seen in (32a)–(32d), Sesotho exhibits all four uses of clitics:

(32)   a. *Ke-a-mo-bón-a.*
            I-pres-him-see
            'I see him'.
        b. *Ngoaná ke-a-mo-bón-a.*
            child   I-pres-him-see
            'The child, I see him'.
        c. *Ngoaná éò   ké-mo-bón-á-ǹg.*
            child   that I-him-see-rel
            'The child that I see (him)'.
        d. *Ke-a-mo-bón-a ngoaná.*
            I-pres-him-see child
            'I see the child'.

Because cliticizability may depend on the MEANS by which a clitic is obtained, it is important to distinguish whether the OM is a true pronoun [e.g., (32a)] or a copy of a noun present in the same construction [e.g.,

(32b)–(32d)]. A particularly clear example of the need to distinguish the different functions of the OM comes from Sukuma (Herman Batibo, personal communication). In this language the following sentence is ungrammatical:

(33)   *A-ka-bii-nh-w-á.
        he-past-them-give-pass-asp
        'He was given them [human cl. 2]'.

This shows that a passive construction will not tolerate a human pronoun in the OM slot. However, as seen in (34), the human OM is acceptable in the passive if a preprefixed (= [+ determined]) coreferential object noun occurs with the clitic.

(34)   A-ka-bii-nh-w-á abaana.
        'He was given the children'.

What cannot cliticize as a pronoun in (33) CAN cliticize as an agreement marker in (34)!

Returning to Sesotho, we observe in (35) that when the affected possessor ngoaná 'child' of (29a) is subjectivized, the possessed part letsóho 'arm' cannot be cliticized as a pronoun:

(35)   *Ngoaná ó-le-róbiloe.
        child   he-it-broke-pass
        Lit.,   'the child was broken it [the arm]'.

However, as seen now in (36), cliticization of 'arm' can cooccur with the subjectivization of 'child', if the clitic OM is the result of relativization rather than pronominalization.

(36)   Letsóhó léò ngoaná á-lé-robíloé-ng
        arm   that child   he-it-broke-pass-rel
        Lit., 'the arm that the child he [it] was broken'.

As we would not want to claim that 'arm' miraculously BECOMES an object in (36), we must conclude that the constraints on cliticization are relaxed depending on the source of the clitic. And, finally, we conclude that if cliticization is to be seen as a determinant of objecthood, then we must further specify that the clitic must be a pronoun, and not simply a resumptive marker required by the relativization process in Sesotho.

In any typology of cliticization in Bantu one must seek to hierarchize these clitic functions and determine the relative strength of each type. Except for the northwestern end of the Bantu zone (and a few exceptional languages), all Bantu languages appear to use the clitic OM slot for pronominalization. In addition, all of the Bantu languages we have examined exhibit clitic OMs with a left dislocation process. Only some Bantu languages require clitic resumptive pronouns in relative clauses or have "true" object agreement.[12] By "true" object agreement we mean that a noun can cooccur with a coreferential OM clitic without there being a syntactic break characteristic of right dislocation.[13] Sesotho permits this kind of object agreement only in the "long" form of the present tense, as seen in (32d) above. In order to show that (32d) is not a case of right dislocation (in which case the sentence would be translated 'I see him, the child'), it is necessary to show that asserted information can follow the coreferential noun and that what precedes is therefore not a complete sentence. A proper frame is provided in (37).

(37)   *Ke-a-mo-bótsa ngoaná lepótso.*
        I-pres-him-ask child   question
        'I am asking the child a question'.

In this sentence 'child' cannot be seen as a right dislocation, because this would automatically imply that the full assertion was what precedes it, that is, *ke-a-mo-bótsa* 'I am asking him'. As the assertion is not completed until the noun *lepótso* 'question' is uttered, *ngoaná* 'child' must be part of the assertion, rather than right dislocation. In (38), however, where 'child' occurs AFTER 'question', the resulting sentence is necessarily analyzed as the assertion 'I am asking him a question' followed by right dislocation 'the child'.

(38)   *Ke-a-mo-bótsa lepótsó   ngoaná.*
        I-pres-him-ask question child
        'I am asking him a question, the child'.

This is necessarily correct, because, as we have seen, the language does not permit a nonhuman postverbal noun to precede a human noun. Thus, (38) must be analyzed as containing a major syntactic break between *lepótsó* and *ngoaná*. In this case the clitic *-mo-* 'him' is a true pronoun and not an object agreement marker.

Turning now to the PA hierarchy, we typologize Bantu languages according to (*a*) the DEGREE to which person and animacy play a role in determining the object properties of arguments, and (*b*) the MEANS by which they do so. Some languages such as Logooli show relatively little

---

[12] The presence of object agreement is required in some languages when the object noun is human (Givón 1979, Wald 1979). When the object noun is nonhuman, the presence of an OM agreeing with the noun may mean that the latter is presupposed information.

[13] For a discussion of right dislocation in Haya, see Byarushengo and Tenenbaum (1976), Byarushengo, Hyman, and Tenenbaum (1976), and Tenenbaum (1977a, 1977b).

concern for animacy, while others (e.g., Sesotho and Shona) make a major effort to organize referential material along the PA scale. In languages where animacy plays a major role, either word order or access to grammatical processes can be affected. We have already seen that Sesotho requires human nouns to precede nonhuman nouns. In addition, in languages with multiple clitics in the OM slot, participants that are higher in the various hierarchies are generally placed closer to the verb radical, as seen in the Haya utterance in (39).

(39)   *N-ka-ga-ba-kú-siig-il-a.*
         I-P$_3$-it-them-you-smear-app
         'I smeared it [oil] on them [people] for you (sg.)'.

In this example we not only have the order instrument–patient–benefactive (following the case hierarchy in reverse), but also 3rd inanimate followed by 3rd human followed by second person, in accordance with the PA hierarchy. As we have mentioned, only some Bantu languages allow more than one clitic in the OM slot.[14] In languages that have multiple clitics, their combinability and relative ordering are determined by case, person–animacy, and determinedness. In Duranti (1979) a rigorous study was made of all of the possible manipulations of these features in both Shambala and Haya. The purpose of the study was to determine how different Bantu languages deal with conflicts arising between the different hierarchies. For example, in a sentence such as *I hit you for him,* the benefactive is third person, and the patient object is second person. According to the case hierarchy, the benefactive is higher than the patient, but according to the PA hierarchy, second person is higher than third person. We thus have a conflict. Duranti (1979) shows that whenever a conflict arises in Shambala, cooccurrence of the two clitics is blocked. In Haya, on the other hand, different strategies are employed to resolve the conflict. Whenever there is a conflict between the case and PA hierarchies, the latter wins out, as seen in (40).

(40)   a.   *A-ka-mu-ku-léét-el-a.*
              he-P$_3$-him-you-bring-app
              'He brought him to you'.
              'He brought you to him'.
         b.   **A-ka-ku-mu-léét-el-a.*
              he-P$_3$-you-him-bring-app

---

[14] In fact, in many languages, for example, Shi (Polak-Bynon 1975), there can be two OM clitics only when one of them is a first person singular or a reflexive. The first person singular is of course highest on the PA and number hierarchies and therefore least likely to begrudge the OM slot to a cooccurring clitic.

While (40b) is ungrammatical because a second person clitic precedes a third person clitic, (40a) has both of the readings indicated. Whenever there is a conflict between animacy and case, it can be resolved with either winning out, as seen in (41).[15]

(41)   a.   *A-ka-bi-ba-léét-el-a*
              he-P$_3$-them-them-bring-APP
              'He brought them (*bi*) to them (*ba*)'.
              'He brought them (*ba*) to them (*bi*)'.
        b.   *A-ka-ba-bi-léét-el-a*
              he-P$_3$-them-them-bring-APP
              'He brought them (*ba*) to them (*bi*)'.
              *'He brought them (*bi*) to them (*ba*)'.

In these examples *ba* is the human clitic, while *bi* is the nonhuman clitic. In (41a) either interpretation is possible: In the first gloss animacy and case line up; in the second gloss, where the human clitic is the patient, it still can appear closer to the verb stem by virtue of its higher position in the animacy hierarchy. In (41b), on the other hand, where the inanimate clitic stands before the verb stem, the only interpretation is that it is the benefactive (i.e., higher on the case hierarchy than the patient). Haya also treats singulars as higher on the determinedness hierarchy. The data in (42) should be thus compared with those in (41).

(42)   a.   *A-ka-ba-mu-léét-el-a*
              he-P$_3$-them-him-bring-app
              'He brought them to him'.
              'He brought him to them'.
        b.   *A-ka-mu-ba-léét-el-a*
              he-P$_3$-him-them-bring-app
              'He brought him to them'.
              *'He brought them to him'.

Both readings are possible in (42a): In the first gloss the singular clitic lines up with the higher case (benefactive) and therefore appears close to the verb. In the second gloss, where the plural clitic is the benefactive (higher case), *mu* still stands closer to the verb because it is singular, whereas *ba* is plural. In (42b), only one reading is possible, as the second gloss violates BOTH the case and determinedness hierarchies. The con-

---

[15] Since Duranti (1979) demonstrates that person is stronger than case whereas animacy and case are equal in strength, this provides some motivation for separating our conflated PA hierarchy into two parts: (*a*) 1st > 2nd > 3rd, and (*b*) 3rd human > 3rd animal > 3rd inanimate.

clusion drawn by Duranti is that person is stronger than case or number, and that case = animacy = number. It is only when case and number COMBINE that their cumulative effect is equal in strength to person.

As far as access to clitic position is concerned, we have said that the subjectivization of a less animate referent can block the cliticization of a more animate referent. Logooli offers an exception to this rule, since sentences such as (43b) are ruled out in most Bantu languages:

(43)   a. *Ichú'kúríá ch-a-ḿ-deek-er-w-a.*
             food   it-past-him-call-app-pass
             'The food was cooked for him'.
         b. *Isúguukú 'y-á-ḿ-'ráának-ir-w-â*
             feast   it-PAST-him-call-APP-PASS
             Lit., 'the feast was called him (for)'.

5. HISTORY OF OBJECT PROPERTIES

It is clear from the preceding discussion that there is considerable variation in how the object relation is treated by different Bantu languages. Not only do the actual criteria for object status vary from one Bantu language to the next, but so do the strategies or factors influencing which arguments will acquire these criteria. In distinguishing between the criteria themselves and the factors influencing the acquiring of these criteria, we hope to have employed a framework which can be applied with success to the typological study of the object relation in all parts of the Bantu zone.

One question that immediately arises is a historical one: Which one, if any, of the languages discussed here or in the literature represents the properties of objects in Proto-Bantu? For example, was Proto-Bantu a case-oriented or an animacy-oriented language? How many objects could occur in the same sentence in Proto-Bantu?

While certain phenomena appear to be recent innovations (e.g., the object agreement found in Swahili, Nyakyusa, and certain coastal languages [see Wald 1979]), the questions are complicated by a number of unresolved side issues which bear on the nature of objects in PB:

1. What was the function of extensions (e.g., the app) in PB?
2. What was the word order in PB?
3. How does PB relate to the rest of Benue- and Niger-Congo (higher order phyla to which it belongs)?

We shall briefly address only questions (1) and (2).

The app extension is perhaps central to the problem of reconstructing the object properties of the protolanguage. While it is apparently always the case that this extension "introduces" or "makes possible" a benefactive or recipient object, its other functions cannot be ignored. In particular, it frequently can introduce an instrument, as in Logooli and in ChiMwi:ni (Kisseberth and Abasheikh 1977), or a locative, as in Tunen (Dugast 1971) and Haya. In Haya, as seen in the following examples, the app extension can even result in a meaning difference (cf. also Trithart 1977).

(44)   a.   *N-ka-gw' ómú-nju.*
              I-P₃-fall   in   -house
              'I fell into the house'.
        b.   *N-ka-gw-el' ómú-nju.*
              I-P₃-fall-app in   -house
              'I fell in the house'.

In (44b) the falling took place while I was in the house, while in (44a) I fell from outside *into* the house.[16] Similar additional examples show that the app extension allows one to "upgrade" a noun to being outside the scope (or selectional restrictions) of the verb. Thus, compare the two sentences in (45).

(45)   a.   *N-ka-bón-a kat'. ómú-nju.*
              I-P₃-see   Kato in   -house
              'I saw Kato [while he was] in the house'.
        b.   *N-ka-bón-el-a kat' ómú-nju.*
              I-P₃-see-APP Kato in   -house
              'I saw Kato [while I was] in the house'.

While it is the case in so many Bantu languages that the app extension introduces an object, it would be hard to argue that the locatives in (44b) and (45b) represent higher CASE relationships than those in (44a) and (45a). Rather, it is their relationship to the CLAUSE that is different: In the (a) sentences the locatives are part of the verb complement; in the (b) sentences they are not part of the verb complement, but rather relate to the entire proposition (including the subject's relationship to the action). Reconsidering sentences with an app extension introducing a benefactive or recipient argument, we can say that the app extension here

---

[16] Since the app extension is normally associated with the dative (recipient) case in Bantu, the parallel situation represented by the following German sentences is particularly striking: *Ich fiel in das [acc.] Haus* 'I fell into the house' versus *Ich fiel in dem [dat.] Haus* 'I fell in(side) the house'.

also elevates its object to being outside the verb complement (e.g., to cook food FOR someone). Thus, instead of saying that the app extension orients the verb toward the benefactive, we may say that it DISORIENTS the verb away from its (patient or locative) complement. In-depth analysis of the app extension in representative Bantu languages is a necessary prerequisite, then, to establishing the nature of the object in PB.

The same is true of word order. It has been hypothesized by Givón (1971) that the reason why the OM clitic position precedes the verb radical is that at an earlier stage PB was an SOV language. The older order is thus preserved when the object is a pronoun, but a new SVO order has come into being when the object is a noun. (The same SVO order is observed with pronouns in the northwestern part of the Bantu zone.) The question that is of relevance here concerns the relative chronology of the development of SVO word order and cliticization (as a criterion for object status). One weakness of Givón's reconstruction is that he has restricted his data base to only one sub-branch of Bantu, which, although admittedly covering a vast geographic expanse, is not representative of the whole family. Most of the languages of the numerous sub-branches of Northwest Bantu show little or no trace of clitics. An extreme example is Tunen, which, as reported by Dugast (1971), not only has full pronouns instead of clitics, but also has SOV word order even when the object is a noun! Two interesting observations about Tunen are (a) the presence of the same extensions found elsewhere in Bantu, and (b) the presence of preverbal tense markers preceding the object noun or pronoun. One of these concerns the same past tense marker seen earlier in the Haya and Sukuma examples:

(46)   *Bá ká nekaka bílíhɔ́ni m^{w}ɔ̄sé málɛ́ndólónum.*
       they past meeting fixed   days   seven
       'They fixed the meeting at seven days'.

There is considerable evidence that Tunen has innovated this SOVX word order, rather than (46) representing a remnant from the PB stage. In either case we would probably have to maintain that prefixed tense/aspect markers such as PB *kà* appeared as separate words rather than as part of what we know today as the agglutinative verbal complex. If this is correct, then it is also possible that PB did not have clitics—that is, that it either had full object pronouns or, more likely, that it only had [+human] object pronouns. The hierarchies that have been exposed in this paper would therefore have come into being as a result of innovating clitics and the OM position itself!

Although the evidence for this view is inconclusive at present, there are important signs in present-day NW Bantu languages that point to such an interdependency between clitics and hierarchies. Consider Basaa, one such language spoken in Cameroon.[17] Basaa is an SVO language having the same extension system noted universally in Bantu. It differs from its easterly relatives, however, in having full pronouns occurring after the verbal complex, whether first, second, or third person. In (47)–(49) we apply our three tests of objecthood to the proposition 'I cooked food for the child'. [As there are no clitics, pronominalization will be substituted for cliticization in (48).]

(47)   a.   *Mɛ nlémbél   máŋgé bijék.*
            I   cooked-app child   food
            'I cooked the child food'.
       b.   *?Me nlémbél   bíjék maŋgé [A].*
            I   cooked-app food   child
            'I cooked food (for) the child'.

(48)   a.   *Mɛ nlémbél   nyé bijék (*bíjék nyέ).*
            I   cooked-app him food   food him
            'I cooked him food'.
       b.   *Mɛ nlémbél   gwɔ́ maŋgé / máŋgé gwɔ́.*
            I   cooked-app it   child   child   it
            'I cooked it (for) the child'.
       c.   *Mɛ nlémbél   nyé gwɔ́.*
            I   cooked-app him it
            'I cooked him it'.
       d.   **Mɛ nlémbél   gwɔ́ nyé [R].*
            I   cooked-app it   him
            'I cooked it (for) him'. (= intended)
            ('I cooked him for it' = actual)

(49)   a.   **Maŋgé i nlémbná   bíjék.*
            child   he was cooked-app food
            'The child was cooked food'.
       b.   *Bijék bí ńlémbná   máŋgé*
            food it was cooked-app child
            'Food was cooked (for) the child'.

The normal word order involving two noun objects is as seen in (47a): The benefactive precedes the patient. In (47b), where the two are reversed, ambiguity results between the intended meaning and the reading

---

[17] The Basaa materials were worked out in conjunction with Marie Anne Boum, to whom we are greatly indebted for this information.

'I cooked the child for the food'. In (48a) and (48b) we observe that the order "pronoun followed by noun" is always possible, and in addition, in (48b), the order "noun followed by pronoun" is acceptable if the noun is the benefactive and the pronoun the patient.[18] Sentence (50c) shows that both the benefactive and the patient can be pronominalized simultaneously, but as seen from the ungrammaticality of (48d) in its intended meaning, the order of the pronouns must be benefactive–patient. (The [R] indicates that only the reverse meaning is inferable, i.e., 'I cooked him for it'.) What is of crucial importance to our study of objecthood is the fact that only the patient can be subjectivized. The passive construction in (49a), where the benefactive has been made subject, is ungrammatical. The construction in (49b), on the other hand, with its patient subject, is completely acceptable. The generalization seems to be as follows: If a Bantu language has clitics, then the benefactive object has equal or greater access to subjectivization. (In fact, as we saw from the Sesotho test sentences, case relations often subside almost completely in the face of the PA hierarchy.) On the other hand, if a Bantu language does not have clitics, the patient object has exclusive access to subjectivization.[19] Thus, Bakundu is another Cameroonian language without clitics and has the same subjectivization properties as Basaa (Erhard Voeltz, personal communication), whereas Bakweri, a nearby Bantu language WITH clitics, looks very Haya-like in character (Hawkinson, personal communication). The conclusion is that, within Bantu as well as without, when a language has clitics, semantic hierarchies acquire an upper hand in determining object properties, while grammatical considerations step to the side.

---

[18] It should be noted that in Tunen, Basaa, Bakundu, Hunde, and other Bantu languages having full object pronouns, these pronouns are clearly derived from demonstratives as secondary and often independent developments.

[19] This statement needs to be tempered somewhat, since the verb 'to give' allows only its recipient object to subjectivize:

(i) *Maŋgé a ntí -bá bíjék.*
   child   he give-pass food
   'The child was given food'.

(ii) **Bíjék bí ńtí -bá   máŋgé.*
   food   it give-pass child
   'The food was given (to) the child'.

While the few verbs like 'to give' are oriented toward the recipient object in all of Bantu, only clitic languages have the property of orienting verbs extended by the app suffix toward the corresponding recipient or benefactive object. Perhaps this is a later innovation occasioned by the development of clitics?

ACKNOWLEDGMENTS

An earlier version of this paper was presented at the Colloque "Expansion Bantu" organized by the L.P. 3-121 team of the Centre National de la Recherche Scientifique in Viviers, France (April 1977). We would like to acknowledge the considerable input of Mr. Ernest Byarushengo and Ms. Malillo Morolong, whose many insights into the analysis of their respective languages (Haya and Sesotho) have led to some of the positions taken in the present study. Research on comparative Bantu syntax, especially within the Cameroonian context, was supported in part by a National Science Foundation grant BNS76-81261.

REFERENCES

Byarushengo, E., L. Hyman, and S. Tenenbaum (1976) "Tone, Accent and Assertion in Haya," in L. Hyman, ed., *Studies in Bantu Tonology* (*Southern California Occasional Papers in Linguistics* 3), Department of Linguistics, University of Southern California, Los Angeles.

Byarushengo, E. and S. Tenenbaum (1976) "Agreement and Word Order: A Case for Pragmatics in Haya," *Proceedings of the Second Annual Meeting of the Berkeley Linguistics Society,* 89–99.

Comrie, B. (1979) "Definite and Animate Direct Objects: A Natural Class," *Linguistica Silesiang* 3, 13–21.

Dalgish, G. (1976a) "Passivizing Locatives in Olutsootso," *Studies in the Linguistic Sciences* 6, 57–68.

Dalgish, G. (1976b) "Locative NPs, Locative Suffixes, and Grammatical Relations," in *Proceedings of the Second Annual Meeting of the Berkeley Linguistics Society,* 139–148.

Dugast, I. (1971) *Grammaire du Tùnεn* (Langues et Littératures de l'Afrique Noire VIII), Editions Klincksieck, Paris.

Duranti, A. (1976) "Contributi delle Lingue Bantu alla Teoria della Grammatica Relazionale," *Rivista de Grammatica Generativa* 1.3, 1–57.

Duranti, A. (1979) "Object Clitic Pronouns in Bantu and the Topicality Hierarchy," *Studies in African Linguistics* 10, 31–45.

Duranti, A. and E. Byarushengo (1977) "On the Notion of 'Direct Object'," in E. Byarushengo, A. Duranti, and L. Hyman, eds., *Haya Grammatical Structure* (*Southern California Occasional Papers in Linguistics* 6), Department of Linguistics, University of Southern California, Los Angeles.

Fεltz, L. M. (1978) "On Indirect Objects in Universal Syntax," in D. Farkas, W. Jacobsen, *Papers from the Fourteenth Regional Meeting of the Chicago Linguistic Society,* Chicago Linguistics Society, University of Chicago.

Fox, B. (1981) "Body Part Syntax: Towards a Universal Characterization," *Studies in Linguistics*.

Gary, J. and E. L. Keenan (1977) "On Collapsing Grammatical Relations in Universal Grammar," in P. Cole and J. Saddock, eds., *Syntax and Semantics 8: Grammatical Relations,* Academic Press, New York.

Givón, T. (1971) "Historical Syntax and Synchronic Morphology: An Archeologist's Field Trip," in Chicago Linguistic Society, University of Chicago. *Papers from the Seventh Regional Meeting of the Chicago Linguistic Society,*

Givón, T. (1979) *On Understanding Grammar,* Academic Press, New York.

Hawkinson, A. and L. Hyman (1974) "Hierarchies of Natural Topic in Shona," *Studies in African Linguistics* 5, 147–170.

Hinnebusch, T. and R. Kirsner (1980) "On the Inference of 'Inalienable Possession' in Swahili," *Journal of African Languages and Linguistics* 2.1, 1–16.

Hopper, P. and S. Thompson (1980) "Transitivity in Grammar and Discourse," *Language* 56, 251–299.

Hyman, L. (1977) "The Syntax of Body Parts," in E. Byarushengo, A. Duranti, and L. Hyman, eds., *Haya Grammatical Structure* (*Southern California Occasional Papers in Linguistics* 6), Department of Linguistics, University of Southern California, Los Angeles.

Kimenyi, A. (1979) *A Relational Grammar of Kinyarwanda,* University of California Press, Los Angeles and Berkeley.

Kisseberth, C. and M. Abasheikh (1977) "The Object Relationship in Chi-Mwi:ni, a Bantu Language," in P. Cole and J. Saddock, eds., *Syntax and Semantics 8: Grammatical Relations,* Academic Press, New York.

Morolong, M. and L. Hyman (1977) "Animacy, Objects, and Clitics in Sesotho," *Studies in African Linguistics* 8, 199–218.

Polak-Bynon, L. (1975) *A Shi Grammar,* Musée Royal de l'Afrique Centrale, Tervuren.

Stucky, S. (1976) "Locatives as Objects in Tshiluba: A Function of Transitivity," *Studies in the Linguistic Sciences* 6, 174–202.

Tenenbaum, S. (1977a) "Left- and Right-Dislocation," in E. Byarushengo, A. Duranti, and L. Hyman, eds., *Haya Grammatical Structure* (*Southern California Occasional Papers in Linguistics* 6), Department of Linguistics, University of Southern California, Los Angeles.

Tenenbaum, S. (1977b) "On Reference in Haya," in E. O. Keenan and T. Bennett, eds., *Discourse across Time and Space* (*Southern California Occasional Papers in Linguistics* 5), Department of Linguistics, University of Southern California, Los Angeles.

Trithart, L. (1975) "Relational Grammar and Chichewa Subjectivization Rules," in R. Grossman, L. J. San, and T. J. Vance, eds., *Papers from the Eleventh Regional Meeting of the Chicago Linguistic Society,* Chicago Linguistic Society, University of Chicago.

Trithart, L. (1976) *Relational Grammar and Chichewa Subjectivization Rules,* unpublished master's thesis, University of California, Los Angeles.

Trithart, L. (1977) "Locatives," in E. Byarushengo, A. Duranti, and L. Hyman, eds., *Haya Grammatical Structure* (*Southern California Occasional Papers in Linguistics* 6), Department of Linguistics, University of Southern California, Los Angeles.

Trithart, L. (1979) "Topicality: An Alternative to the Relational View of Bantu Passive," *Studies in African Linguistics* 10, 1–30.

Voeltz, E. (1976) "Inalienable Possession in Sotho," in L. Hyman, L. Jacobson, and R. Schuh, eds., *Papers in African Linguistics in Honor of Wm. E. Welmers* (*Studies in African Linguistics,* Supplement 6), 255–266.

Wald, B. (1979) "The Development of the Swahili Object Marker: A Study in the Interaction of Syntax and Discourse," in T. Givón, ed., *Syntax and Semantics, 12, Discourse and Syntax,* Academic Press, New York.

TRANSITIVITY IN A CZECH FOLK TALE

IVAN KALMÁR

1. INTRODUCTION

In a major contribution to functional syntax, Hopper and Thompson (1980) communicate an implicational relationship between different characteristics of the clause, which they list as in Table 1. Hopper and Thompson regard these parameters as components of an interrelated complex they call TRANSITIVITY. They claim that (*a*) the presence of one component implies the presence of the others, and that (*b*) high transitivity correlates with the discourse feature of foregrounding, that is, of making some clauses more important than others in terms of their content.

To test the validity of Hopper and Thompson's claims for Czech, I subjected a Czech folk tale to an analysis according to their criteria, and performed tests of significance on the results. In confirmation of Hopper and Thompson's study, I found that an implicational relationship among the 10 categories of Table 1 did on the whole hold for my data. However, my results appear to indicate that our understanding of the correlation between transitivity and foregrounding is in need of further refinement. I found it necessary to separate two elements of foregrounding: the singling out of some clauses as carrying more important information than

241

TABLE 1
List of Transitivity Components (A–Agent, O–Object)

Component	High transitivity	Low transitivity
Participants	2 or more	1 participant
Kinesis	action	nonaction
Aspect	telic (perfective)	atelic (nonperfective)
Punctuality	punctual	nonpunctual
Volitionality	volitional	nonvolitional
Affirmation	affirmative	negative
Mode	realis	irrealis
Agency	A high in potency	A low in potency
Affectedness of O	O totally affected	O not affected
Individuation of O	O highly individuated	O nonindividuated

others, or FOREGROUNDING proper, and the temporal ordering of events, or SEQUENTIALITY.

Foregrounding, thus redefined, could not be proved to correlate with transitivity on the basis of my limited data, although the figures make such correlation quite likely if a larger corpus could have been included. Remarkably, however, sequentiality correlated with foregrounding extremely strongly. I conclude that the primary correlation of transitivity is with sequentiality.

Should transitivity turn out also to correlate with foregrounding, then this could be seen as a consequence of the relationship between sequentiality and foregrounding proper. Temporal ordering is really just one way of highlighting the more salient components of a discourse, and in this sense sequentiality is one element of foregrounding. QUOTATION is another: Much of the crucial information appears in direct and indirect quotes. Unlike sequentiality, however, quotation does not seem to correlate with transitivity. Hence the relationship between transitivity and foregrounding "as a whole" is weaker than that between transitivity and sequentiality alone.

2. THE TEXT

The text is one of the folk tales told in standard spoken Czech recorded in a collection by Tille (1929). Although the tale is short, it yielded surprisingly many relationships that were highly significant statistically. Our text is remarkably similar in style to other texts in Tille's collection, and this facilitates the assumption that the conclusions reached here hold more generally.

For clarity of presentation I give the text first, although some of the notation used in transcribing it cannot be fully explained until later. In the transcription, each clause is preceded by its number. The number is followed by symbols in parentheses, which are to be read as follows: S sequential, $-S$ nonsequential, F foregrounded, $-F$ backgrounded, F' foregrounded continued, $-F'$ backgrounded continued. All these terms are explained in what follows. The numbers following the letters give the transitivity score for each clause, as in the following examples: $S, -F7$ sequential, backgrounded clause with a score of 7; $-S4, F8$ nonsequential clause with a score of 4, which is also the first part of a foregrounded clause with a score of 8. This terminology, too, becomes clear later.

TEXT

1. $(-S, -F4)$ *Jiřík, rytířův   syn, se dobře učí.*
    Jiřík knight-gen son refl well   studies-imperf
    'Jiřík, the son of a knight, is a good student.

2. $(-S, -F7)$ *Jednou přijede   ze   školy   na svátky domů,*
    once   arrives-perf from school-gen on holidays home
    Once he comes home from school for the holidays.

3. $(S4,F5)$ *ráno   na okně   křičí*
    morning on window-loc screams-imperf
    and in the morning a nightingale screams

4. $(S5,F')$ *a třepetá   se slavík*
    and flutters-imperf refl nightingale
    and flutters on the window.

5. $(-S3, -F4)$ *Rodiče se diví,*
    parents refl wonder-imperf
    (Jiřík's) parents are wondering

6. $(-S3, -F')$ *co   chce.*
    what wants-imperf
    what he wants.

7. $(-S5,F9)$ *Jiřík praví,*
    Jiřík says-imperf
    Jiřík says

8. $(-S5,F')$ *že   to ví*
    that it knows-imperf.
    that he knows

9. $(-S, -F3)$ *ale bojí   se   to říci.*
                  but fears-imperf refl it to-tell
                  but is afraid to tell.

10. $(S,F9)$ *Prchlivý otec   mu poručí,*
                  volatile father him orders-perf
                  (His) volatile father orders him

11. $(-S3,F')$ *aby   mluvil.*
                  in-order-to speaks-imperf-subj
                  to speak.

12. $(-S5,F8)$ *Jiřík praví:*
                  Jiřík says-imperf
                  Jiřík says,

13. $(-S5,F')$ *Slavík   křičí,*
                  nightingale screams
                  "The nightingale is saying

14. $(-S2,F')$ *že budu   pánem,*
                  that I-will-be lord-instr
                  that I will be a lord,

15. $(-S7,F')$ *otec že mi bude držet koflík s   vodou k mytí,*
                  father that me he-will hold cup   with water to washing
                  my father will hold up for me a cup to wash myself,

16. $(-S7,F')$ *matka ručník k utření.*
                  mother towel to drying
                  and my mother a towel to dry myself with."

17. $(S,F10)$ *Otec se na něho oboří*
                  father refl on 3acc attacks-perf
                  His father attacks him,

18. $(S,F10)$ *a hodí   ho do vody*
                  and throws-perf 3acc into water-gen
                  and throws him in the water.

19. $(S,F5)$ *Jiřík plove.*
                  swims-imper
                  Jiřík is swimming.

20. $(S,F9)$ *Najdou   ho rybaři*
                  they-find-perf 3acc fishermen
                  Some fishermen find him

21. $(S,F10)$ *a dovedou   k pánovi,*
                  and they-lead-perf to lord-dat
                  and lead him to the lord

22. $(-S, -F7)$ *jemuž chytají   ryby;*
                  that-dat catch-imperf fish-pl
                  that they have been catching fish for;

23. (S,F10)   *pán ho přijme   do služby.*
               lord 3acc accepts-perf into service-gen
               the lord accepts him into his service.

24. (−S, −F3)   *Nedaleko bydlí   král,*
               not-far   lives-imperf king
               Not far off there lives a king,

25. (−S, −F7)   *kterému létají   na okno tři   krkavci;*
               whom-dat fly-imperf on window three ravens
               on whose window three ravens keep flying;

26. (−S, −F4)   *nedají   pokoje.*
               they-give-neg-perf rest-gen
               they give the king no peace.

27. (S,F9)   *Král sezve   panstvo k hostině,*
               king invites-perf lords   to feast-dat
               The king invites the lords to a feast;

28. (S,F10)   *pán   vezme   Jiříka   s   sebou.*
               the-lord takes-perf Jiřík-acc with himself-instr
               the lord takes Jiřík with him.

29. (−S, −F4)   *Když sedí   za   stolem,*
               when sit-imperf behind table-instr
               As they sit at the table,

30. (S,F7)   *přiletí   krkavci*
               arrive-flying-perf ravens
               the ravens arrive

31. (−S, −F5)   *a   křičí.*
               and scream-imperf
               and start screaming.

32. (−S,F8)   *Král slibuje   tomu*
               king promises-imperf that-one-dat
               The king promises to him

33. (−S5,F′)   *kdo uhodne*
               who guesses-perf
               who would guess

34. (−S5,F′)   *co   krkavci chtějí,*
               what ravens want-imperf
               what the ravens want

32. cont.   *dceru   a   půl království.*
               daughter-acc and half kingdom
               his daughter and half his kingdom.

35. (S,F9)   *Jiří oznámí   pánovi,*
               announces-perf lord-dat
               Jiří announces to the lord

36.   (−S6,F′)   *že   to ví,*
                    that it knows-imperf
                    that he knows,

37.   (S,F9)   *pán to řekne   králi;*
                    lord it tells-perf king-dat
                    and the lord tells the king;

38.   (S5,F8)   *král žádá,*
                    king demands-imperf
                    the king demands

39.   (−S8,F′)   *aby   to vyložil*
                    in-order-to it explain-perf-subj
                    that he explain it to him.

40.   (S5,F8)   *Jiří praví,*
                    says-imperf
                    Jiří says

41.   (−S3,F′)   *že   jsou   to rodiče,*
                    that they-are-imperf it parents
                    that it is a couple

42.   (−S3,F′)   *uprostřed nich   je   mládě.*
                    in-between they-gen is-imperf young
                    with their young one between them.

43.   (−S2,F′)   *Když byl   hlad,*
                    when was-imperf famine
                    In a famine

44.   (S10,F′)   *samice opustila   mládě,*
                    female abandoned-perf young
                    the female abandoned their baby,

45.   (S9,F′)   *krkavec   je živil.*
                    raven-masc it kept-alive-imperf
                    and the male raven kept it alive.

46.   (S4,F′)   *Hlad   pominul,*
                    famine passed-perf
                    The famine passed,

47.   (−S6,F′)   *samice chce   mládě,*
                    female wants-imperf young
                    and now the female wants the baby,

48.   (−S9,F′)   *že   je vyseděla,*
                    that it she-sat-perf
                    saying that she sat on it [i.e., on the egg],

49.   (−S4,F′)   *samec se hájí,*
                    male   refl defends-imperf
                    but the male is defending himself,

50. (– S9,F') *že   je zachránil*
that it saved-perf
saying that he saved it

51. (– S9,F') *a   vychoval;*
and brought-up-perf
and brought it up;

52. (– S7,F') *žádají   krále   o   rozhodnutí.'*
request-imperf king-dat for decision
they request a decision from the king.

53. (S6,F9) *Král řekne,*
king says-perf
The king says

54. (– S5,F') *že mládě patří   samci.*
that young belongs-imperf male-dat
that the child belongs to the male.

55. (S,F7) *Krkavci odletí,*
ravens fly-away-perf
The ravens fly away,

56. (– S, – F8) *samec s   mládětem vpravo,*
male   with young-instr rightwards
the male with the child to the right,

57. (– S, – F7) *samice vlevo.*
female leftwards
the female to the left.

58. (S,F9) *Jiří dostane rinceznu,*
gets-perf princess-acc
Jiří gets the princess;

59. (S,F9) *vyloží   králi   svůj život.*
explains-perf king-dat his life
he tells the story of his life to the king.

60. (S,F9) *Oznámí   rodičům,*
announces-perf parents-dat
He announces to his parents

61. (– S9,F') *že je   navštíví král s   královnou.*
that them visit-fut king with queen-instr
that the king and the queen will visit them.

62. (S,F9) *Rodiče sezvou   hosty,*
parents invite-perf guests
His parents invite guests,

63. (S,F10) *ustrojí   hostinu,*
arrange-perf feast-acc
they arrange a feast,

64.   (S,F8)   *ráno   otec   drží   synovi koflík s   vodou,*
                morning father holds-imperf son-dat cup   with water-imperf
                in the morning his father is holding up for him a cup with water,

65.   (S,F8)   *matka ručník.*
                mother towel
                and his mother is holding a towel.

66.   (−S,F7)   *Král se jich vyptává   na děti,*
                king refl them ask-imperf on children
                The king inquires about their children,

67.   (S,F6)   *otec se s   pláčem   přizná,*
                father refl with crying-instr confesses-perf
                the father confesses in tears,

68.   (S,F6)   *syn se dá   poznat,*
                son refl gives-perf to-recognize
                the son lets himself be recognized,

69.   (S,F8)   *otec ho na kolenou prosí   o prominutí.*
                father him on knees-loc begs-imperf for forgiveness
                the father, on his knees, begs forgiveness.

70.   (S,F7)   *Jiřík prosí   rodiče o požehnání.*
                begs-imperf parents for blessing
                Jiřík asks his parents for their blessing.'

3. FOREGROUNDING AND SEQUENTIALITY

Before proceeding with the analysis of the text, a careful examination of Hopper and Thompson's position is necessary. Their claim that high transitivity correlates with foregrounding actually confounds two different phenomena under the heading of "foreground":

> First, the foregrounded portions together comprise the backbone or skeleton of the text, forming its basic structure; the background clauses put flesh on the skeleton, but are extraneous to its structural coherence. Second, the foreground clauses . . . are ordered in a temporal sequence; a change in the order of any two of them signals a change in the order of the real-world events they name. (1980:281)

This assumes that sequentiality and foregroundedness, which are coextensive in some of the texts published in the literature (e.g., Labov and Waletzky 1967) are always so. However, in our text the temporally sequenced clauses do NOT comprise the skeleton of the story. When taken by themselves, these clauses comprise the following "condensed text":

3. *In the morning a nightingale is screaming and fluttering on the window.*
10. *His volatile father orders him* 17. *His father attacks him,* 18. *and throws him in the water.* 19. *Jiřík swims.* 20. *Some fishermen find him.* 21. *and lead him to the lord* 23. *the lord accepts him into his service.* 27. *The king invites the lords to a feast,* 28. *the lord takes Jiřík with him.* 30. *some ravens arrive* 35. *Jiří announces to the lord* 37. *and the lord tells the king* 38. *the king demands* 40. *Jiří says* 44. *the female abandoned their baby* 45. *and the male raven kept it alive* 46. *the famine passed* 53. *The king says* 55. *The ravens fly away* 58. *Jiří gets the princess,* 59. *he tells the story of his life to the king.* 60. *He announces to his parents* 62. *His parents invite guests,* 63. *they arrange a feast,* 64. *in the morning his father is holding up for him a cup with water.* 65. *and his mother is holding a towel.* 67. *the father confesses in tears,* 68. *the son lets himself be recognized,* 69. *the father, on his knees, begs forgiveness.* 70. *Jiřík asks his parents for their blessing.*

Obviously, many crucial events are not included in this sequence, especially in its initial parts. Many direct and indirect quotes are not included because they are not sequentially ordered. For example, the sequence of clauses (7)–(9), 'Jiřík says that he knows but is afraid to tell' is absolutely essential to the plot. But since Jiřík speaks while (presumably) the nightingale is still screaming and fluttering in the window [Clauses (3) and (4)], his act of speaking is contemporaneous with, rather than subsequent to, what precedes in the discourse. Yet although Clauses (7)–(9) are not sequential they are certainly foregrounded, for without them what follows makes little sense. In the following I shall include direct and indirect quotes among the foregrounded clauses, regardless of whether they refer to temporarily ordered events or not.

The necessity of including quotes in the foreground points to the need for a second revision. Note that even when a quoting clause *is* temporally ordered, including it on the list of sequential clauses does not make that list more self-contained as a story. For example, Clause (53), 'The king says', does refer to a temporally ordered event, and thus I included it in the "condensed text". But it is little help. We want to know WHAT the king said. It seems that the content of the quote is at least as important for the story as the act of quoting itself. At least in a language like Czech, where the content is given in a clause grammatically subordinated to the quoting clause ('he says', 'he announces'), the whole sentence should be considered together when separating the foreground from the background information. I see no reason not to generalize from this and introduce our second revision in the following form: We will consider subordinate clauses together with their superordinate clauses.

The classification obtained after these two revisions (including quotes with the sequential clauses and not counting subordinate clauses separately) does separate the "foreground" of the story from the "background." The reader may convince himself or herself of this by following the sequence of clauses marked F. (Recall that these are to be taken together with the subsequent subordinate clauses marked F'.)

It is not an accident that in isolating the true "skeleton" or foreground of the story we had to make special provision for quotation. Clearly, there is a dire need for studies of the text-grammatical role of quotation. But even a precursory examination of narrative in, it seems to me, any language at all is likely to yield the very strong impression that the narrator does not use only temporal sequencing as a means of communicating essential information. Quotation is also used in this manner.[1]

My first conclusion, then, is that sequentiality and foregrounding are not the same thing. Sequential clauses are foregrounded, but not all foregrounded clauses are sequential. Temporal sequencing is one mode of foregrounding, but quotation is another. Accordingly, one can distinguish between a narrower discourse parameter, "sequentiality," and a broader one, "foregrounding." The question now is, with which parameter, if any, does "transitivity" correlate? And, in the event that it correlates with both parameters, in which case is the correlation stronger?

To answer these questions, I have identified the degree of transitivity in each clause, correlated it separately with sequentiality and foregrounding, and then sought some meaning in the comparison of the two.

4. TRANSITIVITY AND SEQUENTIALITY

Dividing the text into sequential and nonsequential clauses was not done without difficulty, for too often the text simply fails to make clear the temporal procession of the events. For example, Clause (5), '(Jiřík's) parents are wondering', follows Clauses (3) and (4), 'and in the morning a nightingale is screaming and fluttering in the window', without any indication as to whether the parents did their wondering at the same time or after the nightingale's display. In fact, there is no indication that the nightingale ever ended its bothersome behavior. In cases like this I simply used my best guess. As my guesses were presumably random, the dif-

---

[1] It is not certain that this is true for all genres, although quotes are, for one thing, as important in a scholarly paper as in a folk tale. Nor is it assuredly true that quoting clauses belong to the foreground in all languages, although they do in many, including a language as different from Czech as Inuktitut (Kalmár, 1982).

ficulty introduced by the occasional vagueness of the time sequence should lead to no more than a tolerable margin of "laboratory error."

I scored each clause as follows: I assigned a rating of + for high kinesis, aspect, etc., and a rating of − for a low degree of each quality, always using Hopper and Thompson's definitions. Apart from making possible the comparison of clauses for individual transitivity parameters, this also made it possible to get an overall "transitivity score" for each clause. This overall score was obtained by adding up all the plus signs associated with a clause, and it appears within the parentheses preceding each clause in the transcription of the text.

As each component of transitivity is fully discussed in Hopper and Thompson's paper, only the following comments need be added here: I interpreted KINESIS strictly according to Hopper and Thompson's instructions, as a "change of place or condition." It is not clear whether a proposition like 'he says' refers to a change of condition. Albeit without much conviction, I decided that it does not, and I classified quoting clauses as [−kinesis]. Under ASPECT I looked at the boundedness of the event in time, again in accordance with Hopper and Thompson's instructions. Note that this quality is not always expressed by the morphological category of perfect/imperfect, which is marked as such in the transcription of the text. Morphological "aspect" in Czech in fact singles out PUNCTUALITY. In gauging the AFFECTEDNESS and the INDIVIDUATION OF THE OBJECT I considered all types of object, although in a more thorough study it might be necessary to separate direct and indirect objects.

Agency and individuation of the object are the two components that are clearly not binary. Hopper and Thompson suggest the following scores for agency: third person pronoun agent: 4; proper name: 3; animate noun: 2; inanimate noun: 1. For individuation of the object they suggest a score of 2 for referential and definite objects; 1 for referential but not definite, or definite but not referential, objects, and 0 for objects that are both nonreferential and indefinite. I used these scores when evaluating agency and individuation of the object separately. However, for the total score of each clause every component had to be assigned a plus or minus rating. I therefore assigned a plus to an agency score of 3 or 4 (proper name or third person pronoun), and to an individuation score of 1 or 2 (referential, definite, or both).

To determine the level of significance of the results I used a chi square test for the contrast within each separate transitivity component, and a t test for the difference in the average overall scores of sequential and nonsequential clauses. In the tables that follow, the fractions in the "significance level" columns refer to the likelihood that the observed difference is due to chance. For example < .005 means that this likelihood is less than 5 in 1000. The greater the chi square, the more significant the difference observed.

A one-by-one comparison of transitivity components in sequential and nonsequential clauses is given in Table 2. Most correlations are just as Hopper and Thompson have claimed. Only AFFIRMATION clearly does not correlate significantly with sequentiality, but this is perhaps due to the near absence of negative clauses in the data. A larger sample might confirm Hopper and Thompson's position. Even more likely to be confirmed with more data is the affectedness of object relationship, which is not fully significant but approaches significance.

The agency and individuation of the object criteria are tabulated separately as they are not binary. A count for agency that assigned clause scores of 1–4 as explained above resulted in Table 3. (Some of the tables also include data on foregrounding, for later reference.) There are too

TABLE 2
TRANSITIVITY COMPONENTS IN SEQUENTIAL AND NONSEQUENTIAL CLAUSES

	Sequential clauses				Nonsequential clauses					
	+		−		+		−		χ^2	Significance
Component	N	(%)	N	(%)	N	(%)	N	(%)	$(df = 1)$	level
Participants	20	(69)	9	(31)	19	(46)	22	(54)	3.18	<.10
Kinesis	17	(59)	12	(41)	15	(37)	26	(63)	3.15	<.10
Aspect	25	(86)	4	(14)	13	(32)	28	(68)	38.87	<.005
Punctuality	22	(76)	7	(24)	9	(22)	32	(78)	18.62	<.005
Volitionality	26	(90)	3	(10)	28	(68)	13	(32)	4.28	<.05
Affirmation	29	(100)	0		40	(98)	1	(2)	.68	N.S.
Mode	29	(100)	0		30	(73)	11	(27)	9.52	<.005
Affectedness of object	18	(100)	0		15	(88)	2	(12)	2.12	>.10

TABLE 3
AGENCY—DETAILED COUNT

	Pronoun		Proper name		Animate noun		Inanimate noun	
Clause in which agent appears	N	(%)	N	(%)	N	(%)	N	(%)
Sequential clause	4	(14)	5	(17)	19	(66)	1	(3)
Nonsequential clause	16	(39)	3	(7)	21	(51)	1	(2)
Foregrounded clause	5	(16)	7	(22)	20	(62.5)	0	
Backgrounded clause	4	(38)	1	(8)	7	(54)	0	

many cells in this table for a significance test, so I paired 3 and 4 against 1 and 2 and also 4 against 1–3 to see which of these differences would turn out to be statistically significant. Table 4 shows that only the count that separates out the pronominal agent (score 4) is significant, although the other division does seem to approach significance, appearing in this way to confirm the gradient quality of the agency criterion.

It was similarly necessary to reduce a detailed count for individuation of the object (Table 5) to a simpler one that would be amenable to a chi square test (Table 6). This difference between sequential and nonsequential clauses on this criterion was found to be significant. However, in this case the reverse of Hopper and Thompson's position has been confirmed! It is the nonsequential rather than the sequential clauses that correlate more strongly with individuation of the object. In other words, indefinite, nonreferential objects are more likely to occur in sequential clauses.

Finally, the overall comparison of the total scores for each type of clause is given in Table 7. The difference, as can be seen, is highly significant.

In summary, then, all and each of Hopper and Thompson's transitivity components either correlated with sequentiality or would apparently have done so given more data. It is a mere footnote on a generally positive result that the relationship between individuation of the object and sequentiality is the reverse of that posited by Hopper and Thompson. It does, however, suggest that this component may have to be eliminated from the transitivity complex.

5. TRANSITIVITY AND FOREGROUNDING

In evaluating the correlation between transitivity and foregrounding I used the same methodology as I used with sequentiality.

The comparison of the total scores is given in Table 8. The t value for this comparison, .57, means that the difference is not statistically significant. There is a tendency for high transitivity to correlate with foregrounding, but the likelihood that it is due to chance is almost 30%. Thus, even if further data confirms a positive relationship, we see that transitivity relates much more strongly to sequentiality than to foregrounding. This effectively answers the main question posed at the beginning of our discussion.

Note that the transitivity–sequentiality correlation is stronger DESPITE the similarity in the average scores for sequential and foregrounded clauses on the one hand (8.07 and 8.19) and nonsequential and back-

TABLE 4
AGENCY—SIMPLIFIED COUNT

Clause in which agent appears	Pronoun N	(%)	Other N	(%)	χ^2 (df = 1)	Significance	Pronoun or proper name N	(%)	Other N	(%)	χ^2 (df = 1)	Significance
Sequential clause	4	(14)	25	(86)	5.18	<.025	9	(31)	20	(69)	1.69	N.S.
Nonsequential clause	16	(39)	25	(61)			19	(46)	22	(54)		
Foregrounded clause	5	(16)	27	(84)	2.73	<.10	12	(38)	20	(62)	.29	N.S.
Backgrounded clause	5	(38)	8	(62)			6	(46)	7	(54)		

TABLE 5

INDIVIDUATION OF OBJECT—DETAILED COUNT

Clause in which object appears	+ referential + definite		+ referential, − definite or + definite, − referential		− referential − definite	
	N	(%)	N	(%)	N	(%)
Sequential clause	15	(83)	1	(6)	2	(11)
Nonsequential clause	17	(100)	0		0	
Foregrounded clause	17	(68)	6	(24)	2	(8)
Backgrounded clause	3	(100)	0		0	

TABLE 6

INDIVIDUATION OF OBJECT—SIMPLIFIED COUNT

Clause in which object appears	+ referential + definite		Other		χ^2 ($df = 1$)	Significance
	N	(%)	N	(%)		
Sequential clause	15	(83)	3	(17)	3.24	<.10
Nonsequential clause	17	(100)	0			
Foregrounded clause	17	(68)	8	(32)	1.08	N.S.
Backgrounded clause	3	(100)	0			

TABLE 7

OVERALL COMPARISON OF SEQUENTIAL AND NONSEQUENTIAL CLAUSES

Type of clause	N	Total score	Average score	Standard deviation	t ($df = 68$)	Significance
Sequential	29	234	8.07	.169	34.41	<.005
Nonsequential	41	226	5.51	.000321		

TABLE 8

OVERALL COMPARISON OF FOREGROUNDED AND BACKGROUNDED CLAUSES

Type of clause	N	Total score	Average score	Standard deviation	t ($df = 44$)	Significance
Foregrounded	32	262	8.19	2.35	.57	<.30
Backgrounded	13	68	5.23	2.78		

grounded clauses on the other (5.51 and 5.23). The large difference in significance is due to the great difference in standard deviation for fore-grounding and sequentiality. The number of clauses whose total "transitivity score" strays far from the average is much larger in the fore-grounded and backgrounded categories than in the sequential and nonsequential. (This is just another way of saying that the correlation is not as strong.) This, in turn, is due to the fact that some transitivity components correlate with foregrounding very strongly indeed, and others not at all. So we need to consider each component separately. The relevant data are given in Table 9, which should be considered together with Tables 3, 4, 5, and 6 where the data on the gradient properties of agency and individuation of the object are given.

When each component is examined separately, we see that although the overall correlation with sequentiality is much stronger, some indi-viduation components correlate more with foregrounding.

6. SOME DETAIL

The correlations for each feature are summarized in Table 10. There are some strong differences favoring sequentiality and others favoring foregrounding.

First, let us consider the correlations that favor sequentiality. Kinesis is slightly significant in the sequentiality correlation, and not at all sig-nificant in the foregrounding correlation. This may be because actions

TABLE 9
TRANSITIVITY COMPONENTS IN FOREGROUNDED AND BACKGROUNDED CLAUSES

Component	Foregrounded clauses				Backgrounded clauses				χ^2 ($df = 1$)	Significance
	+ N	(%)	− N	(%)	+ N	(%)	− N	(%)		
Participants	25	(78)	7	(22)	4	(31)	9	(69)	9.31	<.005
Kinesis	19	(59)	13	(41)	7	(54)	6	(46)	.11	N.S.
Aspect	24	(75)	8	(25)	3	(23)	10	(77)	15.95	<.005
Punctuality	20	(62.5)	12	(37.5)	3	(23)	10	(77)	5.57	<.025
Volitionality	30	(94)	2	(6)	9	(69)	3	(31)	5.03	<.025
Affirmation	32	(100)	0		11	(92)	1	(8)	2.36	>.10
Mode	32	(100)	0		12	(0)	0	—	N.S.	
Affectedness of object	25	(100)	0		3	(43)	4	(57)	15.76	<.005

TABLE 10
THE RELATIVE SIGNIFICANCE OF THE CORRELATION OF TRANSITIVITY COMPONENTS WITH SEQUENTIALITY AND FOREGROUNDEDNESS

Component	Sequentiality	χ^2	Foregroundedness	χ^2
Participants	less significant	3.18	more significant	9.31
Kinesis	slightly significant	3.15	not significant	.11
Aspect	more significant	38.87	less significant	15.95
Punctuality	more significant	18.62	less significant	5.57
Volitionality	less significant	4.28	more significant	5.03
Affirmation	not significant	.68	not significant	2.36
Mode	highly significant	9.52	not significant	—
Agency	more significant	5.18	less significant	2.73
Affectedness of O	approaches significance	2.12	highly significant	15.76
Individuation of O	slightly significant	3.24	not significant	1.08

rather than states are somewhat more likely to constitute the temporally organized sequence of events in a text. Aspect correlates more strongly with sequentiality, presumably because events with a clear beginning and end are easier to string in a temporal sequence. The same is true of punctual events. However, both also correlate with foregrounding, though to a lesser extent; apparently bounded and punctual events are likely to be seen as more important than unbounded and durative ones. Mode probably correlates with sequentiality and (perhaps) not with foregrounding because true facts are more likely to be included in the sequence of "what happened" than suppositions. There is also a difference in favor of sequentiality on the agency and individuation of the object criteria, but here the difference in the chi square values is not large enough to inspire much confidence.

Other transitivity components correlate more strongly with foregrounding. The participants component is a case in point, with almost three times the chi square value of the participants–sequentiality correlation (9.31 versus 3.18). Affectedness of the object—whether total or partial—also correlates more with foregrounding than with sequentiality.

The reason for the anomalous correlations of the participants and affectedness components is not quite clear.[2] It is worth noting, however,

---

[2] That the participants component is anomalous in this sense suggests that the choice of "transitivity" as the name of the whole complex we are dealing with may be problematic. "Transitivity" traditionally refers primarily to the number of participants, yet we see that in our text this component is not as typical of the entire complex as some of the others. This is a surprising result when one considers that, in the languages surveyed by Hopper and Thompson, transitivity in the traditional sense indeed proved to be quite central among the features of the complex.

that the correlations that strongly favor sequentiality—aspect, punctuality, and mode—all relate essentially to the verb, expressing the
"event" or "predication." On the other hand, PARTICIPANTS and AFFECT-
EDNESS OF THE OBJECT concern primarily the NP arguments. At least in
the case of sequentiality, this makes some sense, as it is events that are
sequenced, not arguments.

To recapitulate, then, transitivity as a complex clearly correlates with
the difference between sequential and nonsequential events. However,
our data do not provide sufficient evidence that it correlates with the
foreground–background distinction. Yet two individual components of
transitivity distinguish foreground from background even more strongly
than sequential from nonsequential clauses. These are *affectedness of
the object* and *participants*.

7. CONCLUSIONS

On the whole the statistical analysis of Jiřík's story confirms Hopper
and Thompson's claim that there is an interrelated complex such as they
call TRANSITIVITY. But it also shows that this complex relates more to
sequentiality than to foregrounding proper.

In a more broadly based study one would want to speculate on the
possibility that the discourse functions of transitivity are not unique.
(There may be further, and possibly unrelated, functions in addition to
temporal sequencing and foregrounding.) This would raise the methodological problem of how to determine exactly which, if any, of the complex's discourse functions are primary. Furthermore, as individual features do not correlate with every function that the complex as a whole
correlates with, we need to reflect on exactly how we determine which
features belong to the complex and which features just happen to be
associated with it in some contexts but not others.

As all pioneering work does, Hopper and Thompson's transitivity article raises as many questions as it answers. These can be tackled ef-
ficiently only after extensive empirical research, including statistical analyses, has been undertaken. This study is meant to be a modest contribution
to that end.

ACKNOWLEDGMENTS

I am indebted to Paul Hopper and Sandy Thompson for the original inspiration of this
study and for some incisive criticism. A major part of this paper is the result of my
grappling with their comments, though not necessarily to their full satisfaction. Only I can
be blamed for the remaining errors.

REFERENCES

Hopper, P. and S. Thompson (1980) "Transitivity in Grammar and Discourse," *Language* 56, 251–299.
Kalmár, I. (1982) *The Function of Inuktitut Verb Modes in Narrative,* in P. Hopper, ed., *Tense–Aspect: Between Semantics and Pragmatics,* John Benjamins, Amsterdam and Philadelphia.
Labov, W. and J. Waletzky (1967) "Narrative Analysis: Oral Versions of Personal Experience," in J. Helm, ed., *Essays on the Verbal and Visual Arts,* University of Washington Press, Seattle.
Tille, V. (1929) *Soupis Českých Pohádek 1* (Česká Akademie Věd a Umění, Rozpravy, Třída III, číslo 66), Česká Akademie Věd a Uměni, Prague.

INDIVIDUATION HIERARCHIES IN MANAM

FRANTISEK LICHTENBERK

1. INTRODUCTION

The Manam language, spoken on Manam and Boesa Islands off the north coast of New Guinea, is a member of the Oceanic branch of the Austronesian family. In Manam, verbs index their subjects by means of prefixes that at the same time mark mood: realis (rl) and irrealis (ir). In addition, direct objects are indexed in verbs by means of suffixes; however, NOT ALL types of direct objects are indexed. The purpose of this paper is to examine the criteria that determine the indexing of direct objects in Manam verbs.

It will be shown that whether and how a direct object is indexed in the verb depends on several factors: (*a*) the person and number of the direct object; (*b*) its case relation, as well as the presence or absence, in the same clause, of other direct objects bearing particular case relations; (*c*) whether the referent of the direct object is a "higher animal" or not; (*d*) with one class of verbs, whether the direct object is specific or not; and (*e*) with another class of verbs, whether the direct object is cognate or not. More generally, it will be shown that in many cases the indexing of direct objects in Manam depends on the degree of "individuation" of their referents.

261

Syntax and Semantics, Volume 15

The term "direct object" as used here refers to any argument of a verb that is not the subject or an oblique object. By "oblique object" is meant any argument that carries a case suffix or is followed by a postposition. That is, in Manam, direct objects are contrasted with oblique objects, not with indirect objects: There is no evidence, morphological or syntactic, for the category of "indirect object" in Manam. As will be seen in what follows, up to three direct objects may occur with a Manam verb.

Manam has the following set of suffixes used to index direct objects in verbs:

	sg		pl
1	-a	exc(lusive)	-ʔama
		inc(lusive)	-ʔita
2	-iʔo		-ʔamiŋ
3	-i, -∅		-i (Class I)
			-∅ (Class II)
			-di (Class III)
			-di (higher animals)

The object suffixes that start with a consonant receive an epenthetic *i* after a stem that ends in a consonant other than a nasal. The 1sg object suffix -*a* receives an epenthetic *i*, which then becomes *y*, after a stem that ends in a back vowel (*u, o, a*). The 2sg suffix -*iʔo* has a variant -*ʔo*, which is used optionally after stems that end in a nasal consonant and obligatorily with the verb *te* 'see, find'. The 3sg object marker has two forms: -*i* and -*∅*. The latter is used when the object marking position is directly followed (except for an intervening "buffer element," to be explained in what follows) by a directional, a benefactive, or the source suffix *and* immediately preceded by a front vowel (*i, e*); also *after* the source suffix; and finally with the verb *te* 'see, find'. The -*i* variant is used elsewhere.

Three classes of transitive verbs must be recognized in Manam on the basis of the form of the 3pl object suffix used to index direct objects whose referents are not higher animals: Cl. I -*i*, Cl. II -*∅*, Cl. III -*di*. If the referent of the direct object is a higher animal, the form of the 3pl object suffix is -*di*, regardless of the class of the verb. The category of higher animals traditionally consists of human beings, pigs, dogs, and birds (including fowls), and now also includes goats, horses, and other large animals, which are of relatively recent introduction in New Guinea. However, whereas humans are always considered higher animals, there is some variation with the other members of the category: The latter are always considered higher animals when domestic but only optionally so when wild. (Although the Manam may derogatively speak of certain mainlanders as 'wild', grammatically they nevertheless always treat them as higher animals.)

When word final, some of the object suffixes, namely 1sg, 3sg, and the *-di* variant of the 3pl object marker, require antepenultimate stress, unless the penultimate syllable is closed, in which case *it* will bear the stress. With the remaining object suffixes the position of stress is determined by general phonological rules.[1]

And finally, some of the object suffixes require special "buffer" elements (bf) when followed by another suffix. The only function of these buffer elements appears to be to separate certain suffixes from each other.

The following sentences serve to exemplify the use of the object suffixes (only the relevant morpheme breaks are indicated; ´ indicates stress):

(1)   *Tamóata (ŋáu) í-te-a.*
      man   (me)   3sg(rl)-see-1sg(obj)
      'The man saw me'.

[For simplicity, we will assume here that the use of the independent pronouns—*ŋau* in (1)—is optional. In fact it is not, but the factors that govern the use of the independent pronouns are not germane to our present concern. A discussion of these factors may be found in Lichtenberk, forthcoming.]

(2)   *Áine   údi   í-doʔ-i.*
      woman banana 3sg(rl)-take-3sg(obj)
      'The woman took the banana'.

(3)   *Ógi go-doʔ-∅-a-mái.*
      axe 2sg(ir)-take-3sg(obj)-bf-hither
      'Bring the axe here'.

(4)   *Tamóata di-lele-ʔáma.*
      man   3pl(rl)-look for-exc(obj)
      'The men looked for us'.

---

[1] Stress falls on the closed syllable if there is one. If not, stress is penultimate unless the penultimate vowel is immediately preceded by another vowel and no morpheme boundary intervenes between that vowel and the end of the word; in the latter case stress falls on the antepenultimate vowel. In addition to the three object suffixes listed above, some other suffixes require antepenultimate stress. And finally, no stress can be farther from the end of a word than its antepenultimate syllable.

(5)   *Áine   údi   i-dó²-i*   (*do²* is a Class I verb)
        woman banana 3sg(rl)-take-3pl(obj)
        'The woman took the bananas'.

[Compare the positions of the stress in the verbs in (5) and (2).]

(6)   *Dáu   ²o²ó²o i-gére-∅*   (*gere* is a Class II verb)
        letter many   3sg(rl)-write-3pl(obj)
        'He wrote many letters'.

(7)   *²ái   u-bázi-di.*   (*bazi* is a Class III verb)
        stick 1sg(rl)-carry-3pl(obj)
        'I carried the sticks'.

(8)   *Bóro u-dó²-idi.*   [higher animal; cf. (5)]
        pig   1sg(rl)-take-3pl(obj)
        'I took the pigs'.

(9)   *Nátu ²o²ó²o i-geré-t-idi.*   [higher animal; cf. (6)]
        child many   3sg(rl)-tattoo-thc-3pl(obj)
        'He tattooed many children'.

[The *t* in the verb in (9) is one of the "thematic consonants" (thc) found in many transitive verbs.]

In the next several sections, we will be concerned with the various complications found in the indexing of direct objects in verbs.

2. DITRANSITIVE VERBS

Ditransitive verbs require two direct objects (as defined earlier), unless ellipsis has taken place. Consider the following examples:

(10)   *Tamóata tanépwa bóro té²e dí-an-i.*
        man   chief   pig   one 3pl(rl)-give to-3sg(obj)
        'The men gave the chief one pig'.

(11)   *Tamóata tanépwa bóro tóli dí-an-i.*
        man   chief   pig   three 3pl(rl)-give to-3sg(obj)
        'The men gave the chief three pigs'.

(12)   *Tamóata nátu -∅   márau-∅   i-ti²ín-di.*
        man   child-his sister -his 3sg(rl)-show to-3pl(obj)
        'The man showed his child(ren) to his sisters'.

(13)   *(²ái²o) maraú-gu anúnu²a-∅   m-iti²íŋ-²o*
        (you sg) sister -my picture   -her 1sg(ir)-show to-2sg(obj)
        'I will show you a picture of my sister'.

(14)   *Nátu ʔaŋári   álu   i-sináu-ya.*
        child canarium nut some 3sg(rl)-ask for-1sg(obj)
        'The child asked me for some canarium nuts'.

(15)   *Nátu málo   di-o ʔo-r-á ʔ-idi.*
        child breechclout 3pl(rl)-put on-thc-trans-3pl(obj)
        'They put breechclouts on the children' (i.e., the children—
        boys—underwent an initiation ceremony).

The *-a ʔ* in (15) is a transitivizer (trans), see what follows.]

The important thing to note in (10)–(15) is that even though the verbs have two direct objects (expressed or ellipted), only one of them is indexed in the verb.

One might suggest that with ditransitive verbs it is the indirect, and only the indirect, object that gets indexed in the verb (the indirect object being the NP that encodes the participant to whom something is given, shown, etc.). However, as already mentioned, in Manam there is no independent motivation for distinguishing between direct and indirect objects; for example, any type of argument can be the head of a relative clause, can be thematized, focused, etc. (cf. Faltz 1978 for the absence of the syntactic category of "indirect object" in some languages).[2] And even though it is often the case that what one would call the "indirect object" usually precedes the "direct object," it is not necessarily so; see, for example, Sentence (12). (The unmarked word order of Manam is S*X*P, where S is subject, P is predicator, and *X* is anything else. Word order is, however, quite free in the sense that, all other things being equal, elements that encode new information usually follow those that encode old information—except that the subject never occurs after the predicator.)

According to Böhm (1975), it is the *human* (direct) object that is indexed in a ditransitive verb. Notice, however, that *both* direct objects can be human, as in (12), nevertheless only one is indexed.

From the examples given here, it is evident that with ditransitive verbs it is the direct object which bears a GOAL relation (i.e., the participant to whom something is given, shown, etc.) that is indexed in the verb rather than the direct object that encodes the PATIENT (the participant that is given, shown, etc.). Notice that even though Böhm's statement that it is the human direct object that is indexed is clearly not sufficient, it is nevertheless the case that goal participants are normally human

---

[2] For Faltz, "indirect object" is a semantic rather than a syntactic category. A language may have the semantic category of indirect object even though indirect objects are coded in exactly the same way as are direct objects. In this paper, "direct object" and "indirect object" are considered to be strictly syntactic categories, regardless of the types of participants (patient, goal, beneficiary, etc.) they encode.

beings or at least other higher animals, as in (16), whereas patients are more likely to be non-higher-animal than higher-animal.

(16)   Bóro ʔaníŋa álu   gó-an-i.
        pig food   some 2sg(ir)-give to-3sg(obj)
        'Give some food to the pig'.

3. BENEFACTIVE CONSTRUCTION

The benefactive construction is characterized by the presence of a direct object that encodes a beneficiary; in addition, the verb carries a benefactive suffix (ben): -n if the beneficiary is singular, and -ø if the beneficiary is plural. The beneficiary direct object is indexed in the verb by the appropriate object suffix, which follows the benefactive marker. For reasons that will later become apparent, we will refer to the position of the object suffix that indexes the beneficiary as the "primary object marking position."

The benefactive construction can be used with intransitive, transitive, and ditransitive verbs.

3.1. Intransitive Verbs

(17)   Tamóata (ŋáu) i-nanári-n-a.
        man   (me) 3sg(rl)-tell story-ben-1sg(obj)
        'The man told me a story'. (Lit., 'the man story-told for me'.)

(18)   M-pilai-n-íʔo.
        1sg(ir)-play-ben-2sg(obj)
        'I will play for (instead of) you'.

(19)   Póaʔe ʔoʔóʔo (ʔéʔa)   di-pura-ø-ʔáma.
        sore many   (us-exc) 3pl(rl)-come-ben-exc(obj)
        'We have many sores'. (Lit., 'Many sores have come up on us'; 'on' in its benefactive sense, as in She walked out on me.)

3.2. Transitive Verbs

Transitive verbs in the benefactive construction have two direct objects—one encoding the beneficiary, the other encoding the patient—and both of them are indexed in the verb. The beneficiary is indexed in primary object marking position, whereas the patient is indexed, by the

appropriate object suffix, *before* the benefactive marker. We will refer
to the latter position as the "secondary object marking position."

(20)   *Tamóata tanépwa ?áti   da-sabár-∅-a-n-i.*
        man   chief   canoe 3pl(ir)-hew-3sg(obj)-bf-ben-3sg(obj)
        'The men will hew a canoe for the chief'.

[Recall that the 3sg object marker has a zero form when it is directly
followed—except for an intervening buffer element—by a benefactive
suffix *and* not immediately preceded by a back vowel; cf. (21).]

(21)   *Nátu go-ru?u-í-a-n-a.*
        child 2sg(ir)-wash-3sg(obj)-bf-ben-1sg(obj)
        'Wash the child for me'.

(22)   *Nátu bis?éti u-zaza-dí-a-∅-di.*   (*zaza* is a Class III verb)
        child biscuit 1sg(rl)-buy-3pl(obj)-bf-ben-3pl(obj)
        'I bought biscuits for the children'.

Ditransitive Verbs

Ditransitive verbs in the benefactive construction have three direct
objects—a beneficiary, a patient, and a goal—but only two of them get
indexed in the verb: the beneficiary and the goal. The beneficiary is
indexed in primary object marking position, and the goal in secondary
position. The patient does not get indexed in the verb at all—a property
that carries over from simple ditransitives.

(23)   *Tanépwa maŋ   mi-an-∅-á-ŋ-?o.*
        chief   chicken 1sg(ir)-give to-3sg(obj)-bf-ben-2sg(obj)
        'I will give a chicken/chickens to the chief for you' (e.g.,
            since you don't have any).

Several things should be noted at this point:
First, the benefactive construction is used only with human beneficiaries.
Second, in Manam no more than two object suffixes can occur on a
verb. This means that if a verb has three direct objects, only two of them
can be indexed. Notice that in that case it is the direct objects that are
either human (beneficiary, goal) or other higher-animal (goal) that are
indexed; patient direct objects, whose referents are typically non-higher-
animal, are not. That is, just as is the case with ditransitive verbs not
in the benefactive construction, the "preference" is given to those types
of direct objects whose referents are always higher animals rather than
to those whose referents are typically non-higher-animal.
Finally, notice that in (20)–(23) the patient direct objects are always

third person—singular or plural. In fact, the benefactive construction is
used ONLY with third person patients. If the patient is other than third
person, the beneficiary will not be realized as a direct object but as an
oblique object with the suffix -*lo*. Thus we can have (24a) and (25a) but
NOT (24b) and (25b):

(24)   a.   *ɁaíɁo-lo   dá-te-a.*
              you(sg)-for 3pl(ir)-find-1sg(obj)
              'They will find me for you'.
        b.   **Da-te-a-ú-ŋ-Ɂo.*
              3pl(ir)-find-1sg(obj)-bf-ben-2sg(obj)

(25)   a.   *Ɖáu-lo da-úŋ-Ɂo.*
              me-for 3pl(ir)-beat-2sg(obj)
              'They will beat you up for me'.
        b.   **Da-úŋ-Ɂo-n-a.*
              3pl(ir)-beat-2sg(obj)-ben-1sg(obj)

Several linguists have argued that the semantic category of "individuation of participants" is often relevant to the morphological and/or
syntactic marking of the objects that encode them (e.g., Timberlake 1975,
1977; Morolong and Hyman 1977, Hopper and Thompson 1980; many
of the examples in Moravcsik 1978 as well clearly involve individuation).
The individuation of a participant is "the degree to which the participant
is characterized as a distinct entity or individual in the narrated event"
(Timberlake 1975:124). Individuation is a matter of degree, not of yes
or no: Some types of participants are more individuated than others—
either intrinsically or just in a particular context. Thus, for example,
animate participants are more likely to be viewed as separate entities
than inanimate ones, specific participants more so than nonspecific ones,
singular participants more so than plural participants, and first and second
person participants more so than third person participants. In other
words, it is possible to set up an "individuation hierarchy"—the types
of participants higher on the hierarchy are more likely to be viewed as
separate entities than those lower on the hierarchy.

To account for the behavior of Manam direct objects considered so
far, we can set up the following individuation hierarchy:

        1st/2nd
        3rd   human
                other higher-animal
                non-higher-animal

With ditransitive verbs, it is the goal that is indexed in the verb. Goal
participants are normally human beings or at least other higher animals;

that is, they are the top four categories on the hierarchy. Patients, on the other hand, are typically non-higher-animal; that is, they usually occupy the bottom of the hierarchy.

Beneficiary direct objects are always human—they belong to the top three categories, and they are always indexed in the verb. Recall, furthermore, that only third person patients can appear in the benefactive construction. In other words, the patient can never be higher on the individuation hierarchy than the beneficiary; at the most they can be on the same level—if the patient is human.

We will return to the individuation hierarchy in the following sections.

4. SOURCE CONSTRUCTION

The source construction also uses a special suffix on the verb—the form of this "source" suffix (sorc) is -le. This marker identifies a participant realized as a direct object as a "source," that is, a participant from whom something is removed. Source participants are always human. The source construction can be used only with transitive verbs; it cannot be used with intransitive or ditransitive verbs. Just like the benefactive construction, the source construction can be used only with third person patients. If the patient is other than third person, *it* will be the only direct object, and the source participant will be realized as an oblique object with the suffix -lo [see (28) in what follows].[3]

In the source construction, two object suffixes appear on the verb. The one in primary object marking position (i.e., after the source suffix) indexes the source; the one in secondary object marking position (before the source suffix) indexes the patient.

(26) *Tamóata ógi i-doʔ-í-le-a.*   (Class I verb)
      man   axe 3sg(rl)-take-3pl(obj)-sorc-1sg(obj)
      'The man took the axes away from me'.

(27) *Toʔá   -ŋ   tabíra go-bagá-∅-le-di.*   (Class II verb)
      older brother-your(sg) dish 2sg(ir)-fetch-3pl(obj)-sorc-3pl(obj)
      'Fetch the dishes from your older brothers'.

(28) a. *ʔeʔá-i-lo   da-doʔ-íʔo.*
          us(exc)-bf-from 3pl(ir)-take-2sg(obj)
          'They will take you away from us'.

---

[3] In Manam, -lo is an "all-purpose" case suffix used to express a variety of semantic relationships between participants and events. In this paper it is glossed 'for' when it appears on a noun phrase that encodes a beneficiary, and 'from' when it appears on a noun phrase that encodes a source. It can also indicate a location, an instrument, etc.

b. *Da-do ʔ-i ʔo-le- ʔáma.
3pl(ir)-take-2sg(obj)-sorc-exc(obj)

In other words, just like in the benefactive construction, in the source construction the patient can never be higher on the individuation hierarchy than the source. At the most, they can be on the same level—if the patient is human.

5. VERBS OF MENTAL DISPOSITION

There are several verbs of "mental disposition" in Manam, that is, verbs that refer to attitudes (liking/wanting, disliking/not wanting), knowing, knowing how, and not knowing how. All of these verbs have two variants: an intransitive one and a transitive one.

In Manam, transitive verbs are derived from intransitive sources by means of the transitivizing prefix a ʔa-, and/or a thematic consonant, and/or the transitivizing suffix -a ʔ (trans). In addition, there are many instances of zero derivation—the only difference between the transitive and the intransitive variants is the presence of an object suffix on the former.

Intransitive	Transitive	Gloss
rere	rere-t-a ʔ	'like, want'
	-thc-trans	
sege	sege-a ʔ	'not like, not want'
ʔawa	ʔawa-t-a ʔ	'know'
amaŋ	aman-t-a ʔ	'know how, be skillful (at)'
bebe	bebe-t-a ʔ	'not know how, be clumsy (at)'

For example, compare (29) and (30), (31) and (32), and (33) and (34):

(29) (Ɖáu) u-sége.
      (I)   1sg(rl)-not like
      'I don't like (that/to do that)'.

(30) Tamóata (ŋáu) i-segé-a ʔ-a.
      man   (me)   3sg(rl)-not like-trans-1sg(obj)
      'The man doesn't like me'.

(31) Tágo u- ʔáwa   áine   ŋe nóra   i-púra.
      not 1sg(rl)-know woman this yesterday 3sg(rl)-arrive
      'I didn't know that this woman arrived yesterday'.

(32)   *Áine   ŋe tágo u-ʔawá-t-aʔ-i.*
        woman this not 1sg(rl)-know-thc-trans-3sg(obj)
        'I don't know this woman'.

(33)   *Tamóata i-amáŋ.*
        man   3sg(rl)-be skillful
        'The man is skillful'.

(34)   *ʔáti   tára-ya-∅   tágo t-amán-t-aʔ-i.*
        canoe cut-nom-its not   inc(rl)-be skillful-thc-trans-3sg(obj)
        'We are not doing a good job of making (cutting) the canoe'.
        (Lit., 'We are not skillful at cutting the canoe'; *tara-ya* is a
        nominalization "possessed" by *ʔati* 'canoe'.)

However, the intransitive variants of the verbs of mental disposition
are used not only when there is no direct object in the clause but also
under certain circumstances when there *is* one—expressed or ellipted.
The use of the intransitive and the transitive variants of the verbs of
mental disposition with direct objects is governed by the following rules:

1. If the direct object is both specific and higher-animal, the transitive
   variant must be used.
2. If the direct object is both nonspecific and non-higher-animal, the
   intransitive variant must be used.
3. If the direct object is either nonspecific or non-higher-animal, but
   not both, either the transitive or the intransitive variant may be
   used.[4]

The following sentences exemplify this rule-governed use of transitive
and intransitive variants of verbs of mental disposition:

(35)   *deparóbu u-rerére/   *u-rere-t-áʔ-i.*
        rice   1sg(rl)-like   -thc-trans-3pl(obj)[5]
        'I like rice (in general)'. (nonspecific, non-higher-animal)

(The intransitive variant *rere* is optionally partially reduplicated to indicate the continuative aspect.)

---

[4] Interestingly, according to Timberlake (1975), in Russian, verbs of perception and
emotion ('know', 'see', 'hear', 'think', 'feel', 'want', 'expect') (as well as verbs of existence), when negated, tend to take their direct objects in the genitive rather than the
accusative more than verbs of other semantic classes. And the genitive rather than the
accusative is also more likely to be used with the less individuated members of a number
of oppositions (common versus proper, abstract versus concrete, indefinite versus definite,
etc.), regardless of the semantic class of the verb.

[5] In Manam, mass nouns are considered plural unless they refer to a particular quantity.

(36)   *Tamóata ʔaiboándi u-rére/   u-rere-t-áʔ-idi.*
man   strong   1sg(rl)-like   -thc-trans-3pl(obj)
'I like strong men (in general)'. (higher-animal but nonspecific)

(37)   *ʔána táʔa u-rére/ u-reré-t-aʔ-i.*
thing other 1sg(rl)-want -thc-trans-3sg(obj)
'I want the other thing'. (specific but non-higher-animal)

(38)   *Bóro ŋe u-rere-t-áʔ-idi/*u-rére.*
pig this 1sg(rl)-like-thc-trans-3pl(obj)
'I like these pigs'. (higher-animal and specific)

(39)   *Nanári ŋe u-ʔáwa/u-ʔawá-t-aʔ-i.*
story this 1sg(rl)-know -thc-trans-3sg(obj)
'I know this story'. (specific but non-higher-animal)

(40)   *Tamóata tágo i-ʔawá-t-aʔ-a/*i-ʔáwa*
man   not 3sg(rl)-know-thc-trans-1sg(obj)
'The man doesn't know me'. (higher-animal and specific)

In order to account for this behavior of the verbs of mental disposition, it is necessary to introduce another distinction into our individuation hierarchy: specific versus nonspecific. Specific objects are more individuated than nonspecific ones. The specific versus nonspecific distinction is relevant only to third person objects—first and second person objects are always specific—and it is parallel to the animacy distinctions—the two parameters can combine.

1st/2nd		
3rd	human	specific
	other higher-animal	nonspecific
	non-higher-animal	(with verbs of mental disposition only)

6. VERBS OF EXCRETION/SECRETION

Manam has a number of verbs that refer to various bodily functions: urinating, defecating, sweating, spitting, vomiting, etc. Like the verbs of mental disposition, the verbs of excretion/secretion have both intransitive and transitive variants.

The intransitive variants are used (*a*) if there is no direct object in the clause, and (*b*) with cognate direct objects. The transitive variants are used with noncognate direct objects.

Compare Sentences (41)–(43), as well as Sentences (44)–(46):

(41)   *Áine   i-tamím.*   (no object)
        woman 3sg(rl)-urinate
        'The woman urinated'.

(42)   *Áine   baŋ i-tamimi-r-á?-i.*   (noncognate object)
        woman taro 3sg(rl)-urinate-thc-trans-3pl(obj)
        'The (mythical) woman urinated taros'. (i.e., taros grew out of
            her urine)

        (Certain verbs whose stems end in a nasal receive an epenthetic
        i before a thematic consonant.)

(43)   *Áine   tamím i-tamím.*   (cognate object)
        woman urine   3sg(rl)-urinate
        'The woman urinated'. (i.e., she produced some urine)

(44)   *Áine   i-tabé?a.*   (no object)
        woman 3sg(rl)-defecate
        'The woman defecated'.

(45)   *Áine   pátu i-tabe?á-r-a?-i.*   (noncognate object)
        woman stone 3sg(rl)-defecate-thc-trans-3sg(obj)
        'The woman excreted the stone'.

(46)   *Áine   tá?e i-tabé?a.*   (cognate object)
        woman feces 3sg(rl)-defecate
        'The woman defecated'. (i.e., she produced some feces)

Intransitive constructions without cognate objects appear to be concerned strictly with the activity, whereas those with cognate objects
seem to place more emphasis on the fact that the activity produced (an
unspecified quantity of) whatever that activity normally produces (urine,
feces). Note that cognate objects are not necessarily nonspecific. In (46)
the cognate object is specific; it refers to the feces excreted by the
mythical woman on a particular occasion and out of which Manam Island
later came into being.

Cognate objects are clearly less individuated than noncognate objects;
strictly speaking, they do not contribute any significant information.
Their referents are intimately bound up with, are the normal product of,
the respective activities. It is, then, necessary to introduce yet another
distinction into our individuation hierarchy. This distinction is also relevant only to third person objects.

INDIVIDUATION HIERARCHY FOR DIRECT OBJECTS IN MANAM

1st/2nd			
3rd	human	specific	noncognate
	other higher-animal	nonspecific[a]	cognate[b]
	non-higher-animal		

[a] for verbs of mental disposition only
[b] for verbs of excretion/secretion only

7. SUMMARY

In conclusion, let us summarize the characteristics of Manam direct objects that are relevant to their indexing in verbs:

Person. The grammatical person of an object determines, in conjunction with its number, the form of the object suffix. Moreover, only third person patients can appear in the benefactive and the source constructions.

Number. The number of an object determines, in conjunction with its person, the form of the object suffix.

Case relation. With the exception of certain types of objects of the verbs of mental disposition and the verbs of excretion/secretion (see under *Specificity* and *Cognate objects* in what follows), these rules hold:

1. If there is only one direct object in a clause, it is indexed in the verb regardless of its case relation (patient, beneficiary).
2. If there are two direct objects in a clause, several possibilities exist:
   (a) goal + patient: The goal is indexed in the verb; the patient is not.
   (b) beneficiary + patient: The beneficiary is indexed in primary object marking position; the patient is indexed in secondary object marking position.
   (c) source + patient: The source is indexed in primary object marking position; the patient is indexed in secondary object marking position.
3. If there are three direct objects in a clause—a beneficiary, a goal, and a patient—the beneficiary is indexed in primary object marking position; the goal is indexed in secondary object marking position; and the patient is not indexed.
4. Only third person patients can be indexed in secondary object marking position (see also under *Person*).

Higher animateness. Direct objects whose referents are higher animals take the *-di* form of the 3pl object marker, regardless of the class of the verb (see also under *Specificity*).

Specificity. With the verbs of mental disposition, objects that are both nonspecific and non-higher-animal occur with the intransitive forms of the verbs (and thus do not get indexed). Objects that are both specific and higher-animal require the transitive variants of the verbs (and thus get indexed). Objects that are either nonspecific or non-higher-animal (but not both) may occur with either the transitive or the intransitive variants of the verbs.

Cognate objects. Cognate objects of the verbs of excretion/secretion require the intransitive variants of the verbs.

More generally, the following conclusions may be made for Manam:

1. Patients are direct objects to a lesser degree than are goals, beneficiaries, and sources. If patients cooccur with the other types of participants, either they do not get indexed in the verb at all, or if they do, it is only third person patient NPs that can appear in those constructions.
2. With the verbs of mental disposition, objects that are nonspecific and/or non-higher-animal are direct objects to a lesser degree than are those that are both specific and higher-animal.
3. With the verbs of excretion/secretion, cognate objects are direct objects to a lesser degree than are noncognate objects.

These properties of Manam direct objects are directly relatable to differences in individuation:

1. Goals, beneficiaries, and sources are human (or, in the case of goals, possibly other higher animals), whereas patients are more likely to be non-higher-animal than higher-animal. In other words, the former are more individuated than the latter.
2. Objects that are nonspecific and/or non-higher-animal are less individuated than those that are both specific and higher-animal.
3. Cognate objects are less individuated than noncognate objects.

In other words, of the two members in each opposition—patient versus goal/beneficiary/source; nonspecific versus specific; and cognate versus noncognate—it is always the less individuated member that is a direct object to a lesser degree.

ACKNOWLEDGMENTS

The data given here are based on the material collected during a field trip to Manam Island in 1976–1977. The fieldwork was part of the Oceanic Comparative Linguistics Project supported by NSF Grant 75-19451. I am grateful to Joel Bradshaw, Andrew Pawley, and Stanley Starosta for valuable comments on an earlier version of this paper.

REFERENCES

Böhm, K. (1975) "Grammatik-Skizze der Manam-Sprache," edited by Johannes Z'graggen, in K. Böhm, *Das Leben einiger Inselvölker Neuguineas*, Anthropos-Institut St. Augustin—Haus Völker und Kulturen, St. Augustin.

Faltz, L. M. (1978) "On Indirect Objects in Universal Syntax," in D. Farkas, W. Jacobsen, and C. Todry, eds., *Papers from the Fourteenth Regional Meeting of the Chicago Linguistic Society*, Chicago Linguistic Society, University of Chicago.

Hopper, P. and S. Thompson (1980) "Transitivity in Grammar and Discourse," *Language* 56, 251–299.

Lichtenberk, F. (forthcoming) *A Grammar of Manam*, The University Press of Hawaii, Honolulu, Hawaii.

Moravcsik, E. (1978) "On the Case Marking of Objects," in J. Greenberg, ed., *Universals of Human Language 4: Syntax*, Stanford University Press, Stanford.

Morolong, M. and L. Hyman (1977) "Animacy, Objects and Clitics in Sesotho," *Studies in African Linguistics* 8, 199–218.

Timberlake, A. (1975) "Hierarchies in the Genitive of Negation," *Slavic and East European Journal* 19, 123–138.

Timberlake, A. (1977) "Reanalysis and Actualization in Syntactic Change," in C. Li, ed., *Mechanisms of Syntactic Change*, University of Texas Press, Austin.

THE DEVELOPMENT OF OBJECT MARKERS
IN SERIAL VERB LANGUAGES

CAROL LORD

In West African languages of the Benue-Kwa group, object markers have developed, to varying degrees, from the verb 'take' in the context of serial verb constructions.[1] This diachronic process is paralleled in Mandarin Chinese. In this paper, I discuss first the Mandarin evidence, then data from Benue-Kwa languages. I describe correlations in these languages between object marking, word order, polarity, aspect, and definiteness of objects—correlations consistent with the tendency for diachronic innovation to occur in foregrounded clauses, according to the Transitivity Hypothesis developed by Hopper and Thompson (1980). I then discuss the parallel between the historical development described here and the development of object marking in children learning to speak.

---

[1] Serial verb constructions and related case-marking morphemes have been recognized by many linguists, among them Ansre (1966), Pike (1967), Awobuluyi (1973), Lord (1973), Li and Thompson (1974a), and Givón (1975). Specifically, 'take' as a defective verb or case marker in serial constructions has been noted by, among others, Riis (1854), Zimmermann (1858), Christaller (1875), Stewart (1963), Boadi (1966), Hyman (1971), Trutenau (1973), Li and Thompson (1974b, 1981), Givón (1975), and Leynseele (1978).

277

1. EVIDENCE FROM MANDARIN CHINESE

Although there is no evidence of historical relationship, Mandarin Chinese resembles many Benue-Kwa languages typologically. It tends to be isolating, with little inflectional morphology; it is a tone language; it has VO word order historically, serial verb constructions, and deverbal prepositions. Mandarin Chinese provides an example, documented by written records, of the evolution of an object marker from the verb 'take'. In classical Chinese, *bǎ* was a verb meaning 'take hold of', as in the fifth-century B.C. example given in (1).[2]

(1)   *Yu qīng   bǎ   tīan   zhǐ   ruì-lìng   yǐ zhēn*
          himself take heaven poss mandate to conquer
          you   Miao   (Li and Thompson 1974b:202)
          particle
       'Yu himself took the mandate of heaven to conquer Miao'.

The verb *bǎ* was used in serial verb constructions, as in (2) and (3) from the Tang dynasty (seventh–ninth centuries A.D.).

(2)   *Shī   jù   wú rén   shì   yīn   bǎ*
          poem sentence no man appreciate should hold
          jiàn   kàn.   (Li and Thompson 1974b:202)
          sword see
       'Since no one appreciates poetry, I should take hold of the
          sword to contemplate it'.

(3)   *Zuì   bǎ zhū-gēn-zǐ xì   kàn.* (Li and Thompson 1976a:485)
          drunk   dogwood   careful look
          a.   'While drunk, (I) took the dogwood and carefully looked at
               it'. (serial verb interpretation)
          b.   'While drunk, (I) carefully looked at the
               dogwood'. (object marker interpretation)

For (3), both serial verb and prepositional phrase analyses are possible, as illustrated by readings (3a) and (3b).

In modern Chinese, *bǎ* can not take an aspect marker and can not occur as the predicate of a simple sentence, as (4) illustrates. However, so-called partitive sentences like (5) suggest its earlier verb meaning.

(4)   **Tā bǎ* NP   (Li and Thompson 1976a:485)
          he

---

[2] The marking of tone in examples here follows the conventions used in the sources cited; in some cases tones are left unmarked when they are not relevant to the explanation.

(5)   *Tā bǎ sān-ge jiǎozi   chī-le   liǎng-ge.*
       he   three   dumpling eat-aspect two
       'He ate two of the three dumplings'.
                                        (Li and Thompson 1976a:485)

In modern Chinese, *bǎ* functions as an objective case marker, as in (6).

(6)   *Zhāng-sān bǎ Lǐ-sì pīping   le.*
                             criticize aspect
       'Zhang-san criticized Li-si'.   (Li and Thompson 1976a:485)

As described by Li and Thompson (1976a, 1976b, 1981), *bǎ* has lost all of the syntactic properties of a verb, and its function as an object marker in sentences like (6) is unmistakable. The pathway for the reanalysis was the serial verb construction, where the verb-to-preposition change can be seen taking place in Example (3) from the eighth century.

We do not have written records from West Africa to document language change over long periods. However, internal and comparative evidence provide clues which we can interpret, guided by our growing understanding of universals of linguistic change. The evidence strongly suggests that historical developments similar to those documented for Chinese are taking place in some Benue-Kwa languages—to a considerable degree in Idoma, and to a limited extent in Ga and Akan.

2. EVIDENCE FROM AKAN

Grammars of Akan[3] from the nineteenth century cite sentences with *de* as a verb meaning 'take, hold, possess, use', as in (7)–(10).

(7)   *Abrokirri akoa ni   ho,   von iniara vo-**de***
       Europe   slave is-not there they all   they-**possess**
       von-hu.   (Riis 1854:167)
       their-self
       'In Europe there is no slave, they are all free'.

(8)   *Ɔnó nà   ɔ -**de**   kùró yi.*   (Christaller 1881:68)
       he   focus he-**possess** town this
       'He is the possessor of this town'.

(9)   *Ɔ-n-**dé**   apèmpensí nà   épè n'ádé.*   (Christaller 1881:68)
       he-neg-**use** extortion   conj seek his-thing
       'It is not his manner or way to enrich himself by extortion'.

---

[3] For the major language of southern Ghana, Riis (1854) represented 'Twi' as *Oji;* Christaller (1875) used *Tshi;* current scholars prefer the name *Akan* for the dialect group.

(10)   *Anoma de ako-ne-aba.*   (Christaller 1875:139)
        bird   **use** going-and-coming
        na e-nwene berebuw.
        and it-weave nest
        'By going and coming a bird weaves its nest'.

Today *de* does not occur as a verb in a simple sentence; however, it is
possible that the idiomatic expression in (11) has the verb *de* 'take' as
its historical source, as suggested by Stewart (1963).

(11)   *Ɔkɔm de   me.*   (Stewart 1963:146)
        hunger **takes** me
        'I am hungry'.

The existence of the noun *àdé* 'thing, property, possession', as in (9),
is consistent with that of a cognate verb meaning 'hold, have, possess,
own', since the prefix *a-* on verbs is one of a set of affixes forming
nominals from verbs, as in verb–nominal pairs such as *gòru* (verb) 'play'
and *agóru* (noun) 'game, play, amusement', and *hù* (verb) 'see, discover'
and *ahú* (noun) 'a treasure discovered'. (Although this derivational process is not productive today, it might have been at an earlier period
when *de* was more fully verbal.)

The casemarking morpheme *de* is in complementary distribution with
another morpheme, *fa. De* is used in the indicative, *fa* is used in the
negative and imperative. *Fa,* meaning 'take', has the full range of formal
capabilities of a verb. The fact that *fa* is fully verbal, both semantically
and formally, is consistent with the view of its suppletive partner having
once been so too. As suggested by Riis (1854:96) and Christaller (1875),
since the meaning of *fa* is 'take', it is reasonable to assume that the
meaning of *de* as a verb was similar. The meaning 'take' is in the same
semantic range as 'have, possess, hold, use, employ'. Pragmatically,
after one has completed the act of "taking" something, one "has, holds,
possesses" it, and if one holds it while performing some action and the
item is helpful or instrumental to the performance, a reasonable interpretation is that one "uses" it. As meanings of lexical items reflect the
circumstances of their actual use by people, this sort of semantic range
for a given morpheme (*de* or *fa*) is just what we would expect.

Supporting comparative evidence is found in the related language Anyi,
which uses the verb *fa* 'take' in both negative and affirmative sentences;
in Anyi *de* is a verb meaning 'grab' (Leynseele 1978).

For present-day Akan speakers, the former verb *de* has lost many
semantic and syntactic properties. It does not inflect for tense/aspect,
it has a suppletive negative, and it does not occur as an independent
verb in a simple sentence. Reminiscent of its earlier verb identity is its

occurrence before noun phrases which are in the objective form when pronominalized. *De* is now an invariant, noninflecting morpheme, which functions as a casemarking preposition rather than a verb. Its defective status parallels that of other deverbal prepositional case markers in Benue-Kwa languages. As a preposition, it introduces noun phrases in the semantic role of instrument (including means, material, manner, and comitative relationships, which share common universal semantic ground and can be found to share similar marking in other unrelated languages, as noted in Lord 1973). It also marks semantic patients;[4] according to Stewart (1963:149), it functions as "a mere carrier of a direct object which another verb cannot, or preferably does not, carry itself."

This rather wide range of synchronic functions for *de* can be seen to follow from its former identity as a verb. Most contexts in which it occurs can be given a literal gloss with *de* as a verb meaning 'take' or 'use' in a serial verb construction as in (12)–(16). These sentences illustrate the parallel between the development of case markers from *de* 'take' in Akan and from *bǎ* 'take' in eighth-century Mandarin Chinese, as in (3).

de marking instrument NP:

(12)   *O-de eñkrante tya duabasa.*   (Riis 1854:168)
        he-*de* sword   cut branch
        'He cut off a branch with a sword'.
        (Serial verb reading: 'He took a sword and cut off a branch'.)

de marking comitative NP:

(13)   *Ɔ-de né nnípa fòro   bépow.*   (Christaller 1875:71)
        he-*de* his men   ascend mountain
        'He ascends a mountain with his men'.
        (Serial verb reading: 'He takes his men and ascends a
          mountain'.)

de marking patient NP:

(14)   *O-de mfoníni bi   kyèré nè bá.*   (Christaller 1875:71)
        he-*de* picture certain show his child
        'He shows his child a picture'.
        (Serial verb reading: 'He takes a picture and shows his child'.)

(15)   *Wo-de no yeè   osafohéne.*   (Christaller 1875:117)
        they-*de* him make captain

---

[4] Here I use the semantic case role terminology established in Fillmore (1968), except that I use the label "patient" instead of Fillmore's "objective," in an attempt to avoid muddying further the distinction between semantic patients and syntactic objects.

'They made him captain'.
(Serial verb reading: 'They took him and made him captain'.)

(16)   *Ɔ-de kanéà bí   sii   pónó nó   só.   (Stewart 1963:148)
        he-de lamp   certain stood table that top
        'He stood a lamp on the table'.
        (Serial verb reading: 'He took a lamp and it stood on the
            table'.)

Typically in many Benue-Kwa languages, within a serial verb construction the actions or conditions named by the component verb phrases are necessarily related as elements in a single overall event, where the second verb signifies the intended result or consequence of the first (Lord 1974). Accordingly, if a semantic agent manually takes up a concrete item and carries out an action affecting a semantic patient, where the intention in the taking is for the purpose of carrying out the action (this semantic connection being inherent in the serial verb construction in this language), then the item taken up falls into the semantic role classification of instrument with respect to the action. Thus, the object of the verb 'take' in a serial verb construction of this sort is readily reanalyzable as an argument occupying the semantic role of instrument with respect to the second verb. This is precisely the historical process discernible in (12). With abstract NP objects of *de,* where a better gloss might be 'employ', as in (9) and (10), the instrument role is broadened to include means and manner.

Pragmatic plausibility determines that the NP introduced by *de* in (13) occupies a comitative rather than instrumental role relationship. Many other languages use the same case marker for instrumental and comitative NPs; English does, as illustrated by the English translations for (12) and (13), where *with* marks the instrumental NP in (12) as well as the comitative NP in (13).

The historical reanalysis process in (14)–(16) is similar to that in (12). But in (14)–(16) the second verb does not signify action upon a semantic patient, but rather action involving a semantic dative, factitive, and locative, respectively. In these environments the 'taken' item fills the semantic role of patient with respect to the second verb, and in these contexts *de* is reanalyzed as a case marker for semantic patients.

As noted by nineteenth-century scholars, the presence of *de* makes intransitive motion verbs transitive/causative (Riis 1854:168; Christaller 1875:119). In Akan a verb like *si* 'stand' is classified as a motion verb, occurring independently with a semantic patient as subject and a locative NP complement as in (17), but not with agent subject and patient and locative complements, as the ungrammaticality of (18) illustrates.

(17)   *Duá bi   sì   né dán   aniṁ.*   (Christaller 1875:119)
        tree certain stand his house front
        'A tree stands before his house'.

(18)   a. *O-sii   kanea bi   pono no so.   (Stewart 1963:148)
           he-stood lamp   certain table that top
           'He stood a lamp on the table'.
        b. *O-sii   pono no so kanea bi.
           he-stood table that top lamp   certain
           'He stood a lamp on the table'.

In a serial verb construction like (16) the patient NP 'lamp' is simultaneously the object of *de* 'take' and the understood subject of *si* 'stand'. Here the reanalysis in the serial verb context has the result of adding an agent NP, 'he', to the second verb in the scene represented in (16).

In addition to meaning 'take', the verb *de* meant 'possess, have, get', as in Sentences (7)–(8). In unrelated languages, verbs with these meanings have been utilized to mark causative constructions—note that translations with *have* and *get* provide idiomatic English versions of (16) as 'He had a lamp stand on the table', and 'He got a lamp to stand on the table'.

In an Akan serial verb construction, the understood subject of the second verb is typically the same as that of the first verb. But another reading is possible when the first verb is an action verb (most typically, a verb of physical manipulation with a semantic patient as object) and the second verb is a motion verb. In this alternative reading, the understood subject of the second verb is the first verb's object. For example, in the serial verb reading for (16) the object of *de*, 'lamp', is the understood subject of 'stand'; 'he' did not stand on the table. When the second verb's selectional restrictions for its subject permit either the subject or object of the first verb, ambiguity results (see Boadi 1966). However, given the characteristic action–result meaning of serial verb constructions, usually only one reading is pragmatically plausible, and there is rarely confusion in context. This ambiguity can be seen in (19), where (a) is the same-subject reading and (b) is the causative reading.

(19)   *Kofi de Amma kɔɔe.*   (Boadi 1968:85)
                    went
        'Kofi took Amma away'.
        Serial verb readings:
        a. 'Kofi took Amma and (Kofi) went'.
        b. 'Kofi took Amma and Amma went'.

As Riis and Christaller note, in connection with *de* the meaning of a motion verb becomes causative; *kɔ* 'go' becomes 'take away, take to a place, lead, conduct', and *de . . . ba* (historically 'take . . . come') appears in Christaller's dictionary (1881) as 'bring', as in the following sentence:

(20)   *Kofi de nwoma no   a-ba.*
        Kofi *de* book   that perf-come
        'Kofi has brought the book'.

In terms of semantic roles, the object of *de* in (19) and (20) is a patient with respect to *de*. The *de* NP phrase is reanalyzed as comitative with respect to the second verb in the same-subject reading (19a) 'Kofi went away with Amma'. For the reading (19b) 'Kofi led Amma away', the agentive NP *Kofi* is added to the scene, giving the second verb a transitive/causative reading. In actual language use, establishing a distinction between (a) and (b) is rarely crucial for communication; for example, in the case of (20), whether Kofi arrived with the book, caused it to arrive, or brought it with him is usually either obvious from context or irrelevant to the point of the message. This pragmatic irrelevance may have facilitated the shift from an intransitive reading ('Kofi has arrived with the book') to a transitive reading ('Kofi has brought the book') for motion verbs with *de*.

Clearly, then, sentences like (16), (19), and (20) with the *de* construction and motion verbs have transitive/causative readings. However, the motion verbs themselves are still considered to be intransitive, since they do not take patients as postverbal objects in the established SVO sentence pattern. Although these motion verbs may take locative NP complements, it is only with *de* marking the patient that a transitive/causative reading is possible for these verbs, so *de* can be considered a marker of transitivity in these instances.

With verbs like *kyerɛ* 'show' in (14), *yɛ* 'make' in (15), and others of this class such as *ma* 'give', *bisa* 'ask', *fɛm* 'lend', and *hyɛ* 'wear, put on', the patient in preverbal position is marked by *de*. Unlike motion verbs, these bitransitive verbs can occur in sentences with patient nouns without *de*, but the patient occurs after the verb (if there is a dative, it immediately follows the verb, and the patient follows the dative).

The *de* construction introduces a patient when the subject is an agent. Factitive arguments can not be marked by *de;* (21) does not have a paraphrase with *de*, because the semantic role of the NP 'letter' is factitive.

(21)   *W-a-kyerɛw me nhoma.*   (Christaller 1875:118)
        he-perf-write me letter
        'He has written me a letter'.

This fact follows from the earlier verb meaning of *de,* because a serial verb reading would be 'He has taken the letter and written to me'; since a letter can not be taken, grasped, before it is written, the string is pragmatically anomalous. The former verb meaning of *de* and the action–result meaning of serial verb constructions still determine what can be marked by *de.* At some much later date in the continuum of change, it is conceivable that the influence of the verb meaning of *de* might become weaker, for example, to allow objects of *de* to function as factitives as well as patients with respect to the second verb, or to allow subjects of *de* to function as experiencers as well as agents, in which case the range of possible objects for *de* would be describable syntactically rather than semantically. Just this development appears to have occurred in Idoma, as will be seen later in this paper. The related Ghanaian language Ga, discussed in the next section, shows evidence of historical development similar to Akan.

In Akan, then, as in Mandarin Chinese, the verb 'take' in serial verb constructions has been reanalyzed as a preposition marking semantic patients, and the former construction with two verb phrases has been reanalyzed as a single proposition.

Pike (1966) describes a similar situation in Vagala, where the verb *kpa* 'take' occurs in serial constructions, introducing instrument and patient arguments. Pike differentiates between these case-related constructions ("clause subclusters") and regular serial constructions ("clause clusters") on semantic grounds, noting that in the subclusters "the meaning of the series is *not* the sum of the meanings of the included clauses. Rather, the total function is something above and beyond the individual elements" (1966:13). He considers the subclusters to be new developments, and observes that, since the language is in a state of transition, "only a dynamic view of the total system can do descriptive justice to such data" (1966:45).

3. EVIDENCE FROM GA

The parallels between *kè* in Ga and *de* in Akan suggest similar historical development. The morpheme *kè* has many functions in Ga, including marking instrumental nouns, as in (22), as well as comitative and manner nouns.

(22)   a. *È kè tsò   tswà gbékè lὲ.*
            he *kè* stick hit   child the
            'He hit the child **with a stick**'.

   b. *È tswà gbékè lè   tsò*
       he hit   child the stick
       'He hit the child **with a stick**'.

Instrumental nouns before the verb are marked with *kè*, as in (22a);
instrumental nouns after the verb are not marked prepositionally, as
shown in the alternative sentence pattern in (22b).

This case marker has many properties that suggest that its diachronic
source was a verb:

1. It often occupies the position within the sentence normally occupied
    by the first verb in a serial construction.
2. It is preceded by subject pronouns and is followed by object pro-
    nouns, even in its comitative capacity conjoining NPs.
3. In imperatives corresponding to (22), the verb following *kè* is in
    the subjunctive, as is the case in regular verb sequences in
    imperatives.
4. When a third person singular inanimate object of *kè* is pronomi-
    nalized, it is realized as zero, as is the usual pattern with verbs.

Trutenau (1973) argues for an analysis of *kè* as a verb, and Zimmermann (1858) calls it an auxiliary verb. But *kè* has a number of properties
that distinguish it from regular verbs:

1. It does not occur without another verb in the sentence.
2. It does not inflect; in a regular serial verb sequence the second verb
    is not inflected, but verbs following *kè* are inflected.
3. Unlike regular serial verb sequences, the verb following *kè* never
    has a pronominal subject.
4. When *kè* occurs followed by a high tone verb prefix (e.g., perfect
    or subjunctive), *kè,* unlike regular verbs, assimilates to the high
    tone and the prefix vowel is deleted.

Although Zimmermann (1858) says it was formerly a verb meaning
'take', speakers today do not recognize it as such. Glossing *kè* as 'take'
makes (22a) parallel to the Akan serial verb constructions like (12) with
de marking instrument NPs, giving it the reading 'He took a stick and
hit the child'. As with *de* in Akan, verbs of motion in Ga can appear
in serial-like constructions, where the morpheme *kè* makes possible a
transitive/causative reading, as in (23) and (24).

(23)   *Tètè kè wòló lè   bà.*
        Tete *ke* book the came
        a. 'Tete came **with the book**'.
        b. 'Tete brought **the book**'.

(24)   *È kὲ wòlò ŋmὲ-sî.*
        she *kɛ* book lay- down
        'She put down **a book**'.

Ga verbs are typically CV monosyllables; in some cases a verb +
locative noun has been reanalyzed as a bisyllabic verb, as in (24) where
the second syllable *sî* is recognizable as the former noun 'ground' which
in combination with verbs simply means 'down'. The *kὲ* construction
is required for these polysyllabic verbs. In (24) the motion verb *ŋmὲ-
sî* 'lay down' occurs with the patient noun phrase *wòlò* 'book'. But
historically (24) contains the motion verb *ŋmὲ* 'lay' followed by the
locative noun *sî* 'ground' in object position. As the object position is
already filled by the locative, the *kὲ* construction is used, with the patient
in preverb position, preserving the "favorite" one-object-per-verb pattern. The situation is paralleled in Akan, as can be seen by reexamining
(16) and (18). Even though the Ga verb and its locative object have been
reanalyzed as a polysyllabic verb, the inherited sentence configuration
remains. Similarly, in Mandarin Chinese many polysyllabic verbs, historically from verb + noun compounds and verb + verb compounds,
require the *bǎ* construction.

In the established SVX sentence pattern in Ga, bitransitive verbs like
hǎ 'give' and *wò* 'put' take two postverbal complement NPs, the first
a locative or dative recipient, and the second a patient, as in (25b) and
(26b). The patient can occur before the verb, marked by the preposition
kὲ, as in (25a) and (26a).

(25)   a.   *È kὲ wòlò hǎ   mì.*
             she *kɛ* book gave me
             'She gave me **a book**'.
        b.   *È hǎ   mì wòlò.*
             she gave me book
             'She gave me **a book**'.

(26)   a.   *È kὲ nù   wò tɔ́   lὲ mlî.*
             she *kɛ* water put bottle the inside
             'She put **water** in the bottle'.
        b.   *È wò tɔ́   lὲ mlî   nù.*
             she put bottle the inside water
             'She put **water** in the bottle'.

The *kὲ* construction requires an agent preceding *kὲ* and a patient
following it, consistent with the semantic requirements of an earlier verb
meaning 'take'. For example, neither an agent–factitive combination as

in (27), nor an experiencer–patient combination as in (28), is possible with *kè,* as illustrated by the ungrammaticality of (27a) and (28a).

(27) a. **È kè wɔlɔ ŋmè.*
       she *kɛ* egg lay
       'She laid **an egg**'.
     b. *È ŋmè wɔlɔ.*
       she lay egg
       'She laid **an egg**'.

(28) a. **Tètè kè Kɔkɔ nà.*
       Tete *kɛ* Koko saw
       'Tete saw Koko'.
     b. *Tètè nà Kɔkɔ.*
       Tete saw Koko
       'Tete saw Koko'.

The Ga preposition *kè,* then, parallels the Akan preposition *de* and the Mandarin preposition *bǎ* in historical development.

4. EVIDENCE FROM IDOMA

The Nigerian language Idoma has a morpheme similar to Akan *de,* Ga *kè,* and Mandarin *bǎ* in function and distribution, but rather than a preposition it is a prefix. The range of its functions suggest that it may also have evolved from a former verb 'take' in a serial verb construction.

For both Idoma sentences (29) and (30) the most natural English translation includes an instrumental phrase. Sentence (29) contains a serial verb construction with the verb *bi* 'hold', paralleling the form and meaning of Akan sentence (12) with *de* and Ga sentence (22) with *kè.* The position of the 'take' verb is occupied by the prefix *l-* in (30), suggesting a verb source for the prefix. (All Idoma examples are from Abraham 1951.)

(29) *Ó bī- ēwā gūwā.*
       he hold-knife slash-them
       'He slashed them with a knife'.

(30) *Ǹ l-ēwā gūwā.*
       I *l-*knife slash-them
       'I slashed them with a knife'.

Sentence (30) comprises a single proposition in which the instrumental NP is marked by the prefix *l-.*

This same *l-* prefix provides an alternative to the basic SVO sentence pattern in Idoma. The prefix marks direct objects in preverbal position, as in (31)–(33).

(31)   a. *Ó l-ùwā nū.*
            s/he *l-*them drive-away
            'S/he drove them away'.

    b. *Ó nū   ùwā.*
            s/he drive-away them
            'S/he drove them away'.

(32)   a. *Ó l-ɔyí mà.*
            s/he *l-*child bear
            'She bore a child'.

    b. *Ó mà ɔyí.*
            s/he bear child
            'She bore a child'.

(33)   a. *Ó l-ɔcí má.*
            s/he *l-*tree saw
            'S/he saw the tree'.

    b. *Ó má ɔcí.*
            s/he saw tree
            'She saw the tree'.

The prefix *l-* and the Idoma verb *lè* 'get, possess, have', illustrated in (34) and (35), may be historically related.

(34)   *Ó lè ɔñā.*
         he get wife
         'He has a wife'.

(35)   *Òcí lè īkpō.*
         tree get seeds
         'The tree has seeds'.

The verb *lè* is semantically comparable to Mandarin *bǎ* and Akan *de;* the prefix occurs where we would expect to find a verb in a serial verb construction. Sentence (31a) has an agent and a patient, and if we read it as a serial verb construction with *l-* as 'take', we get 'S/he took them and drove them away'. Sentences (32a) and (33a) do not provide very meaningful paraphrases—'She took a child and bore it', and 'She took a tree and saw it'. But neither (32) nor (33) contains both an agent and a patient, suggesting that, if Idoma has followed the same general path from verb to patient marker as the other languages discussed here, it has gone even farther: It no longer requires that the subject be an agent—

for example, an experiencer is permitted in (33)—and it has generalized
its prefixal marking of semantic patients to include syntactic objects.

In the languages discussed earlier, the verb 'take' has become formally
defective. In Idoma, the former verb has become both semantically and
syntactically defective to the extent that formally it no longer exists even
as a preposition, but has become morphologically attached as a prefix
on the noun it marks.

Evidence for the prefix status of *l-* is found in the processes of elision
and linkage. Verbs participate in the processes, but the prefix *l-* does
not. As illustrated in (36), in the elision process the tone of the verb
appears in the contracted form, but the prefix has no tone to contribute,
not even at an underlying level. Accordingly, the nouns retain their own
tones after *l-*.

(36)   *Elision:*   má + ɔ̀cí → mɔ́cí   'see tree'
         l + ɔ̀cí → lɔ́cí   'obj tree'
         l + ógò → lógò   'obj calabash'

As illustrated in (37), the verb contributes its mora of length, as well as
its tone, to the contracted form in those combinations that undergo the
linkage process, but the prefix has neither length nor tone to contribute.

(37)   *Linkage:*   jè + īlī → jìīlī   'take cloth'
         lè + īkpō → lììkpō   'get seeds'
         l + īlī → līlī   'obj cloth'

From its present form and behavior, we would be unable to reconstruct
the original vowel and tone of the object marker. A possible clue is
provided, however, by its performance with borrowed consonant-initial
nouns, as in (38), where the low tone of the prefix syllable corresponds
to that of the (presumably) related verb *lè*.

(38)   Borrowed noun as object: l + lámpò → lìlámpò   'obj lamp'

In Benue-Kwa and elsewhere, verbs of possession, location, and identification are sometimes historically related; in Idoma the verb *lè* is also
used for membership in a class. The prefix is also used to mark comitative
nouns, and occurs in nominalizations where a possessive/locative source
related to the verb *lè* is plausible. This range of historically related
meanings for *lè* and *l-* is consistent with the universal semantic shifts
proposed by Anderson (1975); he suggests that universal directions of
semantic drift go from 'get' to 'have' to 'with', and from 'get' to 'become'
to 'be'. Possible cognates for *lè* and *l-* in related languages include Nupe
la, Gwari *la,* Bamileke *làh,* and Babanke *lyʉ,* 'take' ('take' and 'get'
are of course very close semantically).

The verb *la* 'take' in Nupe shows a (now familiar) range of uses (George 1975). It functions as a main verb, as in (39), as well as an introducer of instrument, manner, and comitative NPs in serial constructions. With verbs of motion and location, it introduces the patient NP. According to George (1975:60), it signals a causative interpretation. Compare the intransitive (40) with the causative 'take' construction in (41) (from George 1975):

(39)   *Sàlámì là   èbi.*
        took knife
        'Salami took the knife'.

(40)   *Èbi   ta èsákó o.*
        knife be table loc
        'The knife is on the table'.

(41)   *Sàlámì lá   èbi   ta èsákó o.*
        took knife be table loc
        'Salami put the knife on the table'.

In (41) the causal action involves direct manual manipulation (i.e., "taking"); however, *la* functions as a causative in abstract contexts as well, as in (42) and (43).

(42)   *Sàlámì lá   kàràtun yé   mî.*   (**Sàlámì lá kàràtun.*)
        took lesson   be-understood me
        'Salami explained the lesson to me'.

(43)   *Yígídí lá   mángòrò dzú.*   (**Yigidi la mangoro.*)
        sun   took mango   red
        'The sun reddened the mango'.

Corresponding to the causative sentence (41) there exists the literal 'take' sentence (39). The meaning of the causative (41) is not wildly incompatible with a literal interpretation of *la* as 'take'. But for the causative sentences (42) and (43) there is no corresponding 'take' sentence, as the starred strings in parentheses in (42) and (43) illustrate. This indicates the degree to which the function of *la* as a transitive/causative element has diverged from its lexical meaning 'take'. The path of reanalysis of the 'take' morpheme in Nupe parallels the other languages discussed here, but *la* has not progressed as far as the analogous morpheme in Idoma has.

For Idoma, then, I suggest that the meaning of the verb *lè* 'get, have, be' and the range of occurrences of the *l-* prefix are consistent with the claim of a common historical source. The path of historical development of the object marker function of the prefix in Idoma was probably parallel to the development in Mandarin Chinese, Akan, Ga, Vagala, and Nupe, a gradual continuum of change from verb to preposition—and then, in the case of Idoma, from preposition to prefix.[5]

5. WORD ORDER, DEFINITENESS, POLARITY, ASPECT, AND PRAGMATIC FUNCTION IN DISCOURSE

The grammaticization of 'take' in serial verb constructions has resulted in a new option for the order of elements in sentences: A verb-final sentence pattern is possible, in addition to the established verb-medial pattern. A correlation has developed between word order and the definiteness of the object noun phrase. Further correlations are present between word order and polarity and aspect.

In Mandarin there are two word order possibilities: verb medial, as in (44a), and verb final, as in (44b).

(44)   a. *Háizi tàng yīfu   le.*   (Li and Thompson 1976b:177)
            child iron clothes asp
            'The child ironed **some clothes**'.
        b. *Háizi bǎ yīfu   tàng le*   (Li and Thompson 1976b:177)
            child *ba* clothes iron asp
            'The child ironed **the clothes**'.

The historically more recent development, with the object before the verb as in (44b), requires the object to be definite (Li and Thompson 1976b).

In Akan, for bitransitive verbs like *ma* 'give' there are two possible sentence configurations for indefinite patients, as illustrated in (45).

(45)   a. *Ọ-ma   abofra no akutu.*   (Christaller 1875:71)
            he-give child   the orange
            'He gives the child **an orange**'.
        b. *Ọ-de akutu   ma abofra no.*   (Christaller 1875:71)
            he-*de* orange give child   the
            'He gives the child **an orange**'.

---

[5] The native American language Chickasaw has no known historical relationship to either Benue-Kwa or Chinese, yet there is evidence of parallel development in the function of the verb 'take' (Munro and Gordon, to appear, and personal communication). Typologically, Chickasaw allows verbs in series and prefers a relatively low number of noun phrase arguments per verb. 'Take' can mark instruments, as in (12) for Akan, and has the effect of making intransitive motion verbs transitive/causative, as in (20) for Akan. These contexts are just those in which, according to the West African data, we would expect the historical process to begin.

The indefinite patient NP *akutu* 'orange' can occur after the main verb, as in (45a), or before the main verb in the *de* construction as in (45b).

However, when the patient NP is definite, only the *de* construction is grammatical, as illustrated in (46).

(46)   a. *ɔ- maa me siká   nó.*   (Stewart 1963:147)
            he-gave me money def
            'He gave me **the money**'.

        b. *ɔ-de siká   nó maa me.*   (Stewart 1963:147)
            he-*de* money the gave me
            'He gave me **the money**'.

This generalization is true for verbs of transfer involving physical manipulation, such as *ma* 'give', *kyɛ* 'give', *brɛ* 'bring', and *mane* 'send'; the verb *fɛm* 'lend' is exceptional in that it allows both the (a) and (b) configurations for definite patients. But when the definite patient is a pronoun, even with the verb *fɛm* 'lend', the *de* construction is again the only grammatical sentence form, as in (47).

(47)   a. *ɔ-fɛmm me no.*   (Stewart 1963:145)
            he-lent   me it
            'He lent me **it**'.

        b. *ɔ-de nó fɛmm me.*   (Stewart 1963:145)
            he-*de* it lent   me
            'He lent me **it**'.

In Akan, then, as in Mandarin, there is a correlation between preverb position and definiteness for patients. For Akan, this correlation is a property of verbs for which physical manipulation, or "taking," is involved in the action named by the verb, reflecting the original lexical meaning of the object-marking morpheme.

Like Akan, Anyi allows indefinite patients to occur after a bitransitive verb like *ma* 'give', but definite patients must occur before 'give'— specifically, in a serial construction where the definite patient is introduced by the verb *fa* 'take' (Leynseele 1978).

Similarly, in Ga, speakers prefer the *kɛ* construction, with its object in preverb position, for instrumental and patient nouns when they are definite. The consistency of the direction of the historical developments in these languages suggests that the choice of definite objects for preverb position is not idiosyncratic. It stems from the former meaning of the marker as the verb 'take', and follows the universal tendency for definite, "individuated" objects to occur earlier in the utterance and to show overt marking, as observed by Hopper and Thompson (1980). The historical change in each case has established a connection between word order and the definite–indefinite meaning distinction.

Another factor that correlates with word order is polarity. In Idoma the innovative verb-final sentence pattern, morphologically marked with the *l-* prefix and rare in the language family, does not occur in negative sentences. This fact is consistent with Givón's (1979) observation that the negative tends to be conservative syntactically, often accepting innovations more slowly than the affirmative, due to differences in pragmatic function. Hopper and Thompson (1980) have noted that the marking of objects in negative clauses often reflects their low Transitivity; the restriction of overt morphological object marking to affirmative clauses in Idoma is consistent with their Transitivity Hypothesis. Similarly, in Akan, *de* occurs only in affirmative sentences; their negative counterparts use the inflecting verb *fa* 'take' in serial verb constructions.

In Idoma affirmatives the *l-* prefix occurs in the past and future, but not in the imperfective, consistent with Hopper and Thompson's findings. According to Hopper and Thompson, objects in imperfective clauses are less likely to be totally affected by the action of the verb, and less likely to show overt marking. Imperfective clauses are rarely part of the foreground in discourse. Verb-final Idoma sentences are possible in the imperfective, but they use the verb *bi* 'hold', as in (29), instead of the grammaticized prefix *l-*. This usage of *bi* 'hold' in serial verb constructions appears to echo the much earlier use of the verb ancestor of the *l-* for affirmative constructions.

Dagbani, a Gur language of northern Ghana described by Wilson (1970), also shows a correlation between aspect and 'take' as a marker of instruments and patients. The verb *zang* 'take' occurs independently in simplex sentences, and introduces instrument and patient NPs in serial structures like those discussed earlier. In perfective clauses like (48), *zang* 'take' occurs, but imperfective clauses use the verb *mala* 'have' (which also occurs independently in simplexes), as in (49) (examples from Wilson 1970).

(48)   *M zang m suu nmaai nɨmdi.*
        I   took my knife cut-perf meat
        'I cut the meat with my knife' (the knife may already be in
        my hand).

(49)   *M mala m suu nmaara   nɨmdi.*
        I   have my knife cut-imperf meat
        'I am cutting the meat with my knife'.

In (48) *zang* has lost its literal meaning; as the gloss indicates, 'take' is not necessarily an element of the meaning of the sentence. This suggests that in (48) the presence of *zang* in conjunction with the verb morphology may signal perfective aspect (or, at any rate, the language may be headed in that direction).[6]

The use of the verb 'take' with preverbal objects is also correlated with perfective aspect and affirmation in Gwari, as described by Hyman and Magaji (1970). Gwari, a Nigerian language, uses SVO word order for perfective negative sentences and for perfective affirmatives with contrastive emphasis on the object. However, in perfective affirmatives without contrastive emphasis the object occurs before the verb, introduced by 'take'—*la* with singular objects, *ku* with plural objects.

In some serial verb languages the process of grammaticization of 'take' has resulted in a correlation between verb-final word order and definite objects; affirmative and negative clauses accept the new word order differentially, with grammaticization occurring more slowly in the negative; the change develops in perfective aspect constructions before imperfectives. All three of these correlations follow from the fact that languages change as people use them for the purpose of communicating. Utterances that are central to the momentum of the discourse, that advance the story line, that constitute foreground rather than background, are more likely to be affirmative than negative, to be perfective than imperfective, to involve definite rather than indefinite objects, and to mark those objects overtly, as Hopper and Thompson have shown. Utterances that are foregrounded with respect to discourse are likely to be at the forefront in terms of innovative change.

6. PARALLEL BETWEEN DIACHRONIC AND ONTOGENETIC DEVELOPMENT OF OBJECT CODING

According to Hopper and Thompson (1980), a high degree of transitivity is associated with an agent acting volitionally upon a definite or referential object. The verb 'take' is accordingly a good candidate for involvement in high transitivity, as it typically selects objects that are

---

[6] Although the Dagbani verb *zang* 'take' has lost some literal meaning, as demonstrated, its distribution in serial constructions still reflects its literal verb meaning:

(i) *O peenti loori.*   (= *O zang loori peenti.*)
     he paint lorry
     'He painted the lorry'.

(ii) *O peenti duu.*   (**O zang duu peenti.*)
     he paint room
     'He painted the room'.

The 'take' construction is allowable with 'lorry' but not with 'room', as objects in the 'take' construction can not be immovable (non-take-able) (Wilson 1970).

concrete and movable, and 'takers' are typically animate instigators. If transitivity is defined as "the effective carrying over of an activity from an A to a patient" (1980:279), then the meaning of 'take' qualifies admirably. The verb 'take' and its two noun phrase arguments, agent and patient, define a prototypical transitive act, and it is a descendant of this verb that can be found marking transitive/causative constructions and can eventually be generalized to mark syntactic direct objects.

There is some evidence suggesting that the course of this historical development may be paralleled by the progression of successive generalizations about object marking made by children learning to speak. The young child spends a lot of time 'taking' things, grasping objects manually and moving them around. These activities are evident in the play of infants and preschoolers. From observing young children it becomes apparent that these activities are important to the child; performing them successfully gives him satisfaction and pleasure. As the child matures, these activities become more complex and sophisticated; Lyons's observations suggest to him that "as human beings, we are particularly interested in the results of our purposive actions and in the effects that our actions have upon patients" (Lyons 1977:491). And human language reflects human nature. Lyons sees paradigm instances of agentive situations as those in which the action results in a change in the physical condition or location of the patient. Consistent with these observations are the fourteen properties proposed by Lakoff (1977:244) for prototypical agent–patient sentences; among them: an agent volitionally directs his energies and attention toward a single, definite patient, using his hands, body, or some instrument to effect a perceptible change, with spatiotemporal overlap between the agent's action and the patient's change.

Slobin (this volume) suggests that object manipulation, in which a causal agent brings about a change of state or location by means of direct body contact, is a "prototypical event" with significance in the development of language from sensorimotor cognitions in early child language development. According to Slobin, prototypical events, rather than categories, seem to provide the initial conceptual framework for grammatical coding. For example, Slobin cites Gvozdev's 1949 diary study of a child learning Russian: In adult Russian speech, all direct objects carry an accusative suffix, but at first (age 23 months) this child used the suffix only on objects of verbs involving direct physical action (i.e., on 'pick up', 'tear', 'throw away', but not on 'see', 'read'). Slobin also cites Braine's (1976) report of similar undergeneralization in children acquiring Swedish, English, Finnish, and Samoan, in which regularities in word order are present for events involving the moving or holding of objects, but these regularities are not immediately generalized to all events involving action on objects.

The child language data suggest that a grammatical marking initially used for the prototypical event of direct object manipulation becomes generalized later to indicate the action of a verb on an object. The language-internal and comparative evidence from languages with serial verbs shows a corresponding historical progression: The actual verb used for physical object manipulation—for taking—comes to function as a more general semantic patient marker and indicator of causality, and eventually in some cases a grammatical object marker. The history parallels ontogeny in that the causative-marking function is first found in constructions with motion verbs and involves moving an object by means of direct physical manipulation.

Just as the verb 'take' in these languages defines the class of semantic patients historically, the child's act of grasping and moving a physical object defines his earliest coded patient category. These languages later grammaticize the 'take' morpheme for use outside of strictly agent–patient situations, just as the developing child later broadens the scope of his early coding to mark other semantic roles, eventually including all syntactic objects according to the adult model he hears. Developmentally as well as historically, the emergence of the category is firmly grounded in the context of speakers interacting with their environment.

7. CONCLUSIONS

The verb 'take' in serial verb constructions has been reanalyzed historically, to varying degrees, as a preposition marking nouns filling semantic roles of instrument and patient in Benue-Kwa languages as well as in Mandarin Chinese. As a result, objects can occur in preverbal position in addition to the established postverbal position in these languages. Another result of the historical process is the addition of a noun phrase argument (instrument, agent or patient) to the clause, increasing the valence of the other verb in the series. A long-term effect could be a typological shift in sentence structure, from serial verb constructions with typically one noun phrase object per verb, to heavier sentence structures with one verb allowing several noun phrase arguments. That such a shift is already in process can be seen in the gradual change noted previously from serial verb to prepositional marking for locative, comitative, instrument, and dative noun phrases.

As the rate of diachronic innovation is greater in foregrounded clauses, which tend to be affirmative and perfective, the innovative verb-final word order is found earlier in affirmative and perfective clauses. As objects in foregrounded clauses tend to be definite, the verb-final clause pattern is preferred for definite objects, resulting in a correlation between word order and definiteness.

It may be that the child's earliest concept of causation develops through the physical act of grasping an object and causing it to move, and that such a prototypical agent–patient act is the basis for later generalized syntactic marking of objects. If so, the development in the individual child parallels the historical development described here for grammatical marking of transitivity and causation.

ACKNOWLEDGMENTS

Many of the developments described here were reported on earlier in "The Evolution of Object Markers in Benue-Kwa," a paper presented at the International Conference on Historical Linguistics IV, March 1979, Stanford University. I am indebted to Sandra Thompson for helpful comments on that paper.

REFERENCES

Abraham, R. C. (1951) *The Idoma Language,* University of London Press, London.
Anderson, L. B. (1975) "Grammar–Meaning Universals and Proto-Language Reconstruction, of Proto-World NOW!", in R. Grossman, L. J. San, and T. J. Vance, eds., *Papers from the Eleventh Regional Meeting of the Chicago Linguistic Society,* Chicago Linguistic Society, University of Chicago.
Ansre, G. (1966) "The Verbid—A Caveat to 'Serial Verbs'," *Journal of West African Languages* 3.1, 29–32.
Awobuluyi, O. (1973) "The Modifying Serial Construction: A Critique," *Studies in African Linguistics* 4.1, 87–111.
Boadi, L. (1966) *The Syntax of the Twi Verb,* unpublished doctoral dissertation, University of London.
Christaller, J. (1875) *A Grammar of the Asante and Fante Language, Called Tshi,* Basel Evangelical Missionary Society (republished by Gregg Press, 1964).
Christaller, J. (1881) *Dictionary of the Asante and Fante Language Called Tshi,* Basel Evangelical Missionary Society (revised 1933).
Fillmore, C. (1968) "The Case for Case," in E. Bach and R. Harms, eds., *Universals in Linguistic Theory,* Holt, Rinehart and Winston, New York.
George, I. (1975) *A Grammar of Kwa-Type Verb Serialization: Its Nature and Significance in Current Generative Theory,* unpublished doctoral dissertation, University of California, Los Angeles.
Givón, T. (1975) "Serial Verbs and Syntactic Change: Niger-Congo," in C. Li, ed., *Word Order and Word Order Change,* University of Texas Press, Austin.

Givón, T. (1979) *On Understanding Grammar*, Academic Press, New York.
Hopper, P. and S. Thompson (1980) "Transitivity in Grammar and Discourse," *Language* 56, 251–299.
Hyman, L. (1971) "Consecutivization in Fe?fe?," *Journal of African Languages* 10, 29–43.
Hyman, L. and D. Magaji (1970) *Essentials of Gwari Grammar* (Occasional Publication No. 27), Institute of African Studies, University of Ibadan, Nigeria.
Lakoff, G. (1977) "Linguistic Gestalts," in W. Beach, S. Fox, and S. Philosoph, eds., *Papers from the Thirteenth Regional Meeting of the Chicago Linguistic Society*, Chicago Linguistic Society, University of Chicago.
Leynseele, H. van (1978) "Restrictions on Serial Verbs in Anyi," unpublished paper, University of Leiden.
Li, C. and S. Thompson (1974a) "Coverbs in Mandarin Chinese: Verbs or Prepositions?" *Journal of Chinese Linguistics* 2, 257–278.
Li, C. and S. Thompson (1974b) "An Explanation of Word Order Change SVO → SOV," *Foundations of Language* 12, 201–214.
Li, C. and S. Thompson (1976a) "Development of the Causative in Mandarin Chinese: Interaction of Diachronic Processes," in M. Shibatani, ed., *Syntax and Semantics 6: The Grammar of Causative Constructions*, Academic Press, New York.
Li, C. and S. Thompson (1976b) "On the Issue of Word Order in a Synchronic Grammar: A Case Against 'Movement Transformations'," *Lingua* 39, 169–181.
Li, C. and S. Thompson (1981) *A Functional Reference Grammar of Mandarin Chinese*, University of California Press, Berkeley and Los Angeles.
Lord, C. (1973) "Serial Verbs in Transition," *Studies in African Linguistics* 4, 269–296.
Lord, C. (1974) "Causative Constructions in Yoruba," *Studies in African Linguistics* Supplement 5, 195–204.
Lord, C. (1976) "Evidence for Syntactic Reanalysis: From Verb to Complementizer in Kwa," in *Papers from the Parasession on Diachronic Syntax*, Chicago Linguistic Society, University of Chicago.
Lyons, J. (1977) *Semantics* Vol. 2, Cambridge University Press, Cambridge.
Munro, P. and L. Gordon (1982) "Syntactic Relations in Western Muskogean: A Typological Perspective," *Language* 58.
Pike, K. (1966) *Tagmemic and Matrix Linguistics Applied to Selected African Languages*, Summer Institute of Linguistics Publications No. 23.
Riis, H. (1854) *Grammatical Outline and Vocabulary of the Oji-Language*, C. Detloff, Basel.
Slobin, D. (this volume) "The Origins of Grammatical Encoding of Events."
Stewart, J. M. (1963) "Some Restrictions on Objects in Twi," *Journal of African Languages* 2, 145–149.
Trutenau, H. (1973) "The Verbal Status of the NP-linker in Gã," *Studies in African Linguistics* 4, 71–86.
Wilson, W. A. A. (1970) *Verbal Sequences and Case Markers in Dagbani*, unpublished doctoral dissertation, University of Texas, Austin.
Zimmermann, J. (1858) *A Grammatical Sketch and Vocabulary of the Akra- or Ga-Language*, Stuttgart (republished by Gregg Publishers, 1972).

ON THE TRANSITIVITY OF 'SAY' VERBS

PAMELA MUNRO

1. INTRODUCTION

In her paper "The Syntax and Semantics of Quotation" (1973), Partee raises the question of what constituency relationship there is (in English) between a quotation and the associated clause which specifies who said it, concluding provocatively that "the quoted sentence is not syntactically or semantically a part of the sentence which contains it." Partee's argument is based largely on the similarity between quotation sentence structure (particularly the use of anaphora and deixis) and the syntax of conversation, but in her conclusions she counters a long-standing tradition by which quotations and other complements of *say* are analyzed approximately as (cf. Partee 1973:412)

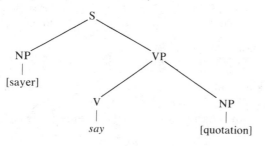

301

—with the quoted material equivalent to a standard object complement. Rosenbaum (1967), for instance, includes *say* as a verb taking object NP complementation; more recently, such sources as Stockwell (1977:105) diagram *say* and its complement just as shown.

There is considerable cross-linguistic evidence, however, that 'say' verbs are often less than perfectly transitive, and that the quotations they introduce are often very different from normal objects or object clauses, all of which tends to support the alternative view hinted at by Partee. I hope to show in this paper that it is by no means unusual for 'say' to be construed as intransitive. In fact, I have found that the normal quotation-ascribing verb has some intransitive or less transitive characteristics in every language I know well enough to survey carefully. Phenomena of the sort I will describe in this paper are often subtle, and unlikely to show up in a cursory survey, but they seem to represent a recurrent pattern in quotation structures, more evidence for which will doubtless be provided by future investigators.

There are many different intransitive characteristics a 'say' sentence may have: The quotation may behave differently from other sorts of direct object constituents, the verb or the sentence may be morphologically marked as intransitive, or the 'say' construction may pattern syntactically with other intransitive constructions. In the next section of this paper, I will discuss a number of these possibilities, illustrating them with examples from a variety of languages. In the last section, I will note some ways other languages manage to avoid the transitivity issue.

2. INTRANSITIVE CHARACTERISTICS OF 'SAY' SENTENCES

2.1. Lack of Marking on Quoted Material

The best known way in which complements of 'say' differ from other syntactic objects is the possibility of leaving quotation complements marked only in the way they would be if uttered in isolation (Givón 1980 and Green 1976 are among those who have remarked the syntactic significance of this fact). For instance, English sentences like

(1)   a.   *He said (*that) "I'm going."*
        b.   *He said (that) I'm going.*

show that the subordinator *that* cannot be inserted before a quotation representing actual speech without changing meaning—in other words, clearly (1a) does not mean the same as (1b). Similarly, in a language like

Chickasaw,[1] which has syntactic object marking, the object marker -$\bar{a}$ cannot follow either a quoted sentence or an utterance consisting only of a noun or noun phrase, as in[2]

(2)   a. *"Ihoo" (*-$\bar{a}$) aachi.*
            woman   obj say
            'He says, "Woman" '.
    b. *"Hilha" (*-$\bar{a}$) aachi.*
            dance   obj say
            'He says, "She's dancing" '.

Every language I have surveyed allows quotations introduced by or associated with 'say' verbs to be completely unmarked (except as they would be in isolation), even in cases where all other complement-taking verbs require overt subordination marking, or at least the possibility of it, as in English. This is one characteristic, perhaps the most important one, which makes quotation complements of 'say' appear very different from those of other verbs.

Up to now I have avoided the issue of "direct" versus "indirect" quotation. The possibility or impossibility of subordination marking, as in (1), often seems to be taken to be a good test for direct versus indirect quotation in English, but I believe that this is not the best universal correlate of the distinction, as many languages allow direct/indirect contrasts on similarly subordinated or unmarked clauses. A better test, which works for every language for which I have data, is what might be termed the transparency of pronominal reference. In indirect quotation, as in (1b) above, pronominal reference is transparent—when the speaker says *I*, he refers to himself, and so on, following normal deixis, exactly as with every other sentence type. Pronominal reference is opaque, on the other hand, in direct quotation—the referent of an *I* within a direct quote, as in (1a), can only be determined with reference to the subject of the associated verb of saying.

In some languages, such as English, the "intransitivity" of 'say' is much more apparent when the verb is used with direct quotations than it is when 'say' introduces indirect quotations and other complements (as in, for instance, *She said a few words*). In other languages, however, the less transitive qualities of 'say' appear in all contexts. Certainly,

---

[1] The Chickasaw data is from Catherine Willmond, to whom I am most grateful.

[2] The abbreviations I use in the examples include 3 = third person, abs = absolutive, art = article, aux = auxiliary, diff = different subject subordinator, erg = ergative, fut = future, incomp = incomplete action, int = interrogative, intr = intransitive, neg = negative, obj = object, obl = oblique, pres = present, quot = quotative, same = same subject subordinator, stat = stative, subj = subject, subr = subordinator, tns = tense.

however, whether it refers only to a subset of quotations or to all of them, the requirement that such 'say' complements appear unmarked is a significant way in which these complements differ from others in a language.[3]

2.2. Restrictions on Possible "Objects" of 'Say' Verbs

A number of languages exhibit the peculiarity of allowing 'say' to take a clausal object, or rather, a quotation, but refusing to allow the same verb to co-occur with a pronominal object like 'it' or a more concrete object than a quotation, such as 'a few words' or 'the name.'

In the Kru language Godié,[4] for example, the usual verb for ascribing quotation is *lʌ*, as in the following sentence:

(3)   *Baalʌ lʌ   ʌ̄ʌ́   lɔ́   kō̄.*
      Baalo say I-neg here be
      'Baalo said, "I'm not here" '.

Other verbs taking clausal objects may occur with an object pronoun 'it',[5] such as *sʉ* 'tell/talk':

(4)   *ɔ   sʉ   nɩ ɔ   tʉ.*
      he tell it his father
      'He told it to his father'.

However, *lʌ* may not. It is also not possible to use an object like *walɩ* 'words' with *lʌ*.

A similar situation occurs in Hausa,[6] where there are two common 'say' verbs, *céè* and *fàɗaa*. The latter may be used with a nonquotation

---

[3] I will not discuss in the text the variation which is subsumed, in some languages, by my general labels "'say'" and "'say' verbs." In some languages verbs semantically close to 'say', like 'think' or 'suppose', adopt the same syntactic patterns that 'say' does (and may thus be subject to being called "intransitive"); in other languages there may be more than one verb that does the work of English *say*. The Hausa examples in the next section illustrate the possibility of different words for reporting direct quotation and for what Laurie Tuller has called characterizations of the same quotation [cf. (5–6)]; other languages use different words if an indirect object is present (cf. English *tell*) or if the quotation has the speaker himself as its subject (in Chickasaw, *miha*, with this meaning, contrasts with the normal 'say' verb *aachi*, which is used in the examples in the text). I have considered all such variation to be within the general domain of "'say' verbs."

[4] This description of the Godié facts was provided by Lynell Marchese.

[5] The object pronoun *nɩ* in Sentence (4) consists of a particle *n* plus the third person plural inanimate pronoun *ɩ*, which is often used to refer to words or messages.

[6] I owe my understanding of the Hausa facts to Laurie Tuller.

object:

(5)   *Yaa fàdì kalmà biyu.*
       he say word two
       'He said two words'.

In contest, *céè* (the verb used to ascribe actual quotations) may not, as shown by Sentence (6), in which the "object," *kalmà biyu,* can only be interpreted as a quotation itself.[7]

(6)   *Yaa céè kalmà biyu.*
       he say word two
       'He said, "Two words" '.

   English comes to mind immediately as a language in which a quotation may (apparently) be easily pronominalized:

(7)   a. *He said, "She's here."*
       b. *He said it/that/something.*
       c. *What did he say?*

The words *it, that, something,* and *what* seem clearly to be pronouns filling an object role in these sentences, and it is indeed odd that English should allow such a range of nonquotation objects for 'say' while other languages do not. However, note that there are contexts in English in which a pronominal object for *say* is difficult or impossible:

(8)   a. *Who says (that/?it)?*
       b. *You don't say (*that/*it)!*
       c. *You said (?that/*it)!*   [indignant child to parent]

Our normal interpretation of an English transitive verb used without an object (in examples like *She's cooking*) is that the general action is of more interest than the specific unspecified object, but I do not think that

---

[7] Michael Hammond has suggested another such example from Classical Chinese, in which the two verbs of direct quotation, *yūe* and *yún,* do not occur with a pronominalized quotation:

(i)   **Kǒngzi yūe zhī.*
       Confucius say it
       'Confucius says/said it'.

—even though *zhī* has some use as a pronominalization in similar contexts, for instance in this proverbial expression using a third 'say' verb, *yán:*

(ii)   *Yán zhī yǒu wù.*
       say it   have substance
       'What (he) says sounds right.'

that is the case with the objectless *say* examples in (8). In each of the cases in (8), the speaker has in mind some particular quotation—yet that quotation is not (for some reason) pronominalized. This odd fact becomes a bit more easily explained if *say* is less than perfectly transitive, and the quotation in a *say* sentence fills some role other than that of the direct object.

And English, of course, is another language in which a second quotation verb fails to occur with a pronominal direct object. In colloquial (juvenile?) English *go* introduces quotations in sentences like

(9)   *And then Mary went/goes, "Well, you'll have to come with us."*

(cf. Partee 1973). This use of *go* is restricted to direct quotations, as the impossibility of (10a)–(10d) show.

(10)   a. **And then Mary went that we'd have to come too.*
       b. **And then Mary went it/that/something.*
       c. **And then Mary went.*
       d. **And then Mary went John's name.*   (Cf. *And then Mary went, "John's name."*)

2.3. Lack of Morphological Agreement with the Object of 'Say'

In languages in which there is morphological agreement with a singular direct object (as opposed to the independent pronominal agreement seen in the preceding section) we would expect such agreement to show up on a 'say' verb used with a quotation, but this is not always the case.

For instance, in the Uto–Aztecan language Cahuilla[8] a third-person singular object, whether concrete or clausal, is marked on the verb with a prefix *pe-*:

(11)   a. *Pe-n-'ayaw-qa mansaana-y.*
         it-I-want-pres   apple-obj
         'I want an apple'.
       b. *Pe-n-'ayaw-qa hen-hichi-ka.*
         it-I-want-pres   I-go-incomp
         'I want to go'.

However, quotations or other objects of the verb 'say' do not trigger

[8] My Cahuilla data is from Katherine Siva Sauvel, whom I thank. (The sentences illustrate the Mountain dialect.)

such agreement in Cahuilla:

(12)   *Ni-ya-qa "Hen-hichi-ka"*
        I-say-pres I-go-incomp
        'I say, "I'm going" '.

2.4. Treatment of the 'Say' Clause as Intransitive

Ergative languages provide another opportunity to see whether 'say' is treated as intransitive, as in such languages case marking or verbal agreement is different for the subject of a transitive verb (ergative) as opposed to the subject of an intransitive one (absolutive). In Samoan,[9] the subject of 'say' is unmarked, or in absolutive form, rather than marked with an ergative preposition:[10]

(13)   *Na fai mai   lātou.*
        past say towards-me they
        'They said it to me'.

A potentially similar fact is that in Yup'ik Eskimo[11] a simple quotation may be used with the proper inflection as an intransitive verb taking absolutive subject agreement:

(14)   *Waqaa-llru-u-nga.*
        "hello"-past-intr-I(abs)
        'I said, "Hello" '.

2.5. Restrictions on the Passivization of 'Say'

The interaction of 'say' with the passive is a topic too large to treat adequately here, even just for one language. In English, though, what is said is certainly the subject of passivized *say:*

(15)   a.   *A few words were said.*
        b.   *It is said (by some) that the house is haunted.*

---

[9] I thank Sandra Chung for drawing this fact to my attention, and for providing the examples.

[10] In fact, if the subject of *fai* is marked as ergative, *fai* means not 'say' but 'do': Thus, in Samoan, 'do' is the transitive form of 'say'.

(i)   *Na fai e   lātou.*
       past do erg they
       'They did it'.

[11] My Yup'ik data is from Joan Hamilton (Pirciralria), to whom I am most grateful.

(Extraposition is required with a clausal subject.) Clearly, though, (15) does not illustrate direct quotation. Passivization seems far less felicitous with actual quoted speech:[12]

(16)   a. ?*"*Help!*" *was said.*
        b. ?*It *was said (to me) (by some), "Your house is haunted."*

This failure of direct quotations to occur as the subject of passives suggests that English *say* is much less transitive with a direct quotation complement than with a nonquotation.

2.6. Treatment of the Quoted Material as an Oblique

The structure of quotation sentences in many languages of the Yuman family has puzzled linguists for some time. In these languages (which I will exemplify here with data from Mojave), there is a switch-reference system which differentiates subordinate clauses whose subject is the same as that of the main clause from subordinate clauses whose subject is different from that of the main clause, generally through the use of a "same-subject" subordinator *-k* and a "different subject" subordinator *-m:*

(17)   a. *'-isay-k   '-suupaw-m.*
            I-fat-same I-know-tns
            'I know I'm fat'.
        b. *M-isay-m   '-suupaw-m.*
            you-fat-diff I-know-tns
            'I know you're fat'.

Quotation clauses of a wide variety of types, whether direct or indirect, however, are often marked with an unexpected *-k* suffix:[13]

(18)   *M-isay-k   '-i'ii-m.*
        you-fat-?? I-say-tns
        'I say you're fat', 'I say, "You're fat" '.

[12] I thank Allen Munro for pointing this out to me.

There seems to be one usage that is not subject to the generalizations just proposed—when *say* is used to mean 'use the word', as in

(i) *"Ain't"* is said by few professors.

The generalizations in the text must also be restricted to contemporary (American?) English, given the following 1780 citation from the OED (IX:152): "*Mirror* No. 75 (1787) III.6. In the very next paragraph it is said, 'We have the pleasure of informing the Public [etc.]'." I find this indubitably direct quotation quite awkward.

[13] I believe that this fact was originally noted by Sandra Chung. For a different treatment of these facts than I present here, see Kendall (1972).

Nellie Brown and others deserve the thanks for teaching me about Mojave.

Semantically, it would be hard to offer an explanation for the occurrence of same-subject -*k* in such an environment. This quotation -*k* is not just some main clause ending, as it occurs on quotation clauses that could never end in -*k* alone;[14] it also seems unlikely to be the same as the switch-reference marker because in the Maricopa language, as Gordon (1980) has shown, the quotation -*k* may follow verbs that never allow suffixation of same-subject -*k* even in a semantically appropriate context.

Mojave 'say' may occur with an oblique nonquotation object in cases like

(19)   *'inyep(-k) i'ii-m.*
         me-obl   say-tns
         'He said it about me'.

'Me' cannot be a direct object in (19), since otherwise the first-person object prefix *ny-* would appear on the verb; its oblique status is optionally marked by the case marker -*k*. It seems likely that this use of -*k* (a case marker reconstructable for Proto-Yuman) to mark the topic of conversation was grammaticized and extended to the marking on full quotation clauses, as seen in (18), which would be consistent with the differences between this -*k* and the switch-reference -*k*. This would mean that in the Yuman languages which mark quotations with -*k* the status of these clauses is explicitly not that of a direct object constituent.

2.7. Treatment of the Quoted Material as a Nonconstituent

The Uto–Aztecan language Pima[15] exhibits some strict restrictions on word order, although the order of major constituents is quite free. In particular, only one constituent may precede the second-position auxiliary element, which codes the person and number of the subject and other features of the sentence, such as mood and aspect:

(20)   a.   *Ian'o   s-ha-hoohit   heg 'u'uvi.*
             Ian 3(aux) stat-them-like art women
        b.   *S-ha-hoohit   'o   heg 'u'uvi heg Ian.*   'Ian likes girls'.
             stat-them-like 3(aux) art women art Ian
        c.   *'u'uvi 'o s-ha-hoohit heg Ian* [etc.]

Thus, although many variations in the order of subject, object, and verb

[14] For instance, in Tolkapaya Yavapai no surface main verb can end in -*k* (cf. Hardy 1979), so quotations comparable to that in (18) could not be uttered on their own.

[15] My Pima data is from Etheleen Rosero, whom I thank.

are possible in Pima sentences like (20), the auxiliary element (here, third-person singular imperfective '*o*) must always be in second position in the sentence, with only one preceding constituent. [As (20) shows, the article *heg* never appears sentence-initially.] The preauxiliary position may also be filled by elements like the deictic particle *b*, in (21b):

(21) a. *Rina 'o-b   heñ-ñeid.*
          Rina 3(aux)-here me-see
      b. *B-o   heñ-ñeid heg Rina.* 'Rina is looking at me'.
          here-3(aux) me-see   art Rina

In this case, the particle cliticizes to the auxiliary—but still, only one element comes in initial position.

Indirect quotations are introduced in Pima with a subordinator *m-* (which, like the *b-* in (21b), counts as the first element in its clause); their auxiliaries end with the quotative element -*ṣ:*

(22) a. *Hegai ceoj 'o-b   kaij m-a-ṣ*
          that   man 3(aux)-here say subr-3(aux)-quot
          s-heepit heg 'uuvi.
          stat-cold art woman
      b. *B-o kaij hegai ceoj m-a-ṣ s-heepit heg 'uuvi.*
          'That man said that the woman is cold'.

But consider direct quotations, like those in (23):

(23) a. *"S-heepit 'añ" b-añ   kaij.*
          stat-cold I(aux) here-I(aux) say
          ' "I'm cold," I said'.
      b. *"Ha'u" b-a-ṣ   kaij heg ban.*
          yes   here-3(aux)-quot say art coyote
          ' "Yes," said the coyote'.[16]

The deictic particle *b* (a form of which almost always appears with *kaij* 'say') is in first position in the 'say' clause in the examples of (23). But in these examples quotations come before this particle, providing the only example I know of in Pima in which more than one constituent element of a clause may precede the auxiliary of that clause. It is almost as though the quotation is being treated as not belonging to the sentence, or to the 'say' clause, for the purpose of auxiliary placement. This example seems clearly to support the idea that Pima 'say' is not transitive in the ordinary way, since if its associated quotation were a direct object,

[16] The quotative appears on the main verb in this sentence because the whole sentence is from a text told in traditional style. Here its meaning is something like 'it is said.'

it would have to function like any other direct object in initial position [cf. (20c)].

2.8. Word Order Differences between Quotations and Other Object Clauses

I have pointed out that leaving quotations completely unmarked is always a syntactic option in the languages I surveyed, even though such a lack of marking is generally not possible with other types of object complements. I have shown how the marking of many 'say' complements is different from that of other object complements in many Yuman languages. Another way in which many languages differentiate quotations from other object clauses is through word order.

In a variety of languages, for example, quotation clauses (direct or indirect) may be "framed"—both preceded and followed by an inflected form of 'say', as in this Chickasaw example:[17]

(24)   *Jan-at   aachi-kat "Ish-ī'sh-a'chi" aash-tok.*
         Jan-subj say-same   you-take-fut   say-past
         'Jan said, "You take it" '.

(The *aachi-/aash-* variation here is phonologically predictable.) I know of no other verb that occurs in this sort of "frame" construction in any of the languages that exhibit this pattern.

A second type of word order difference involves extraposition. In the Yuman language Maricopa, for instance, object clauses are very frequently preposed, as in the following sentence:[18]

(25)   *'-n'ay-sh   va   dany chew-m Heather-sh   shuupaw-sh.*
         my-father-subj house this   make-diff Heather-subj know-perf
         'Heather knows that my father built this house'.

However, extraposition of quotations in front of an overt subject of 'say' is not possible in Maricopa:

(26)   a. *Heather-sh   i-m   '-n'ay-sh   va   dany chew-k*
             Heather-subj say-tns my-father-subj house this make-k
             'Heather said, "My father built this house" ' or 'Heather said that my father built this house'.
        b. *'-n'ay-sh va dany chew-k Heather-sh i-m.

---

[17] Some of the languages in which I have observed this construction or seen it reported are Chickasaw, Lahu (Tibeto-Burman; Matisoff 1973), and Gahuku (New Guinea; Deibler 1971). The frame construction also can be used in every language of the Yuman family for which I have data.

[18] Thanks to Lynn Gordon for noting the significance of this data, and for providing the examples.

Still another difference between the treatment of 'say' complements and other object clauses involves center-embedding. In the Yuman languages a direct object clause may appear center-embedded between the subject and higher verb (in the standard direct object position), as in this Mojave example:

(27)   'iipa-ny-ch   thinya'aak-ny-ch ivaa-m   suupaw-pch.
        man-dem-subj woman-dem-subj arrive-diff know-perf
        'The man knows that the woman is here (has arrived)'.

However, a complement of 'say' never appears center-embedded in this way.

2.9. Similarity of Quotation Syntax to That of Other Intransitive Constructions

Stylistic inversion in English affects a rather motley set of constructions. The types of simple sentence that sound acceptable when inverted, in normal speech, are 'say' sentences with direct quotations,[19] various types of copular sentences [under which heading I include locationals like (28c)], and sentences with certain directional adverbs.

(28)   a.   *"What's up?" said/asked John. / John said/asked, "What's up?"*
        b.   *The capital of New York is Albany. / Albany is the capital of New York.*
        c.   *In front of the fire was/sat my brother. / My brother was/ sat in front of the fire.*
        d.   *Up came Mr. Hopkins. / Mr. Hopkins came up.*

Such inversion is not possible, of course, with normal transitives (in ordinary speech), even when morphology or semantics would rule out any possibility of ambiguity:

(29)   a.   **Linguistics likes Mary.*
        b.   **A pizza were eating the boys.*
        c.   **Herb and Elaine married the minister.*

It appears, then, that the 'say' sentences that can invert[20] are treated along with other sentences which have a Subject–Verb–Complement

---

[19] Or "semi-indirect" quotations:

(i)   *Good heavens, he thought fondly, they really were going to have to stop meeting this way.*

[20] Some of the restrictions on this sort of inversion are described, for instance, by Green (1976, to appear), and Hermon (1979), whose analysis has been replicated and extended in unpublished work by Charles Ulrich.

order which mimics that of ordinary transitives but in which the "complement" is clearly not an ordinary direct object. This is certainly one of the more subtle "intransitive" characteristics that 'say' verbs can exhibit, but it seems likely that as stylistic rules come to be better understood in more exotic languages we will accumulate more such examples.

3. THE NONTRANSITIVE CHARACTER
   OF 'SAY' CONSTRUCTIONS

I have illustrated a wide variety of ways in which 'say' sentences present intransitive characteristics. And yet 'say' really does seem as though it should be a transitive verb: It has a volitional agent, and although the thing said is not a prototypical direct object, it is certainly affected (or effected) by the act of saying. The last examples I will present in this paper are of cases where it appears that particular syntactic patterns have been adopted in various 'say' constructions in order to sidestep the issue of transitivity.

The first set of examples develop from the fact that in many languages the normal way of expressing quotation is not with an ordinary verb (whose transitivity or lack thereof might be apparent from evidence like that considered in the previous section) at all. The most common type of nonverb quotation structure cross-linguistically is probably a "quotative" structure, in which an affix or particle is used instead of a 'say' verb to ascribe quotation, as in this example from Yaqui (from Lindenfeld 1973:105; cf. also Munro 1978):[21]

(30)   *In kuna   si   yuk-ne-tia.*
        my husband much rain-fut-quot
        'My husband says it is going to rain much'.

Chamorro presents a different sort of example: 'say' and a few other imperfect transitives such as 'like' and 'prefer' occur in nonfuture Chamorro sentences in a nominalized construction, shown in (31), in which the formal indications of transitivity that would show up in a finite verb construction are absent:[22]

(31)   *Ilek-ña "Pues maolik."*
        say-his   then good
        'He said, "Then it is good" '.

---

[21] Another common way of reporting quotation, which I cannot consider here, is with no attribution at all.

[22] Sandra Chung told me about this, and provided the examples.

In normal Chamorro transitive sentences, such as (32) the subject is indicated by a proclitic pronoun specified as ergative; absolutive subjects of intransitive verbs trigger no morphological agreement marking.

(32)   *Ha-bisita   si   Maria nigap.*
        he(erg)-visit art Maria yesterday
        'He visited Maria yesterday'.

But in the variant nominalized construction, which is required only for the few verbs listed here, all subjects are indicated by the same set of possessive prefixes—so the suffix *-ña* in (31) could refer to either an ergative or an absolutive subject. A sentence like (31), then, is syntactically vague as to transitivity.[23]

As was noted, the nominalization construction that allows the subject of Chamorro 'say' sentences like (31) to remain unspecified as absolutive or ergative is only used for nonfuture 'say' sentences. But whereas pronominal agreement operates on an ergative basis in nonfuture Chamorro sentences like (32), in future sentences agreement is with the subject, regardless of transitivity. Thus, the nominalized 'say' construction is used only in those cases where a finite verb construction would require an explicit indication of transitivity or its absence.

I have noted a variety of ways in which quotation complements of 'say' act differently from normal direct objects, whether nominal or clausal. Perhaps the most striking example of a "real" object for 'say', when we come to think about it, is with sentences in which the quotation itself is questioned: In *What did you say?* surely *what* must be a syntactic object. But many languages with perfectly good words for 'what' avoid these words in 'say' questions.

In most Yuman languages, for instance, the complement of 'say' can be questioned by prefixation of an indefinite/interrogative morpheme to

---

[23] There is additional evidence that 'say' nominalizations like those in (31) are syntactically intransitive. Although both transitives and intransitives can occur nominalized, as in (31), transitive nominalizations normally require an *-in-* infix for a factive reading, as in (i), whereas transitive nominalizations without *-in-* generally have a manner or instrumental reading, as in (ii):

(i)   *fina'gase-nña*
      nom + wash-his
      '(the fact) that he washed', 'his washing'
(ii) *fa'gase'-ña*
      wash-his
      'the way he washed', 'his washing'

Intransitive nominalizations, however, do not show the *-in-* infix, even for the factive reading. Note that this (transitive) *-in-* does not appear in the 'say' nominalization in (31).

the 'say' verb, as in (33a), a process that cannot be used in a normal 'what' question like (33b)—the examples here are from Mojave:[24]

(33)   a. *Ka-m-i'ii ?*
            int-you-say
            'What did you say?'
        b. *Kuch m-iyuu ?*
            what you-see
            'What did you see?'

Similarly, in a number of Uto–Aztecan languages there is a special interrogative stem for 'say'—the Cahuilla 'say' question in (34a), for instance, has intransitive syntax [like the nonquestion (12)], in contrast to the standard transitive 'what' question in (34b):

(34)   a. *'e-hi-ya-qa'a ?*
            you-int-say-past
            'What did you say?'
        b. *Hich'a-y pe-'-teew-qa'a ?*
            what-obj it-you-see-past
            'What did you see?'

The avoidance of interrogative 'what' in 'say' questions is not confined to exotic languages, of course—consider, for instance, the widespread use of 'how' forms for 'I beg your pardon' in Romance languages, as illustrated by Italian *come* 'how' in

(35)   *Come avete detto?*
        'What did you say?'

The crucial problem raised in this paper is that of the relationship between the 'say' verb and the associated quotation. In the paper I referred to earlier, Partee (1973) shows sympathy with Davidson's (1967) claim that a 'say' sentence with a direct quotation logically includes a demonstrative notion (as in *John said* [*like*] *this/that*)—with the actual quotation corresponding fairly well to the physical gesture that might accompany a sentence like (to use Partee's example) *A circular staircase goes like this.* Indeed, demonstratives are associated with 'say' verbs in some other languages [such as Pima, as shown by (23)],[25] although

[24] Prefixes like this are only used on 'say', 'be', and 'do'. In Mojave it is also possible to add *kuch* 'what' to a question like (33a).

[25] The Pima word order problem raised earlier might be solved if the quotations and the following demonstrative/deictic *b*s in the sentences in (23) formed constituents. However, I know of no other case in Pima in which a demonstrative of any sort follows the element it qualifies.

this is by no means universal. But still we feel that a quotation must be some kind of object.

The meaning of 'say' must, I believe, go beyond the idea of simply communicating facts by uttering words, and must probably include at some level a recognition of the general human reaction to speech as a characteristic indicator of personality and intention. It is the saying of something and what is said together which set people apart, in many circumstances, from each other and from other beings; perhaps a good way to conceptualize the syntactic role of a 'say' sentence is with the 'say' verb and its complement taken together (incorporated, almost) to form a single complex verb which can be used to characterize someone as well as to report an event. This sort of "incorporation" is morphologized (in different ways) only in the Yup'ik and Yaqui examples (14) and (30), but a conception like this may help us to understand the indeterminacy shown by all the intransitive characteristics of the 'say' sentences cited in the previous section. A sentence with an incorporated object certainly has an object, just as our 'say' sentences seem to do, but generally is more or less intransitive by various syntactic tests, just as our 'say' sentences are.

The syntactic intransitivity of 'say' sentences fits in well with Hopper and Thompson's theory of semantic transitivity (1980), which allows the ranking of a sentence for a variety of transitivity features (1980:252), two of which concern the affectedness and individuation of the sentence's object.[26] As already noted, the complement of 'say' is fully effected by the saying, and so the degree of affectedness seems in one sense as great with 'say' as with any other verb of production. However, as often observed, saying that something is true does not make it true (in most cases), and thus the sense of a 'say' complement sentence is very little affected by the act of saying. Complements of 'say' seem to score rather low in "individuation" as well, by Hopper and Thompson's criteria (1980:253): They are clearly neither proper nor animate, and the other individuation features ($\pm$ concrete, $\pm$ singular, $\pm$ count, and $\pm$ referential) seem to make little sense when applied to 'say' complements. Lack of object individuation is associated with many types of morphosyntactic intransitivity surveyed by Hopper and Thompson (1980:256–259), among them object incorporation of the usual sort, and it must certainly be one of the reasons for the unexpected syntactic patterns characteristic of 'say' sentences.

The characterization of 'say' plus a quotation as syntactically intransitive (to different language-specific degrees) appears to be a valid cross-

[26] The transitivity components are listed in the Introduction to this volume.

linguistic generalization with some semantic support, but it is an incomplete generalization at this point. A number of examples have been presented of how the syntax of 'say' verbs is often unique, or nearly so: Not only do they behave unlike ordinary transitives, they also fail to act like ordinary intransitives. So the final explanation for their peculiarities cannot only be their "intransitivity," but what this final explanation is must await further research.

ACKNOWLEDGMENTS

Much of the material I present here was assembled in the course of my preparation for a UCLA seminar on 'say' verbs. I am grateful to Bonnie Glover, Lynn Gordon, Michael Hammond, Lynell Marchese, Carol Lord, Laurie Tuller, and Charles Ulrich, who shared their data or observations with me during this project, and to Allen Munro and Sandra Chung for suggestions about the present paper. Of course, the responsibility for the interpretation of the data presented is my own.

REFERENCES

Davidson, D. (1968/69) "On Saying 'that,'" *Synthese* 19, 130–146.

Deibler, E. (1971) "Uses of the Verb 'to say' in Gahuku," *Kivung* 4, 101–110.

Givón, T. (1980) "Binding, Embedded Agents, and the Typology of Complements," unpublished paper.

Gordon, L. (1980) *Maricopa Morphology and Syntax,* unpublished doctoral dissertation, University of California, Los Angeles.

Green, G. (1976) "Main-clause Phenomena in Subordinate Clauses," *Language* 52, 382–397.

Green, G. (to appear) "Some Wherefores of English Inversions," *Language*.

Hardy, H. (1979) *Tolkapaya Syntax: Aspect, Modality, and Adverbial Modification in a Yavapai Dialect,* unpublished doctoral dissertation, University of California, Los Angeles.

Hermon, G. (1979) *On the Discourse Structure of Direct Quotation,* Center for the Study of Reading, University of Illinois.

Hopper, P. and S. Thompson (1980) "Transitivity in Grammar and Discourse," *Language* 56, 251–299.

Kendall, M. (1972) "The /-k/, /-m/ Problem in Yavapai Syntax," *International Journal of American Linguistics* 41, 1–9.

Lindenfeld, J. (1973) *Yaqui Syntax* (University of California Publications in Linguistics 76).

Matisoff, J. (1973) *The Grammar of Lahu* (University of California Publications in Linguistics 75).

Munro, P. (1978) "Chemehuevi 'Say' and the Uto-Aztecan Quotative Pattern," in D. Tuohy, ed., *Proceedings of the Great Basin Anthropological Conference,* Ballena Press, Socorro, New Mexico.

Partee, B. H. (1973) "The Syntax and Semantics of Quotation," in S. Anderson and P. Kiparsky, eds., *A Festschrift for Morris Halle,* Holt, Rinehart and Winston, New York.

Rosenbaum, P. (1967) *The Grammar of English Predicate Complement Constructions,* MIT Press, Cambridge, Massachusetts.

Stockwell, R. (1977) *Foundations of Syntactic Theory,* Prentice Hall, Englewood Cliffs, New Jersey.

PROMINENCE, COHESION, AND CONTROL: OBJECT-CONTROLLED PREDICATE NOMINALS IN RUSSIAN

JOHANNA NICHOLS

1. OBJECTS AS CONTROLLERS OF PREDICATE NOMINALS

This study investigates objects as controllers of predicate nominals in Russian, and explores the implications of object control for lexical transitivity, types of objects, and Transitivity.[1] Both Transitivity and object control have been described in terms of feature hierarchies. However, although both Transitivity and object control deal crucially with objects and transitivity, for the most part neither the respective hierarchies nor their features coincide. Rather than calling into question the validity of either the system of control conditions or the Transitivity features, the lack of coincidence actually reinforces one's confidence in both analyses. That is because Transitivity features and object control are very different domains of grammar and the hierarchization of features within each of them serves very different ends.

CONTROL is a cover term for the relation holding, for example, between a reflexive pronoun and its antecedent; between an infinitive or a Russian

[1] The term *Transitivity*, with a capital letter, in this paper is the term of Hopper and Thompson (1980). Since it proves necessary to discuss traditional concepts in this paper, I have retained the standard term *transitivity*, without the capital, to refer to government of the accusative direct object.

319

adverbial participle (or, more precisely, between the understood or zero subject of the infinitive or participle) and its main-clause coreferent; and between a secondary predicate noun or adjective and its coreferent. I will use the standard term CONTROLLER for the antecedent or main-clause coreferent, and TARGET for the controlled reflexive, infinitive, or secondary predicate. Control is not a syntactic relation, at least not a relation like subject-of or object-of. Although it rather clearly belongs in the domain of syntax, to describe it one must take account of morphological, syntactic, and semantic factors. The grammar of control in Russian consists of the ranking of controllers for what is called controller strength, the ranking of targets by what is called accessibility, and generalizations, based on strength and accessibility, about what can control what under what conditions.[2] The rankings and the generalizations are stated in terms of a number of different features, or conditions, such as syntactic relations (of controller and target), topicality, subaspectual parameters, referentiality, modality, agency, and stylistic considerations. Most of these features are covert but systematic in that they reappear in several places in the grammar of Russian (see especially Timberlake 1982 in this connection). Each feature has its own hierarchization of its values; for instance, topicality involves the ranking of topic (which favors control) over nontopic (which disfavors control). These features define a multidimensional space within which individual examples can be situated. Unlike Transitivity features, they do not covary.

Predicate nominals in Russian comprise a variety of subtypes, each with its own cutoff point in a hierarchy of syntactic relations defining possible controllers (for the cutoff points and the hierarchy of controllers see Nichols 1979, 1981:68ff.). The present study was undertaken because the occasional examples of object control I came across in earlier work gave the impression of clearly distinguishing direct objects from indirect and/or oblique objects. Specifically, there was a type of predicate nominal that appeared to be easily controlled by direct objects but not by indirect or oblique objects. That type is the instrumental of nouns denoting a stage of life such as *rebenok* 'child', *mal'čik* 'boy', *devočka* 'little girl', *starik* 'old man', *student* '(undergraduate) student', etc., used as secondary predicates of temporal meaning in:

(1)   *My znali ego mal'čikom.*
       we knew him boy (instrumental)
       'We knew him as a boy'.

---

[2] This conception of control is based on the following studies: Timberlake (1979, 1980a, 1980b, 1981, 1982); Rappaport (1979, 1980); Nichols, Rappaport, and Timberlake (1980); Nichols (1979, 1981). These works and the present paper are part of an ongoing joint investigation of control in Russian.

(2)   *On poljubil   ee ešče devočkoj.*
        he fell-in-love her still little-girl (instrumental)
        'He fell in love with her as a little girl', '. . . when she was still
        a little girl'.

Henceforth in this paper the term "predicate nominal" will refer to this
type of predicate nominal only.

In the preliminary survey, both textual and elicited evidence supported
placing the cutoff point for controllers after direct objects. There were
many text examples of subject and direct object controllers, but no
examples of controllers lower on the hierarchy. Speakers rejected indirect
and oblique objects like the dative in (3) as possible controllers:[3]

(3)   **Brat   vsegda pomogal **sestre**   ešče devočkoj.*
        brother always helped   sister (dat) still little girl
        'The brother always helped his sister as a little girl'.

Furthermore, in the preliminary survey objects of verbs which also had
an infinitive ('force', 'let', 'advise', etc.) were rejected as controllers,
regardless of their case (Nichols 1981:79–80):

(4)   ***Ego**   ešče rebenkom roditeli zastavili xodit' na rabotu.*
        him (acc) still child   parents forced   to-go to work
        'His parents forced him to go to work as a child'.

Henceforth in this paper such objects will be termed CO-OBJECTS OF IN-
FINITIVES; the infinitives will be referred to as CODEPENDENT INFINITIVES.

This study tests two hypotheses: (*a*) Only direct objects, not indirect
or oblique objects, can control these predicate nominals. (*b*) Co-objects
of infinitives cannot control predicate nominals. (Neither hypothesis will
be upheld.) It also tests the more general hypothesis that control of
predicate nominals can be diagnostic of syntactic types of object. These
particular predicate nominals are of interest not only for their potential
diagnostic value, but for a methodological reason as well: since there
is no textual evidence for controllers of lower accessibility than direct
objects, all factors favoring controllerhood of indirect objects or disfavoring controllerhood of direct objects would have to be elicited. As the
previous studies of Russian control drew at least part of their evidence
from grammars and text surveys, a study based wholly on elicitation
could provide a useful test case. Text surveys have made important
contributions to control studies, in the areas of heuristics, consistency,

---

[3] In addition to grammaticality marks discussed in what follows, the following conventions are used in examples. The controller is indicated in boldface type. The case of the
controller is identified: (dat) = dative, (acc) = accusative.

and variety of factors uncovered. A study based entirely on elicitation can be expected to show fewer conditioning factors and more individual variation than those also using textual data; this expectation has been borne out in the present study.

The following terms will distinguish types of objects in this paper. A FIRST OBJECT is approximately equivalent to the traditional DIRECT OBJECT, the relational FINAL 2, or Tesnière's SECOND ACTANT (1965:105ff.), and identical to the notion FIRST COMPLEMENT of Mel'čuk (1974:222, 1979). In contrast to traditional and relational usage, I assume that the term FIRST OBJECT has a purely syntactic definition, independent of its morphological realization in the accusative or another case. By this definition, whereas a direct object is necessarily in the accusative case, a first object is not: The dative governed by *zavidovat'* 'envy' or *radovat'sja* 'rejoice (at)', the instrumental governed by *upravljat'* 'manage, rule', and other such obliques are first objects. (This is Mel'čuk's sense also. For a survey of first object constructions see Iomdin and Percov 1975.)

A SECOND OBJECT is approximately equivalent to the traditional INDIRECT OBJECT, the relational FINAL 3 (exclusive of inverse subjects), Tesnière's THIRD ACTANT, and Mel'čuk's SECOND COMPLEMENT. The same proviso about syntactic definitions holds.

A THIRD OBJECT is Mel'čuk's THIRD COMPLEMENT; in traditional and relational grammar it is simply considered an oblique and often classed with adverbials. Some examples of the types of objects follow (objects numbered):

(5)   *He said this to me about you.*
            1   2   3

(6)   *Compare the circle to the square in area.*
                  1   2   3

A further preliminary concerns syntactic categorization of objects. Both traditional Russian grammar and relational grammar base their notions of direct object (final 2) and indirect object (final 3) on nonsyntactic criteria. The primary criterion is a morphological one, namely case: A direct object is in the accusative case, whereas an indirect or oblique object (the two are not distinguished in Russian grammar) is in some other case. A lexical criterion, namely a generalization over governing verb classes, is also used: An indirect object (final 3) is governed by verbs of communication, transfer, and the like. The objects that have received attention in the two traditions are the clearest instances of the criteria used: accusatives with verbs like 'kill', 'break', 'throw' (i.e., prototypical direct objects) and datives with verbs like 'say', 'give', and the like, (i.e., prototypical indirect objects). Neither tradition gives a full discussion of the syntactic relation of co-objects of infinitives. The question is worth raising because in Russian some verbs taking infinitives govern the accusative (*zastavljat'* 'force', *prosit'* 'ask'), whereas others govern the dative (*prikazyvat'* 'order', *velet'* 'order', *davat'* 'let', *pomogat'* 'help'). Do co-objects of infinitives, then, represent one syntactic relation or two? By such purely syntactic criteria as complementary distribution and (apart from case) generalized substitutability (for these criteria see Mel'čuk 1979) they represent a single surface syntactic relation. Is that relation, then, first object, second object, or neither? Since some of them (those in the dative) are prototypical second objects and none are prototypical direct objects, and since all of them are one and the same syntactic relation, then they must all be second objects. Since syntactic relations are usually an important control condition, object control of predicate nominals was chosen as a possible source of diagnostic evidence for the syntactic categorization of objects.

Eleven native speakers of Russian were consulted for this study.[4] The full range of conditions was elicited from only six of them. Their reactions to constructions are symbolized below with the following four degrees of grammaticality and/or acceptability:

(no mark)	fully acceptable, normal, frequent
†	acceptable but less fully so, less frequent
?	dubious, infrequent
*	ungrammatical, unacceptable

These degrees of acceptability are based on speakers' responses, although speakers were not asked to judge sentences according to this schema. The rating 'fully acceptable' is relative to the general context of object-controlled constructions. Subject-controlled predicate nominals are always better than object-controlled ones, as all but one speaker volunteered. (This means that wherever the subject can be interpreted as controller that is the preferred reading. The examples given in what follows are constructed so as to preclude such readings. The subjects and objects always differ in gender and/or number; as the predicate nominal agrees with the controller in gender and number, the object is unambiguously the intended controller.)

Elicitation revealed 13 conditions that affected acceptability of control more or less systematically, plus some idiosyncratic phenomena. (Three

[4] I am grateful to Natalja Zundelevich, Serge Kassatkin, Nelja Dubrovič, Emil Draitser, Vladimir Skomarovskij, Olga Hughes, Simon Karlinsky, Lazar Fleishman, Michael Kreps, Olga Astromova, Olga Sorokina-Vasilieva, Igor Mel'čuk, and Lidia Iordanskaja for their help.

speakers, for example, rejected all but fixed expressions like 'remember as', one of them noting that he personally disliked adverbial predicate nominals, gerunds, and participles.) The 13 conditions fall into two groups, which I will call *rule conditions* and *semantic conditions*. Rule conditions (the notion is based on Timberlake 1979, 1980b) are those referring to inherent aspects of grammatical rules involving a controller and a target. Examples of rule conditions include the restriction of some predicate nominals to subject controllers alone, or the restriction of those investigated here to subject and object controllers; conditions on finiteness of verbs (and thus on the boundedness of control); conditions referring to the part of speech of targets; and so on. Rule conditions uncovered in this study repeat those documented in other control studies. I have loosely labeled the second group *semantic conditions* (it is partly analogous to the propositional conditions of Nichols 1981:141ff.). Some of these are straightforwardly semantic; others are superficially syntactic, but ultimately motivated by semantics. Most of the semantic conditions have not been proposed elsewhere in the literature on control.

2. RULE CONDITIONS

Five rule conditions emerged. They yield a generalization attested in most control studies: More accessible targets, and greater controller strength, favor control.

2.1. Target Accessibility

Only one factor involving target accessibility was found. If the construction is a more or less stable one, and the predicate nominal bears a more or less object-like relation to the verb, control is of course entirely natural. All speakers accepted examples like (7) and (8); these represent fixed constructions 'know as' and 'remember as'. Sentence (9), however, was less acceptable to most speakers and unacceptable to one; the lower acceptability is due to the fact that there is no fixed construction 'love as'.

(7)   *Ona znala **ego**   mal'čikom.*
        she   knew him(acc) boy
        'She knew him as a boy'.

(8)   *Ja pomnju   **ego**   mal'čikom.*
        I   remember him(acc) boy
        'I remember him as a boy'.

(9)   †*On ljubil **ee**   ešče devočkoj.*
         he loved her(acc) still girl
         'He loved her as a little girl', '. . . when she was still a little
            girl'.

This condition coincides in part with the semantic condition on independent temporal reference documented in what follows.
   The remaining rule conditions concern controller strength.

2.2. Case

   An object in the accusative case is a stronger controller than one in another case or one governed by a preposition, other things being equal. As examples of first objects without codependent infinitives, compare (9) with (10): (9), with accusative, is acceptable whereas (10), with dative, is not.

(10)   **On pomogal *ej***   *ešče devočkoj.*
         he helped   her(dat) still girl
         'He helped her as a little girl'.

Accusative versus dative co-objects of infinitives:

(11)   *Roditeli zastavljali **ego**   stirat'   i   myt' posudu*
         parents forced   him(acc) do-laundry and wash dishes
         ešče mal'čikom.
         still boy
         'His parents used to make him do laundry and wash dishes
            as a boy'.

(12)   ?*Roditeli pomogali **ej**   stirat'   i   myt' posudu*
         parents helped   her(dat) do-laundry and wash dishes
         ešče devočkoj.
         still girl
         'Her parents used to help her do laundry and wash dishes as
            a girl'.

2.3. Ranking of Objects: First > Second > Third

   Dative first objects, as in (13), are grammatical and moderately acceptable as controllers; dative second objects, as in (14), are less acceptable and sometimes completely rejected.

(13)   †*Ona zavidovala **emu**   ešče mal'čikom.*
         she envied   him(dat) still boy
         'She envied him as a boy'.

(14)   ?*Sosedi   často davali **emu**   den'gi ešče mal'čikom.*
        neighbors often gave   him(dat) money still boy
        'His neighbors often gave him money as a boy'.

Third objects as in (15) are entirely unacceptable to all speakers. [Example (15) shows a nonminimal contrast because the third object is a prepositional phrase rather than in the dative. No dative third objects could be found. The second object—the dative addressee—is not overt in this example.]

(15)   **Sestra často govorila èto **o**   **nem** ešče mal'čikom.*
        sister often said   this about him still boy
        'His sister often said this about him as a boy'.

2.4. Codependent Infinitive

An object is a stronger controller if it also controls an infinitive, as shown by the following minimal pair:

(16)   **Emu   ešče mal'čikom pomogala sestra.*
        him(dat) still boy   helped   sister
        'His sister used to help him as a boy'.

(17)   *†Emu   ešče rebenkom roditeli pomogali pisat' sočinenija.*
        him(dat) still child   parents helped   write compositions
        'His parents used to help him write his compositions as a
           boy'.

[Compare also (10) and (12).] In general, co-objects of infinitives can control predicate nominals even when those objects are not in the accusative case, whereas for many speakers an object without a codependent infinitive cannot control unless it is accusative (and even then cannot always control).[5] This condition is systematic, and the acceptability ranking of pairs like (16)–(17) was readily apparent to all speakers who would consider dative controllers. The same condition is observed for control of gerunds in Rappaport (1979:35–39): Dative "subjects" of inverse verbs, which would otherwise be poor controllers or noncontrollers for most grammarians, are able to control gerunds if they also control infinitives. Notice that for both gerunds and predicate nominals the controlled target is outside the infinitive phrase. This means that the controller is controlling two targets, the infinitive and the gerund or predicate nominal. The mere presence of a controlled infinitive, then, is evidently

---

[5] These results falsify the claim, made in Nichols (1981:79–80), that co-objects of infinitives are weaker controllers.

the factor strengthening the overall controllerhood of the controller; in more general terms, control favors control. The minimal distinction is evidently the syntactic phenomenon of control rather than the semantics of increased responsibility on the part of the controller which it might suggest, since (as is shown in what follows) greater responsibility on the part of the controller in fact disfavors control.[6]

In both Rappaport's corpus and mine, codependent infinitives favor control primarily, or only, for datives—as in (16)–(17). Although no minimal pairs with accusative controllers could be elicited, a survey of accusative controllers revealed that for most speakers accusative co-objects of infinitives, taken as a group, control no better than plain accusatives; for one speaker there was marginal evidence that accusative co-objects of infinitives are somewhat better controllers. On the whole, however, the codependent infinitive serves primarily to rank dative controllers.

2.5. Topicality

Topicality in Russian is signaled primarily by word order. In (18) the dative controller is preverbal and the construction is more or less acceptable; in (19) the controller is postverbal and the construction is less acceptable.

(18)   †*Ešče mal'čikom* **emu**   *zapretili kurit'*.
        still boy   him(dat) forbade smoke
        'As a boy they forbade him to smoke'.

(19)   ?*Ešče mal'čikom zapretili* **emu**   *kurit'*.
                         forbade him(dat)
        'As a boy they forbade **him** to smoke'.

There are two ways of analyzing the effect of topicality on control. Preverbal position is that of topicalization (specifically, the preverbal NP is usually discourse theme), so we could say control is improved in (18) because the controller is topic. On the other hand, preverbal position is neutral word order for (subject and object) pronouns; therefore we could say that (19) is less acceptable because of the presence of a marked pragmatic component signaled in its word order [the postverbal pronoun of (19) is stressed and would be interpreted, out of context, as focus or contrast]. Either of these two explanations (topicalization of controller

---

[6] Rappaport (1979:35ff.) sees the relevant factor not as an additional instance of control but as an additional predication. This is still a rule condition and not a semantic condition, as the semantics of predication is entirely due to control.

improves control; marked pragmatic division in the construction worsens control) accounts for the difference in acceptability between (18) and (19). We will see in what follows that the former is consistent with the metaprinciple of prominence, the latter with the metaprinciple of cohesion. [The speaker who provided these examples, incidentally, commented on the focus and stress of (19) but not on the topicalization of (18).]

3. SEMANTIC CONDITIONS

3.1. Responsibility of Subject

For two different groups of verbs and thus two construction types, object control is favored by what I will call increased responsibility of the subject (not the controller, NB, but the subject) for the action in question. This is a purely lexical property of verbs, not a matter of the semantic roles of actants. Verbs of emotion can be ranked in the following order, based on the extent to which their (accusative) first objects can control predicate nominals. The strongest verbs are those that most easily permit control; the weakest are those that tend not to permit it.

Strongest:	*poljubit'*	'fall in love' (perfective)
	voznenavidet'	'(start to) hate', 'come to hate' (perfective)
	nenavidet'	'hate' (imperfective)
	ljubit'	'love' (imperfective)
Weakest:	*bojat'sja*	'be afraid' (imperfective)[7]

The following are examples of the differences in acceptability that result:

(20)   *Ona poljubila **ego**   ešče mal' čikom.*
       she fell-in-love him(acc) still boy
       'She fell in love with him as a boy'.

(21)   *Ona voznenavidela **ego**   ešče mal' čikom.*
       she came-to-hate him(acc) still boy
       'She came to hate him as a boy'.

[7] For some speakers *bojat'sja* 'be afraid of' takes the genitive, whereas for the majority it takes the accusative of feminine nouns and the genitive of others. For speakers for whom it takes the genitive, weaker control is of course to be expected on the basis of the nonaccusative object. However, the ranking shown here is also valid for those for whom it takes the accusative, which shows that verbal semantics and not simply case of controller is relevant to the ranking.

(22)   † *Ona nenavidela ego   ešče mal'čikom.*
          she   hated   him(acc) still boy
          'She hated him as a boy'.

(23)   †/? *Ona ljubila ego   ešče mal'čikom.*
          she   loved him(acc) still boy

(24)   ?/* *Ona bojalas' ego   ešče mal'čikom.*
          she   feared   him(acc/gen) still boy
          'She was afraid of him as a boy'.

(The evidence for the relative ranking of *poljubit'* 'fall in love' and *voznenavidet'* 'come to hate', and that of *nenavidet'* 'hate' and *ljubit'* 'love', is least strong. For all other pairs it is clear.) The subject is most responsible when there is a single definable event with which he is associated, as in (20)–(21); less responsible when there is a temporally undelimited state which he is capable of sustaining or counteracting to at least some extent and which can in itself constitute a social relation ('love', 'hate'); and least responsible when there is a less clearly caused state which he is less able to control ('be afraid'). Responsibility as defined here, then, involves as many as four dimensions: more nearly event-like character of the situation for which the individual is responsible; identifiable cause of that situation; an emotion which can be to some extent volitionally or artificially sustained or suppressed; and an emotion which can in itself constitute a social relation. Responsibility is not to be confused with agency: The subjects of all these verbs are experiencers, not agents. Rather, it has to do with societal assessment of the individual in relation to the emotion.

My use of the term *state* here, to refer to temporally unbounded and nonvolitional emotions, should not be confused with the resultant state following a punctual event, the typical cross-linguistic meaning of perfect tenses. I will call this latter resultant or perfect meaning, *stative*. There is evidence that a stative reading favors control: A speaker who felt a clear preference for perfective (20) and (21) over imperfective (22) and (23) commented that (20) and (21) are better because the love or hate continues to the time of speech. This comment enables us to add another stage to the hierarchy, so that the ranking for responsibility is:

(25)   High responsibility: stative result of event
                                  event
                                  caused, temporally delimited state
          Low responsibility: uncaused, temporally undelimited state

Responsibility of the subject may account for the acceptability of (26), where the subject is a true agent:

(26)   *Roditeli trebovali ètogo ot   **menja** ešče rebenkom.*
         parents demanded this   from me   still child
         'My parents demanded this of me as a child'.

A prepositional phrase should be a weaker controller than a dative; yet several speakers for whom even datives were in general weak controllers readily accepted the sentence. One factor influencing this acceptability may be the high responsibility of the subject of 'demand' and the low volition of the controller.[8]

The second group of verbs revealing responsibility is those taking codependent infinitives. For these verbs speakers varied somewhat in their preferences. For all speakers, however, it was clear that verbs could again be classified into strong and weak groups, the strong verbs favoring object control relative to the weak verbs. There was no evidence for ranking within these groups. The verb groups are shown in Table 1.

Although there are some differences among speakers, there is considerable consistency. There are four tendencies, shared by all speakers, which account for the groupings. One of them is responsibility of the subject. The weak group includes only (but not all) verbs which presuppose that the *controller* actually initiated or intended to perform the action: 'help', 'hinder'. (For some speakers 'let' and 'forbid' are also weak; and they also imply controller initiative.) The strong group includes those which presuppose that the action would not have taken place without the *subject's* causal action, and which do not specifically presuppose volition or independent initiation of action on the part of the controller. Initiative on the part of the controller is the converse of subject responsibility. Subject responsibility favors control; controller (object) responsibility disfavors it. [Subject responsibility was also relevant for verbs of emotion which do not take infinitives, as was discussed in conjunction with (20)–(24). For such verbs, since there is no code-

---

[8] Another factor is the fact that *èto* 'this, it' is most easily interpreted as the anaphor of an infinitive phrase rather than of a simple NP. In other words, *ot menja* 'from me' should be grouped with co-objects of infinitives. Substitution of a full, noninfinitive NP for *èto* lowers acceptability:

(i) †/? *Roditeli trebovali xorošie otmetki ot   menja ešče rebenkom.*
        parents demanded good   grades from me   still child
        'My parents demanded good grades of me as a child'.

However, for the speaker in question (26) is more acceptable than many examples with dative co-objects of infinitives; it is this greater acceptability that is accounted for by responsibility of the subject.

TABLE 1

CONTROL STRENGTH FOR CO-OBJECTS OF INFINITIVES, BY MAIN VERB[a]

Control strength	Case of controller			
	Accusative		Dative	
Strong	*zastavljat'*	'force'	*razrešat'*	'allow'
	prosit'	'ask'	*ne davat'*	'not let'
	umoljat'	'implore'		
	posylat'	'send'		
Variable or unclear			*sovetovat'*	'advise'
			pozvoljat'	'permit'
			prikazyvat'	'order'
			zapreščat'[b]	'forbid'
			davat'[b]	'let'
			velet'	'order'
			ne velet'	'order not to'
Weak			*pomogat'*	'help'
			mešat'	'hinder, bother'

[a] Verbs are cited in the imperfective, the usual citation form. Vertical ordering within groups of verbs is not significant.

[b] These two verbs were strong for approximately half the speakers who could discriminate among verbs, and weak for the other half. The other verbs in this class were less clear to speakers or were elicited from fewer speakers than the others.

pendent infinitive, responsibility of the controller is out of the question.] The remaining three tendencies involve aspect and case.

3.2. Aspect

The overt morphological category of aspect for the most part played no direct role in the acceptability of control. (In isolated examples it did affect acceptability; this fact is discussed in the conclusions.) However, a covert subaspectual category of countability (the term proposed in Timberlake 1982) does systematically influence control. If the verb refers to, or may be understood as referring to, a multiple or iterative action, control is disfavored. The second generalization to be made about the ranking of verbs in Table 1 is the following: The weak group will include many (and, for two speakers, it includes only) verbs that bear or favor an interpretation whereby the infinitive action occurs in discrete phases or as discrete events. (This parameter ranks verbs governing the dative but does not apply to those governing the accusative.) For example, for many speakers *davat'* 'let' weakens control. Now the lexical meaning and the imperfective aspect *davat'* 'let' both impose a presupposition that there were various discrete occasions on which the controller asked or began to perform the action, and on each occasion the subject granted him permission. A striking minimal pair is provided by *davat'* 'let' versus *ne davat'* 'not let':

(27)   *Roditeli ne davali **emu**   kurit'   ešče mal'čikom.*
         parents not let   him(dat) smoke still boy
         'His parents didn't let him smoke as a boy'.

(28)   †*Roditeli davali **ej**   stirat'   i   myt' posudu ešče*
         parents let   her(dat) do-laundry and wash dishes still
         malen'koj devočkoj.
         little   girl
         'Her parents let her do laundry and wash dishes as a little girl'.

'Not let' favors control, as in (27); 'let' disfavors it, as in (28). Whereas *davat'* 'let' can imply (and does, in this example) a series of discrete events, *ne davat'* 'not let' does not: It can suggest an overall negative attitude on the part of the parents rather than discrete instances of forbidding, or it can suggest a single instance of forbidding (at an unspecified time, thus the imperfective aspect) which remained in force throughout the son's childhood.

Similarly, *razrešat'* 'allow' is a strong verb whereas its near-synonym *davat'* 'let' is variable; and a subtle difference in the lexical semantics of the two verbs is that *razrešat'* 'allow' (strong) more easily denotes an overall state of mind on the part of the parents than does *davat'* 'let' (variable). Likewise, *ne davat'* 'not let' (strong) readily suggests an attitude, *zapreščat'* 'forbid' (variable) a series of acts. (Readers unfamiliar with Russian should be cautioned that these properties of the Russian verbs are not adequately conveyed by their English translations.)

The same subaspectual parameter accounts for the ranking of first objects without codependent infinitives. A minimal pair is (29)–(30). Both verbs govern the dative, a fact which in itself lowers acceptability. Control with *zavidovat'* 'envy' in (29) is dubious, whereas control with *radovat'sja* 'be glad' in (30) is definitely unacceptable.

(29)   ?*Ona zavidovala **emu**   ešče mal'čikom.*
         she envied   him(dat) still boy
         'She envied him as a boy'.

(30)   **Ona radovalas' **emu**   ešče mal'čikom.*
         she was-glad   him(dat) still child
         'She was (always) glad (to see) him as a boy'.

'Envy' is a predicate that can denote a continuous state or attitude, whereas 'glad' is a short-term response to a specific event; in the imperfective, as in (25), it refers to repeated discrete instances of being glad and not to a single continuous state. These examples show that a continuous state is a possible frame for control, whereas repeated instances of the state are not.

Weaker evidence comes from (31)–(32). For some speakers (31) is acceptable whereas (32) is less so.

(31)   *Roditeli čitali **emu**   skazki ešče mal'čikom.*
       parents read him(dat) stories still boy
       'His parents used to read him stories as a boy'.

(32)   †*Sosedi   davali **emu**   den'gi ešče mal'čikom.*
       neighbors gave   him(dat) money still boy
       'His neighbors used to give him money as a boy'.

Reading stories can be a nightly ritual; the separate events are not well individuated or salient, and the emphasis is on the parent–child relationship rather than on the events of reading. But for neighbors to give a child money is not a frequently repeated ritual and not indicative of a particular social relationship; the emphasis is on the events rather than on the character of a relationship, and the events themselves are probably fewer, less regular, less typical, and hence more salient and more individuated.

3.3. Further Observations on Lexical Classes

Two additional generalizations follow from Table 1. One concerns aspect and will be made in what follows. The other concerns case: All verbs governing the accusative will cluster in the strong class. Verbs governing the dative can be strong, variable, or weak, depending on other factors (and with a certain measure of individual variation).

The ranking of verbs as strong and weak parallels the ranking of verbs given in Timberlake (1979). There the verbs fall into two groups with respect to the ease with which they allow subject-controlled reflexivization into dependent infinitive clauses. The most basic causative verbs allow it most easily: These comprise *davat'* 'let', *pomogat'* 'help' [+dative] and *zastavljat'* 'force' [+accusative]. The less basic verbs allow it less easily; these include such verbs as *prikazyvat'* 'order' [+dative] and *prosit'* 'ask' [+accusative]. Since with regard to the control of predicate nominals verbs governing the accusative are all in the strong group and show little or no evidence of internal diversification, the hierarchy of verbs in Table 1 does not reflect Timberlake's split of *zastavljat'* 'force' from *prosit'* 'ask'. On the other hand, there is fairly convincing confirmation of his ranking of verbs governing the dative. As Timberlake's higher ranked group of basic causatives favors subject control as opposed to object control, we would expect 'let' and 'help' to correspond to the weak and variable groups of Table 1: My weak verbs, and Timberlake's basic causatives, both disfavor object control. Even at first glance we find partial confirmation of this pattern: The weak group includes 'help' and the variable group includes the basic verb for 'let', *davat'*; neither is strong. In fact, for three speakers I found exact confirmation: Both 'help' and 'let' are weak verbs. The less basic verbs are in the strong or variable groups; of the variable verbs, 'advise', 'permit', and 'order' were strong for a few speakers and 'forbid' was unexpectedly weak for two.

The variable position of *davat'* 'let', relative to weak *pomogat'* 'help', can be explained by reference to other factors. The control of *davat'* 'let' is strengthened by the feature of subject responsibility: *pomogat'* 'help' entails greater volition or responsibility on the part of the controller than does *davat'* 'let' (since *davat'* can imply an attitude on the part of the subject rather than actual granting of permission, as discussed earlier). Closely related to this is the relevance of the subaspectual parameter of countability: *pomogat'* 'help' easily refers to discrete incidents in which the controller attempted the action and the subject helped, whereas *davat'* 'let' can indicate an overall attitude. In short, 'let' and 'help' should pattern alike, according to Timberlake's hierarchy; that they do not is due to independently attested factors of aspect and subject responsibility. What is most important is that neither is strong.

In addition, nonbasic *razrešat'* 'allow' is strong whereas basic *davat'* is variable. This ranking is what we would expect, as basic verbs should be weaker. Now, control for *razrešat'* 'allow' is improved by its aspectual properties, as discussed earlier. On the other hand, its control should be weakened by its greater controller responsibility (i.e., its lesser subject responsibility): *razrešat'* 'allow' distinctly presupposes that the controller requested permission; *davat'* 'let' is neutral in this respect. In other words, the two factors of subject responsibility and aspect cancel each other out for these two verbs. Yet *razrešat'* 'allow' is stronger than *davat'* 'let'. This must mean that the nonbasic nature of *razrešat'* is indeed relevant, and that we have a minimal pair here. In summary, then, Table 1 does exhibit an overall conformity to Timberlake's ranking, and this conformity is only strengthened when we take into consideration the influence of subject responsibility and aspect.

3.4. Temporal Coreference

It is a general condition on this type of predicate nominal construction that the time reference of the main verb and that of the predicate nominal must coincide at least in part (Nichols 1981:34ff.). Thus in (31), the time when the parents read stories to their son coincides with the time when he was a child; and in fact it is the very function of these constructions to assert that temporal coincidence. Examples such as (33) are ungrammatical for all speakers because the time reference does not coincide.

(33)   *Ešče mal'čikom ee   často sravnivali   s   bratom.
        still boy   her(acc) often they-compared with brother
        'As a boy they often compared her to her brother'.

The comparison in (33) is between the sister (possibly, but not necessarily, in her childhood) and the brother in his childhood; it involves saying that the sister's present appearance and behavior resemble the brother's past appearance and behavior.

Sentence (33) has an oblique controller; but (34) shows that control is ungrammatical even for direct objects under the same conditions:

(34)   *Ona napominaet otca   ešče mal'čikom.
        she reminds-of father(acc) still boy
        'She reminds (one) of her father as a boy'.

These examples involve comparison. There is nothing in the semantics of comparison per se that precludes control of predicate nominals, however. Sentence (35) is fully acceptable:

(35)   On sejčas vyše rostom, čem byla ego mat'
        he now   taller   than was his mother(nom)
        uže   vzrosloj ženščinoj.
        already adult   woman
        'He is already taller than his mother was as an adult'.

This is because (35) has a separate clause with its own predicate byla 'was'; the predicate nominal is temporally coreferential to this predicate, and the sentence is acceptable. If the comparative clause is reduced the sentence becomes ungrammatical because the temporal reference of the predicate nominal differs from that of the main clause:

(36)   *On sejčas vyše rostom, čem ego mat'   uže
        he now   taller than   his mother(nom) already
        vzrosloj ženščinoj.
        adult   woman
        'He is already taller than his mother as a full-grown woman'.

3.5. Independent Temporal Reference

This factor is not to be confused with temporal coreference. As has been stated, in predicate nominal constructions of this type both the verb and the predicate nominal have temporal reference, and the sentence asserts their (partial) coincidence. Temporal coreference has to do with this (partial) coincidence. Independent temporal reference, on the other hand, has to do with the fact that both the verb and the predicate nominal have their own, independently stated, time reference. That this is so is intuitively fairly clear. More objective evidence comes from examples like (37).

(37)   *Ona poljubila* **ego**   *ešče mal'čikom.*
         she   fell-in-love him(acc) still boy
         'She fell in love with him as a boy'.

The perfective verb *poljubila* '(she) fell in love' refers to a single event; the time reference of *mal'čikom* '(as a) boy' is a longer period of time which frames the single event. The two time references must be independently stated since they differ (although they coincide in part, as required by the construction type).

Although independent temporal reference is definitional of the type of predicate nominal investigated here, it is in itself a factor actually disfavoring control. Predicate nominals which are semantically concessive rather than temporal, and which use the conjunction *daže* 'even' rather than temporal *ešče* 'still', are acceptable where temporal ones are not:

(38)   **Roditeli pomogali emu**   *ešče rebenkom.*
         parents helped   him(dat) still child
         'His parents helped him as a child'.

(39)   *Roditeli pomogali* **emu**   *daže vzroslomu.*
                             him(dat) even adult
         'His parents helped him even as an adult'.

(Such pairs are never minimal, as *daže* 'even' requires agreement whereas *ešče* 'still' is used with the instrumental.)

Three speakers rejected all temporal predicate nominals except for the fixed constructions. For one of them, however, sentences were acceptable if they could be given some reading other than temporal. Whereas for most speakers (40) is ambiguous, with two acceptable readings, for this speaker only the second reading, where the meaning is roughly comparative rather than temporal, was acceptable.

(40) *Ja videl **ego** rebenkom.*
      I   saw him child
      a. 'I saw him when he was a child'.
      b. 'I saw (imagined) him as a child'.

This factor also applies to the fixed constructions. One reason for their acceptability and stability may be the fact that they are ambiguous, permitting nontemporal readings. Sentences (41) and (42) have two meanings:

(41) *Ona znala **ego**   mal'čikom.*
      she knew him(acc) boy
      a. 'She knew him when he was a boy'.
      b. 'She knew (thought of, imagined) him as a boy'.

(42) *Ona pomnit   **ego**   mal'čikom.*
      she remembers him(acc) boy
      a. 'She remembers how he was during his childhood'.
      b. 'She (mistakenly) remembers him as being a boy'.

For each, only the first reading is temporal; the second is roughly comparative.[9] It may well be the availability of the second, nontemporal, reading that favors the existence of the entire construction.

3.6. Word Order

For all speakers word order affected control in at least some examples; but its effect on control differed. For some speakers, preposed predicate nominals favored control; for others, postposed ones favored control. Of the following pair, (43) was preferred by three speakers and (44) by three; two of the speakers who rejected all nonfixed constructions could not rank these two sentences.

(43) *Roditeli pomogali **emu**   pisat' sočinenija   ešče mal'čikom.*
      parents helped   him(dat) write compositions still boy
      'His parents used to help him write his (school) compositions
      as a boy'.

(44) *Ešče mal'čikom roditeli pomogali **emu**   pisat' sočinenija.*
      still boy   parents helped   him(dat) write compositions
      'As a boy his parents used to help him write his (school)
      compositions'.

[9] The first reading of (42) in fact violates the conditions on temporal coreference: The remembering takes place at a time later than, and thus distinct from, the childhood. This reading was not particularly difficult to elicit, although it was never spontaneously offered. It may be an entailment rather than an actual meaning.

3.7. Embedding

Embedding improves the acceptability of control. Sentence (45) is dubious because the controller is dative; the same clause is acceptable when embedded, as in (46).

(45)   ?*Ona zavidovala **emu**   ešče mal'čikom.*
         she envied   him(dat) still boy
         'She envied him when he was a boy'.

(46)   †*Ona pomnit,   kak zavidovala **emu**   ešče mal'čikom.*
         she remembers how envied   him(dat) still boy
         'She remembers how she envied him as a boy'.

This factor evidently applies only when poor control is due to factors other than semantic ones. Embedding did not improve the acceptability of control with *radovat'sja* 'be glad', where control is disfavored by the semantics of aspect:

(47)   **Ona radovalas' **emu**   ešče mal'čikom.*
         she was-glad   him (dat) still boy
         'She was glad (to see) him as a boy'.

(48)   **Ona pomnit,   kak radovalas' **emu**   ešče mal'čikom.*
         she remembers how was-glad   him(dat) still boy
         'She remembers how she was always glad to see him as a
              boy'.

3.8. More Accessible Potential Controller in Sentence

Object control is weakened if the sentence contains a subject that could also be a controller. This is true even where (as in all examples here) the subject and object differ in gender and/or number and the predicate nominal unambiguously agrees only with the object. In (49) the subject, feminine *sestra* 'sister', interferes with control by the object *emu* 'him', although the predicate nominal is masculine and cannot be controlled by *sestra*.

(49)   ?*Ešče mal'čikom sestra vsegda mešala   **emu**   spat'.*
         still boy   sister always bothered him(dat) sleep
         'As a boy, his sister always kept him from sleeping'.

In (50) the subject is neuter *èto* 'this, it', which refers to an entire situation and therefore for semantic reasons could not possibly control a predicate nominal referring to an individual's stage of life; there is no interference and the construction is acceptable to most speakers.

(50)   *Ešče mal'čikom èto vsegda mešalo **emu**   spat'.*
        still boy   this always bothered him(dat) sleep
        'As a boy, this always kept him from sleeping'.

This condition follows from the fact that subjects are stronger controllers than objects. A subject that is semantically plausible as a controller is apparently attended to as a potential controller, suppressing or diminishing attention to the object as a potential controller, during processing of the sentence.

3.9. Conjunction

Apart from fixed constructions, the delimiter *ešče* 'still' favors control, relative to no delimiter.

(51)   *Ona ljubila ego* $\left\{ \begin{array}{l} ? \emptyset \\ \dagger\ ešče \end{array} \right\}$ *mal'čikom.*
        she loved him   boy
        'She loved him as a boy'.

When given examples like (51) in isolation all speakers said that *ešče* is required. However, some speakers, in repeating or trying out various examples at other points in elicitation sessions, would occasionally omit *ešče*. I interpret this as evidence that *ešče* is the grammatical marker of a construction type rather than a fully semantic element: In general, when speakers repeat a construction they feel free to tamper with the grammatical marking but not with the content; thus if *ešče* were semantic it would not be freely omissible. This means that we are justified in regarding *ešče* as the grammatical exponent of the temporal predicate nominal construction when that construction is not governed by the verb. When it is governed by the verb, as in (41)–(42), the conjunction is usually omitted.

As a semantic element *ešče* means 'still' in the sense of 'as long ago as', often with a presupposition that the action or its result continues to the present time. It can often be translated 'even':

(52)   *Moskva byla krupnym torgovym centrom ešče v 15-om veke.*
                 was major   trade   center even in   century
        'Moscow was a major trade center as long ago as the 15th
        century', '. . . even in the 15th century'.

When rejecting examples such as (43)–(44), with *pomogat'* 'help', most speakers pointed out that they were semantically odd just because of the presupposition that the state of affairs is still relevant: (43) or (44) means 'his parents not only help him now, but helped him even in his childhood'. This is odd because sons and daughters are usually helped in childhood and not in adulthood. The fact that *ešče* is interpreted semantically in these sentences, and not as the grammatical marker of a syntactic relation, shows that the syntactic relation is not fully acceptable here. This in itself would justify starring or question-marking such examples. (Further evidence for their lower acceptability is, of course, the explicit rejection of speakers.)

One speaker became progressively sensitized to the semantics of *ešče* and by the final session was rejecting most examples as semantically odd. These judgments (which conflicted with earlier ones by the same speaker) were disregarded in drawing up Table 1.

4. CONCLUSIONS

The various conditions yield two metaconditions which, although not functioning as grammatical rules to predict acceptability of individual sentences, do provide meaningful generalizations over the conditions and thus provide some assurance of the plausibility of the analysis. These two metaconditions are prominence, which is a property of controllers, and cohesion, which is a property of events. The conditioning factors are summarized in Table 2.

Although all conditions listed in Table 2 appear to be systematic, some are evidently more salient than others. All speakers reacted strongly to case of controller and most reacted confidently and consistently, although with less ability to explicitly identify the relevant factor, to codependent infinitives. The conditions of controller responsibility, aspect, temporal coreference, and independent temporal reference were harder to elicit, and much of the evidence for them comes from generalizations over lexical classes (see the discussion of Table 1). No speaker reversed the orderings shown on Table 2, but not all speakers gave evidence for all of them.

4.1. Prominence

The rule conditions of target accessibility and controller strength rank the target and the controller for prominence along several axes. (For this approach see Nichols, Rappaport, and Timberlake 1980; also Rappaport

TABLE 2
CONDITIONING FACTORS FOR CONTROL

Rule conditions
Target accessibility
  fixed > open construction
Controller strength
  case: accusative > oblique
  object type: first > second > third
  codependent infinitive > $\cdots$
  topic > nontopic

Semantic conditions
responsibility of subject > $\cdots$
aspect: $\cdots$ > discrete events
temporal coreference > $\cdots$
$\cdots$ > independent temporal reference
word order
embedding > $\cdots$
$\cdots$ > more accessible NP in sentence
delimiter > no delimiter

Metaconditions: cohesion > lack of cohesion
               prominence > lack of prominence

Legend: > separates ranked factors in the order: favors > disfavors control; $\cdots$ = lack of same, other, non-, etc.

1979:59ff., Timberlake 1980b.) The axes and types of prominence are shown in Table 3. All of them apply to controllers; only the syntactic axis was shown here to apply to targets (in that a more object-like target is more prominent). There are at least four further types of prominence which are not shown in Table 3. Prominence along the axes of discourse thematicity and person–number categories were not tested in this study. Lexical prominence, which includes such properties as animacy, was

TABLE 3
TYPES OF PROMINENCE

Axis	Prominence ranking
Syntactic	(subject) > first object > second object > third object > $\cdots$
Morphological	(nominative) > accusative > dative > $\cdots$
Communicative	topic > nontopic
Metacondition:	prominent > less prominent

Legend: ( ) = head of hierarchy, not tested in this study; > ranks properties in order: favors control > disfavors control.

also not tested. Animacy may be said to vacuously apply to object control, in that only animates have phases of life such as childhood, but this is hardly a grammatical condition on control. More interesting is the semantic-role axis, for which prominence is agency. For object control of predicate nominals, the hierarchy of agency is reversed in that volition and thus implicit agency of the controller disfavor control. The reason for the reversal lies in what I will call cohesion, specifically in the responsibility of the subject for the action.

4.2. Cohesion

Cohesion is a measure of the overall unity or "tightness" of the event and its participants. Greater cohesion favors object control of predicate nominals. We may speak of syntactic cohesion and semantic cohesion. SYNTACTIC COHESION is the generalization to be made over the rule conditions. Although controller strength and target accessibility, taken separately, each involve prominence, the conjunction of these notions yields a measure of the syntactic closeness of the controller and the target. It is this syntactic closeness that the term *cohesion* is intended to capture. Prior to the explicit distinction of control strength from target accessibility, a single notion akin or identical to cohesion was pursued in the literature. The very term *cohesion* is used in Comrie (1974) to refer to syntactic cohesion. The present paper differs from such earlier studies not in the substance of the notion of cohesion but in that it is regarded here as a metagrammatical generalization rather than as a primary or invariant grammatical condition.

The semantic conditions yield a generalization which can be labeled *semantic cohesion*. The various conditions reduce to a single semantic metacondition on the event, its properties, and its participants, applicable at a level of considerable abstraction. A highly cohesive event has the following characteristics: The agent is highly responsible for the (controller's) performance of the action; there is temporal coreference between the main verb and other parts of the sentence such as infinitives and predicate nominals; no subordinate part of the sentence has particularly salient independent temporal reference; neither the main verb nor any subordinate predicate refers to discrete multiple individual actions; relationships among verbs and actants—the relation of main verb to infinitive, that of any verb to its object, that of controller to predicate nominal, etc.—are lexically and extralinguistically natural (and in the most cohesive events some of them are lexicalized or grammaticalized); there is no strong internal topic–comment division or other clause-internal pause. The fewer possible controllers, the more cohesive the event (since possible controllers evidently receive significant attention in processing). Embedding favors cohesion in that it precludes independent time reference, strong internal topicalization, and other types of semantic splitting.

One speaker disliked examples with perfective main verbs and imperfective infinitives; he idiosyncratically ranked (53) and (54) as follows:

(53)   *Roditeli zapreščali*   **emu**   *vodit'*   *mašinu*
        parents forbade(impf) him(dat) drive(impf) car
        ešče mal'čikom.
        still boy
        'His parents forbade him to drive as a boy'.

(54)   ?*Roditeli zapretili*   *emu*   *kurit'*   *ešče mal'čikom.*
        parents forbade(pf) him(dat) smoke(impf) still boy
        'His parents forbade him to smoke as a boy'.

This pattern, although not systematic, also follows from semantic cohesion. The sequence of perfective verb (which implies a single, referential event) plus imperfective verb (duration or repetition, possibly nonreferential) gives the two verbs distinct temporal reference (although the two coincide in part, as required by the construction type). In addition, it implies greater agency on the part of the controller and predication of a discrete event: (53) suggests a state of mind of the parents, not simply a succession of acts of forbidding; (54) indicates an act of forbidding, which presupposes that the child tried or asked to smoke.

Semantic cohesion is the semantic analog to syntactic cohesion: Both involve some sort of impressionistic tightness and unity of the construction or the narrated event. Notice that among my features there is no obvious semantic analog to controller strength or to target accessibility; but the global notion of syntactic cohesion does find an analog in the global notion of semantic cohesion.

Prominence and cohesion would appear to be opposed concepts: The prominence of a participant, especially a nonsubject participant, is the very type of factor that has been described here as decreasing cohesion. Yet both prominence and cohesion favor control. It may well be that this paradox is only rhetorical, that is, that further study will demonstrate that prominence as it has been defined is entirely unrelated to the kinds of salience that disrupt cohesion. Even now it is obvious that the domains of application of the two notions are distinct: Prominence pertains to controllers alone, whereas cohesion is a property of events.

A highly cohesive event is in some sense streamlined and presumably suited for smooth, efficient processing. A noncohesive event is presumably more difficult to process in that various separate threads must be kept track of and the hearer is likely to lose track of control relations. This means that cohesion and prominence have similar functional values in processing: prominence is a measure of the extent to which the controller stands out and is retained in the memory; cohesion measures the lack of factors that might distract from the salience of the controller. Therefore prominence and cohesion might be unified in a psycholinguistic description. For a strictly grammatical analysis like the present one, however, they remain distinct.

4.3. Implications for Aspect

As was pointed out in the discussion of Table 1 and in connection with (53)–(54), control with codependent infinitives is stronger when the verb denotes an attitude than when it denotes an event, and stronger when the verb denotes a single event than when it denotes multiple events. Since *attitude* in this context is a specialized synonym of *state,* we can generalize by saying that control is strongest when the verb denotes a state, as shown in (55):[10]

(55)   State   > Event > Multiple events
         (strongest control)   (weakest control)

As a hierarchy, this ranking departs from what might be expected. With regard to Transitivity, for example, we would expect the hierarchy to be headed by single events, which should outrank states and multiple events (whatever order the latter two might assume). The formal marking of the category of aspect in Russian might also lead us to expect that

---

[10] "State" in this context is a generalization over lexical meanings. I have used it simply to draw parallels to other aspect hierarchizations, and not with the intention of contributing to linguistic terminology. It is not to be confused with "stative" (resultant, perfect-like) meaning as the term is used in (25). The hierarchy involving stativity bears some gross similarity to, but is distinct from, that for aspect shown in (55). Nor should state be confused with the impersonal passive construction available to verbs that take dative co-objects of infinitives:

(i)   *ešče mal'čikom emu   bylo   zapreščeno kurit'.
      still boy   him (dat) (it)was forbidden   smoke
      'As a boy he was forbidden to smoke',
      'As a boy it was forbidden to him to smoke'.

As passives, such forms are sometimes called stative. These impersonal passives are much worse in the predicate nominal construction than the corresponding active verbs. The reason for the lower acceptability, apparently, is not aspect but the feature of subject responsibility: As there is no subject or (demoted) agent in the construction, that actant cannot have high responsibility. [Note, incidentally, that this account of the unacceptability of such examples suggests that they involve, not deletion of an unspecified agent, but its absolute semantic absence from the construction. This example differs from (18)–(19), where the unspecified agent is semantically present and identifiable as responsible.]

single events would be isolated at the end of the category: Most often single events are signaled with the perfective, whereas states and multiple events are marked with the imperfective.[11] The pattern of (55) is reminiscent of that found by Timberlake (1982): In both instances, the imperfective is split and the hierarchical ranking shows the perfective flanked by imperfective categories. An important difference is that Timberlake's hierarchy ranks meanings of inflectional aspect, whereas (55) involves verbal lexical semantics.

4.4. Implications for Syntactic Relations

The traditional view of direct objects in Russian draws a sharp distinction between direct and other objects, and it bases this classification wholly on morphological marking of objects (rather than, say, on semantic roles, derivational history, or consideration of the rest of the valence). The results of this study support such a view of objects: We have seen that direct objects are distinct from others in that direct objects are always possible controllers whereas others usually are not, and that there is a clear distinction in the acceptability of accusatives over other controllers.

On the other hand, clearly there is a certain syntactic unity, not captured in traditional or more recent grammatical terminology, underlying the notion *co-object of infinitive*. For Russian, co-objects of infinitives are distinctly better controllers than are plain objects. Recall that in Russian at least some co-objects of infinitives are dative indirect objects and thus plainly second objects, and that there are syntactic grounds for claiming that all co-objects, dative and accusative alike, are second objects. If we assume for the sake of argument that co-objects are second objects, then we can say that this kind of second object as a class outranks the class of objects without infinitives, which includes first objects. A minimal pair like (16) versus (17) shows a second object in (17) controlling better than, and thus outranking, a first object in (16). This pattern may be significant in that it is reminiscent of a cross-linguistic tendency. It is not rare to read that in one or another language indirect objects outrank direct objects for purposes of accessibility and/or control, and it may be that the higher ranking of co-objects of infinitives in Russian is a variant of that kind of ranking. Usually the higher rankings of indirect objects can be ascribed to their necessary animacy; but for

---

[11] This should not be taken to mean that the sole function of aspect in Russian is to mark single events versus other predications. This is merely a conspicuous and frequent function of aspect marking.

Russian, although animacy is involved (in that co-objects of infinitives are normally agent and thus animate), the minimal relevant factor is the codependent infinitive.

This raises the question of syntactic categorization and the surface syntactic relations of Russian. Is co-object of infinitive a distinct syntactic relation? There are three possible ways we might set up the inventory of surface syntactic relations. First, we could follow the traditional, morphosyntactic, approach and speak of direct, indirect, and oblique objects. Second, we could follow Tesnière, Mel'čuk, and relational grammar, simply numbering and ranking objects as first object (second actant or 2), second object (third actant or 3), and so on. Or, third, we could distinguish co-objects of infinitives from other objects (which would then presumably be subdivided by case or valence rank). As far as describing control of predicate nominals is concerned, case is the more fundamental distinction: First objects control well only if they are accusative; the codependent infinitive does not in itself guarantee strong control but merely favors control when the basic condition on case is not met. (It is worth repeating that a statement based on case alone would account for all of the written corpus, all normative judgments on elicited examples, and many nonnormative judgments.)

In other words, to describe control we need to distinguish direct objects from indirect and oblique objects, and only then do we need to distinguish co-objects of infinitives from others, and second from third objects. This does not, however, answer the question of syntactic categorization. It merely tells us that we need, at least as essential input to the formation of hypotheses, a better cross-linguistic understanding of the role of morphology in determining control strength, more application of strictly syntactic criteria such as those of Mel'čuk mentioned earlier, and more inquiry into the extent to which control phenomena define syntactic relations (they are usually accepted as criterial by relational grammarians, although that approach is challenged by Timberlake 1980a and Nichols *et al.* 1980).

The literature on Russian grammar mentions the following three properties of direct objects:

1. *Passivization.* Only (but not all) accusative objects may become derived subjects of passives. (The few counterexamples where oblique first objects become passive subjects can be disregarded as lexicalized.) Passivization is properly a fact about clauses and verbs rather than about objects per se; and in fact passivization is often arguably a lexical process in Russian (see Babby and Brecht 1975).

2. *Accessibility*. Some direct objects, and no oblique or indirect objects, are accessible to the genitive of negation (see Timberlake 1975), the partitive genitive, and the distributive construction with the preposition *po*. These properties are also shared by (final nominative) subjects (Sidorov and Il'inskaja 1949, Chvany 1975:121–140). In addition, the genitive of negation and the distributive are available to adverbial accusatives. Accessibility to these three kinds of quantification, then, is based primarily on cases. Accessibility has obvious similarities to prominence, and ranks direct objects together with subjects rather than distinguishing direct objects from all other relations.

3. *Semantics*. Traditionally, a direct object is said to be more fully affected by the verbal action than are other objects. Although there exist minimal pairs for which this notion can be given precise content in terms of implicativity, consequence, and patienthood, there are also many counterexamples. The statement has some intuitive validity, but is of dubious grammatical merit and predictive value; probably it is best regarded as a second-order generalization over such phenomena as accessibility and control. Impressionistically, at least, it is aligned with the control condition on responsibility of the subject: Both point to a prototypical configuration involving an agent subject acting on a patient object. The traditional statement is probably nothing more than the articulation of this prototype.

In short, the genuinely syntactic properties (control, accessibility) of direct objects rank them with subjects. For passivization, accessibility, and semantics, as for control, the relevant notion of direct object could be characterized in terms of case alone; none of these properties requires setting up any syntactic category of objects distinct from those marked by the morphology. (The traditional statement about semantics, of course, takes the morphology as given and generalizes over instances of it.) All of this suggests that the concepts first object, second object, etc. are convenient generalizations over lexical valence patterns but do not define the syntactic relations needed to account for syntactic phenomena such as control, accessibility, and passivization. If the only contrasts among objects relevant to syntactic behavior are morphological ones, then the syntax of objecthood in Russian merits further inquiry. It may be that we do not need to distinguish types of objects as distinct syntactic relations. Perhaps it suffices to distinguish only subject, objects, and adverbials, allowing morphological and semantic criteria to rank objects for control strength and accessibility without defining discrete surface-syntactic relations.

4.5. Implications for Transitivity

The prominence conditions (which are the rule conditions of controller strength and target accessibility) have no obvious parallels to the Transitivity features of Hopper and Thompson (1980) (in which the following are the high-Transitivity features: two or more participants; action predicate; telic predicate; punctual predicate; volitional predicate; affirmative predicate; realis predicate; agent high in potency; object totally affected; object highly individuated). This is to be expected, as Transitivity is a discourse-motivated property of clauses, whereas prominence is a property of actants.

The cohesion conditions (which include the rule conditions and the semantic conditions of Table 2) also fail to coincide with the Transitivity features. The description of cohesion does sound rather like the description of the prototypical Transitive clause in that both involve a responsible agent subject and an object of lesser responsibility or volition. But such comparisons of individual Transitivity features and individual cohesion features border on the meaningless. Transitivity was advanced as a discourse-motivated property of clauses; Transitivity properties covary to achieve what may be seen as a teleological goal of improving the overall plot-advancing potential of clauses. Object control of predicate nominals is very different from plot advancement: It involves particular syntactic relations linked by the syntactic phenomenon of control. It may be able to tell us something about objecthood—that assumption motivated this paper—but it has no discourse function. We may view Transitivity as an isolable domain of grammar, one in which features covary. Control of predicate nominals is an entirely different domain of grammar. Furthermore, studies of Russian control have never described conditions or features as covarying; the features vary independently of each other to establish a multidimensional space. Hierarchical values of features can be aligned so that those favoring control outrank those disfavoring it; but this alignment is an aspect of the organization of charts like Table 2, not covariance attested in real sentences of Russian. The absence of covariance is due to the fact that neither control nor the syntactic relation of predicate nominal has any function analogous to that of advancing plot; features affect the acceptability of the construction (and, for other types of predicate nominals, its morphological marking) but not its efficacy in some larger functional plan, so there is no teleological value to aligning them identically. Because there is no real alignment of features and no covariance in the domain of control, the hierarchization of control conditions and that of Transitivity features are not comparable. Furthermore, hierarchical ordering aside, there is very little coincidence in the substantive content of the features relevant to the two domains: Of the various features involved in control, only the prominence conditions and the cohesion condition of aspect have any real similarity to Transitivity features.

In fact, it would be suspicious if we found Transitivity features and control conditions to resemble each other significantly, in either their substantive content or their hierarchization. That would suggest that there was some basic cluster of (let us call them) subgrammatical features with inherent covariance tendencies, which pervade all (or much) of language and thus show up in unrelated domains. We might even have to assume any such covariance was an artifact of linguistic analysis or the reflex of a particular theoretical system. If Transitivity features and their covariance were to be found in domains other than Transitivity and discourse foregrounding, we would have reason to question whether the covariance really serves the specific discourse function of foregrounding. In other words, the lack of coincidence in Transitivity features and control conditions serves as a plausibility check on both analyses: As the functions are different, coincidences in features would have to emanate from language in general or from the analysis, not from particular functions or constructions; differences in features tell us that we have probably uncovered genuine properties of the functions and the constructions in question.

In summary, there is no reason to expect Transitivity features to apply to domains of grammar other than Transitivity, even if those domains do crucially involve direct objects and questions of objecthood, as does the domain of object control. Transitivity features do not strengthen object control; prominence and cohesion features do not increase the Transitivity of clauses. Prominence and cohesion are metaprinciples defining optimal configurations for object control. Their relevance to other kinds of control should now be tested. (Timberlake 1981 shows that object control of Russian reflexivization does involve something like cohesion.) And, finally, object control does not suffice to define syntactic relations as distinct from their morphological marking.[12]

REFERENCES

Babby, L. H. and R. D. Brecht (1975) "The Syntax of Voice in Russian," *Language* 51, 342–367.

[12] I am grateful to Alan Timberlake, Igor Mel'čuk, and Farrell Ackerman for comments on this paper.

Chvany, C. V. (1975) *On the Syntax of BE-sentences in Russian,* Slavica, Cambridge, Massachusetts.
Comrie, B. (1974) "The Second Dative: A Transformational Approach," in R. Brecht and C. Chvany, eds., *Slavic Transformational Syntax* (Michigan Slavic Materials 10), University of Michigan, Ann Arbor.
Hopper, P. and S. Thompson (1980) "Transitivity in Grammar and Discourse," *Language* 56, 251–299.
Iomdin, L. L. and N. V. Percov (1975) "Fragment Modeli Russkogo Poverxnostnogo Sintaksisa, II: Kompletivnye i Prisvjazočnye Konstrukcii," *Naučno-Texničeskaja Informacija,* ser. 2, 22–32.
Mel'čuk, I. A. (1974) Opyt Teorii lingvističeskix Modelej "Smysl ⇔ Tekst," Nauka, Moscow.
Mel'čuk, I. A. (1979) *Studies in Dependency Syntax* (Linguistica Extranea: Studia 2), Karoma, Ann Arbor.
Nichols, J. (1979) "Subjects and Controllers in Russian," in *Papers from the Fifteenth Regional Meeting of the Chicago Linguistic Society,* Chicago Linguistics Society, University of Chicago.
Nichols, J. (1981) *Predicate Nominals: A Partial Surface Syntax of Russian.* (University of California Publications in Linguistics 97), University of California Press, Berkeley–Los Angeles.
Nichols, J., G. Rappaport, and A. Timberlake (1980) "Subject, Topic, and Control in Russian," in *Proceedings of the Sixth Annual Meeting of the Berkeley Linguistics Society,* Department of Linguistics, University of California, Berkeley.
Rappaport, G. (1979) *Detachment and Adverbial Participle Clauses in Russian,* unpublished doctoral dissertation, University of California, Los Angeles.
Rappaport, G. (1980) "Deixis and Detachment in the Adverbial Participles in Russian," in R. Brecht and C. Chvany, eds., *Morphosyntax in Slavic,* Slavica, Columbus, Ohio.
Sidorov, V. and I. Il'inskaja (1949) "K Voprosu o Vyraženii Sub''ekta i Ob''ekta Dejstvija v Sovremennom Russkom Jazyke, Izvestija AN SSSR, *Otd. lit. i jaz.,* VIII:4.
Tesnière, L. (1965) *Eléments de Syntaxe Structurale,* Klincksieck, Paris.
Timberlake, A. (1975) "Hierarchies in the Genitive of Negation," *Slavic and East European Journal* 19, 123–138.
Timberlake, A. (1979) "Reflexivization and the Cycle in Russian," *Linguistic Inquiry* 10, 109–141.
Timberlake, A. (1980a) "Oblique Control of Russian Reflexivization," in R. Brecht and C. Chvany, eds., *Morphosyntax in Slavic,* Slavica, Columbus, Ohio.
Timberlake, A. (1980b) "Reference Conditions on Russian Reflexivization," *Language* 56, 777–796.
Timberlake, A. (1981) "Objects as Controllers (Russian Reflexivization)," unpublished paper, University of California, Los Angeles.
Timberlake, A. (1982) "Invariance and the Syntax of Russian Aspect," in P. Hopper, ed., *Tense–Aspect: Between Semantics and Pragmatics,* Benjamins, Amsterdam, The Netherlands.

CHICKASAW AGREEMENT MORPHOLOGY: A FUNCTIONAL EXPLANATION

DORIS L. PAYNE

Chickasaw, a Muskogean language spoken in Oklahoma and parts of the southeastern United States, has a rich system of agreement affixes that show the person and number of verbal arguments and possessors of items.[1] The purpose of this paper is to discuss the forms and uses of the different nonnegative agreement affix sets and to show that the use of an affix from one set rather than another can be explained by the concept of "transitivity" as outlined in Hopper and Thompson (1980), and by the concept of "involvement." I will argue that the affix sets *e* form a hierarchy such that the agent (ag) set indicates a higher degree of transitivity in a clause than does the patient (p) set, while the patient set indicates a higher degree of transitivity and/or involvement than does the dative (d) set. Although in general these affix sets do correlate closely with the semantic role of the arguments in a given clause, there are

---

[1] Abbreviations used in this paper are as follows: agentive agreement affix (ag), comitative (com), complementizer on subordinate clause (comp), dative agreement affix (d), different reference (dr), nonsubject argument (ns), patient agreement affix (p), same reference (sr), subject argument (sub), topic of contrast (top).

351

exceptions with particular verbs and it should be kept in mind that by use of the terms "agent," "patient," and "dative" I am primarily referring to the morphological affixes and only secondarily to any semantic meaning they might carry.

By way of introduction, it may be helpful to note that Chickasaw is an SOV language[2] which has a nominative–accusative case-marking system for free noun phrases. In contrast to the agreement affixes, this case system is primarily sensitive to syntactic, rather than semantic, categories. Subjects (sub) are marked with *-at* or *-t* on the final element in the noun phrase under consideration. Nonsubjects (ns) (either direct objects, indirect objects, or obliques) are either unmarked, indicated by *-ak*, or indicated by *-ā* (or simply nasalization on vowel-final verbs). Whether a nonsubject nominal is marked or unmarked seems to be dependent on discourse considerations which are beyond the scope of this paper.

(1)   *Hattak yamm-at malili.*
        man   that-sub run
        'That man runs'.

(2)   Larry-*at*   *sa-shki'*   *pīs-tok.*
                -sub 1sg$_P$-mother see-past
        Larry-at sa-shki'-ā pīs-tok.
                        -ns
        'Larry saw my mother'.

The case marking is homophonous with the most widely used set of switch-reference morphemes, which uses a *-t* to indicate same reference (sr) and nasalization on a final vowel to indicate different reference (dr) (Payne, 1980).

In discussing the agreement affixes it will be helpful to refer to the three basic semantico-syntactic relations that an argument may have to a verb. These relations will be referred to as A, S, and O, following Dixon (1979). The symbol A stands for the participant in a two-argument clause which is the most agent-like in terms of animacy and control of the action of the verb; S stands for the single argument in an intransitive clause. Together, A and S constitute the category "subject" in Chickasaw; both are marked with the subject case marking *-at*.[3] Finally, O

---

[2] In some elicited sentences, object complements and, rarely, object noun phrases follow the verb. In textual material, however, such variant clause orders are quite rare. The discourse function(s) of such orders have not yet been ascertained.

[3] A possessor of an (original) A or S participant may be "raised" and marked with *-at* in addition to or instead of the (original) A/S participant. When the possessor is so marked it functions as the syntactic subject of the clause   (Gordon 1979; Munro and Gordon, (1982). This construction is discussed further in what follows.

stands for the participant in a two-argument clause which is most patient-like in terms of receiving the action of the verb. An O may be marked with the nonsubject case marking.

In Chickasaw, the presence, person, and number of an A or S nominal in a clause is indicated on the verb by an affix from either the agent (ag), patient (p), or dative (d) paradigms. The presence, person, and number of an O nominal in a clause may be indicated by an affix from either the patient or dative paradigms, although under certain circumstances (discussed in what follows) the presence of an O will be unmarked. It should also be noted that in the agent and patient paradigms third person is generally unmarked.[4] The presence of locative, comitative, and instrument obliques in a clause may be marked on the verb by distinct affixes, but the person and number of these nominals (when not third person) are indicated by the patient affixes. For terminological simplicity, in this paper I will use the term "nominal" to mean either an agreement affix or any noun or noun phrase in the construction which may or may not be coreferential with such an affix.

The organization of the paper is as follows. Presented first are the construction types in which the agreement affixes are used and their morphological forms. The discussion then turns to the transitivity and functional differences correlated with the use of one set of affixes rather than another. Finally, some suggestions are presented regarding the relationship between "involvement" and "transitivity."

1. CHICKASAW AGREEMENT AFFIXES

1.1. Agent Affixes

Agent affixes are used only to refer to the syntactic subject of a verb. In most cases they refer to a participant which is the potentially volitional instigator of the action of the verb. This includes virtually all A nominals and volitional S nominals.[5]

(3)   *Has-sa-shoo-tok.*
      2pl$_{AG}$-1sg$_{P}$-hug-past
      A
      'You all hugged me'.

---

[4] Third person plural subject in all three paradigms may be indicated by the affix *hoo-*, but the conditions under which this is required are unclear (Munro and Gordon, 1982).

[5] There are a few verbs that do not use the agent affixes to refer to what might be thought of as the agent participant. These are discussed in what follows.

(4)   *Hash*-*malili-tok.*
        2pl_{AG}-run-past
        S
        'You all ran'.

(5)   *Chokma-li.*
        good-**1sg**_{AG}
        S
        'I act good'.

There are some exceptional verbal roots which consistently require the agent affixes and for which it is difficult to see any possibility of volitional control on the part of the participant so indicated. This set of verbs includes quantifiers such as numbers, *mooma* 'be many/all', *fokha'si* 'only about (some amount)', and a few verbs like *īla* 'different/strange'.[6]

1.2. Patient Affixes

Patient affixes are used in four different situations. First, they mark the majority of S nominals which are less likely to be seen as potentially volitional instigators of the action or state expressed by the verb than would those participants referred to by agent affixes. In many cases, the state expressed by the verb can be seen as a predominant, if not permanent, characteristic of the S, or some characteristic that could be seen as involving the participant completely. [In verbs beginning with the vowel *a*, as in examples (7) and (9), the patient affix is infixed after the *a*.]

(6)   *Sa*-*chokma.*
        1sg_P-good
        'I'm good'.

(7)   A*sa*biika.
        1sg_P sick
        'I'm sick'.

(8)   *Sa*-lhinko   minna-ttook.
        1sg_P-fat   habitual-distant(past)
        'I used to be fat'.

---

[6] The number of such nonvolitional verbs which require agent affixes is small, and although they do not directly support the transitivity claims to be made in this paper, neither do they stand as counterexamples to these claims. For some such verbs there appear to be historical reasons for their taking the agent affixes, such as frozen reflexive or reciprocal affixes (Munro and Gordon, 1982).

(9)   *Asokchãã.*
        1sg_P alive
        'I'm alive'.

(10)   *Chikashsha   sa-ya.*
        Chickasaw   1sg_P-be
        'I'm a Chickasaw'.

Secondly, patient affixes are used to mark Os which are directly affected by the action of the verb, which are highly involved in the action of the verb, or where the action is aimed directly at the O.

(11)   *Is-sa-shõ'ka.*
        2sg_AG-1sg_P-kiss
        'You kiss me'.

(12)   *Hash-po-pĩs-tok.*
        2sg_AG-1pl_P-see-past
        'You all saw us'.

(13)   *An-chipota-t   sa-sipokni-chi.*
        1sg_D-child-sub   1sg_P-old-cause
        'My child is making me old'.

In examples such as the following one, the presence of a comitative (com) nominal is indicated by *iba* (or *ba*) but the person and number of this nominal are indicated by a patient affix. Clearly, the comitative participant is as equally involved in the action of the verb as is the agent participant:

(14)   *Chi-ba-nowa-l-a'chi.*
        2sg_P-com-walk-1sg_AG-future
        'I'm going to walk with you'.

At this point it is possible to observe that Chickasaw is one of those languages known as "fluid" S languages (Dixon 1979). The agreement marking for certain intransitive verbs is "fluid" in that the single participant may be marked either like an A or an O, depending on the meaning to be conveyed [cf. (5) and (6)]. Note, however, that the marking for many intransitive verbs is fixed in Chickasaw, where the single participant can only be marked like the O of a transitive verb [compare (7)–(10) with (11)–(14)], or like the A of a transitive verb [cf. (3) and (4)].

Third, patient affixes are used on nouns that are inalienably possessed to show the person and number of the possessor. (There are some kinship

terms and body parts which exceptionally take the dative affixes used
to show alienable possession.)

(15)   *sa-haknip*   'my body'
         1sg$_P$-body

         sa-shki'   'my mother'
         1sg$_P$-mother

         sa-holba'   'my picture' (i.e., a picture of me)
         1sg$_P$-picture

         sa-holhchifo   'my name'
         1sg$_P$-name

Finally, patient affixes can be used to mark the A of some nonvolitional
two-argument verbs such as *nokfonkha* 'remember'. We will return to
this use of patient affixes in what follows.

1.3. Dative Affixes

Dative affixes function like the patient affixes in that they are used to
mark Os of transitive verbs, Ss of intransitives, are used on nouns to
show possession, and mark the As of (very few) nonvolitional two-
argument verbs. In addition, dative affixes are used on verbs to show
the person and number of "raised" possessors.

For some verbs that always require dative rather than patient affixes
to refer to Ss, it is difficult to see any clear semantic distinction (e.g.,
in terms of permanency) between patient and dative verbs. For instance,
compare the following with (7) and (8), given earlier:

(16)   *An-tako'bi.*
         1sg$_D$-lazy
         'I'm lazy'.

(17)   *An-chokm-ishto.*
         1sg$_D$-good-big
         'I'm healthy'.

For other verbs that require dative affixes, however, the verb can
more easily be interpreted as describing a temporary or nonpredominant
characteristic of the S.

(18)   *Am-alhtaha.*
         1sg$_D$-ready
         'I'm ready'.

(19)   *Sa-sipokni **am**-ahoba-tok.*
         1sg$_P$-old   1sg$_D$-appear-past
         'I felt old'.

(20)   *Am**-āālhi.*
         1sg$_D$-tired
         'I'm tired/worn out'.

(21)   *An**-chokma.*
         1sg$_D$-good
         'I feel good'.

Comparison of (21) with (6) clearly shows the less permanent/more permanent distinction conveyed by use of dative versus patient affixes.

The use of dative affixes on verbs may also correlate with the idea of possession on the part of the participant indicated. Munro and Gordon (1982) discuss a very interesting and productive process which they term "Possessor Raising." In this construction a possessor may be marked with the subject-marking -*at* in addition to or instead of the possessed item. Often, the verb is then marked with a dative affix agreeing with the possessor (in Munro and Gordon's terms, "III-Subjectivalization"). These two processes relate sentences like (22a) and (22b).

(22)   a.   *Jan ipāshi'-at   tapa.*
            hair-   sub be cut
            'Jan's hair was cut/Jan got a haircut'.
       b.   *Jan-at   ipashi'-(at) in-tapa.*
            -sub hair-(sub)   3$_D$-be cut
            'Jan got a haircut'.

Consider now the following examples which show that the participants referred to by dative affixes in this type of construction must be considered the subjects.

(23)   *Ala-**li**-ttook.*
         come-1sg$_{AG}$-distant(past)
         'I was born'.

(24)   a.   *Chipota-t **am**-al-a'chi.*
            child-sub 1sg$_D$-come-future
            'I'm going to have a baby'.
       b.   *Doris-**at**   chipota-(t) **im**-al-a'chi.*
            -sub child-(sub) 3$_D$-come-future
            'Doris is going to have a baby'.

In (23) the person who was born and who is referred to by the agent affix must be interpreted as the subject. (Note also that *ala* 'come' is not a passive verb form and therefore the agent-marked participant could not be thought of as a "derived" subject.) In (24a)–(24b), then, we might expect *chipota* 'child' to be the subject as this is similarly the participant to be born. There is good evidence, however, that the possessors of *chipota*, that is, those participants referred to by the dative affixes, must be considered the subjects here. First, it is the possessor (when not simply pronominal) which must be marked with the subject case marking *-at*. The possessed item *chipota* can be either marked or unmarked. Further, there is good evidence from the switch-reference system that *Doris* in (24b) functions as the syntactic subject in that this nominal will control switch-reference marking whereas *chipota* will not (for details, see Gordon 1979; Munro and Gordon 1982; Payne 1980). Similarly, *Jan* in (22b) can be proved to be the syntactic subject of that clause.

In sum, the two related processes of possessor raising and marking the verb with a dative prefix which agrees with the possessor give prominence to the (typically human) possessor by bringing it into a grammatical relationship with the verb and giving it subject status. The failure to use agent affixes to refer to these "raised" possessors is consistent with the fact that these subjects do not volitionally control the action of the verb. In other words, this suggests that a defining characteristic of dative affixes is that (like patient affixes) they may be used to mark nonvolitional subject nominals.

In addition to marking of subject nominals, dative affixes are used to mark O nominals that are less directly affected by the action of the verb than those Os marked with patient affixes. Thus, they encode recipients, benefactives, goals, etc. (i.e., "indirect objects").

(25)   *Am-ambi-tok.*
         1sg$_D$-kill-past
         'He killed it for me'.

(26)   *Chim-a-li-tok.*
         2sg$_D$-give-1sg$_{AG}$-past
         'I gave it to you'.

(27)   *In-nokshoopo-li.*
         3$_D$-afraid-1sg$_{AG}$
         'I'm afraid of him'.

(28)   *Is-sam-ollaha'li.*
         2sg$_{AG}$-1sg$_D$-smile
         'You're smiling at me'.

Finally, dative affixes are used on nouns to show alienable possession.

(29)   *im-amboha*   'his house'
        3$_D$-house
        Tom im-ofi'   'Tom's dog'
           3$_D$-dog
        ã-holba'   'my picture' (i.e., a picture
        1$_D$-picture   that I own, but not of me)

Later in this paper I return to a discussion of the functional unity between the use of dative affixes to indicate both possession and noun–verb predication, and try to suggest some explanation for use of the same affixes to indicate both relationships.

The forms of the nonnegative agreement affixes are listed in the following chart.[7]

Nonnegative Agreement Affix Paradigms

	Agent	Patient	Dative
1singular	*-li*	*sa-*	*am-, sam-/* C—
2singular	*ish-, is-/* —*s*	*chi-*	*chim-*
3singular	∅	∅	*im-*
1plural	*(k)il-, (k)ii-/* —C	*po-*	*pom-*
2plural	*hash-, has-/* —*s*	*hachchi-*	*hachchim-*
3plural	∅	∅	*im-*

Note: Our Chickasaw consultant sometimes used the first person plural forms *(k)il(o)-, hapo-,* and *hapom-* when she wished to emphasize that more than two or three people were involved in the action. The forms given in the chart, however, are more frequently used for simply "plural". The dative affixes lose the nasal before continuants, resulting in a nasalized vowel. Before noncontinuants the nasal assimilates in point of articulation.

[7] Different sets of agreement affixes are used when the verb is negated, but I will not be discussing these except to note their morphological forms here. If the verb in the nonnegative form takes an agent affix, that affix is replaced by a negative (n) agreement affix: *ak-* (1sg), *chik-* (2sg), *ik-* (3sg), *(k)il-/(k)ii-* (1dual/plural), *(k)il(o)-* (1pl), *hachchik-* (2pl), *ik-* (3pl). In addition, a glottal stop is infixed after the penultimate vowel of the verb root, and the final vowel of the root is replaced by *o; ki* or *k* is infixed before any tense marker: *Ak-mali'lo-ka'chi* (1sg$_N$-run:neg-future:neg) 'I won't run'.

If the nonnegative form of the verb takes a patient or dative affix to refer to the subject, the regular patient/dative affix is retained but the third person negative affix *ik-* is prefixed to it: *ik-sa-llo* (3$_N$-1sg$_P$-die:neg) 'I didn't die', *ik-chim-alhkani'yo* (3$_N$-2sg$_D$-forget:neg) 'you don't forget'.

2. THE USE OF AGREEMENT AFFIXES AS A FUNCTION
OF TRANSITIVITY AND INVOLVEMENT

In this section I would like to explore the hypothesis that the three sets of nonnegative agreement affixes form the following hierarchy such that choice of an affix from higher on the hierarchy is correlated with some increase in the transitivity of the clause.[8]

(30)   Agent > Patient > Dative

The definition of "transitivity" used here is that of Hopper and Thompson (1980) who loosely define transitivity as the "carrying over" or transferring of an action from the semantic agent to the semantic patient. More precisely, transitivity is seen as a number of (partially independent) components which are concerned with different aspects of the effectiveness or intensity with which the action is carried out. (See the Introduction to this volume for a statement of the Transitivity Hypothesis and a list of the ten components.)

Hopper and Thompson hypothesize that, given any two clauses in a language, if clause A is higher in transitivity with regard to one of these components than clause B, then any concomitant difference between the two clauses with respect to some other component will also show clause A to be higher in transitivity. My purpose here is not to directly argue for or against Hopper and Thompson's Transitivity Hypothesis (which they have already substantiated from a variety of languages); rather I will take their components more or less as given and attempt to show for Chickasaw that, overall, the use of one set of affixes rather than another can be explained in terms of the hierarchy proposed in (30). Those transitivity components which correlate with use of one set of affixes over another in Chickasaw include number of participants, kinesis, volitionality, individuation of O, and affectedness of O.

2.1. Transitivity Features Concerned with the Verbal State
or Event and Verbal Valency

The first transitivity component concerns the valency of the verb or the number of participants (potentially) present in a clause. An increase in transitivity can be marked by an increase from one to two (or more) participants, in that action cannot be transferred unless there is more than one participant. The second component, kinesis, is concerned with

[8] Heath (1977) suggests this hierarchy as a basis for subject selection in Choctaw (in his terms, Actor > Patient > Dative).

whether the verb expresses a state or action and the intensity of the action. The transitivity of an active clause is greater than that of a stative clause in that actions can be carried over or transferred from one participant to another, whereas in a stative clause nothing is transferred from one participant to another. If the intensity of an action is greater in one clause than another, the transitivity is similarly increased in the first clause, in that an object is generally more completely affected by a more intense action.

In Chickasaw the transitivity of a clause can be increased with respect to both these components by addition of the causative morpheme -*chi*. In the following examples the (a) clauses contain the causative -*chi*, are active, and have two participants, whereas the (b) clauses lack -*chi*, are stative, and have only one participant. Thus, the (a) clauses are higher in transitivity than the (b) clauses. These differences in transitivity are correlated with the use of agent affixes to refer to the subjects of the (a) clauses but patient affixes to refer to the subjects of the (b) clauses. (Recall that third person patient is unmarked.)

(31) a. *Achiyoppa-**chi**-li.*
          $2sg_P$ happy-cause-$1sg_{AG}$
          'I speak to you (i.e., I'm on speaking terms with you)'.
      b. *Asayoppa.*
          $1sg_P$ happy/friendly
          'I'm happy/friendly'.

(32) a. *Himitta-**chi**-li.*
          new-cause-$1sg_{AG}$
          'I make it new'.
      b. *Sa-himitta.*
          $1sg_P$-new
          'I'm young'.

(33) a. *Tikahbi-**chi**-li.*
          tired-cause-$1sg_{AG}$
          'I make him tired'.
      b. *Tikahbi.*
          tired
          'He's tired'.

The "active" derivational morpheme -*li*[9] has the effect of increasing

[9] The function of this "active" morpheme is not to derive active verbs/clauses from (lexical) passives, though some translations might give this impression. There does not appear to be any highly productive way to derive passives in Chickasaw, though there are a good number of active–passive pairs.

kinesis by indicating:

1. Derivation of noun to verb: *anompa* versus 'language/word'
                                anompoli   'to talk'
2. Change from state to action: *taha*   versus 'to be finished'
                                 tahli   'to finish'

Like *-chi*, *-li* can also increase the valency of a verb. In this case an agent affix rather than a patient affix is used to mark the subject of the clause.

(34)   a. *Asayoppa.*
            1sg$_P$ happy/friendly.
            'I'm happy/friendly'.
        b. *Ayoppa-li-li.*
            happy-active-1sg$_{AG}$
            'I make him happy'.

Li can also indicate volitionality on the part of the subject, which, for a verb such as *lhatapa* 'spill', is correlated with the use of an agent, rather than a dative, affix.[10] The question of volitionality will be discussed more fully in the following section. (Third person agent is unmarked in the following examples.)

(35)   a. *Pam-at   okka' ī-lhatapa.*
                -sub water 3$_D$-spill
            'Pam spilled the water (by accident)/Pam's water spilled'.
        b. *Pam-at   okka' lhatab-li.*
                -sub water spill-active
            'Pam spilled/poured the water (on purpose)'.

In summary, the use of agent affixes is correlated with higher transitivity in terms of increased kinesis, an increase in number of participants or in volitionality. The use of patient and dative affixes correlates with lower transitivity in terms of these three parameters. This, then, supports the hypothesis in (30) that agent affixes rank higher than patient or dative affixes in terms of the transitivity of the clause.

[10] The verb agreement in examples like (35) may result from what Munro and Gordon (1982) term III-Subjectivalization, where *okka'* 'water' is the original subject, but the possessor *Pam* has been "raised" to this status and the verb is accordingly marked to agree with *Pam*. Because dative affixes are used with this construction, a volitional reading could not occur, prohibiting cooccurrence of the active *-li* suffix which indicates volitionality.

2.2. Transitivity Features Concerned with the A/S

Hopper and Thompson argue from a number of different languages that when an agent is presented as willfully performing some action, the effect of that action on the patient is likely to be more complete and thus the transitivity of the clause increased. Even if there is just one participant the action may be viewed as more transitive. As noted previously, greater volitionality on the part of a participant is correlated with use of agent rather than patient or dative affixes. This is true even when the clause may be "intransitive" in the sense of having only one possible participant. Compare, for instance, the following pairs.

(36) a. *Pilla-yamma-li-t   howita-li-tok.*
          on purpose-do-1sg$_{AG}$-sr throw up-1sg$_{AG}$-past
          'I threw up on purpose'.
      b. *Sa-howita.*
          1sg$_P$-throw up
          'I threw up (accidentally)'.

(37) a. *Alikch-ak ī-hotolhko-li.*
          doctor-ns 3$_D$-cough-1sg$_{AG}$
          'I coughed for the doctor'.
      b. *Sa-hotolhko.*
          1sg$_P$-cough
          'I coughed (accidentally)'.

The (b) sentences here were elicited in the context of the subject participant being sick and not being able to avoid the action. This is in contrast to the (a) sentences which are clearly purposeful on the part of the subject.

Some actions, such as falling, are not normally intentional and thus *ittola* 'fall' normally occurs with the patient prefix. If, however, the agent intentionally falls, the agent affix again occurs. Example (38b) could thus be used in the context of a baseball game where the agent intentionally dives for the base. Example (38c) is an imperative which presupposes that the agent has some control over the action she/he is commanded to do.

(38) a. *Sa-ttola.*
          1sg$_P$-fall
          'I fell (accidentally)'.
      b. *Ott-ittola-li-tok.*
          towards-fall-1sg$_{AG}$-past
          'I fell down (on purpose)'.

    c. *Ish-ittol-a'ni.*
       2sg$_{AG}$-fall-modal
       'Fall down!'

    As Hopper and Thompson point out, volitionality on the part of an agent is often closely correlated with the kinesis of the clause. Choice of agent affixes over patient or dative for some verbs signals not only a change in volitionality but also a change from a state to an action.[11] For example, compare (5) with (6) and (21), and also the following pair.

(39)   a. *Sa-sipokni **am**-ahoba-tok.*
          1sg$_P$-old   1sg$_D$-appear-past   (state)
          'I felt old'.
    b. *Ayoppa il-ahoba-**li**.*
          happy   reflexive-appear-1sg$_{AG}$ (action)
          'I act happy' (lit., 'I (make) myself appear happy').

    In addition to an alternation between agent and patient or dative affixes to refer to an S participant depending on the volitionality of the S, Chickasaw also shows alternations between nonvolitional Ss that are marked with patient and nonvolitional Ss that are marked with dative. This alternation and its possible explanation will be returned to following a discussion of transitivity features associated with Os.

2.3. Transitivity Features Concerned with the O

    One functional distinction between the use of patient versus dative affixes concerns the degree to which an O is affected by the action of the verb. Hopper and Thompson claim that the more completely an O (i.e., a potential semantic patient) is affected by an action, the more completely that action has been carried over to the O. Thus a clause in which a patient is more affected is higher in transitivity than a clause in which the patient is less affected.

    As noted earlier, dative affixes are used to mark benefactives, recipients, and goals. Patient affixes, on the other hand, mark participants that are more clearly the semantic patient or undergoer of an action. It is clear that semantic patients are in general more affected by the action

---

[11] This particular use of agent versus patient affixes to indicate the difference between an action and a state does not seem highly productive in Chickasaw. For example, *ayoppa-li* (happy-1sg$_{AG}$) and *himitta-li* (young-1sg$_{AG}$) are simply ungrammatical and do not mean 'I act happy' or 'I act young' respectively. To get these readings, a separate verb must be added and *ayoppa/himitta* may simply lack person affixes: *Ayoppa il-ahoba-li* (happy reflexive-appear-1sg$_{AG}$) 'I act happy'; *Himitta chiimi-li* (young act-1sg$_{AG}$) 'I act young'.

of a verb than are benefactives, recipients, or goals. The following examples show this distinction and the alternation between patient affixes to mark the more directly affected participant and dative affixes to mark the less directly affected participant. (The alternation in the verb root is phonologically predictable on the basis of changes in stress placement.)

(40)   a.   *Pit-**po**-pilachi-tok.*
           direction-1pl$_P$-send-past
           'He sent us (to someplace)'.
   b.   ***Pom**-pilash-tok.*
           1pl$_D$-send-past
           'He sent it to us'.

There are other examples where it is difficult to make a distinction between a semantic patient and anything like a recipient, goal, or benefactive, and yet the use of patient versus dative affixes can be well motivated by considering the differences in affectedness of the O.[12] For example, compare (41) with (42)–(43).

(41)   *Chihow-at **sa**-kbi-tok.*
      God-sub   1sg$_P$-make-past
      'God made me'.

(42)   *Sa-shk-at   ā-hollo.*
      1sg$_P$-mother-sub 1sg$_D$-love
      'My mother loves me'.

(43)   ***Chī**-yimmi-li.*
      2sg$_D$-trust-1sg$_{AG}$
      'I believe/trust you'.

In (41) the first person participant is clearly affected by the action. Although the action of the verb is directed toward the first person participant in (42) and the second person participant in (43), its effect (if any) on the O is potentially much less than in (41). Note that the "ac-

---

[12] There are some examples involving alternations between patient and dative affixes where, at first glance, differences in potential affectedness might seem counter to this claim: for example, (a) *Am-aabachi* (1sg$_D$-teach) 'He's teaching me', versus (b) *Sa-pīsa* (1sg$_P$-see) 'He sees me'. Example (a) uses a dative affix to refer to the O whereas Example (b) uses a patient affix, and yet it might seem that the O in (a) would potentially be more affected by the action of the verb than the O in (b). It is not unreasonable, however, that examples like (a) should be read 'He is teaching (something) to me', where the expressed O is in fact viewed in a more oblique relation to the verbal action itself than is the O in example (b). In other words, this could be the (very regular) usage of dative affixes to mark "indirect objects" such as benefactives, recipients, and goals.

tions" in (42)–(43) are very low in kinesis compared to the idea of "making," and thus we would expect the O to be less affected.

Dative affixes are consistently used in comparatives where there is clearly no effect on the O, as for example in:

(44)   *Abika-ka-t   am-mayya.*
       sick-comp-sr 1sg_D-ahead of
       'She is sicker than me'.

Compare now the following pair of clauses. Both are high in kinesis and both involve the same root *abi* 'kill'; yet an alternation between use of patient and dative affixes occurs. (The *m* in *ambi* is phonologically predictable and is not a morphological change.)

(45)   a.   *Is-sa-bi-tok.*
            2sg_AG-1sg_P-kill-past
            'You killed me'.
       b.   *Bonnie-at   am-ambi-tok.*
            -sub 1sg_D-kill-past
            'Bonnie beat me (e.g., in a race)'.

In Chickasaw the idea of 'beat' or 'win' is expressed by the same root as 'kill', but the dative prefix must be used. It seems reasonable that the patient or O is more completely affected if it is killed than if it has been outdone in a contest of some type such as a race. Again, the use of the patient affix is correlated with the more fully affected O.

There are other pairs of examples which are low in kinesis and where the alternation between patient and dative can again be motivated by the degree of affectedness or involvement in the verbal action attributed to the O.

(46)   a.   *Asanokfilli.*
            1sg_P think
            'He's thinking about me'.
       b.   *Am-anokfilli.*
            1sg_D-think
            'He's thinking for me (i.e., so I don't have to think)'.

Although no participant is physically affected in either of these clauses, it is clear that in (46a) the O is the actual object of thinking, that is, the participant which directly undergoes thought, whereas in (46b) the O participant does not undergo the action of the verb. Further, in (46a) the O is more highly integral or involved in the verbal idea that in (46b) in that one cannot think without thinking about something or someone, whereas thinking for someone is unnecessary to the act of thinking itself.

2.4. Cooccurrence of Agreement Affixes

With regard to marking of nominals on the verb, Chickasaw has two restrictions. First, person and number of no more than two nominals may actually be marked on any one verb. Second, two patients, two datives, or a patient and dative both may not occur on any one verb. An apparent implication following from these two restrictions is that whenever there is more than one argument in a clause, one of these arguments must be referred to by an agent affix. This, in fact, is true for the vast majority of cases.

There is, however, a small group of verbs which at first glance look like exceptions to these generalizations in that they appear to be able to take both an A and an O and yet no nominal is cross-referenced on the verb by an agent affix. What looks like the A nominal in such a clause is rather referred to by either a patient or dative affix and the O nominal is simply unmarked. This group of verbs includes *alhkaniya* 'forget', *nokfonkha/nokfoyyokha* 'remember', *yimmi* 'believe', and *banna* 'want'. *Alhkaniya* 'forget' normally takes the dative affix to refer to what might be thought of as the A participant while the other verbs normally use the patient set of affixes for the same purpose.[13]

The seemingly idiosyncratic behavior of these verbs can be described in terms of three of the transitivity components which Hopper and Thompson suggest, namely volitionality of the A, kinesis of the verbal action, and individuation of the O. The degree of "individuation" of an O is the degree to which it stands out as different from the agent and from its own background. A participant that is referred to by a noun that is proper, human or animate, concrete, singular, count, referential, and/or definite is more highly individuated than is a participant that is referred to by a common, inanimate, abstract, plural, mass, and/or non-referential noun (Timberlake 1977; Hopper and Thompson 1980). With regard to transitivity, Hopper and Thompson suggest that an action is more effectively carried over to a more highly individuated patient than

---

[13] Etymologically, *alhkaniya* 'forget' is a passive of *kaniya* 'go away/lose' which can only take a dative O, as in *Ofi'-at an-kaniya* (dog-sub 1sg$_D$-go:away) 'I lost my dog/The dog is gone from me'. Thus, it seems reasonable that the "derived" subject (the former O) of *alhkaniya* would be referred to by a dative affix. There is no evidence that the other verbs discussed in this section should be considered passives.

one that is less individuated, and thus a definite O, for example, is often viewed as more completely affected than an indefinite one.

The verbs mentioned above take subjects that are relatively low in volitionality, are nonkinetic, and further, are of the sort that can take clausal complements as their O.[14] The clausal complements are extremely low in individuation in that they refer to an event or state and not to a concrete object.

(47)   *Ish-ollali-kā*   ***sa-nokfonkha.***
       $2sg_{AG}$-smile-comp(dr) $1sg_P$-remember
       'I remember your smile' (lit., 'You smile, I remember it'.)

(48)   *Doris-at   nann-aachi-kā*   ***sa-yimmi.***
       -sub something-say-comp(dr) $1sg_P$-believe
       'I believe what Doris says'.

(49)   *Yamm-ako-t ay-a'ni   ik-**sa-banno**.*
       that-top-sr   go-modal 3_N-$1sg_P$-want(neg)
       'I don't want him to go'.

(50)   ***Am-alhkaniya**-tok kii-yamish-to-kā.*
       $1sg_D$-forget-past $1pl_{AG}$-do-past-comp(dr)
       'I forgot we did it'.

It appears that because of their low volitionality and kinesis and the fact that they do take clausal complements, the morphology that is used to mark nonvolitional subjects of single-argument verbs has become gram-maticized for these verbs. That is, they require patient or dative affixes to refer to the S/A. Even in imperative mood, the agreement marking does not change:

(51)   ***Chi-nokfoyyakh**-a'shki!*
       $2sg_P$-remember-imperative
       'You remember that!'

(52)   ***Chim-alhkaniy**-a'shki!*
       $2sg_D$-forget-imperative
       'Forget it!'

It could be argued that the clausal complements in Examples (47)–(50) are not really "Os" and, therefore, these really are single-argument verbs. Interestingly, however, they can take third persons as their Os—

---

[14] It must be noted that there are many verbs such as *ithaana* 'know', *pīsa* 'see', etc., which can take clausal complements but which have grammaticized the agent affixes to refer to their A/S argument.

that is, just those persons for which there is no verbal affix in the patient paradigm:

(53)   *Am-alhkaniya holhchifoh-ā.*
       1sg$_D$-forget   name-ns
       'I forgot her name'.

(54)   *An-nani'-ak hachchi-banna.*
       1sg$_D$-fish-ns 2pl$_P$-want
       'You all want my fish'.

Here, there is no way to plausibly argue for second clauses which contain the Os, and there are clearly two nominals in the clauses, as evidenced by the free noun phrases and the noncoreferential verbal agreement affixes. A possible explanation for the lack of marking in examples like these would be that the free noun phrases simply are not arguments of the verb and thus do not merit cross-referencing on the verb. Sandra Thompson (personal communication) has observed that this alternative is unlikely for examples (53) and (54) given the degree of individuation that these definite Os have. Thus, it appears that the restriction is against using more than one patient or dative affix on a given verb—not against how many arguments these particular verbs may take.

Similar behavior is evidenced by some three-argument verbs such as *ima* 'give' (which cannot occur without a dative affix). Here, two Os may cooccur provided that the most highly affected O (which would otherwise elicit a patient affix) is a nonhuman third person and therefore cannot be marked on the verb:

(55)   *Pam-ā   an-to'wa' ima-li-tok.*
       -ns 1sg$_D$-ball 3$_D$ give-1sg$_{AG}$-past
       'I gave my ball to Pam'.

It is impossible to express something like 'I gave you to him', where the O is human.

Similarly, two obliques or a dative and an oblique may cooccur in a clause only if the oblique is third person and therefore cannot be marked for person and number by the patient affixes.

(56)   *Pam-ā   aboha' ano'ka' yamm-akō aa-im-anompoli-li-tok.*
       -ns house inside   that-top:ns loc-3$_D$-talk-1sg$_{AG}$-past
       'I talked to Pam in the house'.

(57)   *Jan-ā   aboha' ano'k-akō   aa-iba-chokoshkomo-li.*
       -ns house inside-top:ns loc-com-play-1sg$_{AG}$
       'I'm playing with Jan in the house'.

The most highly individuated type of O would be a human participant, particularly when first or second person. For these verbs which typically use a patient or dative affix to mark the A/S participant, two strategies can be used when the O is human. Commonly, the circuitous route is taken in which the O will be expressed as part of an entirely separate proposition and the marking on the higher verb will remain the same. This neatly avoids the problem of how to mark the two nominals on a single verb, both of which should be referred to by patient and/or dative affixes.

(58)   *Am-alhkani'ya-cha aya-li-tok   ish-hikki'ya-kā.*
       1sg$_D$-forget-and:sr go-1sg$_{AG}$-past 2sg$_{AG}$-stand-comp(dr)
       'I forgot you' (lit., 'I forgot and went away while you
          stood there'.)

       *Achilhkaniya-li. / **Am-achilhkaniya.*
       2sg$_P$ forget-1sg$_{AG}$ 1sg$_D$-2sg$_P$ forget
       'I forget you'.

(59)   *Chi-pīs-li-to-ka-t*   *sa-nokfoyyakha-ka-t*   *immo'ma.*
       2sg$_P$-see-1sg$_{AG}$-past-comp-sr 1sg$_P$-remember-comp-sr still
       'I still remember you' (lit., 'I still remember I saw you'.)

       *Chi-nokfoyyakha-li / **Chi-sa-nokfoyyakha.*
       2sg$_P$-remember-1sg$_{AG}$ 2sg$_P$-1sg$_P$-remember
       'I remember you'.

A second strategy for some verbs when the O is human is to "promote" the A participant and refer to it by means of an agent affix, while using the dative affix to refer to the O.

(60)   *Chī-yimmi-li.*
       2sg$_D$-believe-1sg$_{AG}$
       'I believe you'.

Here, both of the nominals trigger agreement for person and number. Thus, the clause formally becomes a transitive clause in which the O is not highly affected. In other words, the clause is midway in transitivity between a clause that has two arguments, referred to by agent and patient affixes, and a clause that has only one argument, referred to by a patient or dative affix.

There are other verbs which can take a human O only if the clause is reflexive or reciprocal in nature. Hopper and Thompson (1980) describe reflexive and reciprocal actions as being relatively lower in transitivity than otherwise identical nonreflexives/reciprocals in that the O in these cases is not highly individuated from the A. In Chickasaw, this lower degree of transitivity again correlates with the use of dative prefixes to refer to the O (and/or A).

(61)   *Itt-im-alhkaniya-tok.*
         reciprocal-3$_D$-forget-past
         'They forgot each other'.

(62)   *Ili-m-alhkaniya-li-tok.*
         reflexive-$_D$-forget-1sg$_{AG}$-past
         'I forgot myself'.

The behavior of verbs like those in Examples (60)–(62) may demonstrate that there is some "fluidity" of marking for A nominals in Chickasaw, rather than just for S nominals.[15] That is, although the majority of As in Chickasaw are cross-referenced on the verb by agent affixes, for a few verbs where there is the semantic combination of low kinesis, low volitionality, and an O that is relatively low in individuation (or absent), the A is cross-referenced by a patient or dative affix. The language-specific restrictions on affix cooccurrence then require that when the A is thus referred to by a patient or dative affix, the O (if present) can only be a (nonhuman) third person which is perforce unmarked. These verbs can take agent affixes if and only if the O is a highly individuated human participant, in which case the O must be referred to by a dative affix. In sum, unlike the fluidity of marking for S nominals which correlates with a change in volitionality of the S, the choice between use of agent versus patient/dative affixes for marking the A of these (potentially) two-argument verbs correlates with a change in degree of individuation of the O.

2.5. The Functional Unity between Possession and Verbal Agreement

Thus far I have been concerned with describing the agreement marking system of Chickasaw and providing an explanation for the uses of and alternations between the agent, patient, and dative sets of affixes in terms of Hopper and Thompson's (1980) Transitivity Hypothesis. It has been shown that for marking A or S participants, agent affixes are correlated with features of higher transitivity than are patient or dative affixes, and that patient affixes correlate with features of higher transitivity for the marking of Os than do dative affixes. There remain, however, two situations in which both patient and dative affixes can be used, namely to

---

[15] This suggestion was made by Sandra Thompson.

mark nonvolitional S arguments and possessors of items. None of the transitivity components that Hopper and Thompson propose directly explains these alternations, and it is to these two situations that I now turn my attention. In the following discussion I will use the term "argument" to refer to either the possessor in a possessive construction or to the noun in a noun–verb relation; and the term "function" to refer to the possessed item in a possessive construction or to the verb in a noun–verb relation.[16]

There is, first of all, a great deal of cross-linguistic evidence that there is some unity of function between possessor–possessed and noun–verb relations in that languages frequently use the same devices or morphology to indicate both the person and number of arguments of the verb as they do to show person and number of the possessor of an item (cf. Allen 1964). Some languages use the same morphology for possession as they do for subjects (the A or S) of verbs—for example, Yagua (data from Powlison and Powlison 1978), and most languages of the Yuman family (Pam Munro, personal communication). Other languages use the same morphology for both objects (the O) and possession—for example, Pima (Pam Munro, personal communication). Still others use the same morphology to indicate possession as they do for both subjects and objects—for example, Chickasaw.

As a step toward explaining this similarity in morphology in communicative or functional terms, I would like to suggest that the argument in a construction is perceived and/or presented by the speaker as in some way being INVOLVED in or with the function of that construction. That is, the speaker presents the argument as being associated with or participating in the function. The argument can be involved in the instigation of an action or event, involved in the experiencing of an action, state, or abstract quality, or involved with a more concrete item in terms of possessing it. For example, in *John hit Bill, Bill,* the O, is involved in the experience or state of "being hit," while *John,* the A, is involved in the event of "hitting Bill." In *John fell, John,* the S, is presented as being involved in the state of having fallen and/or the event of falling

[16] This terminology is taken from Keenan and Faltz (1978). They discuss a number of constructions, including possessor–possessed and noun–verb relations, which are composed of arguments and functions. According to Keenan and Faltz, the logical unity underlying all argument–function relations is that the semantic interpretation and form of a function may vary depending on the choice of argument. They do not, however, suggest any unitary semantic or cognitive basis as to when or why the interpretation of one constituent in a construction will be dependent on another. Although the concept of "involvement" (discussed in what follows) could be claimed to motivate this dependency in Chickasaw, it does not appear that this concept could be associated with all the various constructions which Keenan and Faltz describe in terms of argument–function relationships.

(regardless of whether it was accidental or volitional). Similarly, in *John's dog* or *John's goodness, dog* and *goodness* are viewed as items and qualities which, in the speaker's view, John is claimed to have some involvement with. The concept of involvement thus stands as a unified semantic function behind all those cases where, in Chickasaw, agreement affixes are used, whether the affix refers to an S, A, O, or possessor.

2.6. The Functional Distinction between Patient and Dative Affixes

In preceding sections we have seen that volitional involvement for the most part characterizes those cases where agent affixes are used. The agent affixes are restricted to referring only to A and S nominals. Nonvolitional involvement for the most part covers all the uses of patient and dative affixes, whether they refer to an S, O, or possessor. A unified functional or semantic motivation differentiating all the uses of patient from dative affixes remains to be discussed. I would like to suggest that this distinction can be motivated in terms of MORE VERSUS LESS INVOLVE-MENT on the part of the argument indicated. If the degree of involvement is indeed the significant factor governing all the uses of patient versus dative affixes, then the following hypothesis should hold:

(63)   Given any two constructions J and K such that $J = jx$ and
         $K = ky$ where x and y are arguments of the functions j and k
         respectively, and j may or may not be identical with k, and
         such that there is a difference in degree of involvement
         between J and K,
         if x is referred to by a patient affix and y is referred to by
                a dative affix,
         then   there will be a higher degree of involvement between x
                and its function j in J than there will be between y and
                its function k in K.

It has already been shown that with regard to Os, use of patient versus dative affixes correlates with the degree to which the O is affected by the action of the verb. Differences in affectedness would be predicted by the concept of involvement in that the more highly involved an O is in an event (i.e., the more it is seen as somehow participating in the event), the more we can expect that O to be affected by the action of the event. More highly affected or involved Os are referred to by patient affixes, whereas less highly affected or involved Os are referred to by dative affixes. In the following subsections I will try to show that the hypothesis in (63) is also supported by the use of patient and dative affixes to refer to nonvolitional Ss and possessors.

A. ALIENABLE AND INALIENABLE POSSESSION

In addition to affectedness of an O, a difference in degree of involvement can be seen in the distinction languages sometimes make between alienable and inalienable possession. The relationship between kinship members or between a body part and the person to whom it belongs may often be viewed as so tight and permanent that the language has some special device to indicate the permanence of this relation. Sandra Thompson (personal communication) has noted that in one sense, a participant is highly involved with his body parts in that body parts are not highly distinguished from the possessor, that is, they are low in individuation relative to the possessor.

Chickasaw is a language that formally distinguishes between alienable and inalienable possession and, in line with the hypothesis in (63), we would predict that patient affixes should be used to indicate inalienable possession, whereas dative affixes should be used to indicate alienable possession. Chickasaw is, in fact, quite consistent in using the two sets of affixes in just these ways: Most body parts and kinship terms are marked with patient affixes [other items which are similarly inalienable include one's name and pictures of one's self—cf. the examples in (15)], and items which can be disowned consistently take the dative affixes [cf. the examples in (29)].[17]

B. PATIENT AND DATIVE AFFIXES USED TO MARK NONVOLITIONAL SUBJECTS

A third type of difference in degree of involvement concerns states, qualities, or nonvolitional actions which are attributed to participants. In *Tom is good,* "goodness" is seen as a more predominant or pervasive characteristic of Tom's personality than in *Tom feels good,* where "goodness" is likely to be interpreted as a more temporary or nonintegral characteristic. In other words, Tom is presented by the speaker as being more highly involved in the state or quality of "goodness" in the first case than in the second. The hypothesis in (63) predicts that instances of the second type will correlate with the use of dative affixes whereas instances of the first type will correlate with the use of patient affixes. Just these correspondences were, in fact, claimed earlier in the paper.

It was noted, however, that it is sometimes difficult to see any clear semantic difference in terms of pervasiveness or permanence between some stative verbs that consistently take dative affixes and some that

---

[17] There are exceptions to this generalization in that some supposedly inalienable kinship terms, such as 'father', and some body parts, are marked with dative affixes.

consistently take patient affixes. Even in terms of degree of involvement it is difficult to see much difference between *An-tako'bi* 'I'm lazy' versus *Sa-kostinni* 'I'm sober' or *Chi-haksi* 'You're drunk' (the latter two consistently take patient affixes whereas the first takes the dative affixes). The number of examples that evidence this seemingly unmotivated distinction between use of patient and dative affixes seems relatively small, however, and for now I will assume that it is dependent on some (synchronically) arbitrary lexical categorization.

The significant thing to note is that there are no examples that disprove the hypothesis in (63), that is, where use of a dative affix correlates with a *higher* degree of involvement than does a patient affix, whereas there are many examples that support it. As is shown by examples like (9) and (10), patient affixes do indicate states and characteristics that are viewed as basic or integral (if not permanent) to the participant. In contrast to such examples, dative affixes connote a lesser degree of involvement between the verbal idea and the S participant—compare, for example, (18)–(21) with (6)–(10). Example (18), *Am-alhtaha* 'I'm ready', does not imply that "readiness" is a basic or predominant characteristic of the subject, or that it is an integral characteristic of the participant's personality or physical make-up. It simply means that at a given point in time the participant is finished with whatever he/she may have been doing and is ready for whatever comes next. This correlates with use of the dative affix. Similarly, in (19), *Sasipokni am-ahobatok* 'I felt old', the speaker is not claiming that she/he is old but only that she/he felt that way (perhaps even temporarily). Thus, the degree of involvement is less. Example (20) *Am-āālhi* 'I'm tired/worn out' is perhaps less clear in that "worn out" implies the S is totally involved in that particular state, at least at the time of the utterance. Nevertheless, the dative affixes have been grammaticized for *āālhi* and this may be because in the norm "tiredness" is not a basic or predominant characteristic of persons, but is usually viewed as temporary and due to a hard day or some trying circumstances.

Finally, it was suggested that a dative affix may be used on a verb to refer to the possessor of that item about which the verb is making a predication. Patient affixes on verbs never have this function. It seems reasonable that if the verb is asserting something primarily about the possessed item but is just marked to agree with the possessor in order to give some type of pragmatic prominence to the possessor, the possessor's involvement in the verbal action or state itself is still less than that of the possessed item. This lesser degree of involvement in the verbal state or action provides a semantic explanation for the use of dative rather than patient affixes to refer to these "raised" possessors.

3. TRANSITIVITY AND INVOLVEMENT: CONCLUSIONS

This paper has been concerned with the forms and uses of agreement affixes in Chickasaw. We have seen that the concept of transitivity as outlined by Hopper and Thompson (1980) has been able to explain in a motivated way some of the uses of agent, patient, and dative affixes. In particular, higher kinesis and valency of the verb, greater volitionality on the part of the semantic agent, and for some verbs degree of individuation of the O correlate with the use of agent rather than patient or dative affixes to refer to A/S nominals. The use of patient versus dative affixes to refer to O nominals correlates with a higher degree of affectedness of the O. Thus, the hypothesis that agent affixes rank higher than patient or dative affixes and patient affixes rank higher than dative affixes in terms of the overall transitivity of the clause, is supported.

It does not appear, however, that any of the transitivity components that Hopper and Thompson propose directly account for the use of patient versus dative affixes to refer to nonvolitional Ss and possessors of items. Instead, it has been suggested that a higher degree of involvement between an argument and its function will correlate with use of a patient rather than dative affix. It has been argued, in fact, that the degree of involvement provides a unified semantic explanation for all the uses of patient versus dative affixes.

There are two questions which I would now like to very briefly address, though they cannot be pursued in detail here:

1. Can the use of agent versus patient/dative affixes also be explained in terms of degree of involvement?
2. Should involvement be considered another component of transitivity?

With regard to Question (1), it is not clear to me that the volitionality of a participant necessarily correlates with either higher or lower involvement in an action or state. Consider, for example, (32a)–(32b), where there is an alternation between agent and patient affixes with a corresponding change in volitionality on the part of the subject. Despite the higher volitionality, valency, and overall transitivity of (32a) *Him-ittachi-li* 'I make it new' in comparison with (32b) *Sa-himitta* 'I'm young', it is not clear to me that the first person singular participant is any more or less involved in the action of (32a) than in experiencing the state of (32b).[18]

---

[18] In a legal sense we may attribute more culpability to someone who acts volitionally (and with premeditation) than to someone who does not. But I do not think it necessarily follows that the nonvolitional actor is any less involved in the act than the volitional actor.

The second question, regarding the relationship between transitivity in general and an involvement parameter, is one that needs more discussion and research than can be pursued in this paper. Nevertheless, I would like to present the following suggestion.[19] There are certain semantic parallels between a high degree of involvement and a high degree of transitivity with regard to various of the components suggested by Hopper and Thompson. In particular, I have argued above that permanence can be one manifestation of a high degree of involvement, whereas transitoriness is a manifestation of a lower degree of involvement. Permanence has semantic correlations with perfective aspect, total affectedness, and individuation in that each of these deals with wholeness or completion in some sense: Permanence is concerned with wholeness of time; perfectivity indicates that an event is viewed in its entirety; a highly individuated participant is seen as a whole rather than in terms of its parts; and, of course, a participant can be wholly affected by an action. Nonpermanence or transitoriness, on the other hand, is semantically related to imperfectivity or ongoingness, partitivity, and partial affectedness. Thus, from a semantic viewpoint, a high degree of involvement would be expected to correlate with a high degree of transitivity. Insofar as the concept of transitivity could thus be shown to have an involvement parameter, transitivity would stand as a unified explanation behind the very interesting agreement affix system of Chickasaw.

ACKNOWLEDGMENTS

The data for this paper were gathered over a period of a year, partly in the context of a 1979 UCLA field methods class. The dialect of Chickasaw described is that of Catherine Willmond from Marshall County, Oklahoma. I would like to express my appreciation to Catherine for her patience and helpfulness and also to Pamela Munro and Sandra Thompson for their valuable suggestions and comments, though they may not agree with everything I have said.

REFERENCES

Allen, W. S. (1964) "Transitivity and Possession," *Language* 40, 337–343.
Dixon, R. M. W. (1979) "Ergativity," *Language* 55, 59–138.
Gordon, L. (1979) "Possessive constructions in Chickasaw," unpublished paper, University of California, Los Angeles.
Heath, J. (1977) "Choctaw Cases," in K. Whistler *et al.*, eds., *Proceedings of the Third Annual Meeting of the Berkeley Linguistics Society,* 204–213.

[19] Thanks are due to David Gil for this suggestion.

Hopper, P. and S. Thompson (1980) "Transitivity in Grammar and Discourse," *Language* 56, 251–299.

Keenan, E. L. and L. M. Faltz (1978) *Logical Types for Natural Language* (UCLA Occasional Papers in Linguistics, No. 3), University of California, Los Angeles.

Munro, P. and L. Gordon (1982) "Syntactic Relations in Western Muskogean: A Typological Perspective," *Language* 58.

Payne, D. (1980) "Switch-reference in Chickasaw," in P. Munro, ed., *Studies of Switch-reference* (UCLA Papers in Syntax, No. 8), University of California, Los Angeles.

Powlison, P. and E. G. Powlison (1978) "Yagua," in E. Loos, ed., *Materiales Para Estudios Fonológicos, Tomo II,* Ministerio de Educación (Perú), and Instituto Lingüístico de Verano, Lima.

Timberlake, A. (1977) "Reanalysis and Actualization in Syntactic Change," in C. Li, ed., *Mechanisms of Syntactic Change,* University of Texas Press, Austin.

SOME SEMANTIC ASPECTS OF *YI-* AND *BI-* IN SAN CARLOS APACHE

JOANNE SHAYNE

A phenomenon that some Athabaskan languages have in common is the occurrence of the verbal prefixes *yi-* and *bi-*, one or the other of which must appear in transitive verb sentences where two third persons interact. These prefixes apparently are pronouns that refer to one of the two nouns or pronouns in the sentence, and the question of what conditions the appearance of one versus the other has stirred particular controversy among investigators of Navajo, where the major concentration of work on this topic has been done. The present study examines the behavior of these prefixes in Western Apache—specifically, the dialect that is spoken on the San Carlos Reservation in Arizona.[1] It will be shown that the hypotheses put forth by the investigators of Navajo do not account for the Apache phenomenon, and an alternative approach will be proposed.

1. DESCRIPTIONS OF *YI-* AND *BI-* IN NAVAJO

Let us begin by looking at the verb itself. Edward Sapir and Harry Hoijer (1967) did an in-depth analysis of the structure of the Navajo verb

[1] Although little work has been published on this dialect of Western Apache, there are other reliable sources of data. Two of these are Goddard (1919) and Hill (1963), although neither was used in this study.

379

Syntax and Semantics, Volume 15

(this was preceded by Hoijer, 1945, in which the structure of the verb in all the Apachean[2] languages was shown to be the same) and identified 10 positions on the verb complex:[3]

1. adverbial prefixes (0, 1, or more)
2. iterative prefix
3. plural prefix
4. direct object prefix
5. deictic subject prefix
6. adverbial prefixes (0, 1, or 2)
7. mode, tense, or aspect prefix
8. subject prefix
9. classifier prefix
10. verb stem

One never finds all 10 positions filled on one verb, but those which do occur must do so in the order listed here. Positions 5 or 8 and position 9 are obligatorily filled but may appear as zero morphemes.[4]

Positions 4 (direct object), 5 (deictic subject), and 8 (subject), if they are filled at all, must be filled by pronominal prefixes. In the case of position 4, the prefixes generally have the same form as the independent pronouns, although there are some exceptions which will be noted as they become relevant. There is no variation between the subject and object forms of the independent pronouns. The Navajo and Apache independent pronoun forms are as follows:

Navajo		Apache	
shi	'I'	*shi*	'I'
ni	'you (sg.)'	*ni*	'you (sg.)',

[2] The Apachean languages are Navajo, Western Apache, Chiricahua, Mescalero, Kiowa-Apache, Jicarilla, and Lipan.

[3] Hoijer's original hypothesis (1945) suggested 14 positions on the verb complex, including an indirect object prefix and a postposition in positions 1 and 2 respectively (these were removed as free forms), a theme prefix in position 4 (later grouped with the adverbial prefixes), and separate positions for the tense and modal prefixes. Aspect was not included.

[4] I want to mention here that throughout this paper I have taken the liberty of breaking down the Navajo data in greater detail than did the linguists who originally presented it. I did this so that I might be able to indicate which positions are filled on a given verb complex, thus enabling the reader to see the object prefixes within their structural context. Each morpheme on each verb complex has been assigned a number according to the position list. In addition, I inserted zero morphemes into the transcriptions of the data so that these positions could be numbered. I am, therefore, fully responsible for any errors either in the literal translation of the Navajo material or in the insertion of zero morphemes. My translations appear in brackets.

bi	'he, she, it'	*bi*	'he, she, it'
		an[5]	'he, she'
ho	'he, she (indef.)'	*ki*	'he, she (indef.)'
nihi	'we'	$\left\{ \begin{array}{l} nohwi \\ nee \end{array} \right.$	'we'
nihi	'you (pl.)'	*nohwi*	'you (pl.)'
bi	'they'	*bi*	'they'
daaho	'they (indef.)'	*ki*	'they (indef.')'

Notice that *yi-* does not occur as an independent pronoun in either Navajo or Apache. The question that must be answered is, why does a prefix *yi-* appear where we would normally expect to find only *bi-*, given the fact that the object prefixes usually have the same form as the independent pronouns? In their analysis of Navajo, Sapir and Hoijer (1967) called *yi-* and *bi-* third person object markers and stated that they occur when the subject is also third person. If the subject is other than third person, the object prefix position (position 4) is filled by ∅ (Young and Morgan, 1943, give the same analysis). They provide the following Navajo examples:

(1) a. ∅-   dĭ-   š-∅-   tèèh.
         4   6   8 9   10

     [*him-incept-I-class-carry*]
     'I begin to carry him'.

   b. ∅-   dí-   ł-   tèèh.
       4   6,8   9   10

     [him-$\left\{ \begin{array}{l} incept \\ you \end{array} \right\}$-class-carry]
     'You begin to carry him'.

[in (1b), the subject 'you' appears as a high tone on the preceding morpheme, *di-*]

   c. *Yĭ-*   *dĭ-*   *∅- ł-*   *tèèh.*
       4   6   8 9   10

     [him-incept-he-class-carry]
     'He (A) begins to carry him (B)'.

   d. *Bĭ-*   *dĭ-*   *∅- ł-*   *tèèh*
       4   6   8 9   10

     [him-incept-he-class-carry]
     'He (B) begins to carry him (A)'.

[5] Apache *an* never appears as a prefix.

In order to better exemplify the difference between (1c) and (1d), they present phrases of the structure NV and phrases of the structure NNV. Compare (2a) with (2b) and (3a) with (3b):

(2)   a.   *Ꞌàškíí yĭ-   dĭ-   ∅- ł-   tèèh.
            4   6   8   9   10
          [boy   him-incept-he-class-carry]
          'He begins to carry the boy'.

      b.   *Ꞌàškíí bĭ   dĭ-   ∅- ł   tèèh.
            4   6   8   9   10
          [boy   him-incept-he-class-carry]
          'The boy begins to carry him'.

(3)   a.   *Dĭné àškíí yĭ-   dĭ-   ∅- ł-   tèèh.
            man boy 4   6   8   9   10
          [man boy   him-incept-he-class-carry]
          'The man begins to carry the boy'.

      b.   *Dĭné àškíí bĭ-   dĭ-   ∅- ł-   tèèh.
            man boy 4   6   8   9   10
          [man boy   him-incept-he-class-carry]
          'The boy begins to carry the man'.

These examples make it clear that where *yi-* occurs, the noun immediately before the verb is the object, and where *bi-* occurs, the noun immediately before the verb is the subject.[6]

This description does account for the given data, but it does not offer any explanation for the existence of two third person object markers that seem to be semantically equivalent. While we can see in Examples (2a) and (3a) that *yi-* indicates that the noun preceding the verb is the object, and in Examples (2b) and (3b) that the *bi-* indicates the noun preceding the verb is the subject, how are we to understand 'A' and 'B' in Examples (1c) and (1d)? Moreover, as we shall see, there are some Navajo transitive verb sentences that cannot be predicated by the Sapir–Hoijer analysis. It is this fact which led to the current controversy over the function of *yi-* versus *bi-*. The debate started when Kenneth Hale (1972) related the occurrence of *yi-* and *bi-* in Navajo to a process he labeled "subject–object inversion." The word order in Navajo is typically SOV. According to Hale, when subject and object occur in this order, *yi-* is prefixed to the verb. When the subject and the object are inverted, however, the verbal prefix is *bi-*.

---

[6] Sapir and Hoijer go on to say that there is a group of verbs where *bi-* occurs regardless of the fact that the subject pronoun is other than third person. They do not describe the nature of these verbs, which Sapir labeled "transitivized," and they use only one such verb in their examples.

(4)   a.   *ł̨į́į́   dzaanééz yi-   z-   ∅- ∅-   tał.*   SOV

                     4   7   8   9   10

      [horse mule   him-perf-he-class-kick]

      'The horse kicked the mule'.

   b.   *Dzaanééz ł̨į́į́   bi-   z-   ∅- ∅-   tał.*   OSV

                          4   7   8   9   10

      [mule   horse him-perf-he-class-kick]

      'The mule was kicked by the horse'.

Hale notes that while there are cases in which noun inversion may optionally occur, there are also cases in which it is blocked. In Example (5), the (b) sentence is ungrammatical:

(5)   a.   *łééchąą'í łeets'aa' yi-∅- ł-   naad.*   SOV

                            4 8 9   10

      [dog   plate   it- he-class-lick]

      'The dog is licking the plate'.

   b.   **łeets'aa' łééchąą'í bi-∅- ł-   naad.*   OSV

                          4 8 9   10

      [plate   dog   it- he-class-lick]

      'The dog is licking the plate'.

Finally, Hale presents evidence that subject–object inversion is sometimes obligatory:

(6)   a.   **Yas   łééchąą'í' yi-   s-   ∅-∅-   tin.*   SOV

                            4   7   8 9   10

      [snow dog   him-perf-it-class-freeze]

      'The snow froze the dog'.

   b.   *łééchąą'í' yas   bi-   s-   ∅-∅-   tin.*   OSV

                      4   7   8 9   10

      [dog   snow him-perf-it-class-freeze]

      'The snow froze the dog'.

Here the only acceptable word order is OSV (6b).

Hale hypothesized that these facts are related to the apparent existence in Navajo of a hierarchy of noun classes in which humans rank highest, followed by animates, with inanimates ranking lowest on the scale. The hierarchy is significant in the sense that it appears that in the Navajo view of life, certain nouns have more or less power to act on other nouns, depending on their relative rank. Lynn Salego (1977) suggested that the noun hierarchy is based on an "innate power to act upon other entities . . . expressed by strength, aggressiveness, potency, rationality and animacy." (See Creamer 1974, p. 6, for a slightly different categorization of noun hierarchy in Navajo.) Thus, a noun may act upon another noun of equal or lower rank, but its power to act decreases or disappears in interaction with nouns that rank higher on the scale.

Hale stated that if the subject and object of a sentence are of equal rank, inversion is optional; if the subject is ranked higher than the object, inversion cannot take place; and if the object is ranked higher than the subject, inversion is obligatory. When inversion does take place, only *bi-* can appear on the verb. If this hypothesis is correct, then the order of elements in a transitive sentence reflects the Navajo concept of noun hierarchy: A noun of lower rank may not precede a higher ranked noun.

Nancy Frishberg (1972) examined a more complex set of data, and concluded that Hale's conditions were not sufficient to predict all the occurrences of *yi-* and *bi-* in Navajo. She claimed that contrary to what Hale suggested, *yi-* and *bi-* are not synonymous markers that separate inverted from uninverted sentences. She devised a slightly different hypothesis. She suggested that *yi-* can refer to any object NP in a transitive sentence, as in Examples (7) and (8):

(7)   *Mósí łééchaa'i yi-   zi-   Ø- Ø-   ghaas.*   SO*yi*
                          4   7   8   9   10

        [cat   dog   him-perf-he-class-scratch]
        'The cat scratched the dog'.

(8)   *łeezh naltsos tsits'aa yi- sh-   Ø- Ø-   jįzh.*   SO*yi*
                               4   7   8 9   10

        [sand   carton   it- perf- it- class-crush]
        'The sand crushed the carton'.

However, *bi-* can occur only when the object is human or animate and is the first of two NPs in the sentence. Thus, Examples (9) and (10) are grammatical because they fulfill both conditions for *bi-*:

(9)   *Shinaaí   ana'i   bi-   z-   Ø- Ø-   tał.*   OS*bi*
                            4   7   8 9   10

        [my-brother enemy him-perf-he-class-kick]
        'The enemy kicked my brother'.

(10)   *Shilį́į́   shinaaí   bi-   z-   Ø- Ø-   tał.*   OS*bi*
                                4   7   8 9   10

        [my-horse my-brother him-perf-he-class-kick]
        'My brother kicked my horse'.

The object in each of these sentences is human or animate and is the first NP in the sentence. Example (11), however, is ungrammatical because the first NP is inanimate:

(11)   **Naltsos tsits'aa łeezh yi-sh-   Ø- Ø-   jįzh.*   OS*bi*
                                 4 7   8 9   10

        [carton   sand it- perf-it- class-crush]
        'The sand crushed the carton'.

Frishberg claimed that the OS*bi* sentences can be translated with the English passive.

Suzette Elgin (1973) took a different approach. She called *bi-* a "topicalization"[7] marker indicating that the object of a transitive verb sentence is the noun that is being emphasized: "When a pronoun prefix is semantically important because it conveys emphasis or contrast, as for the independent subject pronouns and for the object pronoun prefix of a verb marked by emphatic /ji/, such a pronoun is lexicalized as /bi/ [p. 170]."[8] She suggested that *yi-* is phonologically motivated and therefore semantically empty. Where *yi-* occurs without phonological justification, Elgin stated, it is probably present by analogy to regularize a paradigm. Thus *yi-* has no meaning whatsoever, and *bi-* indicates that the emphasis is on the object. Her topicalization rule moves the object in front of the subject and prefixes *bi-* to the verb stem.

Elgin notes that where *bi-* is obligatory on the verb, her consultants consistently prefer an active rather than a passive translation, and further, that her consultants will accept for *all bi-* sentences an active as well as a passive translation. Therefore, the *yi-/bi-* distinction cannot be called an active–passive one.

Munro *et al.* (1976) raised the question of how to accommodate sentences like (12a) and (12b), which cannot be accounted for by any of the preceding hypotheses:

(12)   a.   *łį́į́   John yi-   z-   ∅-   ∅-   tał.*   OS*yi*
                        4   7   8   9   10

[horse John him-perf-he-class-kick]
'John kicked the horse'.

   b.   *łį́į́   John bi-   z-   ∅-   ∅-   tał.*   SO*bi*
                        4   7   8   9   10

[horse John him-perf-he-class-kick]
'The horse kicked John'.

They claim that sentences like these may be accommodated "if we assume that the meaning of *yi-* and *bi-*, in sentences with nouns of unequal rank, makes no reference to word order at all, but rather specifies only whether the higher-ranked noun is subject or object." Thus, the presence of *yi-* in (12a) indicates that the higher ranked noun ('John') is the subject, and the presence of *bi-* in (12b) indicates that the higher ranked noun is the object.

Obviously, the function of *yi-* and *bi-* in Navajo is more complex than it first appeared, and the literature discussed represents only a sampling of the proposed solutions. Let us begin our investigation of *yi-* and *bi-* in Western Apache by finding out if any of the hypotheses discussed for Navajo provide an adequate description of the Apache data.

[7] It is assumed that Elgin's use of the word "topicalization" is not to be confused with "topic," a concept that has generated a good deal of discussion among linguists (see Li and Thompson 1976, among others). She is apparently equating topicalization with emphasis.

[8] Elgin analyzed *ji-*, commonly called a "4th person" marker, as an "emphatic prefix."

2. INADEQUACY OF NAVAJO HYPOTHESES FOR WESTERN APACHE

I shall return to the Sapir–Hoijer analysis near the end of this discussion. Let us look first at Hale's ranking constraints on NP inversion. The first constraint states that if the subject and object in a sentence are of equal rank, inversion is optional. In Apache, this is true only if the object NP is human or animate.[9]

(13) a. *Istsaan mé   yi- ∅- ł-   chį.*   SOyi
                    4   8   9   10   human–human
         woman baby him-she-class-give.birth
         'The woman gave birth to a baby'.

      b. *Mé istsaan bi- ∅- ł-   chį.*   OSbi
                      4   8   9   10   human–human
         baby woman him-she-class-give birth
         'The baby was given birth to by the woman'.
         'The woman gave birth to the baby'.

(14) a. *Tłį[10] dzanééẓi yi-s-   ∅-∅-   tał.*   SOyi
                   4 7   8 9   10   animate–animate
         horse mule   it- perf-it-class-kick
         'The horse kicked the mule'.

      b. *Dzanééẓi tłį   bi-s-   ∅- ∅- tał.*   OSbi
                      4 7   8 9   10   animate–animate
         mule   horse it- perf-it- class-kick
         'The mule was kicked by the horse'.
         'The horse kicked the mule'.

(15) a. *Tú   soł   yi- ye[11]- s- ∅-∅- hį.*   SOyi
                 4   6   7   8 9   10   inanimate–
         water plants them-adverb-perf-it-class-kill inanimate
         'Water killed the plants'.

      b. **Soł   tú   bi- ye-   s- ∅-∅- hį.*   OSbi
                 4   6   7   8 9   10   inanimate–
         plants water them-adverb-perf-it-class-kill inanimate
         'The plants were killed by water'.
         'Water killed the plants'.

[9] Paul Kroskrity (1977:175–177) discovered a similar phenomenon in Arizona Tewa.

[10] Both of my consultants insist that the Apache word for 'horse' is *łį*, but in context they almost always produce *tłį*.

[11] The meaning of *ye-* in this example is not clear. We can assume that it is an adverbial, however, given its position on the verb. This morpheme may also appear as *be-* when it occurs after the object pronoun *bi-*. The two forms appear to be in free variation in that environment.

Notice that the (b) sentences may be translated as either active or passive. My consultants strongly prefer the passive translation of these out-of-context examples, although they have stated that the passive is used only because it represents the closest English approximation to the real meaning of each of these sentences. What is actually expressed here is a "feeling" of passivity, resulting from the fact that the entity in subject position in the sentence is the goal rather than the agent of the verb. Notice also that Sentence (15b) is ungrammatical because inversion places an inanimate object in subject position.

Hale's second constraint states that if the subject is ranked higher than the object, inversion is blocked. Here his predictions and the Apache data begin to diverge. It is quite acceptable for inversion to take place where the subject is of a higher rank than the object, but again, the object NP must be human or animate:

(16) a. *Hastin tłį yi- ye- s- ∅- ∅- hí.* SO*yi*
$\quad\quad\quad\quad\quad\quad$ 4 $\quad$ 6 $\quad$ 7 $\;$ 8 $\;$ 9 $\;$ 10 $\quad$ human–animate
$\quad\quad$ old man horse him-adverb-perf-he-class-kill
$\quad\quad$ 'The old man killed the horse'.

b. *Tłį hastin bi- ye- s- ∅- ∅- hí.* OS*bi*
$\quad\quad\quad\quad\quad\quad$ 4 $\quad$ 6 $\quad$ 7 $\;$ 8 $\;$ 9 $\;$ 10 $\quad$ animate–human
$\quad\quad$ horse old man him-adverb-perf-he-class-kill
$\quad\quad$ 'The horse was killed by the old man'.
$\quad\quad$ 'The old man killed the horse'.

(17) a. *Ishkiin gah yi- zá- ná- z- ∅-*
$\quad\quad\quad\quad\quad\quad\quad\;$ 4 $\;$ 6 $\;$ 6 $\;$ 7 $\;$ 8
$\quad\quad$ boy $\quad$ rabbit him-move-around-imperf-he-
$\quad\quad$ *∅- ni'.* $\quad\quad$ SO*yi*
$\quad\quad\;$ 9 $\;$ 10 $\quad\quad$ human–
$\quad\quad$ class-squeeze $\quad$ animate
$\quad\quad$ 'The boy is hugging the rabbit'.

b. *Gah ishkiin bi- zá- ná- z- ∅-*
$\quad\quad\quad\quad\quad\quad\quad$ 4 $\;$ 6 $\;$ 6 $\;$ 7 $\;$ 8
$\quad\quad$ rabbit boy $\quad$ him-move-around-imperf-he-
$\quad\quad$ *∅- ni'* $\quad\quad$ OS*bi*
$\quad\quad\;$ 9 $\;$ 10 $\quad\quad$ animate–human
$\quad\quad$ class-squeeze
$\quad\quad$ 'The rabbit is being hugged by the boy'.
$\quad\quad$ 'The boy is hugging the rabbit'.

(18) a. *Itídé kábas yi-dn[12]-∅- ∅- łiit.* SO*yi*
             4   7   8   9   10   human–inanimate
        girl potato it- perf-she-class-burn
        'The girl burned the potato'.

     b. **Kábas itídé bi-dn- ∅- ∅- łiit.* OS*bi*
             4   7   8   9   10   inanimate–human
        potato girl it- perf-she-class-burn
        'The potato was burned by the girl'.
        'The girl burned the potato'.

In each of the preceding examples, inversion is optional, with the exception of (18b), where the object is inanimate.

Hale's third and last constraint states that inversion is obligatory if the object is ranked higher than the subject. Again, the claim fails to account for the Apache data, as the following examples demonstrate:

(19) a. *Kósé iné y- o[13]- ∅- ∅- 'į̄.* SO*yi*
             4   7   8   9   10   animate–human
        dog man-him-prog-he-class-see
        'The dog sees the man'.

     b. *Iné kósé b- o- ∅- ∅- 'į̄.* OS*bi*
             4   7   8   9   10   human–animate
        man dog him-prog-he-class-see
        'The man is seen by the dog'.
        'The dog sees the man'.

(20) a. *Izee ncho'í itídé yi- ye- s- ∅-*
                      4   6   7   8
        medicine bad girl her-adverb-perf-it-
        ∅- hį̄. SO*yi*
        9   10   inanimate–human
        class-kill
        'Poison killed the girl'.

     b. *Itídé izee ncho'í bi- ye- s- ∅-*
                      4   6   7   8
        girl medicine bad her-adverb-perf-it-
        ∅- hį̄. OS*bi*
        9   10   human–inanimate
        class-kill
        'The girl was killed by poison'.
        'Poison killed the girl'.

---

[12] There is alternation between *n-* and *dn-* in what is called the *ni-* perfective. It is not clear what conditions the change, but the two forms do not appear to be in free variation.

[13] My consultants were unable to explain the morpheme *o-*; however, Sapir and Hoijer (1967:93) imply that in the Navajo sentence this is a form of the progressive prefix *yi-*, so I have tentatively glossed it as such for Apache.

(21)   a.   *Izee   ncho'í gídí yi-   ye-   s-   ∅-*
                                    4   6   7   8
           medicine bad   cat him-adverb-perf-it-

           ∅-   hį́.   SO*yi*
            9   10   inanimate–animate
           class-kill
           'Poison killed the cat'.

       b.   *Gídí izee   ncho'í bi-   ye-   s-   ∅-*
                                     4   6   7   8
           cat   medicine bad   him-adverb-perf-it-

           ∅-   hį́.   OS*bi*
            9   10   animate–inanimate
           class-kill
           'The cat was killed by poison'.
           'Poison killed the cat'.

Again, inversion is optional. Clearly, the generalization that Hale has proposed for Navajo does not account for the Apache data.

Frishberg's suggestion that *yi-* can refer to any object in a transitive sentence is proven incorrect for Apache by Examples (22a)–(25a):

(22a)   **Mé   istsaan yi-   ni-   ∅-   l-   há.*   SO*yi*
                             4   7   8   9   10   human–human
           baby woman her-perf-he-class-worry
           'The baby worried the woman'.

(23a)   **Kosnih mé   tsí-   yi-   ni-   ∅- ł-   hiiz.*   SO*yi*
                            1   4   7   8   9   10   animate–
           bee   child adverb-him-perf-it- class-surprise   human
           'The bee surprised the child'.

(24a)   **Kábas itídé yi-   dn-   ∅-∅-   łiit.*   SO*yi*
                          4   7   8 9   10   inanimate–human
           potato girl   her-perf-it-class-burn
           'The potato burned the girl'.

(25a)   **Hastin tłį́   yi-ye-   s-   ∅- ∅-   hí.*   SO*yi*
                             4 6   7   8 9   10   inanimate–
           old age horse it- adverb-perf-it- class-kill   animate
           'Old age killed the horse'.

Only *bi-* can be prefixed to the verb in these sentences, and it appears without noun inversion. Thus, in Examples (22b)–(25b), *bi-* is referring to an object that is not the first NP in the sentence:

(22b)   *Mé   istsaan bi-   ni-   ∅-   l-   há.*   SO*bi*
                            4   7   8   9   10   human–human
           baby woman her-perf-he-class-worry
           'The baby worried the woman'.

(23b)   *Kosnih mé   tsí   bi- ni- ∅- ł-   hiiz.*   SO*bi*
                                    1   4   7   8 9   10   animate–
          bee   child adverb-him-perf-it- class-surprise   human
          'The bee surprised the child'.

(24b)   *Kábas itídé bi- dn- ∅-∅-   łiit.*   SO*bi*
                               4   7   8 9   10   inanimate–human
          potato girl   her-perf-it-class-burn
          'The potato burned the girl'.

(25b)   *Hastin tłį̀   bi- ye-   s-   ∅-∅-   hí.*   SO*bi*
                             4   6   7   8 9   10   inanimate–
          old age horse him-adverb-perf-it-class-kill   animate
          'Old age killed the horse'.

The NPs in these sentences may be inverted, as demonstrated in
(22c)–(25c). (The braces indicate that neither translation is preferred over
the other.)

(22c)   *Istsaan mé   bi- ni- ∅- l-   há.*   OS*bi*
                            4   7   8 9   10   human–human
          woman baby her-perf-he-class-worry
          { 'The baby worried the woman'.
          { 'The woman was worried by the baby'. }

(23c)   *Mé   kosnih tsí-   bi- ni- ∅-ł-   hiiz.*   OS*bi*
                            1   4   7   8 9   10   human–
          child bee   adverb-him-perf-it- class-surprise   animate
          { 'The bee surprised the child'.
          { 'The child was surprised by the bee'. }

(24c)   *Itídé kábas bi- dn- ∅-∅-   łiit.*   OS*bi*
                            4   7   8 9   10   human–inanimate
          girl   potato her-perf-it-class-burn
          { 'The potato burned the girl'.
          { 'The girl was burned by the potato'. }

(25c)   *Tłį̀   hastin bi-ye-   s-   ∅-∅-   hí.*   OS*bi*
                            4 6   7   8 9   10   animate–
          horse old age it- adverb-perf-it-class-kill   inanimate
          { 'Old age killed the horse'.
          { 'The horse was killed by old age'. }

However, if the object in any of these sentences were inanimate, inversion would be blocked. Compare Sentence (26) with Sentence (25c):

(26)   **Ch'eł hastin bi-ye-   s-   ∅-∅-   hí.*   OS*bi*
                            4 6   7   8 9   10   inanimate–
          tree   old age it- adverb-perf-it-class-kill   inanimate
          'Old age killed the tree'.
          'The tree was killed by old age'.

Frishberg's hypothesis for Navajo clearly does not account for the Apache data: *yi-* cannot refer to just any object NP in a transitive sentence, and *bi-* can refer to a noun in second-NP position. The only restriction is that if *bi-* does refer to the first NP, that noun cannot be inanimate.

Elgin's hypothesis that *bi-* indicates that the object is the noun that is being emphasized or contrasted, whereas *yi-* is meaningless, is also disproven when applied to Apache. My consultants are unable to say that one NP or the other is being emphasized or contrasted in any of the sentences that have been presented here. They prefer to say that the first NP in the sentence is the one that is being talked about—"the important one." Moreover, in Examples (22b)–(25b), *bi-* is prefixed to the verb regardless of the fact that the object has not been moved in front of the subject. Thus, Elgin's topicalization rule does not describe the behavior of *yi-* and *bi-* in Apache.

Finally, recall the hypothesis put forth by Munro *et al.* to the effect that *yi-* and *bi-* have no relevance to word order, but rather indicate whether the higher ranked noun is subject or object. The structure OS*yi* (12a) does not occur in Western Apache. If *yi-* is prefixed to the verb, the order of elements must be SO*yi*. I will also show that the structure SO*bi* (12b) may not occur with a verb like 'kick', which expresses physical action. If *bi-* is prefixed to such a verb (among others, as we will see), the order of elements must be OS*bi*. Therefore, word order does play a role in the *yi-*/*bi-* phenomenon in Apache.

The evidence suggests that the prefixes *yi-* and *bi-*, which exist in both Navajo and Apache, may be governed by markedly different constraints in each language. If so, there must be another way to account for *yi-* and *bi-*, concomitant noun inversion, and active versus passive translation of this type of sentence in Western Apache. I will show that there is indeed another explanation.

3. SEMANTIC BASIS FOR *YI-*/*BI-* DISTINCTION

Consider the Apache data which has been presented. It can be divided into two groups: Examples (13)–(21), which I shall refer to as Group I, and Examples (22)–(25), which I shall refer to as Group II. The examples in Group I each consist of a pair of sentences. In the (a) sentences, the subject is the first NP, *yi-* is prefixed to the verb, and the translation can only be active. In the (b) sentences, the object, if human or animate, is the first NP, *bi-* is prefixed to the verb, and the preferred translation is passive, although an active translation is also acceptable. If we look only at these sentences, we might assume that *yi-* occurs when the order of elements in the sentence is SOV, and *bi-* occurs when the order is OSV—that is, when the human or animate object has been moved into subject position in the sentence. This theory would also account for sentences where only one noun appears. Remember that Sapir and Hoijer (1967) implied that *yi-* in such sentences indicates the stated noun is the object, and *bi-* indicates that it is the subject of the verb. Thus we get sentences like (2a) and (2b). We find the same kind of data in Apache:

(27) a. *Mé y- o- ∅- ∅- 'į̇.*
              4   7   8   9   10
          baby him-prog-he-class-see
          'He sees the baby'.
      b. *Mé b- o- ∅- ∅- 'į̇.*
              4   7   8   9   10
          baby him- prog-he-class-see
          'The baby sees him'.

(28) a. *Hastin yi- ye-   s- ∅- ∅- hį̇.*
                   4   6   7   8   9   10
          old man him-adverb-perf-he-class-kill
          'He killed the old man'.
      b. *Hastin bi- ye-   s- ∅- ∅- hį̇.*
                   4   6   7   8   9   10
          old man him-adverb-perf-he-class-kill
          'The old man killed him'.

This data shows that when only one noun appears in a transitive sentence in which either *yi-* or *bi-* may appear on the verb (depending upon who is acting on whom), that noun always fulfills the function of the second noun phrase in the corresponding sentence of the structure NNV. It is important to point out that we are speaking here of sentences in which either *yi-* or *bi-* can occur. As yet, I have been unable to elicit single-noun transitives for the type of sentence in Group II—that is, for sentences in which *yi-* as an object prefix is not possible.

A corollary to the fact that the given noun in a single-noun transitive sentence always fulfills the role of the second noun in the corresponding NNV sentence is the fact that a noun in an NNV sentence whose verb can be marked with either *yi-* or *bi-* may be deleted only if it is the first NP in the sentence.

This rule of NP deletion is fully optional and applies, as we would expect, to the independent pronouns as well. If the independent pronoun

NPs are not deleted from Examples (27) and (28), we get the sentences of (29) and (30). Such structures function to emphasize the pronominalized NP:

(29) a. *Bi mé   y-   o-   Ø- Ø-   'į̃.*
          ₄   ₇   ₈   ₉   ₁₀
          he baby-him-prog-he-class-see
          '**He** sees the baby'.

      b. *Bi mé   b-   o-   Ø- Ø-   'į̃.*
          ₄   ₇   ₈   ₉   ₁₀
          him baby him-prog-he-class-see
          'The baby sees **him**'.

(30) a. *Bi hastin   yi- ye-   s-   Ø- Ø-   hį̃.*
          ₄   ₆   ₇   ₈   ₉   ₁₀
          he old man him-adverb-perf-he-class-kill
          '**He** killed the old man'.

      b. *Bi   hastin   bi- ye-   s-   Ø- Ø-   hį̃.*
          ₄   ₆   ₇   ₈   ₉   ₁₀
          him-old man him-adverb-perf-he-class-kill
          'The old man killed **him**'.

Examples (31) and (32) show that an independent pronoun that is not the first NP in the sentence may not be deleted:

(31) a. *Mé   bi[14] y-   o-   Ø- Ø-   'į̃.*
          ₄   ₇   ₈   ₉   ₁₀
          baby him him-prog-he-class-see
          'The baby sees him'.

      b. *Mé   bi b-   o-   Ø- Ø-   'į̃.*
          ₄   ₇   ₈   ₉   ₁₀
          baby he him-prog-he-class-see
          'The baby is seen by him'.
          'He sees the baby'.

      c. **Mé   y-   o-   Ø- Ø-   'į̃.*
          ₄   ₇   ₈   ₉   ₁₀
          baby him-prog-he-class-see
          'The baby sees him'.

      d. **Mé   b-   o-   Ø- Ø-   'į̃.*
          ₄   ₇   ₈   ₉   ₁₀
          baby him-prog-he-class-see
          'The baby is seen by him'.
          'He sees the baby'.

[14] *an* may also be used here.

(32)   a.   *Hastin bi yi- ye- s- Ø- Ø- hį́.*
                    4   6   7   8   9   10
         old man him him-adverb-perf-he-class-kill
         'The old man killed him'.

   b.   *Hastin bi bi- ye- s- Ø- Ø- hį́.*
                    4   6   7   8   9   10
         old man him him-adverb-perf-he-class-kill
         'The old man was killed by him'.
         'He killed the old man'.

   c.   **Hastin yi- ye- s- Ø- Ø- hį́.*
                  4   6   7   8   9   10
         old man him-adverb-perf-he-class-kill
         'The old man killed him'.

   d.   **Hastin bi- ye- s- Ø- Ø- hį́.*
                  4   6   7   8   9   10
         old man him-adverb-perf-he-class-kill
         'The old man was killed by him'.
         'He killed the old man'.

Notice that those sentences in which *bi-* is marked on the verb cannot be translated by the English passive if the object NP is a pronoun. There is no passive translation possible for the (b) sentences of Examples (27)–(30). A passive translation is acceptable only if the object is a noun, as in Examples (31) and (32). We shall return to this point shortly.

The preceding description works for the sentences in Group I, but what happens when we are faced with the more complex set of data in Group II? In these examples, *yi-* cannot occur at all, even where the subject is the first NP, as shown by the ungrammaticality of the (a) sentences. Moreover, *bi-* may occur without moving the object to subject position, resulting in an SO*bi* structure, as in the (b) sentences. And unlike the (b) sentences of Group I, where a passive translation is preferred after noun inversion, the NPs of the Group II sentences may be inverted, if the object is human or animate, with no priority of translation, as shown by the (c) sentences. I will demonstrate that it is possible to account for the sentences of Group II and still have one description that accounts for both groups. To do this, we need only accept that the rules governing the appearance of *yi-* and *bi-* in any given sentence are basically semantic in nature. More specifically, the role that each noun plays in the achievement of the verb is a determining factor in the occurrence of *yi-* or *bi-*. Throughout the remainder of this paper I will refer to subject and object as agent and goal respectively, except where the discussion concerns syntax rather than semantics.

Look again at the data in Group I. Notice that in these sentences the "control" of the verb can be attributed to the agent alone. That is, the agent, either willingly or inadvertently, achieves the event by means of an intrinsic or seemingly intrinsic[15] power to do so, without the participation of the goal. The goal may be a necessary aspect of the realization of the verb but, in the Apache view, it does not contribute to that realization. I shall call such agents "potent."

In the Group II sentences, on the other hand, the agent does not have that kind of power. It will perhaps be easiest to understand this if we consider the Group II sentences individually. For the moment, we will bypass the question of noun inversion and consider only the (a) and (b) sentences of each example. In Example (22), although the baby as agent[16] caused the mother to worry, it was the mother—the goal—who actually worried, not the baby. Therefore, 'baby' in this example is not a potent agent, according to our definition. Example (23) is a similar kind of sentence. Although the bee aroused surprise in the boy, it was the boy who experienced the feeling, so 'bee' could not be considered a potent agent in this context.

Example (24) is both interesting and revealing when compared with Example (18). The same nouns and verb appear in both, but the semantic roles of the nouns are reversed. In Example (18), the girl as agent controls the action of burning, without the participation of the goal. But in Example (24), not only is the potato not a potent agent, but in the Apache view, the girl is seen as having participated in getting herself burned by it! As a human being, she has the ability to avoid an inanimate object such as a hot potato. If she does not do so and gets burned as a result, then she contributes to the realization of the burning. Gary Witherspoon (1977:65–68) found a somewhat similar phenomenon in Navajo. In that language, however, it seems to be related to whether or not one noun may precede another in an NNV sentence (regardless of whether *yi-* or *bi-* is prefixed to the verb), the idea being that the first NP in the sentence either controls the other or allows the other to act upon it. He presented the following two examples, among others:

(33)   *Hastiin łı́į́   bi- z-   Ø- Ø-   tał.*
                        4   7   8 9   10
        [man   horse him-perf-it- class-kick]
        'The man was kicked by the horse'.

[15] It is necessary to use the word "seemingly" here because the Apaches categorize entities which *appear* to be capable of self-induced motion (wind, rain, lightning, cars, trains, etc.) as animate objects (this point is supported by Basso 1967). Such entities may function as potent agents.

[16] There is certainly a question about whether or not the entities which I have chosen to call agents in the Group II sentences could be called agents at all. I do not wish to enter into the controversy over what constitutes agency, so I admit to using the term quite loosely and leave it at that.

(34)   łį́į́   hastiin yi- z-   ∅- ∅-   tał.
                    4   7   8 9   10
          [horse man   him-perf-it- class-kick]
          'The horse kicked the man'.

He states that although both sentences are grammatical, Sentence (34)
is culturally unacceptable. He says of Sentence (33) that it "should be
translated 'the man let the horse kick him'. Here the assumption is that
the man with greater intelligence could have, by using his mental powers
and resources, prevented the horse from kicking him. Nevertheless,
through acquiescence or inadvertence, the man at least consented and
may have even encouraged or caused the horse to kick him." He goes
on to say of Sentence (34) that it is "absurd because it claims that the
horse can both decide to kick the man and accomplish the feat without
the man's consent, either openly provided or inadvertently given. It
means that the horse was intellectually dominating the man and had the
man under its control, with the man unable to resist. Again such notions
about the relationship between horses and men seem absurd to the
Navajo."

   We could not say that there is any implication in Apache that the first
NP controls the other or allows the other to act upon it, and we have
seen that there is no constraint on what category of noun may precede
another in a transitive sentence. The only rule is that inversion may not
occur if the goal is inanimate. But we do find the same kind of concept
with slightly different manifestations in Example (24), where the goal is
considered to have contributed to the achievement of the verb by virtue
of having allowed herself to come in contact with the agent. In a sense,
she "let" the potato burn her. In Apache, the manifestation of that
concept is in the prefixing of bi- to the verb, indicating participation of
the goal. If yi- were prefixed to the verb in this sentence, it would make
it appear as if the potato controlled the burning of the girl, which is not
semantically possible. Remember that control as defined earlier refers
to an intrinsic or seemingly intrinsic power to willingly or inadvertently
achieve an event without the participation of the goal. The power to
cause something to burn or to be burned is not intrinsic to the potato,
so it is not a potent agent of that particular verb. In Example (20), on
the other hand, the power to kill is intrinsic to the poison, so it is seen
as achieving that event without the participation of the girl. Even though
she may have had the ability to avoid the poison just as she had the
ability to avoid the potato, the poison, intrinsically potent, is seen as
controlling that event.

   Example (25) is also interesting, especially when compared with Example (16). The word hastin means both 'old man' and 'old age' in

Apache. In Example (16), the meaning is 'old man', and *yi-* is prefixed to the verb, so we can see that the old man is considered to be a potent agent of the event of killing. The goal is a necessary component of the verb in this case, but it is not seen as having contributed to its realization. But in Example (25), where *hastin* means 'old age', a different picture emerges. Old age is not a separate entity that acts on the horse in some way to kill it. It is an inherent characteristic of the horse itself. Through the process of maturing, the horse eventually becomes old and dies as a result. In that sense, it is the horse that controls, albeit inadvertently, the realization of the verb. It has within it the power to do so through the natural and intrinsic process of aging. Therefore, *bi-* is prefixed to the verb, indicating that the "goal" somehow participated in the event.

By now it should be clear that in San Carlos Apache, the question of who or what is credited with achieving a given verb is of primary importance in determining the appearance of *yi-* versus *bi-* in position 4 of that verb. The realization of an event is attributed to the agent only if that agent is potent. If it is not, the realization of the event is credited at least in part to the goal. Notice that the claim I am making differs somewhat from the one that has commonly been proposed for Navajo, where it seems that the crucial point is which entity is seen as somehow outranking or "controlling" the other—see Hale (1972), Frishberg (1972), Creamer (1974), Salego (1977), Witherspoon (1977), and others. The concept of a noun hierarchy in some sense of the word has played a role in the proposals of all of these investigators. Although a more limited set of examples might give the impression that the same concept affects the structure of transitive verbs in Western Apache, the data presented here shows that is not the case. The only restriction we have seen is that noun inversion may not occur if the goal is an inanimate object. This fact, however, appears to be related not to a complex hierarchical ranking of nouns, but rather to a simple constraint on foregrounding something that is neither human nor animate. If a hierarchy were involved, we could say that inversion was blocked if the agent was human or animate and thus ranked higher than the goal. In that case, we would expect inversion to be possible if the agent were also inanimate; but Example (26) shows that inversion is blocked in that case as well. Both 'old age' and 'tree' are inanimate entities, but inversion is unacceptable. An inanimate object may not be foregrounded. Beyond that, we need not concern ourselves with the question of ranking, and we certainly need not consider the relative rank of agent and goal in a sentence. I might add at this point that, as Pamela Munro (personal communication) has pointed out, if my hypothesis proves to be correct, then we need not posit a hierarchical ranking of nouns as a determining factor in the appearance of *yi-* or *bi-*, and we avoid the necessity of complicating the grammar with a "list" of elements.

We are now ready to return to the question of noun inversion. I stated earlier that my consultants have said that the first NP in the sentence, that is, the NP in subject position, is the one that is being talked about—"the important one." This means that fronting foregrounds the goal NP, making it the entity about which something is being said. Let us now examine the sentences in which noun inversion has occurred—that is, the (b) sentences of Group I and the (c) sentences of Group II. We will look first at the significance of active versus passive translations of these sentences.

Note that in the (b) sentences of Group I, the preferred translation is the English passive. There seem to be two reasons for this: First, foregrounding of an object NP is best expressed by the passive in English; and, second, because the agents of these sentences are potent, the goals are seen as playing completely passive roles in the achievement of the given verbs. When such a goal is moved into subject position (first NP), the entity that is being talked about does not participate in the event denoted by the verb, and the result, as mentioned earlier, is a "feeling" of passivity. Therefore, the passive translation is preferred, at least when such a sentence occurs in isolation. However, such sentences are not true passives in Apache, and an active translation is also acceptable. The choice of translation appears to be somewhat context sensitive, but as I have not yet done any significant discourse analysis, I am unable to elaborate on this point.

In the (c) sentences of Group II, the translation may be either active or passive without preference. Unlike the examples in Group I, there is no "feeling" of passivity arising from the fact that the goal has been moved to subject position in the sentence, because the goals in the sentences of Group II are seen as participating in the event denoted by the verb. As a result, the only factor that makes a passive translation possible in these sentences is the fact that the goal has been foregrounded, and it is the passive that is used to foreground an object NP in English. This factor alone, however, is not strong enough to lead to a preference for that translation.

I have presented evidence that in an SOV sentence, *bi-* must appear in position 4 on the verb if the agent does not have the power to realize the verb alone, and the goal is therefore seen as somehow participating in the event. But how can we explain the occurrence of *bi-* in sentences with inverted NPs? In such sentences, *yi-* cannot be prefixed to the verb, even if it appears in the corresponding SOV sentence [Examples (13)–(21)]; therefore, the potency of the agent is not the determining factor in the occurrence of *bi-* in sentences of the structure OSV. It is not difficult, however, to find a solution to this problem. We know that foregrounding makes the goal the prominent entity in a sentence. In that sense, it gives added significance to the goal. But we can say that a goal that participates in the realization of the verb, that is, a goal that requires *bi-* on the verb of an SOV structure, is also of special consequence, at least in relation to the given event. Remember that the question of who or what controls the realization of the verb is an important one to the Apaches. If we assume that *bi-* functions to mark the goal as being especially significant, either as the foregrounded entity in the sentence or as a participant in the event, we can then account for the appearance of *bi-* in every case. *Bi-* is prefixed to the verb in all sentences with inverted NPs because the foregrounding of the goal has increased its importance in the sentence, and it is prefixed to the verb in sentences of the structure SOV if the goal participates in the achievement of the verb and, therefore, bears a special relationship to the given event.

At the beginning of this paper, I mentioned that *yi-* is the only "object pronoun" prefix that never appears as an independent pronoun. We have since seen that, in addition, it must be replaced by *bi-* if the goal is in any way of special significance. These two points make the pronominal status of *yi-* highly suspect. In fact, I suggest that *yi-* is not a pronoun at all. Rather, I propose that it is a marker that appears in the direct object position on a verb, thus marking that verb as transitive, but indicating at the same time that the entity which gets the credit for the realization of the verb, and the entity which is being talked about, is the agent. This hypothesis, if correct, would also explain the fact that although there is no doubt in their minds that *bi-* refers to the goal, my consultants insist that whenever *yi-* appears in the direct object position on the verb, it "refers" to the agent. I am suggesting, in effect, that only if the goal bears a special relationship either to the stated event or to the sentence as a whole, is it marked by a pronoun on the verb.

With this hypothesis in mind, we can now go back to Examples (27)–(30), where we found that a passive translation was unacceptable for the (b) sentences. Consider first Examples (27) and (28). We have said that the sentence structure OSV foregrounds the goal NP. We have also said that the given noun in a single-noun transitive sentence always fulfills the function of a second noun in the corresponding sentence of the structure NNV. If *bi-* is prefixed to the verb in a single-noun transitive sentence, that sentence could be said to correspond to an OSV structure, with the agent in what could be said to be the object position in the sentence. However, a pronominalized goal can never be foregrounded. The mere fact that it is a pronoun means that it is, in effect, "backgrounded." Therefore, a passive translation is unacceptable. But if a pronominalized goal cannot be foregrounded, then why do we find *bi*-prefixed to the verb of a single-noun transitive sentence with a pronominalized goal, as in Sentences (27b) and (28b)? The answer is that if we accept the proposal that only *bi*- is a pronominal prefix, then we expect to find *bi*- rather than *yi*- in the direct object position on the verb in a sentence in which there is no other overt manifestation of the goal. Such is the case for any transitive sentence in which only the agent noun appears before the verb. If *yi*- appeared, there would be no goal in the sentence—only the implication that there is a goal by virtue of the fact that the occurrence of *yi*- in position 4 marks the verb as transitive. This appears to be a correct assumption, as evidenced by the following structure, which is an incomplete sentence if *mé* is the agent of the verb:

(35)   **Mé* *y-*   *o-*   *∅-*   *∅-*   *'į́*
              4   7   8   9   10
           baby trans-prog-he-class-see
           'The baby sees _____'

In short, if the given noun of a single-noun transitive sentence is the agent, the pronoun prefix *bi*- must appear on the verb to represent the goal. If *yi*- appears in such a structure, the sentence is incomplete because *yi*- is not an object pronoun, and, therefore, there is no goal in the sentence.

In Sentences (29b) and (30b), we are once again looking at sentences of the structure NNV. Here we find the pronominalized goal appears as an independent NP, but only to emphasize the goal. We can say in this case that *bi*- is prefixed to the verb—that is, the goal is pronominalized on the verb—because it is the emphasized NP and is therefore of special significance in the sentence.

We are now able to characterize the occurrence of *yi*- and *bi*- in third person transitive verb sentences, and we can do so in the following manner: IF A POTENT AGENT IS IN SUBJECT POSITION OF A GIVEN SENTENCE, *yi*- MUST BE PREFIXED TO THE VERB. IN ALL OTHER CASES, THE PREFIX MUST BE *bi*-. We find additional support for this hypothesis in Examples (36) and (37). In Sentences (36a) and (36b), where the agent is in subject position, we see that either *yi*- or *bi*- may be prefixed to the verb, depending on the connotation of the word 'bother':

(36)   a.   *Ishkiin nayilín y-*   *o-*   *∅-*   *∅-*   *keesh.*
                            4   7   8   9   10
                boy   girl   her-prog-he-class-bother
                'The boy bothers the girl'.
                (The boy is purposely doing something to bother the girl)

b. *Ishkiin nayilín b- o-   ∅- ∅-   keesh.*
                    4   7   8   9   10

boy   girl   her-prog-he-class-bother
'The boy bothers the girl'.
(The girl is allowing herself to be bothered by the boy,
     who may not be trying to bother her at all—and, in
     fact, may not even be present.)

In (36a), the boy is controlling the bothering and is, therefore, a potent agent. In (36b), however, it is the girl, the goal, who controls the event, so *bi-* must appear on the verb to indicate the participation of the goal.

In Example (37), only *bi-* can occur in position 4. The verb 'envy' in these sentences not only implies but states on the verb (position 1) that some kind of "effect" is taking place, and the goal, as the one who is causing the effect, is seen as participating in the event:

(37)   a. **Ishkiin nayilín a-   yi- ∅- ł-   si.*
                       1   4   8   9   10

boy   girl   effect-her-he-class-envy
'The boy envies the girl'.

b. *Ishkiin nayilín a-   bi- ∅- ł-   si.*
                   1   4   8   9   10

boy   girl   effect-her-he-class-envy
'The boy envies the girl'.

In Example (37), even though the boy is the one who is doing the envying, he is not a potent agent because the girl is affecting him in some way that causes him to have that reaction.

Returning now to Sapir and Hoijer's original analysis of Navajo, we can see that their description can be applied successfully to all of the Apache data except the sentences of Group II. Excluding those, we can certainly say that *yi-* appears when the noun immediately preceding the verb is the object, whereas *bi-* appears when the noun immediately preceding the verb is the subject. The inadequacy of their analysis, when we attempt to apply it to Apache, lies in the fact that it does not describe the behavior of *yi-* and *bi-* in sentences such as those of Group II, which cannot be ignored.

To summarize: I have presented evidence that the distribution of the verbal prefixes *yi-* and *bi-* in third person transitive sentences of San Carlos Apache is a semantically based phenomenon. I have argued that the determining factor in the form of the prefix is the significance of the goal NP either to the realization of the verb or to the sentence as a whole, and I have suggested that where full credit for the achievement of the verb goes to the agent, and the goal has not been foregrounded, the goal is not marked pronominally on the verb.

4. *YI-* AS MARKER OF HIGH TRANSITIVITY

To conclude this discussion, I will show that the observations that have been made about third person transitive sentences in San Carlos Apache can be related to a broader concept of transitivity in general. Paul Hopper and Sandra Thompson (1980)[17] present evidence that transitivity involves more than the mere presence of an object. They present a list of ten defining properties which may be correlated with the degree of transitivity of the sentence as a whole.[18] Of these ten, four have particular relevance in Apache:

	Parameter	High transitivity	Low transitivity
(i)	Participants	2 or more, $A + O$[19]	1
(ii)	Agency	A high in potency	A low in potency
(iii)	Kinesis	action	nonaction
(iv)	Affectedness of O	O totally affected	O not affected

Traditionally, the concept of transitivity involves the "transference" of an activity from an agent to a goal, and no transfer can occur if there is only one participant. In Apache, if a sentence has two or more participants, A and O, and both are third person, *yi-* or *bi-* must appear on the verb. If it appears in position 4, the verb is transitive. All of the data supports this statement. Of the other three parameters listed, a sentence with features in the "high transitivity" column has a greater degree of transitivity than does one with features in the "low transitivity" column. Let us take a brief look at the data in terms of these three properties.

I have already discussed in some detail the concept of potency in an agent as it relates to the choice of *yi-* or *bi-* on the verb, and as I need add only a few additional comments to tie our previous conclusions into the Transitivity Hypothesis, we will look first at agency. Earlier, we defined "potency" as control of the realization of an event, and it was shown that potency of the agent is a condition for prefixing *yi-* rather than *bi-* to the verb. In all cases where the agent is potent, as in the

[17] I am grateful to Pamela Munro for her excellent suggestion that I consider my data in terms of the Transitivity Hypothesis put forth by Hopper and Thompson.

[18] See the Introduction to this volume for a complete list. Hopper and Thompson (1980) also discuss the concept of transitivity as a discourse phenomenon, claiming that the defining properties are discourse determined. I have not yet investigated the Apache data from this perspective, but such an investigation is certainly called for.

[19] Hopper and Thompson follow Dixon (1979) in using 'A' for agent and 'O' for object and make no claims about the grammatical relations these two participants bear to the verb.

Group I sentences, *yi-* must appear on the verb. If the agent is nonpotent, as in the sentences of Group II, *yi-* cannot occur. Example (36), where the same sentence may be marked with either *yi-* or *bi-* depending on the potency of the agent in the achievement of the verb, demonstrates this difference quite clearly. In short, if a sentence is assigned the "high transitivity" feature for agency, *yi-* must be prefixed to the verb. Of the four relevant features, only participants and agency *must* be marked in the high column if *yi-* is to occur.

Hopper and Thompson define kinesis as "the degree of directed physical activity in the event to which the verb refers." Looking again at the data in Group I, we can see that sentences in which *yi-* is obligatory on the verb tend to involve some degree of physical activity directed toward the goal. Even in Examples (15), (20), and (21), where there is no visible motion, water and poison kill by means of some kind of physical process, and a physical process entails motion, even if it is too slow to observe. In fact, the only example in the Group I data that appears to be an exception is Example (19), where it is difficult to imagine that 'seeing', a verb of perception, involves any directed physical activity. I do not intend to claim here that it does, but I will suggest that it is possible that the Apaches do not look at this verb in quite the same way as someone whose native language is, for example, English. It is possible that they consider the verb 'see' to be a verb of motion. Gladys Reichard (1949:67) made this observation about Navajo:

> One reason that Navaho has always seemed so hard to learn is that apparently simple examples in English are least typical in Navaho. One gets into difficulties with the verb 'see', for which Navaho has several stems, none exactly equivalent; they too illustrate the exaggeration of motion. One means 'sight moves, get sight in motion, bring vision against, focus against (-'į · ł). This may be roughly interpreted as 'look at', whereas another stem (-tsé · ł) means 'see'; it is actually a cessative, literally, 'pause in sighting'.

Later, while discussing stems of sense and perception, she goes on to say the following (p. 71):

> Some ideas that we should classify here, such as seeing, belong more properly to the category of motion. A stem (-dla · ł) that indicates penetration of the atmosphere seems to denote a process rather than a perception, since it means 'bright light, harsh sound rips (the air).' It is perhaps true that even the stems listed in this category are primarily verbs of motion insofar as the idea is compatible with the expression of sensibility.

If Reichard is correct, then it is likely that the Apache interpretation of the activity of 'seeing' is at least similar to that of the Navajo.

The verbs of the Group II sentences, on the other hand, are classified in the "low transitivity" column for kinesis. The fact that the woman was worried by the baby and the child was surprised by the bee in Examples (22) and (23) respectively does not imply that the baby or the bee was actively doing anything to cause these reactions. In Example (24), the potato is seen as a passive entity that burned the girl because she brought herself in contact with it. And in Example (25), old age is an abstract entity and therefore not capable of physical activity. We can assume, then, that if a sentence falls in the "high transitivity" column for kinesis, it is likely that yi- will be prefixed to the verb.

Hopper and Thompson state that "the degree to which an action is transferred to a patient is a function of how completely that patient is AFFECTED." The implication is that the goal is affected as a result of some physical activity on the part of the agent, although actual contact is not a necessary aspect of affectedness of O. With the exception again of Example (19), the goal in each sentence in Group I is totally affected by the transference of an action from the agent, whereas the goals of the sentences of Group II could not be said to be affected at all, according to the above definition. Example (36) demonstrates this difference nicely. In (36a), the boy is actively doing something to bother the girl and affects her by placing her in that state of mind. In (36b), however, the boy may not be doing anything—he may not even be present—and the girl is seen as creating her own state of mind. Similarly, the woman in Example (22) created her own worry, the child in Example (23) created his own surprise, the girl in Example (24) was responsible for her own burning, and the horse in Example (25) was killed by some internal condition.

The fact that Example (19) differs from the other examples in Group I in that it is classified in the "low transitivity" column for affectedness of O (and possibly for kinesis) indicates that it is less transitive than the other sentences of Group I. On the other hand, it is more transitive than the sentences of Group II because it has more features in the "high transitivity" column. The Transitivity Hypothesis predicts that we will find varying degrees of transitivity among sentences of any natural language, and if we had more data, we would probably see greater variation in Apache than we have found in the limited set of examples presented here. However, we can certainly say that the sentences of Group I in general are more transitive than the sentences of Group II. Given this fact, we can make the following assumption about San Carlos Apache: SENTENCES THAT ARE HIGH IN TRANSITIVITY ARE MARKED WITH yi- IN POSITION 4; SENTENCES THAT ARE LOW IN TRANSITIVITY ARE MARKED WITH bi- IN POSITION 4.

We have said that a sentence is transitive if it has two or more participants, A and O. Let us look now at some sentences with two participants that are marked as intransitive in Apache:

(38)   *Iné istsaan b- it   n-   ∅- ∅-   jǫ.*
                              7   8 9   10
        man woman her-with imperf-he-class-love
        'The man loves the woman'.

In Example (38), the pronominal prefix *bi-* is an indirect object occurring before the postposition *-it* 'with'.[20] There is no direct object. We find similar marking in Examples (39), (40) and (41):

(39)   *Mé   chuskisí b- it   n-   ∅- ł   té.*
                                 7   8 9   10
        child candy   it- with imperf-he-class-like
        'The child likes candy'.

(40)   *John kósé bi-na   s-   ∅- ∅-   nah.*
                             7   8 9   10
        John dog it- about perf-he-class-forget
        'John forgot the dog'.

(41)   *Mary téhgochi   bí-ná   ∅- ł-   ni.*
                                  8 9   10
        Mary San Carlos it- about she-class-remember
        'The girl remembered San Carlos'.

In each of these examples, the given pronominal prefix is an indirect object attached to a postposition. I shall refer to Examples (38)–(41) as Group III.

The question that must be answered is, how do the sentences of Group III, the intransitive sentences, differ from the transitive sentences of Group I and Group II? Why are the events of 'loving', 'liking', 'forgetting' and 'remembering' considered to be *intransitive?* Notice that the Group I sentences tend to involve some kind of physical activity directed toward the goal, and the goal tends to be affected in some way by that activity. In the Group II sentences, there does not tend to be any directed physical activity and the goal is not affected, but the goal does participate in some way in the realization of the verb. Therefore, in both Group I and Group II, there is some kind of interaction between the agent and the goal, either because the agent affects the goal, or because both agent and goal participate in the achievement of the event. In the sentences

---

[20] The significance of 'with' here is somewhat elusive, as there is not necessarily any implication of reciprocity.

of Group III, however, there is no directed physical activity, the Os are not affected by the As, and the Os do not participate in the event. In short, there is no interaction between A and O. As a result, the O is marked as an indirect object. The three different relationships involving A, event and O may be summarized as follows:

Group I: A ⟶ event ⟶ O   Transitive
Group II: A ⟶ event ⟵ O   Transitive
Group III: A ⟶ event   O   Intransitive

In summary: We have looked at both transitive and intransitive sentences involving two or more third person participants and we have seen that there are varying degrees of transitivity, depending on whether a sentence is "high" or "low" for certain parameters. We have also seen that in San Carlos Apache, a sentence with two third person participants that is high in transitivity is marked with *yi-* in direct object position on the verb, and a sentence that is low in transitivity is marked with *bi-* in that position. If there are two participants, A and O, and there is no interaction between them, the O will be marked as an indirect object and the sentence will be intransitive.

If my proposals about the semantic function of *yi-* and *bi-* and the relationship between those prefixes and the degree of transitivity of a sentence are correct, then it would seem that the function of *yi-* and *bi-*, which was almost certainly the same at one time in Apache and Navajo, is now somewhat different in the two languages, for the theory as presented does not account for most of the Navajo data. It seems clear, however, that in both Western Apache and Navajo the appearance of *yi-* versus *bi-* on the verb is a phenomenon that reflects the strong interaction between grammar and cognition.

ACKNOWLEDGMENTS

There are not words enough to thank Pam Munro, whose invaluable comments on this paper took almost as much time and thinking on her part as the paper did on mine.

I also owe a special debt of gratitude to Sandra Thompson for her time, suggestions, and guidance, and to the following people who read, and/or discussed this paper with me at various stages and offered very helpful comments: Bill Bright, Lynn Gordon, Martin Huld, Ron Kendis, Paul Kroskrity, Herb Landar, and Ed Unanue.

My Apache consultants for this study were Mr. John Dawson and Mr. Earl Sisto, who chose to work with me because they felt it would benefit their people. I am deeply grateful for their time and patience and hope that I have not misrepresented in any way what they have taught me.

REFERENCES

Basso, K. (1967) "Semantic Aspects of Linguistic Acculturation," *American Anthropologist* 69,

Creamer, M. (1974) "Ranking in Navajo Nouns," in P. Platero, ed., *Dine Bizaad Nanil'iih/ Navajo Language Review 1,* Center For Applied Linguistics, Washington, D.C.

Dixon, R. M. W. (1979) "Ergativity," *Language* 55, 59–138.

Elgin, S. (1973) *Some Topics in Navajo Syntax,* unpublished doctoral dissertation, University of California, San Diego.

Frishberg, N. (1972) "Navajo Object Markers and the Great Chain of Being," in J. Kimball, ed., *Syntax and Semantics 1,* Academic Press, New York.

Goddard, P. (1919) "San Carlos Apache Texts," *Anthropological Papers, American Museum of Natural History,* Vol. 34, 147–283.

Hale, K. (1972) "A Note on Subject–Object Inversion in Navajo," in B. Kachru, ed., *Issues in Linguistics: Papers in Linguistics in Honor of Henry and Renee Kahane,* University of Illinois Press, Urbana.

Hill, F. (1963) "Some Comparisons between San Carlos and White Mountain Dialects of Western Apache," in H. Hoijer, ed., *Studies in the Athabaskan Languages* (University of California Publications in Linguistics 29), Berkeley.

Hoijer, H. (1945) "The Apachean Verb, Part I: Verb Structure and Pronominal Prefixes," *International Journal of American Linguistics* 11, 193–203.

Hopper, P. and S. Thompson (1980) "Transitivity in Grammar and Discourse," *Language* 56, 251–299.

Kroskrity, P. (1977) *Aspects of Arizona Tewa Language Structure and Language Use,* unpublished doctoral dissertation, Indiana University.

Li, C. and S. Thompson (1976) "Subject and Topic: A New Typology of Language," in C. Li, ed., *Subject and Topic,* Academic Press, New York.

Munro, P., D. Bradshaw, H. George, R. Begaye, and N. Begaye (1976). Untitled, unpublished abstract, University of California, Los Angeles.

Reichard, G. (1949) "The Character of the Navajo Verb Stem," *Word* 5, 55–76.

Salego, L. (1977) "The Hierarchical Classification of Nouns in Navajo," unpublished paper, University of California, Los Angeles.

Sapir, E. and H. Hoijer (1967) *The Phonology and Morphology of the Navajo Language* (University of California Publications in Linguistics 50), Berkeley.

Witherspoon, G. (1977) *Language and Art in the Navajo Universe,* The University of Michigan Press, Ann Arbor.

Young, R. and W. Morgan (1943) *The Navajo Language,* Education Division, U.S. Indian Service, Washington, D.C.

THE ORIGINS OF GRAMMATICAL ENCODING
OF EVENTS[1]

DAN I. SLOBIN

Some time after the child begins to combine words, he or she begins
to mark these combinations grammatically, through the use of word order
regularities and grammatical particles. I suggest that the range of notions
encoded simply by word combination is broader than the range of notions
that first receive grammatical expression. That is, while two- and three-
word utterances may express a number of conceptual relations, only
some of those relations are candidates for grammaticization at the earliest
phase of structured speech. Those notions that are first marked grammatically are in some sense *salient* to the child, and I shall refer to them
as prototypical. Furthermore, I suggest that prototypical situations are
encoded in the most basic grammatical forms available in a language,
and I shall refer to such basic forms as *canonical*.

The way into grammar involves attention to both prototypical situations in the world of reference and canonical forms in the world of
language. I will develop this point by examining one intersection of
meaning and form: the encoding of transitive events. The same argument

[1] This paper was presented to the Symposium "Beyond Description in Child Language,"
Max-Planck-Gesellschaft Projektgruppe für Psycholinguistik, Nijmegen, The Netherlands,
1979. It appeared in *The Child's Construction of Language*, edited by Werner Deutsch,
Academic Press, 1981.

409

could be made for various semantic domains—for example, locative relations, situations that involve beneficiaries, and many others. The general picture I wish to elaborate is the following: The child is anchored to a narrow meaning–form correspondence in the earliest phase. The meaning can be characterized as a highly salient, "prototypical" event type, such as object transfer, physical manipulation, voluntary movement, and the like. I will not attempt to explain why such events have special status for the child, but take such general cognitive representations as given for purposes of the present discussion. Their special status is to be found in an intersection of factors involving basic perceptual categories, emotion, and habitual activities and interactions. The input language encodes such prototypical event types in a canonical way—say, the encoding of transitive events by means of a basic SVO declarative sentence in English, or the use of an accusative inflection and variable word order in Turkish. Growth proceeds from this initial pairing of prototypical event and canonical form.[2] I propose that the meaning of the form is gradually extended—through metaphorical and semantic extension of the sort discussed by Schlesinger (1981)—while the form is held constant. Later in development the form changes as well, and other variants are mastered.

1. PROTOTYPICAL EVENTS

These ideas can be explored through a close examination of *transitive events*—first looking at the prototypical transitive situation, and then at the canonical forms used to encode this situation in various types of languages. Paul Hopper and Sandra Thompson (1980) argue that transitivity can be seen as a continuum, in which clauses highest in transitivity involve object nouns that are proper, human, animate, concrete, singular, count, referential, and definite; and in which actions are willful, punctual, and concrete. They demonstrate a number of linguistic consequences of high transitivity in various types of languages. For example, in Spanish

[2] What I refer to as a "pairing of prototypical event and canonical form" is a special instance of what Fillmore (1975, 1977) refers to as the association of *scenes* with linguistic *frames*. Prototypical events are scenes involving high perceptual salience and kinetic-emotional loading for the child. They are, in Fillmore's terms, "familiar kinds of interpersonal transactions" and "standard scenarios defined by the culture" (1975, p. 124). Canonical sentence forms are privileged linguistic frames—namely, those frames that most reliably embody the language-specific syntactic and morphological means of encoding salient scenes. Such forms are probably also those used most frequently and reliably by adults to encode prototypical events. Thus, in Fillmorean terms, this essay can be understood as an elaboration of the claim that the association of scenes with frames has its origins in the association of prototypical scenes with prototypical frames.

direct objects are marked by a particle, *a,* only if they are human or human-like and referential. In many languages, including Turkish, Hebrew, Amharic, and Persian, objects are morphologically marked only if definite. On the side of the agent and action, in many languages special means are employed to mark clauses that encode a high degree of "directed physical activity"—what Hopper and Thompson call the kinetic quality of the event, and the degree of deliberateness or spontaneity of the agent—the *volitional* quality of the event. I will not review the many linguistic arguments, embracing such forms as accusative and ergative markers, passives and antipassives, perfectives, and so forth. The important point is that Hopper and Thompson have, on linguistic grounds, identified a "highly transitive clause type" characterized by a human-like agent "behaving actively, volitionally, and totally to a definite or referential object." The languages of the world have chosen—in one way or another—to give special status to such clauses in their grammars.

I suggest that children, also, give special status to such clauses in the earliest phases of grammatical development. On the basis of evidence from both linguistics and child language, we can define the prototypical transitive event as one in which an animate agent willfully brings about a physical and perceptible change of state or location in a patient by means of direct body contact. Such events are encoded in consistent grammatical fashion by about age 2, whether the means of encoding be regular word order, accusative case marking, or ergative case marking.

Let us begin with ergative case marking, for here the situation is clearest. The input language clearly distinguishes transitive events in grammatical terms. One of the few ergative languages that has been studied developmentally is Kaluli—a language of Papua New Guinea, investigated in detail by Bambi Schieffelin (1979a, 1979b). In Kaluli there is a special grammar marker—an ergative noun suffix—that indicates the agent of action. This suffix is typically used in situations where someone does something with an effect, as when an agent acts on some object or person to change its state or location. The ergative suffix would thus be attached to agent nouns in sentences such as the following:

'Mother is cooking food'.

'Father is cutting wood'.

'The pig knocked over the bucket'.

But if someone acts without effect on another entity, the ergative suffix is not allowed. Thus it would be lacking in sentences such as:

'Mother is sleeping'.

'Father is thinking'.

'The pig is running'.

That is, the ergative suffix marks only the subjects of transitive verbs.

The subjects of intransitive verbs (and the objects of transitive verbs) are unmarked or marked with a neutral particle (absolutive or nominative).

The acquisition of this marker reveals the special status of high transitive situations. It is acquired early: In all of Schieffelin's samples it is present by age 26 months in two-word utterances. It commonly appears on the agents of verbs such as 'give', 'grab', 'take', and 'hit'—that is, highly kinetic, direct actions. It tends to be lacking in utterances of lower transitivity, with verbs such as 'say', 'call out', and 'see'. Additional evidence for the importance of high transitivity is provided when we ask about the extension of the ergative suffix to the subjects of *in*transitive verbs.

On the basis of what has been written about the acquisition of non-ergative languages (such as English) and the cognitive bases of grammar, we might expect the ergative suffix to be overextended at first to all actors, whether they are causal agents or not. In almost all semantic characterizations of early child speech in the American psycholinguistic literature, it is assumed that 'human actor' is a basic prelinguistic category. On these grounds it would not be surprising if Kaluli children incorrectly applied the suffix to the subjects of intransitive sentences, such as 'Mother is sleeping', 'Father is thinking', and 'The pig is running'. However, this sort of error NEVER occurs in Schieffelin's extensive data.[3]

I suggest that this lack of overextension is due to the fact that the Kaluli child has begun with what Martin Braine (1976) has called a "limited scope formula." I find this notion more useful than an approach based on semantic case categories or a priori categories of infant cognition. It seems that the child does not begin with categories, such as 'actor' or 'agent', looking for the linguistic expressions of such notions in his or her native language. What the child may begin with is much more limited and childlike ways of conceiving of basic events and situations, at first matching grammatical expression to primary or basic event schemata. Many psycholinguistic accounts have depicted the child on the threshold of structured language already equipped with a prelinguistic analysis of events into the categories required for linguistic expression. Perhaps it is not the categories which are primitive, however, but the basic events and parameters out of which the linguistic categories will be built. The fact that Kaluli children limit their use of the ergative suffix to the encoding of prototypical transitive events is consistent with

---

[3] Recent work by Pye (1979, 1980) on the acquisition of another ergative language, the Mayan language Quiche, presents a similar picture. In this language, ergativity is marked on the verb by a choice of ergative or absolutive person markers. As in Kaluli, children did not extend the ergative markers from transitive to intransitive constructions.

the suggestion that the basic notion is not something like 'human actor', but 'causal agent'. 'Causal agent', however, is not an isolated notion in itself; it is part of an entire scene or event in which the agent is embedded. It is such prototypical events, rather than case categories, that seem to provide the initial conceptual framework for grammatical marking.

Now consider the opposite sort of language from Kaluli—the sort of language in which the object, rather than the agent, receives grammatical marking. In such languages—accusative languages—the input does not provide a clear guide to the marking of objects involved in prototypical transitive events. Accusative inflections or placement of direct objects in sentence frames apply to the objects of all types of verbs. In Russian, for example, the direct object (in an affirmative sentence) is marked by an accusative inflection regardless of the type of action involved. The word for 'book' would receive the accusative suffix in all of the following sentences:

'I read the book'.
'I saw the book'.
'I picked up the book'.
'I tore the book'.
'I threw away the book'.

If the suffix corresponds to some underlying semantic notion of 'patient', it should be applied in all such utterances by children. In the case of the child studied by Gvozdev (1949), however, the accusative was at first limited to a particular subset of events—namely, those of high transitivity. The suffix emerged when the child was 23 months old, and was only applied to the objects of verbs involving direct, physical action on things—verbs such as 'give', 'carry', 'put', and 'throw'. Thus the child would say things like 'I picked up the book', 'I tore the book', and 'I threw away the book'—all with an accusative suffix on the word 'book'; but he would not use this suffix when saying things like 'I read the book' and 'I saw the book'.

The Russian UNDERextension makes the same point as the Kaluli lack of OVERextension, although in one language we are concerned with object marking and in the other with agent marking. In both cases the child seems to be using grammar to encode a prototypical event of physical object manipulation.

It is hard to find additional data, as most child language studies do not subcategorize grammatical devices on the basis of the semantics of the lexical items in utterances. The most useful data come from Martin Braine's (1976) reanalyses of two-word combinations in various languages, arguing for limited range semantic categories. At this stage one would look for limited-scope formulae which reflect a saliency of prototypical transitive events. The clearest example comes from Braine's analysis of two-word utterances in the Samoan child, Tofi, studied by Keith Kernan (1969). This analysis suggests an early word-order pattern for talking about moving or holding objects—a pattern apparently not immediately generalized to all events involving action on objects. In examining the Finnish speech of Seppo, studied by Bowerman (1973), Braine suggests that "Seppo is groping for the means of expressing movement in a way that permits both the object that moves and the agent of movement." A similar analysis is presented for the Swedish child, Embla, studied by Lange and Larsson (1973). Braine concludes (1976, p. 67) that an early limited-scope formula may be described as "act + object-moved-or-manipulated-during-the-act." So even in the case of early word order regularities, there seems to be some evidence that limitation of grammatical patterning may reflect a sensitivity to events of high transitivity.[4]

Evidence from historical linguistics is also strikingly consistent with these notions. In some cases it has been possible to trace the origins of grammatical case markers back to meaningful words. Both in Chinese and in a number of West African languages direct object markers have been developed from verbs that originally meant 'take' or 'hold' (Givón, 1975, 1979; Li and Thompson, 1973; Lord, 1973, this volume). These verbs, of course, are drawn from the prototypical transitive event, and are the same verbs which first received accusative marking in child Russian and ergative marking in child Kaluli. And, like child Russian and child Kaluli, in Mandarin 'take' to mark direct object cannot be used with verbs such as 'see', 'hear', 'read', and others in which the object is not a patient which is acted upon in a more directly manipulable manner.

Both in historical language change and in child language development such semantically transparent applications of grammatical forms are gradually extended, at first metaphorically, and ultimately becoming more or less opaque. Accusative inflections, for example, are eventually ex-

---

[4] Recent work by Berman (1980, forthcoming) on Hebrew acquisition shows children's sensitivity to transitivity in another area of grammar. Hebrew verb patterns alternate to derive forms expressing causative, middle-voice, reflexive, reciprocal, passive, and inchoative. Four- and five-year-olds, however, make productive errors that indicate they have divided the system into a simple transitive–nontransitive opposition, using one set of forms to encode active, transitive, and causative events, and the other set to refer to situations that are passive, intransitive, reflexive/reciprocal, and inchoative. As Berman notes (1980, p. 693): "Thus, children's construal of the system captures the traditional division of verbs into transitive versus intransitive, and accords well with more contemporary treatments of the transitivity axis as a crucial one across languages."

tended to mark the direct objects of verbs that are not part of the prototypical event of physical object manipulation, as in the examples from adult Russian cited earlier. That is to say, in learning such a language the child must extend his prototypical event category to include events of lower transitivity until the notion of transitivity has become fully grammaticized.

2. CANONICAL SENTENCE FORMS

While carrying out such semantic extensions, the child at first remains syntactically anchored in the canonical sentence form used to encode the prototypical notion. This is perhaps clearest in the case of English transitive sentences, where the active sentence form is predominant in both child and adult speech. Noncanonical forms, such as passives and clefts, are later acquisitions, in both speech and comprehension. A large and familiar body of research data shows that English-speaking children at first respond randomly to passive sentences, apparently not even treating them as interpretable, and later impose the canonical SVO order, leading to misinterpretation of passives (Bever, 1970; deVilliers and deVilliers, 1973; Maratsos, 1974; and others).

In inflectional languages the definition of canonical sentence form is more complex. In Indo-European, where inflectional systems are no longer fully functional, both inflectional and word order information are necessary components in the sentence processing system, although some sentences can be interpreted with only inflectional or only word order cues. In such languages, children appear to define the canonical sentence as one in which both sorts of information are consistently present. For example, when the Serbo-Croatian-speaking children studied by Radulović (1975) began to apply the accusative inflection regularly in their speech, they adhered to standard SVO word order for several months, only later employing the variability in word order allowed by the input language. In Serbo-Croatian not all nouns have a distinctive accusative inflection. In sentences that have a clearly marked direct object, variation in word order is possible; lacking such marking, SVO order is generally required. Thus both devices—word order and inflection—are necessary for the interpretation of transitive sentences in general throughout the language. What these children have done is to take the canonical transitive sentence to be one with two syntactic features: fixed SVO word order and direct object inflection.

By contrast, consider a language such as Turkish, in which nominal inflections are regularly and consistently applied. Here word order is free to function pragmatically while case inflections signal semantic relations. In such languages children, early on, define the canonical transitive sentence form as one with two nouns and a verb—in any order—provided one of the nouns is inflected for direct object and the other is in the unmarked, or nominative form.

The issue of sensitivity to canonical sentence forms is most easily explored in comprehension studies, rather than in the exploration of corpora of speech production. It is, of course, suggestive that English-speaking children use many active sentences; that Serbo-Croatian children go through a phase of using fixed SVO order with inflected objects; that Turkish children freely vary word order while maintaining inflected objects in all positions; and so on. In comprehension studies, however, it is possible to probe the limits of a child's sentence-processing strategies, revealing the range of forms that children are willing to entertain as possible sentences in their language. In the remainder of the paper I explore several such comprehension studies—from our research at Berkeley and several other projects—indicating that at an early stage of development children respond consistently to transitive sentences in experimental situations only if those sentences are presented in canonical form. Canonical form always includes the requisite finite inflection on the verb, and some indication of the semantic roles of the participants—word order and/or case inflections, depending on the language (for details, see Slobin and Bever, in press; Slobin, 1982).

The basic experimental setting in all of these studies is one in which the child is presented with a reversible sentence comprised of two animate nouns and a verb, such that either noun could be agent or patient of the scene; and the child is given referent objects for the two nouns and asked to act out the sentence. For example, when given a toy cow and a toy horse, the child is asked to show: *The cow kicks the horse*.

Let us consider the role of word order in languages that lack nominal case inflections, such as English, Italian, and French. As a part of our Berkeley cross-linguistic studies, we presented American and Italian children with strings in the three possible orders, NVN, NNV, and VNN, using the appropriate articles and subject verb agreement (e.g., *The dog scratches the cat, Il gatto graffia il cane*). Overall, children between the ages of 2;0 and 4;8 responded consistently only to sentences in NVN order, corresponding to the standard SVO order of those languages. Apparently, strings in nonstandard order, such as *The dog the cat scratches* and *Scratches the dog the cat,* were simply not heard as sentences. That is, they were not treated as stimuli capable of linguistic analysis. Note that this finding is different from the usual finding in regard to passive sentences in English. Passives correspond to canonical NVN order, but the inflectional morphology is noncanonical—both in regard to the verb and the second noun. A stimulus such as *The cat is scratched by the dog* is, at first, simply not heard as a possible English sentence, as the canonical definition of a sentence is limited to the two noun phrases and an appropriately inflected verb. At a later stage, when the additional morphology of a passive sentence can be assimilated as within the bounds of interpretable English, it falls prey to the canonical SVO interpretation.

The French findings of Sinclair and Bronckart (1972) can be understood from this point of view. In their studies, children were also presented with sentences in the three possible orders, NVN, NNV, and VNN, but, unlike the Berkeley studies, the stimuli lacked all morphological markers. Nouns were presented without articles, and the verb was in the infinitive (e.g., *garçon pousser fille*). Whereas we found consistent response to NVN stimuli by about age 3 in English and Italian, Sinclair and Bronckart did not find consistent response to their corresponding French stimuli until later than age 5. I suggest that their younger subjects simply did not hear three-word strings lacking in standard morphology as sentences, just as English-speaking children at first do not apply consistent sentence interpretation strategies to passives. The canonical sentence form requires that the verb be inflected in standard form (probably third person singular), thus excluding the French infinitive and the English auxiliary-participle construction.

The French stimuli also lacked articles, but it is not clear what role this omission played, as the verb morphology was also noncanonical, and as proper nouns can occur without articles. In languages with inflectional nominal morphology, however, it is clear that the canonical sentence form requires that the appropriate morphology be present. Relevant evidence comes from our experiments on Turkish. In those studies we presented children with all six orders of S, V, and O, with appropriate accusative inflection on the object noun. Children as young as 2;0 performed consistently and appropriately in response to all six sentence types. We also presented them with ungrammatical strings in which neither noun was inflected: NVN, NNV, and VNN. Children's response to such stimuli was random, reflecting the fact that word order does not play a significant role in identifying semantic relations in Turkish, but that case inflections are essential. For these children a canonical transitive sentence must have inflectional marking of the patient, but may be in any order.

Similar evidence, though not as clear, is also available for Japanese. Hakuta (1977), using the three possible orders of two nouns and a verb, presented children with three-word strings in which both nouns lacked the postposed inflectional particles and the verb was in the infinitive. Four-year-olds performed inconsistently to these noncanonical strings, though three-and-a-half-year-olds correctly responded to SOV sentences with the accusative particle. However, we cannot separate the results of the deviance in verb and noun morphology in this study. At any rate, the canonical Japanese sentence form must have grammatical markers.

In Serbo-Croatian, as in other inflectional Indo-European languages, it is possible to consider the contributions of both word order and nominal inflection to the child's definition of canonical sentence form. We have already seen that in early production Serbo-Croatian children adhere to standard word order when first acquiring the accusative inflection. Our comprehension studies reinforce this impression. In Serbo-Croatian many nouns no longer have a distinctive form in the accusative. That is, in some instances nominative and accusative are morphologically distinct (generally true of masculine animate and feminine nouns), whereas in other instances there is no distinction (masculine inanimate and neuter nouns). Thus, depending on the nouns involved, in any particular transitive sentence distinctive case inflection may appear on either subject or object, or both, or neither. When there is no clear surface marking of case roles, an SVO word order rule generally applies. We presented children with most of the major possibilities for transitive, reversible sentences. Using the three orders of NVN, NNV, and VNN, there were five possibilities for each of the three word orders—for example, for NVN order: (a) SVO with subject marked, (b) SVO with object marked, (c) OVS with subject marked, (d) OVS with object marked, and (e) NVN, with neither subject nor object distinctively marked. Accordingly, there were 15 different sentence types, as shown in Table 1. The youngest children, 2;0–2;8, responded consistently to only one of these 15 types—namely, the most canonical in their language: SVO with object

TABLE 1
SERBO-CROATIAN STIMULI[a]

S̲VO	SO̲V	VS̲O
SVO̲	SO̲V	VS̲O
O̲VS	O̲SV	VOS̲
OVS̲	OSV̲	VO̲S
NVN	NNV	VNN

[a] In sentences containing S and O, the underlined element represents a feminine noun, thus distinctively marked morphologically as either subject or object, while the other noun is neuter, with no morphological distinction of subject and object. Sentences with two Ns have two neuter nouns, and can only be interpreted on the basis of word order.

marked. This sentence conforms to standard order, and has inflectional marking on the salient case in this accusative-type language. Apparently none of the other sentence forms is, at first, heard as an interpretable string.

As Serbo-Croatian development continues, it becomes clear that the accusative inflection plays a salient role. In a later phase of development, reversed object–subject orders are only comprehended if it is the object that is morphologically marked. That is, an accusative inflection on the first noun can indicate to the child that the first noun is not the agent, resulting in an appropriate object–subject order interpretation. However, if the first noun is unmarked and the second noun has a distinctive subject inflection, a word order strategy overrides inflectional information, and the first noun is incorrectly chosen as agent. Thus later development reveals that the canonical sentence form includes a more salient status of object marking, in relation to subject marking.

Further development also reveals a special status for the canonical word order, NVN. The development of patient-first strategies for sentences in which the first noun is in the accusative is most rapid for sentences in standard word order. Thus, in a language with mixed word order and inflectional marking of semantic relations, the definition of canonical sentence form relies on both sorts of information. As children move beyond the canonical pattern, they remain anchored in the crucial features of that pattern—in this case, NVN order and accusative inflection. They thus include verb medial position in their definition of canonical sentence form.

A similar developmental pattern has been recently documented in Hebrew development by Daniel Frankel and co-workers (Frankel, Amir, Frenkel, and Arbel, 1980; Frankel and Arbel, 1979). In Hebrew the direct object is a preposed particle, preceding the object noun phrase. The verb agrees with the subject in number and gender. Children's responses to reversible transitive sentences is most consistent when all of the grammatical cues are present and in agreement—that is, SVO order with the object particle and with appropriate subject–verb agreement by gender. (This was tested by having masculine and feminine participants in the sentences.) Response was most consistent if all three types of grammatical information were present: word order, object marking, and gender agreement. By systematically varying these features, however, Frankel and co-workers were able to show that word order is the most salient feature of the canonical sentence form for Hebrew children, followed by object marking, with subject–verb gender agreement the least central feature of the basic sentence form.

This is exactly the same pattern we found in Serbo-Croatian. The two languages are unrelated, and the grammatical expressions are quite different. Object marking is by suffix in Serbo-Croatian; by preposed particle in Hebrew. Subject marking is based on the nominative form of the noun in Serbo-Croatian; on subject–verb gender agreement in Hebrew. But both languages are accusative in type, and allow varying word order while adhering to a predominant standard order. In both cases, children's canonical sentence form includes both order and inflectional features, weighting order most heavily, object marking next, and subject marking least. A similar weighting of inflectional cues has been found for German by Mills (1977), who also found that the tendency to pick first noun as agent was more readily blocked by an initial object inflection (in this case a masculine accusative article) than by subject marking on the second noun (a masculine nominative article) in sentences where the first noun was neutral in regard to subject or object marking. The roles of subject and object inflection on nouns is the same in both Indo-European languages, Serbo-Croatian and German, although the sentential position of these inflections differs. These cross-linguistic similarities suggest that there may be some very general principles on which children come to form expectancies, or Gestalten, in regard to the basic sentence forms of their language. Table 2 summarizes the canonical sentence forms that emerge from these studies. Presumably there are other canonical sentence forms for other prototypical events in early experience.

In conclusion, although the data are still scanty I hope to have shown that there is some commonality in the ways in which children conceive of basic events; and that, in each type of language, children initially isolate and generalize basic sentence forms. Furthermore, I believe there are some important links, however shadowy, between these two pro-

TABLE 2

CHILDREN'S CANONICAL SENTENCE FORMS FOR TRANSITIVE EVENTS[a]

English, Italian
    Article   Noun $Verb_{person}$ Article   Noun

Turkish
    any order of Noun, Noun, and $Verb_{person}$,
    provided one Noun is $Noun_{accusative}$

Serbo-Croatian
    $Noun_{nominative}$ $Verb_{person}$ $Noun_{accusative}$

German
    $Article_{nominative}$ Noun $Verb_{person}$ $Article_{accusative}$ Noun

Hebrew
    Article   Noun $Verb_{person, gender}$ Accusative Particle   Article   Noun

[a] In these sentence schemas, the verb always agrees with the first noun.

cesses of pattern formation, such that prototypical events and canonical sentence forms constitute a nucleus for the growth of language.

REFERENCES

Berman, R. A. (1980) "Child Language as Evidence for Grammatical Description: Preschoolers' Construal of Transitivity in the Verb System of Hebrew," *Linguistics*, 18, 677–701.

Berman, R. A. (forthcoming) "Acquisition of Hebrew," in D. I. Slobin, ed., *The Crosslinguistic Study of Language Acquisition*, Lawrence Erlbaum, Hillsdale, New Jersey.

Bever, T. G. (1970) "The Cognitive Basis for Linguistic Structures," in J. R. Hayes, ed., *Cognition and the Development of Language*, Wiley, New York.

Bowerman, M. (1973) *Early Syntactic Development: A Cross-Linguistic Study with Special Reference to Finnish*, Cambridge University Press, Cambridge.

Braine, M. D. S. (1976) Children's First Word Combinations (*Monographs of the Society for Research in Child Development* 41).

de Villiers, J. G. and P. A. de Villiers (1973) "A Cross-Sectional Study of the Development of Grammatical Morphemes in Child Speech," *Journal of Psycholinguistic Research* 2, 267–278.

Fillmore, C. J. (1975) "An Alternative to Checklist Theories of Meaning," in C. Cogen, H. Thompson, G. Thurgood, K. Whistler, and J. Wright, eds., *Proceedings of the First Annual Meeting of the Berkeley Linguistics Society*, Berkeley Linguistics Society, Institute of Human Learning, University of California, Berkeley.

Fillmore, C. J. (1977) "Topics in Lexical Semantics," in R. W. Cole, ed., *Current Issues in Linguistic Theory*, Indiana University Press, Bloomington.

Frankel, D. G., M. Amir, E. Frenkel, and T. Arbel (1980) "A Developmental Study of the Role of Word Order in Comprehending Hebrew," *Journal of Experimental Child Psychology* 29, 23–35.

Frankel, D. G., and T. Arbel (1979) "A Developmental Study of Children's Assignments of Sentence Relations on the Basis of Conflicting and Complementary Strategies," unpublished paper, Hebrew University, Jerusalem.

Givón, T. (1975) "Serial Verbs and Syntactic Change: Niger-Congo," in C. N. Li, ed., *Word Order and Word Order Change*, University of Texas Press, Austin.

Givón, T. (1979) *On Understanding Grammar*, Academic Press, New York.

Gvozdev, A. N. (1949) *Formirovaniye u Rebenka Grammaticheskogo Stroya Russkogo Yazyka*, Izd-vo Akademii Pedagogicheskikh Nauk RSFSR, Moscow.

Hakuta, K. (1977) "Word Order and Particles in the Acquisition of Japanese," in *Papers and Reports on Child Language Development* 13, Department of Linguistics, Stanford University, Stanford, California.

Hopper, P. and S. Thompson (1980) "Transitivity in Grammar and Discourse," *Language* 56, 251–299.

Kernan, K. T. (1969) *The Acquisition of Language by Samoan Children*, unpublished doctoral dissertation, University of California, Berkeley [Working Paper No. 21 (1969), Language-Behavior Research Laboratory, University of California, Berkeley].

Lange, S. and K. Larsson (1973) "Syntactical Development of a Swedish Girl Embla, between 20 and 42 Months of Age, I: Age 20–25 Months" (*Report No. 1, Project Child Language Syntax*), Institutionem for Nordiska Sprak, University of Stockholm.

Li, C. and S. Thompson (1973) "Serial Verb Constructions in Mandarin Chinese: Subordination or Coordination, *You Take the High Node and I'll Take the Low Node,* Chicago Linguistic Society, University of Chicago.

Lord, C. (1973) "Serial Verbs in Transition," *Studies in African Linguistics* 4, 269–296.

Lord, C. (this volume) "The Development of Object Markers in Serial Verb Languages."

Maratsos, M. P. (1974) "Children Who Get Worse at Understanding the Passive: A Replication of Bever," *Journal of Psycholinguistic Research* 3, 65–74.

Mills, A. E. (1977) "First and Second Language Acquisition in German: A Parallel Study," *Ludwigsburg Studies in Language and Linguistics* 2.

Pye, C. L. (1979) *The Acquisition of Grammatical Morphemes in Quiche Mayan,* unpublished doctoral dissertation, University of Pittsburgh.

Pye, C. (1980) "The Acquisition of Person Markers in Quiche Mayan," in *Papers and Reports on Child Language Development* 19, Department of Linguistics, Stanford University, Stanford, California.

Radulovic, L. (1975) *Acquisition of Language: Studies of Dubrovnik Children,* unpublished doctoral dissertation, University of California, Berkeley.

Schieffelin, B. B. (1979a) "A Developmental Study of Word Order and Casemarking in an Ergative Language," in *Papers and Reports on Child Language Development* 17, Department of Linguistics, Stanford University, Stanford, California.

Schieffelin, B. B. (1979b) "How Kaluli Children Learn What to Say, What to Do, and How to Feel: An Ethnographic Study of the Development of Communicative Competence," unpublished doctoral dissertation, Columbia University, Teachers College (Revised version to be published by Cambridge University Press).

Schlesinger, I. M. (1981) "Semantic Assimilation and the Development of Rational Categories," in W. Deutsch, ed., *The Child's Construction of Language,* Academic Press, London.

Sinclair, H. and J. P. Bronckart (1972) "S.V.O. A linguistic universal? A study in developmental psycholinguistics," *Journal of Experimental Child Psychology* 14, 329–348.

Slobin, D. I. (1982) "Universal and Particular in the Acquisition of Language," in L. Gleitman and E. Wanner, eds., *Language Acquisition: State of the Art,* Cambridge University Press, Cambridge.

Slobin, D. I. and T. G. Bever (in press) "Children Use Canonical Sentence Schemas: A Cross-linguistic Study of Word Order and Inflections," *Cognition.*

TRANSITIVITY AND OBJECTHOOD IN JAPANESE

NOBUKO SUGAMOTO

1. INTRODUCTION

This paper concerns itself with two types of two-argument sentences in Japanese, one in which the object NP is case marked by a postposition *o* and another in which the NP which appears to be the object is case marked by a postposition *ga*.[1] It is generally understood that *ga* is a nominative case marker for a subject NP and *o* is an accusative case marker for an object NP.[2] Hence, the identification of the apparent object

---

[1] For example, as in

(i) *Watashi wa shitsumon o rikaisuru.*
    I   question   understand
    'I understand the question'.
(ii) *Watashi wa shitsumon ga wakaru.*
     I   question   understand
     'I understand the question'.

[2] In order to distinguish between cases and syntactic functions, "nominative," "accusative," and so forth will be used to refer to NPs with respect to their case markers and "subject," "object," and so forth to refer to them with respect to their syntactic functions. In the same manner, "topic" will be used as a case category and "theme" as a syntactic function. See also Footnote 5.

423

NP marked by a subject marker is a point of controversy among Japanese grammarians. Traditionally, Japanese grammarians took this NP to be a subject (Kieda 1936, Martin 1958, Mitsuya 1934, Oono *et al.* 1975, Yuzawa 1962). Transformational grammarians regard this as an object (Kuno 1973a, 1973b; Kuroda 1978; Shibatani 1977); for example, Kuno defines it as the object of a stative transitive predicate.[3] Tokieda (1947) proposes to recognize a special case for this particular NP and names it the *taishoo* "objective" case.[4] Regardless of the viewpoint taken, however, no explanation has been given to account for this conflict between the case marking and syntactic function of the NP in question.

The purpose of this paper, then, is to determine (*a*) whether the NP marked by *ga* is in fact a subject or an object; (*b*) if it is an object, and *ga* has a dual role of a subject marker and an object marker, how an object marked by *o* and an object marked by *ga* differ from each other; and (*c*) whether the two roles of *ga* are in any way related to each other.

2. CASE MARKING OF THEME, SUBJECT, AND OBJECT NPs

As a preliminary to the discussion to follow, I will first explain relevant points of case marking in Japanese. Case marking of theme, subject, and object NPs involves the topical postposition *wa* as well as the nominative *ga* and the accusative *o*. A subject NP is typically marked by *ga* as in (1).

(1)   *Kono tochi ga   takai.*
       this   land nom expensive
       'This land is expensive'.

An object NP is typically marked by *o* as in (2).

(2)   *Watashi ga   kono tochi o   kau.*
       I   nom this land acc buy
       'I will buy this land'.

---

[3] The stativity of predicates that take an NP-*ga* "object" has been recognized by other grammarians such as Sakuma (1967) and Shibatani (1978a).

[4] Tokieda states that "it is appropriate to call it a *taishoo* word which refers to the thing that gives rise to the feelings of a person . . ." (p. 376) and that "it becomes necessary to distinguish between a genuine subject word and a *taishoo* word which is a subject and yet different from it . . ." (p. 377). (Translation by Sugamoto.)

A theme NP of a theme–comment sentence structure may also be marked by *ga*.[5]

(3)   *Kono atari ga   tochi ga   takai.*[6]
        this   area nom land nom expensive
        '(It is) this area (where) land is expensive'.

A topic NP of a sentence is marked by topical *wa*. In (4) the subject NP of (2), *watashi* 'I', is the topic.

(4)   *Watashi wa   kono tochi o   kau.*
        I   topic this land acc buy
        'I will buy this land'.

In (5), it is the theme NP of (3) *kono atari* 'this area' that is the topic.

(5)   *Kono atari wa   tochi ga   takai.*
        this   area topic land nom expensive
        'As for this area, land is expensive'.

The difference between (2) and (4) and the difference between (3) and (5) are essentially the same. A topic NP-*wa* is defocused or backgrounded in the message of the sentence while a nontopic NP-*ga* is itself a focus of the sentence. Kuno (1973a, 1973b) notes the function of *ga* as a designator of "new, unpredictable information" in a discourse. In English this difference could be shown by stress, which would fall on 'Í' in (2), on 'thís area' in (3), on 'thís land' in (4), and on 'lánd' in (5). In an isolated sentence the first NP is most likely to be topical (except in presentative-existential sentences).[7] Whether a NP will be marked by

---

[5] Since there is some terminological nonuniformity in the uses of "topic" and "theme" in Japanese, it must be understood that a "theme" NP is used here as the syntactic category of an initial NP in the structure, NP[S], which is commonly known as a topic–comment sentence structure (cf. Li and Thompson, 1976). "Topic," on the other hand, refers to the case of an NP (not only a theme or subject NP but also NPs of other syntactic functions) that is marked by the topical case marker *wa*. Elsewhere, "topic" and "theme" have been used interchangeably or ambiguously as to this morpho-syntactic distinction.

[6] According to Kuno (1973a, 1973b) this sentence is a multiple subject construction in which the first NP, *kono atari* 'this area' is derived from the underlying genitive construction *kono atari no tochi* 'the land of this area' through a subjectivization transformation. Shibatani (1977), however, has claimed that the first NP-*ga* in this type of sentence is not a subject.

[7] See Givón (1979) for discourse-governed word order: "shared, presupposed, 'more topical' information must appear earlier than newer information . . . . The re-established topic thus appears, most commonly, as a left-dislocated element, that is, the first element, followed by the relevant assertion [p. 300]."

topical *wa* or by nontopical *ga* is primarily a discourse–pragmatic rather than syntactic matter, and as it is not our present concern it suffices here to say that a theme NP and a subject NP are alike as to their case markers; they both take either *ga* or *wa*.

Now, consider Sentences (3) and (5). These intransitive sentences contain two major NPs, one the topic, *kono atari* 'this area', and the other the subject, *tochi* 'land'. Intransitive (3) and (5) resemble transitive (2) and (4) in the sense that both contain two NPs and a predicate. For convenience of reference, let us think of a schema,

$$NP_1 \quad NP_2 \quad P(redicate)$$

for all two-NP sentences of types (2)–(5), disregarding the grammatical functions of the constituents of the structure.[8]

2.1. NP$_2$-*o*, NP$_2$-*ga*

Sentences (1)–(5) illustrated canonical cases of nominative *ga* for a nontopical theme or subject NP, accusative *o* for an object NP, and topical *wa* for a topical theme or subject NP in a two-NP sentence.[9] There are, however, a group of two-NP sentences in which the function of NP$_2$ and the role of *ga* for it are not as clear. The following minimal sets of sentences—(6a)–(6c), (7a)–(7b), (8a)–(8b), (9a)–(9b), (10a)–(10c), (11a)–(11b), (12a)–(12b)—are intended to highlight the case-marking contrasts of NP$_2$. The (a) and (c) versions in these sets have the case-marking morphology NP$_1$-*wa* NP$_2$-*o* P, and the (b) versions have NP$_1$-*wa* NP$_2$-*ga* P. The examples are shown categorized by the semantics and forms of the predicates in the (b) sentences.

(6)   Adjectives of internal feeling:
    a. *Watashi wa   kokyoo no machi o   kou.*
        I   topic home   of town   acc miss
        'I miss my home town'.
    b. *Watashi wa   kokyoo no machi ga   koishii.*
        I   topic home   of town   nom homesick-for
        'I am homesick for my home town'.
    c. *Ano hito   wa   kokyoo no machi o   koishi-garu.*
        that person topic home   of town   acc miss -manif
        'He misses his home town'.

[8] The two two-NP sentence types, transitive (2) and (4), and intransitive theme–comment (3) and (5), can be characterized as having the constituent relationships [NP$_1$[NP$_2$ P$_t$]$_{pred}$]$_S$ and [NP$_1$[NP$_2$ P$_i$]$_S$]$_S$, respectively.

[9] This does not mean that only a theme or subject NP may be topical nor that *wa*'s only use is topical.

These sentences express one's subjective, internal feelings. In (6a), P is a transitive verb; in (6b) it is an adjective; and in (6c) it is an adjective plus a verbal auxiliary of manifestation *garu*, which expresses a situation in which a third or second person manifests his feelings. Some further examples of verbs, adjectives, and derived verbs of this type are the following:[10]

Verbs in (a)	Adjectives in (b)	Derived adjectives in (c)
urayamu	*urayamashii*	*urayamashi-garu*
'envy'	'enviable, envious'	'envy'
kanashimu	*kanashii*	*kanashi-garu*
'grieve'	'grievous'	'grieve'
ayashimu	*ayashii*	*ayashi-garu*
'suspect'	'suspicious'	'suspect'
hossuru	*hoshii*	*hoshi-garu*
'want'	'desirous'	'want'
suku/kirau	*suki/kirai*	—
'like/dislike'	'fond of/not fond of'	
kuyamu	*kuyashii*	*kuyashi-garu*
'regret'	'regrettable, regretful'	'regret'
—	*zan'nen*	*zan'nen-garu*
	'disappointing, disappointed'	'feel disappointed'

(7)   Intransitive verbs:[11]
    a.   *Sono toki watashi wa   shima o   mita.*
          that   time I   topic island acc saw
          'Then I saw an island'.
    b.   *Sono toki watashi wa   shima ga   mieta.*
          that   time I   topic island nom appeared
          'Then I caught sight of an island / an island appeared'.

Whereas in (7a) P is a transitive verb, in (7b) it is an intransitive verb. Sentence (7b) translates literally something like 'As for me, an island appeared' to describe a situation in which an island became visible to the speaker. Some further examples of intransitive verbs of this sort include:

[10] The class of predicates in Japanese known as "adjectival nominals" or "nominal adjectives" are referred to simply as "adjectives" in this paper.
[11] Following Kuroda (1978) I will provisionally call this class of verbs "ergative" to distinguish them from other lexically intransitive verbs.

Verbs in (a)	Verbs in (b)
kiku	*kikoeru*
'hear'	'audible, be heard'
toku	*tokeru*
'solve'	'be solved'
—	*iru*
	'be needed'
—	*wakaru*
	'become clear, understood'
—	*tariru*
	'suffice'
—	*niau*
	'suit'
—	*aru*[12]
	'exist'

(8)   Derived adjectives of desire:
      a. *Watashi wa   kono tochi o   kau.*
         I   topic this land acc buy
         'I will buy this land'.
      b. *Watashi wa   kono tochi ga   kai -tai.*
         I   topic this land nom buy-des
         'I want to buy this land'.
      c. *Ano hito   wa   kono tochi o   kai-ta -garu*
         that person topic this   land acc buy-des-manif
         'He wants to buy this land'.

In (8a) P is a transitive verb; in (8b) it is a verb plus an adjectival auxiliary of desire, *tai*, which means 'desirous'; and in (8c) it is a verb plus the adjectival auxiliary, *tai*, plus the verbal auxiliary of manifestation of feeling, *garu*.

(9)   Derived verbs of spontaneity:
      a. *Watashi wa   ima mo   sono koto o   kuyamu.*
         I   topic now even that   thing acc regret
         'I still regret it'.
      b. *Watashi wa   ima mo   sono koto ga   kuyam-areru.*
         I   topic now even that   thing nom regret -spon
         'I still cannot help regretting it'.

In (9a) P is a transitive verb; in (9b) P is a verb plus a verbal auxiliary of spontaneity, *(ar)eru*. Derived verbs of spontaneity signify an action or state that occurs spontaneously irrespective of the subject's intention.

---

[12] See Clark (1971) for a shift in the meaning of the existential 'be', such as *aru*, to the possessive 'have'.

(10)   Derived verbs of potentiality:
   a.   *Watashi wa   kono tochi o   kau.*
        I   topic this   land acc buy
        'I will buy this land'.
   b.   *Watashi wa   kono tochi ga   ka -eru.*
        I   topic this   land nom buy-pot
        'I can buy this land'.

In (10a) P is a transitive verb; in (10b) P is a verb plus a verbal auxiliary of potentiality, *(ar)eru*.[13] Derived verbs of potentiality signify an action that the subject has the potentiality or ability to do. The potential form of the verb *suru* 'do' is suppletive *dekiru* 'can'. This pair of verbs also shows the same case marking contrast, as in (11a)–(11b).

(11)   *Dekiru* of potentiality:
   a.   *Watashi wa   ryoori o   suru.*
        I   topic dishes acc do
        'I cook'.
   b.   *Watashi wa   ryoori ga   dekiru.*
        I   topic dishes nom can-do
        'I can cook'.

(12)   Adjectives of competency:
   a.   —
   b.   *Watashi wa   e   ga   umai.*
        I   topic painting nom good
        'I am good at painting'.

Adjectives of this type do not have corresponding verbs. Some other adjectives of this sort are:

Verbs in (a)	Adjectives in (b)
—	*joozu/heta*
	'skillful/unskillful'
—	*ete/fuete*
	'strong point/weak point'
—	*tokui/futokui*
	'strong point/weak point'
—	*umai/mazui*
	'good/poor'

[13] The distinction between *(ar)eru* of spontaneity and *(ar)eru* of potentiality is a semantic one in most cases depending on the context and the nature of the verb. However, with certain verbs, one form of inflection is preferable for the meaning of spontaneity and another for the meaning of potentiality; for example, *omoidas-areru* 'cannot help recalling' and *omoidas-eru* 'can recall'.

On the basis of the examples that have been presented, let us now, in the following sections, discuss the structural and semantic contrasts between the sentences in (a) and (c) on the one hand and those in (b) on the other. In the course of discussion, the (b) sentence types from (6)–(12) and predicates that fit in one of those sentence types will be referred to collectively as sentence or predicate type (b).

3. THE DUAL ROLE OF NP$_2$-*ga*

First, there are two reasons for considering the NP$_2$-*ga* in the (b) sentences as the subject. One is its nominative case marker and the other is the syntactic fact that many (b)-predicates make good, nonelliptic one-NP sentences. For example, see (13)–(17) which correspond to the sentence types (6b), (7b), (10b), (11b), and (12b), respectively.

(13) a. *Asoko ga   ayashii.*
          there nom suspicious
          'That place looks suspicious'.
      b. *Sono shissaku wa   oshii.*
          that blunder topic regrettable
          'That blunder is regrettable'.
      c. *Ano ko   wa   aware da.*
          that child topic pitiful be
          'That child is pitiful'.

(14) a. *Shima ga   mieru.*
          island nom appear
          'An island is visible'.
      b. *Kane ga   tariru.*
          money nom suffice
          'Money suffices'.
      c. *Giwaku ga   toketa.*
          doubt nom cleared
          'A doubt cleared'.
      d. *Tochi ga   aru.*
          land nom is
          'There is land'.

(15) a. *Kono pen wa   yoku kak -eru.*
          this pen topic well write-pot
          'This pen (can) write well'.
      b. *Kono mizu wa   nom -eru.*
          this water topic drink-pot
          'This water is drinkable'.

(16)   a. *Ryoori ga   dekita.*
            dishes nom become-done
            'Food is done (ready)'.
        b. *Mizutamari ga   dekita.*
            puddle   nom formed
            'A puddle formed'.

(17)   *Kono e   wa   umai.*
        this   painting topic skillful
        'This painting is skillfully done'.

This suggests that the (b) sentences have the same theme–comment structure as (3) or (5), in which the NP_1 is the theme, the NP_2 the subject, and the P the predicate of the NP_2.

3.2. NP₂-*ga* as the Object

Contrary to what we have just observed, syntactic phenomena concerning relativization, reflexivization, and honorification indicate the NP_2-*ga* as a nonsubject.[14] First, despite the similarities in case marking and structure, (3) or (5) and the (b) sentences are dissimilar as to relativization with the NP_2 as the head noun of the relative clause. Observe that (18), which is derived from (3) or (5), is ungrammatical, whereas (19)–(25), derived from (6b)–(12b), are grammatical.

(18)   *[kono atari ga   takai]   tochi
         this   area nom expensive land
        'land [that this area is expensive]'

(19)   [watashi ga   koishii] kokyoo no machi
         I   nom miss   home   of town
        'my home town [that I miss]'

(20)   [watashi ga   mieta]   shima
         I   nom caught-sight-of island
        'the island [that I caught sight of]'

(21)   [watashi ga   kai -tai] tochi
         I   nom buy-des land
        'the land [that I want to buy]'

---

[14] I am assuming here that a subject is a grammatical function and that there is only one of each kind of function in a sentence (whereas there can be more than one theme NP). Following Shibatani (1978b) I will hold the syntactic definition of the subject in Japanese, namely, the controller of the subject honorification and reflexivization processes.

(22)   [*watashi ga   ima mo   kuyam-areru*] *koto*
          I   nom now even regret -spon   thing
          'the thing [that I still cannot help regretting]'

(23)   [*watashi ga   ka -eru*] *tochi*
          I   nom buy-pot land
          'the land [that I can buy]'

(24)   [*watashi ga   dekiru*] *ryoori*
          I   nom can-do dish
          'the food [that I can cook/make]'

(25)   [*watashi ga   umai*] *e*
          I   nom good painting
          'the (kind of) painting [that I am good at]'

The ungrammaticality of (18) is due to the fact that *kono atari* 'this area', the NP_1, and *takai* 'expensive', the P, cannot be taken to constitute a subject–predicate relationship. On the other hand, (19)–(25) are grammatical because the NP_1 and the P in these examples can be interpreted to be the subject and its predicate. This difference in relativizability between (3) or (5) and the (b) sentences suggests that in spite of the similarity in case marking, the constituent relationships in the (b) sentences are different from those in (3) and (5).

Another piece of syntactic evidence concerns reflexivization. Reflexivization in Japanese is controlled by a subject NP.[15] Thus in (26) the reflexive pronoun, *jibun* 'self', may only be coreferential with the subject NP_1, *watashi* 'I', and not to the object NP_2, *byoonin* 'patient'.

(26)   *Watashi$_i$ wa   byoonin$_j$ o   watashi$_i$/kare$_j$/jibun$_{i/*j}$ no*
          I   topic patient acc I   he   self   of
          tanjoobi ni mimatta.
          birthday on visited
          I$_i$ visited the patient$_j$ on my$_i$/his$_j$/my$_i$ own/*his$_j$ own birthday'.

Consider now (27). In this theme–comment sentence, the antecedent of the reflexive pronoun, *jibunjishin* 'oneself', is the NP_2, *musuko* 'son'.

(27)   *Tanaka-san$_i$ wa   musuko$_j$ ga   jibunjishin$_{*i/j}$ ni hoken*
          Tanaka-Mr. topic son   nom oneself   on insurance
          o   kaketa.
          acc placed
          'As for Mr. Tanaka$_i$, (his) son$_j$ insured himself$_{*i/j}$'.

[15] See N. McCawley (1976) for a transformational treatment of Japanese reflexivization.

Compare this to the following sentences, (28) and (29), which correspond to the sentence types (6b) and (7b), respectively.

(28)   *Watashi$_i$ ga Taroo$_j$ ga   jibun$_{i/*j}$ no guruupu de ichiban*
         I   nom   nom self   of group   in best
         suki   da.[16]
         fond-of be
         'I$_i$ like Taroo$_j$ the best in my$_i$ own/*his$_j$ own group'.

(29)   *Watashi$_i$ wa   ano hito$_j$ ga   jibun$_{i/*j}$ no imooto to*
         I   topic that person nom self   of sister   as
         onaji ni mieru.
         same as seem
         'She$_j$ seems to me$_i$ the same as my$_i$ own/*her$_j$ own sister'.

In these two sentences, the reflexivized NPs are coreferential with the NP$_1$ instead of the NP$_2$.

Third, subject honorification.[17] Subject honorification in Japanese is triggered by the subject NP and places its verbal predicate between honorific prefix *(g)o* and an honorific verbal *ni-naru*. For example, in (30) the honorific predicate *omimai-ni-natta* 'visited' takes *koogoo* 'empress' as its subject.

(30)   *Koogoo$_i$ ga   byoonin$_j$ o   omimai$_i$-ni-natta.*
         empress nom patient   acc visited
         'The empress$_i$ visited$_i$ the sick$_j$'.

Now, observe the theme–comment sentence (31) which is ungrammatical because the predicate, *o-nakunari-ni-natta* 'died' may only refer to the NP$_2$, *kai inu* 'pet dog', as its subject, and yet this specific form of honorification does not apply to nonhuman subjects.

(31)   **Tanaka-sensei$_i$ wa   kai inu$_j$ ga   o-nakunari$_j$-ni-natta.*
         Tanaka-Prof.   topic pet dog nom died
         Intended reading: 'As for Prof. Tanaka$_i$, (his) pet dog$_j$ died$_j$'.

Compare this to grammatical (32) and (33), which correspond to the sentence types (7b) and (11b), respectively.

---

[16] This sentence is from Shibatani (1977) for his claim that the NP$_2$-*ga* in this type of sentence is not a subject.

[17] See Harada (1976) for a transformational account of Japanese honorification.

(32)   *Tanaka-sensei$_i$ wa   eigo$_j$ ga   o-wakari$_i$-ni-naru.*
        Tanaka-Prof.   topic English nom understand
        'Prof. Tanaka$_i$ understands$_i$ English$_j$'.

(33)   *Tanaka-sensei$_i$ wa   ryoori$_j$ ga   o-deki$_i$-ni-naru.*
        Tanaka-Prof.   topic dishes nom can-do hon
        'Prof. Tanaka$_i$ can cook$_i$ food$_j$'.

The only possible subject for (32) and (33) is 'Prof. Tanaka', since the honorific form of the predicates necessarily refers to him.

The preceding observations about relativization, reflexivization, and honorification applied to the (b) sentences points to the NP$_1$ in these sentences as subject and the NP$_2$ as something other than a subject, which I provisionally take as an object now and ask the next question of how the nominative object, NP$_2$-*ga*, differs from the accusative object, NP$_2$-*o*.

4. OBJECTHOOD IN JAPANESE

Traditionally it has been assumed that the accusative *o* is the only object marker in Japanese. What then counts as "object" in the grammar of Japanese will be considered in this section by examining the conditions under which an NP$_2$ is case marked by *o* or by *ga*. Predicates that take NP$_2$-*o* are all nonstative verbs. Predicates that take NP$_2$-*ga*—that is, those of the (b) sentences—are either verbs or adjectives. Those verbs may be either stative (e.g., *iru* 'need', *aru* 'have, exist') or nonstative (e.g., *mieru* 'appear').[18] Whether stative or nonstative, these verbs describe situations in which the subject NP is minimally agentive. For example, verbs of the sentence type (9b) are intransitive, low action verbs. Others are derived verbs of spontaneity (9b) and potentiality [(10b) and (11b)]. As explained earlier, verbs of spontaneity indicate an unintentional, spontaneous occurrence of an action or state. In the sense that the subject is not the controller of the situation, the agency of the subject must be regarded as low. Verbs of potentiality indicate one's potentiality or ability to perform an action. That one's capability is not necessarily governable by one's volition can be seen in a sentence like the following:

---

[18] The stativity of Japanese verbs is determined by the syntactic criterion of whether or not a given verb can take a stative and progressive auxiliary *iru*. Nonstative verbs such as *mieru* 'appear' take it: *miete-iru* but stative verbs such as *iru* 'need' and *aru* 'have, exist' do not: *itte-iru* and *atte-iru*. [See Kuno (1973a) for the semantic criterion of stativity of Japanese verbs.]

(34) *Tabe-yoo to   shi-ta ga, tabe-rare-nakatta.*
      eat- int comp did   but eat- pot- neg
      '(I) intended to eat, but (I) could not eat'.

Whether one is able or not able to do something is somehow a separate question from one's intent to do so. Furthermore, verbs of potentiality are in the irrealis mode and hence do not make reference to whether or not the subject actually performed the action. In these senses, the agency of the subject of this class of predicates is also low. Adjectives [(6b) and (12b)] are stative and take NP$_2$-*ga*. Derived adjectives (8b) change the active meaning of a verb to the irrealis state of desire. Note that, although both adjectives and derived adjectives take NP$_2$-*ga*, once the nonstative verbal auxiliary of manifestation is attached [(6c) and (8c)], the case marking changes to *o*. In sum, predicates that take NP$_2$-*o* and those that take NP$_2$-*ga* contrast in one or more of the following semantic features:

Verbs that take NP$_2$-*o*	Verbs and adjectives that take NP$_2$-*ga*
nonstative	stative or nonstative
realis	irrealis
action	nonaction
volitional	nonvolitional
agentive	nonagentive

4.2. Transitivity and Accusative *o*

Hopper and Thompson (1980) propose that transitivity is a notion that consists of certain component parts that covary with one another for varying degrees of transitivity of a clause as a whole. Among the transitivity components suggested are participants, kinesis, volitionality, mode, agency, and affectedness. Each of these components is a scale ranging from high to low degrees of transitivity. For participants in an event or state, two (or more) registers higher in transitivity than one; for kinesis, the higher the predicate is in action the higher it is in transitivity; for volitionality, volitional actions are higher than nonvolitional actions; for mode, realis mode is higher than irrealis mode; for agency, the higher the agent is in potency the higher it is in transitivity; for affectedness and individuation, the more affected, distinct, or definite the object NP, the higher the transitivity. The features we noted about predicates that take NP$_2$-*o* rank high and the features of predicates that take NP$_2$-*ga* rank low on this scale of transitivity. That is to say, accusative *o* marks the object NP$_2$ of a high transitivity sentence.

That high volitionality of the subject is one of the semantic factors of the concept of the accusative NP in Japanese is shown by the difference in the acceptability of (35a,b) and (36a,b). One of the verbs mentioned previously for the sentence type (9b) is *wakaru*. Although it is usually translated into English as a transitive 'understand', it is originally an intransitive verb meaning literally 'become separate, individuated, distinguishable', and takes a nominative object as in (35b) instead of an accusative object as in (35a).

(35) a. *Watashi wa   anata no kimochi o   wakaru.*
          I   topic you   of feeling acc understand
          Intended reading: 'I understand your feeling'.
      b. *Watashi wa   anata no kimochi ga   wakaru.*
          I   topic you   of feeling nom understand
          'I understand your feeling'.

However, when *wakaru* takes the verbal auxiliary, *(y)oo*, of intent, the acceptability of case marking for the NP_2 reverses, as in (36a) and (36b).

(36) a. *Watashi wa   anata no kimochi o   wakar-oo*
          I   topic you   of feeling acc understand-intent
          to   shita.
          comp did
          'I tried to understand your feeling'.
      b. *Watashi wa   anato no kimochi ga   wakar-oo*
          I   topic you   of feeling nom understand-intent
          to   shita.
          comp did
          Intended reading: 'I tried to understand your feeling'.

The difference in case marking between (35a)–(35b) and (36a)–(36b) can be correlated with the high volitionality added to the meaning of the verb by the auxiliary, *(y)oo*, which signifies the subject's "will" or "intent" to perform the action.[19]

---

[19] On the other hand, one may take the verb *shita* 'did' as a subject-to-object raising verb because of its uses in sentences like:

(i) *Isha   wa   Taroo ga/o   byooki da to   shita.*
     doctor topic Taroo nom/acc sick   be comp considered
     'The doctor considered that Taroo was sick'.
     'The doctor considered Taroo to be sick'.

(ii) *Taroo wa   sono kotae ga/o   tadashii to   shita.*
     Taroo topic that answer nom/acc correct comp considered
     'Taroo considered that the answer was correct'.
     'Taroo considered the answer to be correct'.

and argue that accusative *o* in (36a) marks *kimochi* 'feeling' as the object of *shita* rather than as the object of *wakar-oo*. However, the fact that *ga* makes (36b) ungrammatical

The co-relation between an accusative NP and its affectedness, another component of high transitivity, can be seen in the use of *o* that is known as *o* of "passage" in traditional Japanese grammar.[20] Kuno (1973b) summarizes this use of *o* as: "some verbs of motion take NP-*o* as their object. . . . (NP-*o*) indicates that the motion designated by the verb takes place covering the entire dimension (or the major portion thereof) of the NP continuously and unidirectionally" (pp. 96–97). He gives the following examples, among others, for comparison of this use of *o* to other locative postpositions, *ni* and *de:*

(37)   a.   *michi ni aruku*
             street to walk
             'walk to the street'
        b.   *michi de aruku*
             street on walk
             'walk on the street (probably back and forth, and across)'
        c.   *michi o   aruku*
             street acc walk
             'walk (along) the street'

Ni 'to' in (37a) and *de* 'on, at, in' in (37b) are locative case markers; the former indicates the goal point and the latter the spatial limits within which the action takes place. The interrelationship between the space and the action designated by the predicate is perceived as partial in (37a)–(37b), but in (37c), in which *michi* is marked by *o*, it is perceived as more total (as the quotation from Kuno describes it). The following examples further corroborate this point.[21]

(38)   *umi *ni/*de/o   oyogi-kiru*
        sea   to in acc swim compl
        'swim the ocean'

(39)   *umi *ni/*de/o   oyoide mukoo gawa e iku*
        sea   to in acc swim   yonder side to go
        'swim the ocean and go to the other side'

Kiru in (38) is a verbal auxiliary indicating "completeness" or "thoroughness" of the action of a verb, similar in meaning to *out* and *up* in such English expressions as *be tired out* and *finish it up*. In a context

---

[while both *ga* and *o* are acceptable in (i) and (ii) above] suggests that the grammatical use of *o* in (36a) and the ungrammatical use of *ga* in (36b) need be explained with respect to the presence of the auxiliary *oo* in these sentences.

[20] This was brought to my attention by Hopper.

[21] I am indebted to Tomiko Hayashi for these examples.

in which the predicate has this auxiliary of completion, the NP may only be marked by *o*. Similarly, in a context like (39) in which the action necessarily extends over the whole distance, the NP may only be marked by *o*. Total affectedness of the object-space relative to partial affectedness of locative-space is also true of other predicates than motion verbs:

(40)   a.   *kabe ni nuru*
            wall on paint
            'paint on the wall'
    b.   *kabe o   nuru*
            wall acc paint
            'paint the wall'

Whereas (40a) implies that a small portion of *kabe* 'wall' is painted, the normal reading of (40b) is that the entire wall is painted.

Another use of *o* is for individuation or definitization of space and time:

(41)   a.   *10 kiro   aruku*
            kilometers walk
            'walk ten kilometers'
    b.   *10 kiro   o   aruku*
            kilometers acc walk
            'walk the (whole distance of) ten kilometers'

(42)   a.   *Yamada-san wa Tanaka-san ga   inai   aida*
                     topic   nom absent duration
            no ichi jikan hanashi tsuzuketa.
            of one hour talk   continued
            'Mr. Yamada continued to talk for an hour while
            Mr. Tanaka was gone'.
    b.   *Yamada-san wa Tanaka-san ga   inai   aida   no ichi*
                     topic   nom absent duration of one
            jikan o   hanashi tsuzuketa.
            hour acc talk   continued
            'Mr. Yamada continued to talk for the hour while
            Mr. Tanaka was gone'.

In (41a), *10 kiro* is an adverbial quantifier which measures the extent of walking. In (41b), *10 kiro o* implies the entire distance of walking viewed as a whole sum. For example, *10 kiro o* is suitable in the following context:

(43)   *Asoko kara koko made no 10 kiro   o   aruita.*
        there from here to   of   kilometers acc walk
        '(I) walked the ten kilometers from there to here'.

The difference between (42a) and (42b) is a similar one. Whereas (42b), with *ichi jikan o* 'one hour', implies that Mr. Yamada talked for the whole hour during which Mr. Tanaka was gone, in (42a) this implication is absent, or at least less apparent. In (42a) it is possible that Mr. Tanaka was gone for more than one hour. In both pairs, (41) and (42), the (a) versions are the normal way of speaking. The use of *o* for space and time as in the (b) versions emphasizes the definiteness of the particular stretch of space or time.

In this section I have shown that accusative *o* signifies a high transitivity of the sentence and I have exemplified cases in which the affectedness or definiteness of a spatial or temporal NP is reflected by its accusative case. It might be of interest to take note here of the historical background of *o*.[22] Ancient texts of Japanese (dating from the eighth century) lack a subject or an object case marker. The origin of the present object marker *o* is said to be related to postpositional *wo*, which served the general purpose of expressing wonder, emotion, or emphasis.[23] To cite some examples from *Kojiki*[24] (712 A.D.):

(44)   *Ana-ni-yashi e   otoko o*
        (exclamation) dear man   excl
        '[Ana-ni-yashi], how good a lad!'

(45)   *Tachi hake mashi o   kinu   kise   mashi o   hitotsu*
        sword wear aux   excl clothes dress aux   excl one
        matsu ase o
        pine   you excl
        'I would give you a sword to wear, I would dress you with
        clothes, O lone pine, O my brother!'

---

[22] For historical and etymological studies of Japanese, I have relied on Hayashi (1955), Ikegami (1978), Matsuo (1970), Nishida (1977), Oono, Satake and Maeda (1975), Oono (1977), Ootsuki (1979), Saeki (1966, 1970), Uchio (1973), Yasuda (1977) and Yuzawa (1970).

[23] *Wo* is said to be related to the Tungus *wa/wə*, Mongolian *ba*, and Manchu *be* for exclamation and emphasis. (Murayama and Oobayashi, 1973). Miller (1971) pointed out that the Tungus languages also use their accusative particle for time and space. Murayama posits *ba/*bə of emotion and emphasis for primitive-Tungus, -Japanese, and -Mongolian.

[24] Modern Romanization is used to transcribe Old Japanese, i.e., *o:wo*. These examples are cited from *Kojiki* edited by Takeda (1957). The English translations are from *Kojiki* by Philippi (1968). *Mashi* is an auxiliary of unrealizable wishes.

(46)   *Tsumagomi ni yaegaki   tsukuru sono yaegaki   o*
        spouse-dwell for many-fences build   that many-fences excl
        'To dwell there with my spouse, do I build a many-fenced
        palace: Ah, that many-fenced palace!'

(47)   *Kaganabete yoru ni wa   kokono yo   hi   ni wa*
        days together night at topic nine   night day at topic
        too ka o
        ten day excl
        'The number of days is, altogether, of nights, nine, and of
        days, ten'.[25]

Some of the uses of emotive, emphatic *wo*—that is, just those uses
of *wo* after direct objects—were later grammaticized as the object
marker.[26] Although *o* as the object marker in Modern Japanese has lost
its emphatic sense, this sense is still felt in such optional uses of *o* as
those after time and space that we have seen in (41b) and (42b). Old
Japanese had uses of normally intransitive verbs with an NP marked by
o, as shown by the following examples from Matsuo (1970):

(48)   *ne   o   naku*
        voice acc cry
        Lit., 'cry a voice'

(49)   *hito   o   wakaru*
        person acc part
        Lit., 'part a person'

Such uses of *o* have the effect of intensifying the expressions compared
to saying, for instance, (50), which is a normal way of speaking in Modern
Japanese.

(50)   *hito   to   wakareru*
        person comitative part
        'part from a person'

The use of *o* as an adversative postposition in an expression like (51)
also indicates a rather intense emotion.

(51)   *sekkaku   kita mono o*
        at-great-pains came comp adv
        'for all the trouble I took to come'

[25] The use of *wa* as a contrastive-topic marker, which the *wa* in this example may be,
is subsumed in its use as a topic marker in the gloss of this paper.
[26] See Akiba (1978) for an explanation how *wo* as a general emphatic marker developed
to be an object marker.

5. REANALYSIS OF THEME AND SUBJECT NPs

Our next question to ask, then, is whether or not the two case-marking roles of nominative *ga*—for the subject and for the object—are related to each other, and if so, how. To consider this question I will briefly outline the development of *ga* as a subject case marker in Modern Japanese and then propose an explanation for the dual role of *ga*.

In Old Japanese *ga* was a linking postposition of NPs. In the structure NP_x *ga* NP_y, NP_x is a nominal modifier of NP_y (similar in structure and meaning to English NP_y *of* NP_x). Nominals thus linked may have various semantic relationships—possession, location, material, time, or relatedness in general. The use of *ga* as a linking postposition remains in Modern Japanese in proper names and fossilized forms, as in (52)–(55).

(52)   *wa ga ya*
        I   of house
        'the house of mine, my house'

(53)   *san   ga nichi*
        three of day
        'the (first) three days (of the year)'

(54)   *wa ga mama*
        I   of way
        'my own way, selfishness'

(55)   *Kiri ga Mine*
        mist of peak
        'the Peak of Mist'

The head NP_y may be a noun proper or a nominal form of a predicate. When the head NP_y is a nominal form of a predicate, the structure looks like: NP_x *ga* (nominal form of)P, as in (56).

(56)   *Tanetsugu ga kitarikeru*
        (name)   of coming
        'coming of Tanetsugu'

At a later stage in the development of the language (around the eleventh century) the distinction between the nominal form and the sentence final predicative form of a predicate was lost. Consequently, the original nominal structure which then had the appearance NP_x *ga* P was taken as a sentence in itself with the NP_x as the subject, *ga* the subject marker, and the P as the predicate of the NP_x, as in (57).

(57)   *Tanetsugu ga   kitarikeru.*
         Tanetsugu nom has-come
         'Tanetsugu has come'.

In Modern Japanese *ga* has come to be recognized generally to identify a subject NP. Earlier I gave (1) and (13)–(16) as examples of intransitive, one-NP sentences in which the subject NP was marked by *ga*. I also pointed out the fact that Japanese has a theme–comment sentence structure, and gave (3) and (5) as examples of a nonargument theme NP_1, a subject NP_2, and an intransitive P put together to compose a sentence. The (b) sentences have the same structure underlying them. The underlying semantic composition of (6b), (7b), and (10b), for example, are, respectively, 'As for me, my home town is to be missed', 'As for me, an island was visible', and 'As for me, the land is purchasable', which can be paraphrased as 'I (find) my home town (to be) missed,' 'I (find) an island (to be) visible', and 'I (find) the land (to be) purchasable', respectively.

The derived adjectives and derived verbs of (8b)–(10b) are also intransitive in their original meanings. Etymologically the adjectival auxiliary of desire, *tai*, comes from an adjective *itashi* in Old Japanese which meant 'excessive, intense, extreme' (Oono *et al.*, 1975). The structure of (8b), *Watashi wa kono tochi ga kai-tai* 'I want to buy this land', is analyzable as a theme NP and an intransitive sentence which in turn consists of a subordinate transitive clause and an intransitive main predicate looking like $[NP_1[[NP_2 \ P_t]_S P_i]_S]_S$. By predicate merger, this transforms to look like $[NP_1[NP_2(P_t\text{-})P_i]_S]_S$. The NP_2 predicated of the $(P_t\text{-})P_i$ is then case marked by the nominative *ga*. Occasionally the NP_2 in this structure is marked by accusative *o* when transitiveness of $(P_t\text{-})$ prevails over intransitiveness of P_i in the speaker's mind.

Derived verbs of spontaneity (9b) and potentiality (10b) have the same structure. The verbal auxiliary of spontaneity and potentiality, *(ar)eru*, is related to an intransitive verb *aru* 'be, arise, come into being' and functions as a detransitivizer (as it does also as a passive auxiliary, e.g., *keru* 'kick' versus *ker-areru* 'be kicked'). Potential *dekiru* in (11b), which is translated as 'can do' in English, means literally 'come forth, emerge, form'. Its intransitive use was shown in (16). Adjective *umai* in (12b) has the original meaning of 'good or pleasant to the mind and sensory organs', hence 'beautiful, dexterous'. Its intransitive use was shown in (17). Thus (12b) means underlyingly 'As for me, painting is good'.

Now, consider the fact that a theme NP_1 may be marked by either topical *wa* or nominative *ga* just as a subject NP_1 may be marked by either one of the two case markers. This is to say that a NP_1-*wa/ga* in a two-NP sentence may or may not bear a grammatical relationship to the predicate of the sentence. This ambiguity as to the grammatical function of the NP_1 allows speakers to take a nonargument theme NP_1 for an argument NP_1 and push the readings of (6b), (7b), and (10b) further to mean 'I miss my home town', 'I can see an island', and 'I can buy the land', respectively. In these interpretations of these sentences, the NP_1-*wa* is understood as the subject, the NP_2-*ga* as the object, and the P as the predicate of the NP_1-*wa*. Along with this reanalysis of the constituent relationship of the (b) sentences, the meaning of the P shifts from an intransitive one to a transitive one. To summarize, the subject likeness of the theme NP in its position and case allows it to be reanalyzed as the subject NP of the sentence, thereby demoting the original subject NP to a nonsubject NP, which is then taken as the object as a consequence of the meaning of the predicate.[27]

5.2. Transitivity as a Continuum

Besides the ambiguity of NP_1, there is another factor that makes this reanalysis possible. It is a factor that explains why certain sentences of the structure theme NP_1 subject NP_2 P_i, like the (b) sentences, undergo the reanalysis and certain others, like (3) and (5), do not. This has to do with degrees of transitivity of the grammatically intransitive P. To take the sentence type (6b) as an example, predicates of this sentence type are adjectives that express one's subjective, internal feelings concerning some other object or person. Suppose that a situation in which something appears to be a certain way to someone involves two participants, one that is perceived and the other that perceives. Adjectives that describe the situation serve both to describe the feeling or impression that the observer holds about the object and to describe the attribute of the observed, subjective though it may be.[28] Take the intransitive *kowai* 'fearful', for example. For something to be frightening there must be someone to be frightened and vice versa. Although the word is intransitive in the grammatical dichotomy of transitive versus intransitive,

---

[27] The reanalysis of a theme NP as a subject NP I am describing here is fundamentally related to the long-standing question in Japanese concerning the uses of *wa* and *ga* and a theme NP and a Subject NP. But since this is not a place to deal with the subject in detail, I will just mention that the connection between a topic NP and a subject NP has been noted and discussed, for example, as a topic-to-subject shift by Givón (1976a, 1979), as topicality as a subjectlike property by Keenan (1976), and as the typology of a topic or subject prominent language by Li and Thompson (1976).

[28] Tokieda (1947) first took note of this dual semantic nature of adjectives of subjective feelings.

there is thus some transitivity in our understanding of its meaning that facilitates the reanalysis. Examples of typically intransitive adjectives would be those of objective description such as sizes, colors, shapes, etc. Their transitivity is minimal and it is unlikely for the reanalysis to apply to two-NP sentences with these predicates. By more transitive or less transitive here I mean degrees of interaction between assumed participants as mentioned by Hopper and Thompson as one of the parameters of transitivity. Reanalyzability of a two-NP sentence varies according to the degree of assumed transitivity of the intransitive predicate in it. The higher it is the higher the possibility of the reanalysis. Table 1 attempts to show a correlation between the degree of transitivity of the P, the case marking of the object NP$_2$, and the transitive reanalyzability of the two-NP sentence. A plus or a minus in the second column indicates whether a one-NP sentence with that particular predicate is elliptic or not; a plus is for elliptic and a minus is for nonelliptic. The third column shows the case marking of the NP$_2$ in a two-NP sentence. The fourth, fifth, and sixth columns show subjecthood of the NP$_1$ based on the relativizability, reflexivization, and honorification, as discussed earlier. A minus in these columns indicates that the relativization, reflexivization, or honorification disproves subjecthood of the NP$_1$, and a plus indicates the contrary. The seventh column is a scale of transitivity. A plus and a minus occurring together indicates an intermediate level of the predicate as to the particular criterion. For example, the reanalizability of a two-NP sentence with the predicate *ii* 'good' depends on the context. Where *o* and *ga* are both given, the NP$_2$ may take either one of them. Note the gradualness of the change of the case marking of the NP$_2$, the transitive interpretability of a two-NP sentence, and the related syntactic phenomena according to the fine scale of transitivity.

SUMMARY

I have presented a reanalytical account for the question of two ways of object case marking in Japanese. The reanalytical account was based on the following general assumptions:

1. Japanese has as one of its basic sentence types a nonargument theme NP plus a sentential comment structure.
2. A subject is a grammatical function that is definable by its control strength over certain syntactic processes (cf. Shibatani 1979).
3. There is only one of each kind of grammatical function in a sentence (except for theme NPs).
4. Transitivity is a matter of degree (Hopper and Thompson 1980).

TABLE 1

CORRELATION AMONG DEGREE OF PREDICATE TRANSITIVITY, NP₂ OBJECTHOOD, AND CASE MARKING

Predicates	Ellipticality of one-NP sentence	NP₂-ga NP₂-o	Relativiz- ability	Reflexivi- zation	Honorifi- cation	Transi- tivity
akai 'red'	−	ga	−	−	.ᵃ	low
nagai 'long'	−	ga	−	−	.	↑
chiisai 'small'	−	ga	−	−	.	
shinu 'die'	−	ga	−	−	−	
kuru 'come'	−	ga	−	−	−	
ii 'good'	−	ga	−,+	+	.	
kawaii 'lovely'	−	ga	−,+	+	.	
aware 'pitiful'	−	ga	−,+	+	.	
kowai 'fearful'	−	ga	+	+	.	
zyoozu 'skillful'	−	ga	+	+	.	
mieru 'appear, can see'	−,+	ga	+	+	.	
dekiru 'can (do)'	−,+	ga	+	+	+	
hoshii 'want' (adj.)	+	ga	+	+	.	
omow-areru 'cannot help thinking'	+	ga	+	+	.	
nomi-tai 'want to drink'	+	ga,(o)ᵇ	+	+	+	
hanas-eru 'able to speak'	+	ga,(o)	+	+	+	
suki 'fond of'	+	ga,(o)	+	+	.	
omou 'think'	+	o	+	+	+	
hanasu 'speak'	+	o	+	+	+	high
nomu 'drink'	+	o			+	↓

ᵃ The symbol . indicates that this particular form of honorification is not applicable to adjectives and *omow-areru*, a derived verb of spontaneity.

ᵇ The *o* in parentheses, (*o*), signifies the form is possible but not preferred.

The following claims were made:

1. The reanalysis takes the sentence structure that is composed of a theme NP₁-*ga/wa* a subject NP₂-*ga/wa* and an intransitive predicate and reanalyzes it as one that is composed of a subject NP₁-*ga/wa* an object NP₂-*ga/wa* and a transitive predicate.

2. The reanalysis was motivated by the subjectlikeness in position and case of the theme NP and the degree of transitivity of the predicate.

3. The predicates of the sentences that undergo the reanalysis are

predicates of intermediate transitivity which are intransitive originally but allow a transitive interpretation because of some transitive
sense in their meanings.
4. The sentence structure reanalysis results in producing two ways of
object case marking in Japanese, one by accusative *o* and the other
by nominative *ga*.
5. Accusative *o* reflects the high transitivity of the sentence; it marks
the object of a highly transitive predicate and the temporal and
spatial NP which are definite or highly affected by the action designated by the predicate.
6. A nominative object is the object of a predicate of intermediate
transitivity.
7. The covariation between transitivity and the case marking of object,
space and time NPs observed in Japanese is consistent with the
transitivity hypothesis of Hopper and Thompson.

The reanalytical account of the nominative object in Japanese has the
advantages of accounting for (*a*) the semantic nature of the predicates
that take a nominative object, and (*b*) the dual role of nominative *ga* as
a subject marker and an object marker.

ACKNOWLEDGMENTS

I would like to thank Sandra Thompson for her continuing support during the preparation
of this paper, and Paul Hopper, George Bedell, and Pamela Munro for reading and providing
many valuable comments on an earlier version of this paper.

REFERENCES

Akiba, K. (1978) *A Historical Study of Old Japanese Syntax,* unpublished doctoral dissertation, University of California, Los Angeles.
Clark, E. (1971) "Locationals: A Study of the Relations between 'Existential,' 'Locative'
and 'Possessive' Constructions," Working Papers on Language Universals, December
1971, Stanford.
Givón, T. (1976) "Topic, Pronoun, and Grammatical Agreement," in C. Li, ed., *Subject
and Topic,* Academic Press, New York.
Givón, T. (1979) *On Understanding Grammar,* Academic Press, New York.
Harada, S. (1976) "Honorifics," in M. Shibatani, ed., *Syntax and Semantics 5,* Academic
Press, New York.
Hayashi, M. (1955) "Manyooshuu no Joshi," *Manyooshuu Taisei 6, Gengo-hen,* Heibon-
sha, Tokyo.
Hopper, P. and S. Thompson (1980) "Transitivity in Grammar and Discourse," *Language*
56.2, 251–299.

Ikegami, J. (1978) "Arutaigo Keitooron," *Iwanami Kooza, Nihongo 12, Nohongo no Keitoo to Rekishi,* Iwanami Shoten, Tokyo.

Keenan, E. (1976) "Toward a Universal Definition of Subject," in C. Li, ed., *Subject and Topic,* Academic Press, New York.

Kieda, M. (1936) *Kootoo Kokubunpoo Shinkoo, Hinshi-hen,* Tooyoo Tosho, Tokyo.

Kuno, S. (1973a) *The Structure of the Japanese Language,* MIT Press, Cambridge.

Kuno, S. (1973b) *Nihonbunpoo Kenkyuu,* Taishuukan Shoten, Tokyo.

Kuroda, S. (1978) "Case Marking, Canonical Sentence Patterns, and Counter Equi in Japanese," in J. Hinds and I. Howard, eds., *Problems in Japanese Syntax and Semantics,* Kaitakusha, Tokyo.

Li, C. and S. Thompson (1976) "Subject and Topic: A New Typology of Language," in C. Li, ed., *Subject and Topic,* Academic Press, New York.

Martin, S. (1958) *Essential Japanese,* Tuttle, Tokyo.

Matsuo, S. (1970) *Kokugohoo Ronkoo, Tsuiho-han,* Hakuteisha, Tokyo.

McCawley, N. (1976) "Reflexivization: A Transformational Approach," in M. Shibatani, ed., *Syntax and Semantics 5,* Academic Press, New York.

Miller, R. (1971) *Japanese and the Other Altaic Languages,* University of Chicago Press, Chicago.

Mitsuya, S. (1934) *Kootoo Nihon Bunpoo,* Meiji Shoten, Tokyo.

Murayama, S. and T. Oobayashi (1973) *Nihongo no Kigen,* Koobundoo, Tokyo.

Nishida, N. (1977) "Joshi 1," *Iwanami Kooza, Nihongo 7, Bunpoo II,* Iwanami Shoten, Tokyo.

Oono, S., A. Satake and K. Maeda, eds. (1975) *Iwanami Kogo Jiten,* Iwanami Shoten, Tokyo.

Oono, S. (1977) "Shukaku-joshi Ga no Seiritsu," *Bungaku* 6.45, 7.46, Iwanami Shoten, Tokyo.

Ootsuki, F. (1979) *Shintei Daigenkai,* Fuzanboo, Tokyo.

Philippi, D. (1968) *Kojiki,* University of Tokyo Press, Tokyo.

Saeki, B. (1966) *Joodai Kokugohoo Kenkyuu,* Daitoo Bunka Daigaku Tokyo Kenkyuusho, Tokyo.

Saeki, B. (1970) "Ga, No, Tsu," *Kokubungaku Kaishaku to Kanshoo* 11, Shibundoo, Tokyo.

Sakuma, K. (1967) *Nihonteki Hyoogen no Gengokagaku,* Kooseisha Kooseikaku, Tokyo.

Shibatani, M. (1977) "Grammatical Relations and Surface Cases," *Language* 53.4, 789–809.

Shibatani, M. (1978a) *Nihongo no Bunseki,* Taishuukan Shoten, Tokyo.

Shibatani, M. (1978b) "Mikami Akira and the Notion of 'Subject' in Japanese Grammar," in J. Hinds and I. Howard, eds., *Problems in Japanese Syntax and Semantics,* Kaitakusha, Tokyo.

Takeda, Y., ed. (1957) *Kojiki·Fudoki, Kiki, Kayoo,* Kadokawa Shoten, Tokyo.

Tokieda, M. (1947) *Kokugogaku Genron,* Iwanami Shoten, Tokyo.

Tokieda, M. (1978) *Nihonbunpoo, Koogohen,* Iwanami Zensho 114, Iwanami Shoten, Tokyo.

Uchio, K. (1973) "Joshi no Hensen," K. Suzuki and T. Hayashi, eds., *Hinshibetsu Nihonbunpoo Kooza, Joshi,* Meiji Shoin, Tokyo.

Yasuda, A. (1977) "Joshi 2," *Iwanami Kooza Nihongo 7, Bunpoo II,* Iwanami Shoten, Tokyo.

Yuzawa, K. (1962) *Bungobunpoo Shoosetsu,* Yuubun Shoin, Tokyo.

Yuzawa, K. (1970) *Tokugawajidai Gengo no Kenkyuu,* Kazama Shoboo, Tokyo.

INDEX

CONTENTS OF PREVIOUS VOLUMES

Contents of Previous Volumes

Volume 14